GLOBAL STUDIES

LATIN AMERICA

EIGHTH EDITION

Dr. Paul B. Goodwin Jr.
University of Connecticut, Storrs

Dushkin/McGraw-Hill
Sluice Dock, Guilford, Connecticut 06437
Visit us on the internet—http://www.dushkin.com

Latin America

OTHER BOOKS IN THE GLOBAL STUDIES SERIES

Africa
China
India and South Asia
Japan and the Pacific Rim
The Middle East
Russia, the Eurasian Republics,
  and Central/Eastern Europe
Western Europe

Cataloging in Publication Data
Main entry under title: Global studies: Latin America. 8/E
    1. Latin America—History. 2. Central America—History. 3. South America— History. I. Title: Latin America. II.
Goodwin, Paul, Jr., *comp.*
ISBN 0–697–39291–0   954   94–71536

Eighth Edition

Printed in the United States of America

 Printed on recycled paper

Latin America

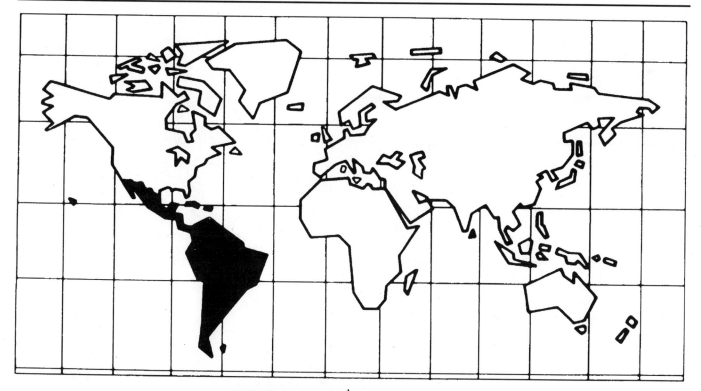

AUTHOR/EDITOR

Dr. Paul B. Goodwin Jr.

The author/editor for *Global Studies: Latin America* is Associate Dean of Arts and Sciences at the University of Connecticut at Storrs. Dr. Goodwin has written, reviewed, and lectured extensively at universities in the United States and many other countries. His particular area of interest is modern Argentina and Anglo–Latin American relations. Dr. Goodwin's work with the Center for Latin American and Caribbean Studies has included running workshops and mini-courses designed to develop a better understanding of Latin America among educators. Dr. Goodwin also contributed numerous articles to the five-volume *Encyclopedia of Latin American History* (Scribner's, 1995).

SERIES CONSULTANT

H. Thomas Collins
PROJECT LINKS
George Washington University

STAFF

Ian A. Nielsen	Publisher
Brenda S. Filley	Production Manager
Lisa M. Clyde	Developmental Editor
Roberta Monaco	Editor
Charles Vitelli	Designer
Cheryl Greenleaf	Permissions Coordinator
Lisa Holmes-Doebrick	Administrative Coordinator
Shawn Callahan	Graphics Coordinator
Lara M. Johnson	Graphics Coordinator
Laura Levine	Graphics Coordinator
Michael Campbell	Graphics Coordinator
Joseph Offredi	Graphics Coordinator
Juliana Arbo	Typesetting Supervisor

Selected World Wide Web Sites for GS: Latin America

All of these Web sites are hot-linked through the *Global Studies* home page:
http://www.dushkin.com/globalstudies (just click on a book).

Some Web sites are continually changing their structure and content, so the information listed may not always be available.

General Sites

1. CNN Online Page—*http://www.cnn.com*—U.S. 24-hour video news channel. News is updated every few hours.

2. C-SPAN Online —*http://www.c-span.org/*—See especially C-SPAN International on the Web for International Programming Highlights and archived C-SPAN programs.

3. International Network Information Center at University of Texas—*http://inic.utexas.edu*—Gateway has pointers to international sites, including all Latin American countries.

4. I-Trade International Trade Resources & Data Exchange—*http://www.i-trade.com/*—Monthly exchange-rate data, U.S. Document Export Market Information (GEMS), U.S. Global Trade Outlook, and World Fact Book.

5. Political Science RESOURCES—*http://www.keele.ac.uk:80/depts/po/psr.htm*—Dynamic gateway to sources available via European addresses. Listed by country name, this site includes official government pages, official documents, speeches, election information, and political events.

6. ReliefWeb—*http://www.reliefweb.int*—UN's Department of Humanitarian Affairs clearinghouse for international humanitarian emergencies. It has daily updates, including Reuters, VOA, and PANA.

7. Social Science Information Gateway (SOSIG)—*http://sosig.esrc.bris.ac.uk/*—Project of the Economic and Social Research Council (ESRC). It catalogs 22 subjects and lists developing-countries' URL addresses.

8. United Nations System—*http://www.unsystem.org/*—The official Web site for the United Nations system of organizations. Everything is listed alphabetically, and data on UNICC and Food and Agriculture Organization are available.

9. UN Development Programme (UNDP)—*http://www.undp.org/*—Publications and current information on world poverty, Mission Statement, UN Development Fund for Women, and much more. Be sure to see the Poverty Clock.

10. UN Environmental Programme (UNEP)—*http://www.unchs.unon.org/*—Official site of UNEP with information on UN environmental programs, products, services, events, and a search engine.

11. U.S. Agency for International Development (USAID)—*http://www.info.usaid.gov/*—Graphically presented U.S. trade statistics with Latin America and the Caribbean.

12. U.S. Central Intelligence Agency Home Page—*http://www.odci.gov/cia*—This site includes publications of the CIA, such as the 1997 World Fact Book, 1997 Fact Book on Intelligence, Handbook of International Economic Statistics, CIA maps and publications, and much more.

13. U.S. Department of State Home Page—*http://www.state.gov/index.html/*—Organized by categories: Hot Topics (i.e., 1997 Country Reports on Human Rights Practices), International Policy, Business Services, and much more.

14. World Bank Group—*www.worldbank.org/html/Welcome.html/*—News (i.e., press releases, summary of new projects, speeches), publications, topics in development, and countries and regions. Links to other financial organizations are available.

15. World Health Organization (WHO)—*http://www.who.ch/*—Maintained by WHO's headquarters in Geneva, Switzerland, the site uses Excite search engine to conduct keyword searches.

16. World Trade Organization—*http://www.wto.org/*—Topics include foundation of world trade systems, data on textiles, intellectual property rights, legal frameworks, trade and environmental policies, and recent agreement.

Mexico

17. The Mexican Government—*http://www.presidencia.gob.mx/welcome/gov_hp.htm*—This site offers a brief overview of the organization of the Mexican Republic, including the executive, legislative, and judicial branches of the federal government.

18. Documents on Mexican Politics—*http://daisy.uwaterloo.ca/~alopz-o/polind.html*—An archive of a large number of articles on Mexican democracy, freedom of the press, political parties, NAFTA, the economy, Chiapas, and so forth can be found on this Web site.

Central America

19. Meso-American Studies—*http://www.icubed.net/usr/bjones/default.htm*—Documentation on political, social, economic, and environmental issues in Central America and Mexico can be referenced here.

South America

20. South American Cybertour—*http://www.wp.com/virtualvoyager/*—Current South American culture is this Web site's topic. The browser can get a feel for all the countries of South America by taking a virtual voyage.

Caribbean

21. Caribbean Studies—*http://www.hist.unt.edu/09w-blk4.htm*—A complete site for information about the Caribbean. Topics include: general information, Caribbean religions, english Caribbean islands, Dutch Caribbean islands, French Caribbean islands, Hispanic Caribbean islands, and the U.S. Virgin Islands.

We highly recommend that you review our Web site for expanded information and our other product lines. We are continually updating and adding links to our Web site in order to offer you the most usable and useful information that will support and expand the value of your book. You can reach us at: http://www.dushkin.com/

Contents

Global Studies: Latin America

Page 3

Page 33

Page 68

Page 89

Page 96

Page 101

Introduction

THE GLOBAL AGE

As we approach the end of the twentieth century, it is clear that the future we face will be considerably more international in nature than was ever believed possible in the past. Each day, print and broadcast journalists make us aware that our world is becoming increasingly smaller and substantially more interdependent.

The energy crisis, world food shortages, nuclear proliferation, and regional conflicts in Central America, the Middle East, and other areas that threaten to involve us all make it clear that the distinctions between domestic and foreign problems are all too often artificial—that many seemingly domestic problems no longer stop at national boundaries. As Rene Dubos, the 1969 Pulitzer Prize recipient, stated: "[I]t becomes obvious that each [of us] has two countries, [our] own and planet Earth." As global interdependence has become a reality, it has become vital for the citizens of this world to develop literacy in global matters.

THE GLOBAL STUDIES SERIES

It is the aim of the Global Studies series to help readers acquire a basic knowledge and understanding of the regions and countries in the world. Each volume provides a foundation of information—geographic, cultural, economic, political, historical, artistic, and religious—that allows readers to better understand the current and future problems within these countries and regions and to comprehend how events there might affect their own well-being. In short, these volumes provide background information necessary to respond to the realities of our global age.

Author/Editor
Each of the volumes in the Global Studies series is crafted under the careful direction of an author/editor—an expert in the area under study. The author/editors teach and conduct research and have traveled extensively in the regions about which they are writing.

The author/editor of *Global Studies: Latin America, Eighth Edition,* has written the umbrella regional essay introducing the area. He has also written the subregional essays and the country reports. In addition, he has been instrumental in the selection of the world press articles.

Contents and Features
The Global Studies volumes are organized to provide concise information and current world press articles on the regions and countries within those areas under study.

Regional and Subregional Essays
Global Studies: Latin America, Eighth Edition, covers Mexico, Central America, South America, and the Caribbean. For each of these subregions, the author/editor has written an essay focusing on the geographical, cultural, sociopolitical, and economic differences and similarities of the countries and people in the region. The purpose of the *subregional essays* is to provide readers with an effective sense of the diversity of the area as well as an understanding of its common cultural and historical backgrounds. Accompanying each of the narratives is a full-page map showing the political boundaries of each of the countries within the subregion.

In addition to these subregional essays, the author provides a brief introductory narrative on Latin America. This *regional essay* examines a number of broad themes in an attempt to define what constitutes "Latin America."

Country Reports
Concise reports on the individual countries within the region follow each of the subregional essays. These reports are the heart of each Global Studies volume. *Global Studies: Latin America, Eighth Edition,* contains 33 *country reports,* including a Mexico report, seven reports for Central America, 12 for South America, and 13 for the Caribbean region. The reports cover each *independent country* within the Latin American area.

The country reports are comprised of six standard elements. Each report contains a small, detailed map visually

(United Nations/Yutaka Nagata)
The global age is making all countries and all peoples more interdependent.

positioning the country among its neighboring states; a summary of statistical information; a brief "wildcard" that describes an interesting facet of the country under study; an essay providing important historical, geographical, political, cultural, and economic information; a historical timeline offering a convenient visual survey of a few key historical events; and four graphic indicators, with summary statements about the country in terms of development, freedom, health/welfare, and achievements, at the end of each report.

All of these elements have been updated to reflect the most current state of affairs in today's Latin American world. Since the first edition of *Global Studies: Latin America* was published, we have had a tremendous and positive response from both students and teachers alike. This important input is reflected in *Global Studies: Latin America, Eighth Edition.*

A Note on the Statistical Summaries

The statistical information provided for each country has been drawn from a wide range of sources (the most frequently referenced are listed on page 220). Every effort has been made to provide the most current and accurate information available. However, occasionally the information cited by these sources differs significantly; and, all too often, the only information available for some countries is quite dated. Aside from these difficulties, the statistical summary for each country is generally quite complete and reasonably current. (Care should be taken, however, in using these statistics—or, for that matter, any published statistics—in making hard comparisons among countries.) We have also included comparable statistics on Canada and the United States, which follow on the next two pages.

World Press Articles

Within each Global Studies volume is reprinted a number of articles carefully selected by our editorial staff and the author/editor from a broad range of international periodicals and newspapers. The articles have been chosen for currency, interest, and their diverse perspectives on the subject countries and regions. There are 19 articles in *Global Studies: Latin America, Eighth Edition*—two regional articles, five articles pertaining to Mexico, five to Central America, four to South America, and three to the Caribbean.

The articles section is preceded by an *annotated table of contents* as well as a *topic guide*. The intent of the annotated table of contents is to offer a brief summary of each article, while the topic guide indicates the main theme(s) of each of the articles reprinted. Thus, readers desiring to focus on articles dealing with a particular theme, say, human rights, may refer to the topic guide to find those articles.

WWW Sites, Glossary, Bibliography, Index

An annotated list of selected World Wide Web Sites can be found on page v in this edition of *Global Studies: Latin America.*

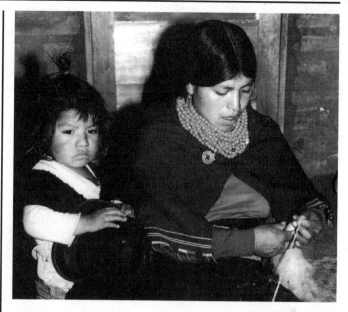

(United Nations photo)
Understanding the problems and lifestyles of other countries will help make us literate in global matters.

At the back of each Global Studies volume, readers will find a *glossary of terms and abbreviations*, which provides quick reference to the specialized vocabulary of the area under study and to the standard abbreviations (UN, OAS, GATT, etc.) used throughout the volume.

Following the glossary is a *bibliography*, which contains specific references for most of the literary works mentioned in the body of the text. The bibliography is organized into general reference volumes, national and regional histories, novels in translation, current events publications, and periodicals that provide regular coverage on Latin America.

The *index* at the end of the volume is an accurate reference to the contents of the volume. Readers seeking specific information and citations should consult this standard index.

Currency and Usefulness

Global Studies: Latin America, Eighth Edition, is intended to provide the most current and useful information available necessary to understand the events that are shaping the cultures of Latin America today.

We plan to issue this volume on a regular basis. The statistics will be updated, essays rewritten, country reports revised, and articles completely replaced as new information becomes available. In order to accomplish this task, we will turn to our author/editors, our advisory boards, and—hopefully—to you, the users of this volume. Your comments are more than welcome. If you have an idea that you think will make the volume more useful; an article or bit of information that will make it more up to date; or a general comment on its organization, content, or features that you would like to share with us, please send it to us for serious consideration for the next edition.

Canada

GEOGRAPHY
Area in Square Kilometers (Miles):
9,976,140 (3,850,790) (slightly larger
than the United States)
Capital (Population): Ottawa (920,000)
Climate: from temperate in south to
subarctic and arctic in north

PEOPLE

Population
Total: 28,820,700
Annual Growth Rate: 1.06%
Rural/Urban Population Ratio: 23/77
Ethnic Makeup: 40% British Isles ori-
gin; 27% French origin; 20% other
European; 1.5% indigenous Indian and
Eskimo; 11.5% mixed
Major Languages: both English and
French are official

Health
Life Expectancy at Birth: 76 years
(male); 83 years (female)
Infant Mortality Rate (Ratio): 6/1,000
Average Caloric Intake: 127% of FAO
minimum
Physicians Available (Ratio): 1/464

Religions
46% Roman Catholic; 16% United
Church; 10% Anglican; 28% others

Education
Adult Literacy Rate: 97%

COMMUNICATION
Telephones: 18,000,000
Newspapers: 96 in English; 11 in
French

TRANSPORTATION
Highways—Kilometers (Miles):
849,404 (530,028)
Railroads—Kilometers (Miles): 70,176
(48,764)
Usable Airfields: 1,138

GOVERNMENT
Type: confederation with parliamentary
democracy
Independence Date: July 1, 1867
Head of State/Government: Queen
Elizabeth II; Prime Minister Jean
Chrétien
Political Parties: Progressive Conserva-
tive Party; Liberal Party; New Demo-
cratic Party; Reform Party; Bloc
Québécois
Suffrage: universal at 18

MILITARY
Number of Armed Forces: 88,000
*Military Expenditures (% of Central
Government Expenditures):* 1.6%
Current Hostilities: none

ECONOMY
Currency ($U.S. Equivalent): 1.41
Canadian dollars = $1
Per Capita Income/GDP:
$24,400/$694 billion
Inflation Rate: 2.4%
Total Foreign Debt: $233 billion
Natural Resources: petroleum; natural
gas; fish; minerals; cement; forestry
products; fur
Agriculture: grains; livestock; dairy
products; potatoes; hogs; poultry and
eggs; tobacco
Industry: oil production and refining;
natural-gas development; fish products;
wood and paper products; chemicals;
transportation equipment

FOREIGN TRADE
Exports: $185 billion
Imports: $166.7 billion

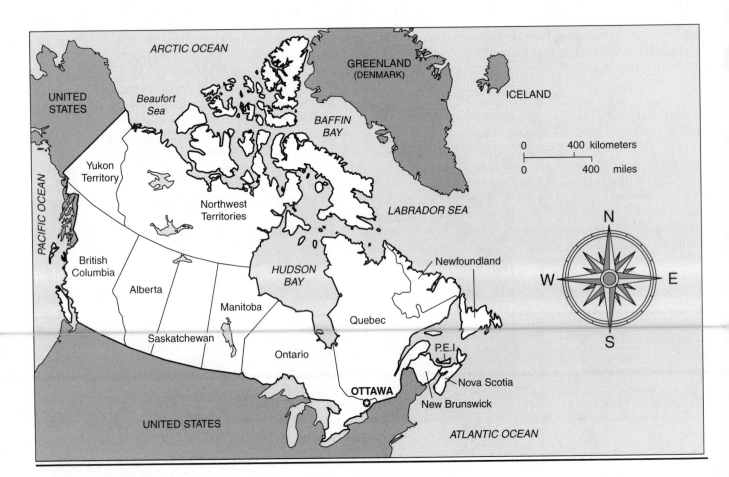

The United States

GEOGRAPHY

Area in Square Kilometers (Miles):
9,578,626 (3,618,770)
Capital (Population): Washington, D.C.
(606,900)
Climate: temperate

PEOPLE

Population

Total: 266,476,300
Annual Growth Rate: 0.91%
Rural/Urban Population Ratio: 25/75
Ethnic Makeup: 73% white; 12%
black; 10% Latino; 5% Asian, Pacific
Islander, American Indian, Eskimo,
and Aleut
Major Languages: predominantly
English; a sizable Spanish-speaking
minority; many others

Health

Life Expectancy at Birth: 73 years
(male); 79 years (female)
Infant Mortality Rate (Ratio): 6.7/1,000
Average Caloric Intake: 138% of FAO
minimum
Physicians Available (Ratio): 1/391

Religions

56% Protestant; 28% Roman Catholic;
4% Muslim; 2% Jewish; 10% others or
unaffiliated

Education

Adult Literacy Rate: 97.9% (official)
(estimates vary widely)

COMMUNICATION

Telephones: 182,558,000
Newspapers: 1,679 dailies;
approximately 63,000,000 circulation

TRANSPORTATION

Highways—Kilometers (Miles):
6,284,488 (3,895,733)
Railroads—Kilometers (Miles):
240,000 (149,760)
Usable Airfields: 13,387

GOVERNMENT

Type: federal republic
Independence Date: July 4, 1776
Head of State: President William
("Bill") Jefferson Clinton
Political Parties: Democratic Party;
Republican Party; others of minor
political significance
Suffrage: universal at 18

MILITARY

Number of Armed Forces: 1,807,177
*Military Expenditures (% of Central
Government Expenditures):* 3.8%
Current Hostilities: none

ECONOMY

Per Capita Income/GDP:
$27,500/$7.25 trillion
Inflation Rate: 2.5%
Natural Resources: metallic and
nonmetallic minerals; petroleum;
arable land
Agriculture: food grains; feed crops;
oil-bearing crops; livestock;
dairy products
Industry: diversified in both capital-
and consumer-goods industries

FOREIGN TRADE

Exports: $578 billion
Imports: $751 billion

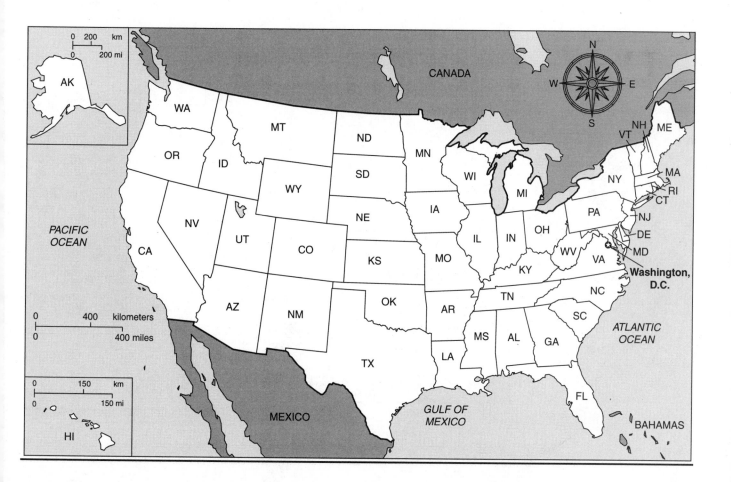

GLOBAL STUDIES

This map of the world highlights the Latin American and Caribbean countries that are discussed in this volume. We include *only independent countries* of the Caribbean and exclude French departments, Dutch territories, British associate states, and U.S. possessions. All of the following essays are written from a cultural perspective in order to give the readers a sense of what life is like in these countries. The essays are designed to present the most current and useful information available. Other books in the Global Studies series cover different global areas and examine the current state of affairs of the countries within those regions.

Scale: 1 to 125,000,000

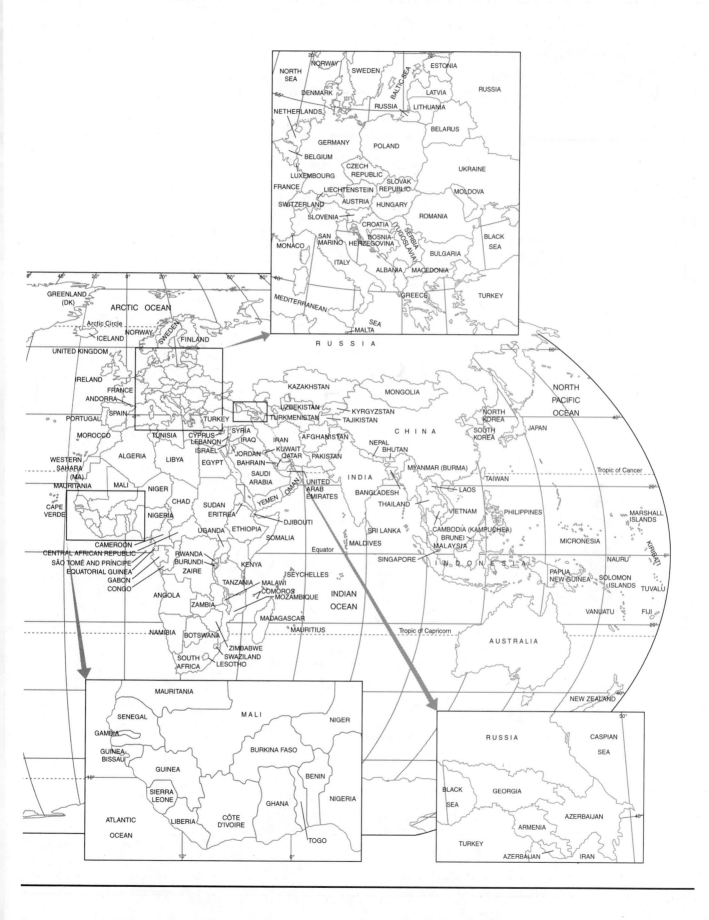

Latin America

Latin America: Myth and Reality

Much of the world still tends to view Latin Americans in terms of stereotypes. The popular image of the mustachioed bandit wearing a large sombrero and draped with cartridge belts has been replaced by the figure of the modern-day guerrilla. But the same essential image, of lawlessness and violence, persists. Another common stereotype is that of the lazy Latin American who constantly puts things off until *mañana* ("tomorrow"). The implied message here is that Latin Americans lack industry and do not know how to make the best use of their time. A third widespread image is that of the Latin lover and the cult of machismo.

Many of those outside the culture find it difficult to conceive of Latin America as a mixture of peoples and cultures, each one distinct from the others. Indeed, it was not so long ago that then–U.S. president Ronald Reagan, after a tour of the region, remarked with some surprise that all of the countries were "different." Stereotypes spring from ignorance and bias; images are not necessarily a reflection of reality. In the words of Spanish philosopher José Ortega y Gasset: "In politics and history, if one takes accepted statements at face value, one will be sadly misled."

THE LATIN AMERICAN REALITY

The reality of Latin America's multiplicity of cultures is, in a word, complexity. Europeans, Africans, and the indigenous people of Latin America have all contributed substantially to these cultures. If one sets aside non-Hispanic influences for a moment, is it possible to argue, as does historian Claudio Veliz, that "the Iberian [Spanish and Portuguese] inheritance is an essential part of our lives and customs; Brazil and Spanish America [i.e., Spanish-speaking] have derived their personality from Iberia"? Many scholars would disagree. For example, political scientist Lawrence S. Graham argues that "what is clear is that generalizations about Latin American cultural unity are no longer tenable." And that "one of the effects of nationalism has been to . . . lead growing numbers of individuals within the region to identify with their own nation-state before they think in terms of a more amorphous land mass called Latin America."

Granted, Argentines speak of their Argentinity and Mexicans of their *mejicanidad*. It is true that there are profound differences that separate the nations of the region. But there exists a cultural bedrock that ties Latin America to Spain and Portugal, and beyond—to the Roman Empire and the great cultures of the Mediterranean world. African influence, too, is substantial in many parts of the region. Latin America's Indians, of course, trace their roots to indigenous sources.

To understand the nature of Latin American culture, one must remember that there exist many exceptions to the generalizations; the cultural mold is not rigid. Much of what has happened in Latin America, including the evolution of its cultures, is the result of a fortunate—and sometimes an unfortunate—combination of various factors.

THE FAMILY

Let us first consider the Latin American family. The family unit has survived even Latin America's economic development and the pressures of modernization. Family ties are strong and dominant. These bonds are not confined to the nuclear family of father, mother, and children. The same close ties are found in the extended family (a network of second cousins, godparents, and close friends of blood relatives). In times of difficulty, the family can be counted on to help. It is a fortress against the misery of the outside world; it is the repository of dignity, honor, and respect.

AN URBAN CIVILIZATION

In a region where the interaction of networks of families is the rule and where frequent human contact is sought out, it is not surprising to find that Latin Americans are, above all, an urban people. There are more cities of more than half a million people in Latin America than in the United States.

(United Nations photo)

In Latin America, the family is an important element in the cultural context. These children, who live in a poor section of Santiago, Chile, come from caring families.

Latin America's high urban population is unusual, for urbanization is usually associated with industrialization. In Latin America, urban culture was not created by industrial growth; it actually pre-dated it. As soon as the opportunity presented itself, the Spanish conquerors of the New World, in Veliz's words, "founded cities in which to take refuge from the barbaric, harsh, uncivilized, and rural world outside. . . . For those men civilization was strictly and uniquely a function of well-ordered city life." The city, from the Spanish conquest until the present, has dominated the social and cultural horizon of Latin America. Opportunity is found in the city, not in the countryside. This cultural fact of life, in addition to economic motives, accounts for the continuing flow of population from rural to urban areas in Latin America.

A WORLD OF APPEARANCES

Because in their urban environment Latin Americans are in close contact with many people, appearances are important to them. There is a constant quest for prestige, dignity, status, and honor. People are forever trying to impress one another with their public worth. Hence, it is not unusual to see a blue-collar worker traveling to work dressed in a suit, briefcase in hand. It is not uncommon to see jungles of television antennas over shantytowns, although many are not connected to anything. It is a society that, in the opinion of writer Octavio Paz, hides behind masks. Latin Americans convey an impression of importance, no matter how menial their position. Glen Dealy, a political scientist, writes: "And those of the lower class who must wait on tables, wash cars, and do gardening for a living can help to gain back a measure of self-respect by having their shoes shined by someone else, buying a drink for a friend . . . , or concealing their occupation by wearing a tie to and from work."

MACHISMO

Closely related to appearances is *machismo*. The term is usually understood solely, and mistakenly, in terms of virility—the image of the Latin lover, for example. But machismo also connotes generosity, dignity, and honor. In many respects, macho behavior is indulged in because of social convention; it is expected of men. Machismo is also one of those cultural traits that cuts through class lines, for the macho is admired regardless of his social position.

THE ROLE OF WOMEN

If the complex nature of machismo is misunderstood by those outside the culture, so too is the role of women. The commonly held stereotype is that Latin American women are submissive and that the culture is dominated by males. Again, appearances mask a far more complex reality, for Latin American cultures actually allow for strong female roles. Political scientist Evelyn Stevens, for example, has found that *marianismo*—the female counterpart of machismo—permeates all strata of Latin American society. Marianismo is the

cult of feminine spiritual superiority that "teaches that women are semi-divine, morally superior to and spiritually stronger than men."

When Mexico's war for independence broke out in 1810, a religious symbol—the Virgin of Guadeloupe—was identified with the rebels and became a rallying point for the first stirrings of Mexican nationalism. Earlier in this century, it was not uncommon in Argentine textbooks to portray Eva Perón (1919–1952), the president's wife, in the image of the Virgin Mary, complete with a blue veil and halo. In less religious terms, one of Latin America's most popular novels, *Doña Barbara,* by Rómulo Gallegos, is the story of a female *caudillo* ("man on horseback") on the plains of Venezuela.

The Latin American woman dominates the family because of a deep-seated respect for motherhood. Personal identity is less of a problem for her because she retains her family name upon marriage and passes it on to her children. Women who work outside the home are also supposed to retain respect for their motherhood, which is sacred. In any conflict between a woman's job and the needs of her family, the employer, by custom, must grant her a leave to tend to the family's needs. Recent historical scholarship has also revealed that Latin American women have long enjoyed rights denied to women in other, more "advanced" parts of the world. For example, women were allowed to own property and to sign for mortgages in their own names even in colonial days. In the 1920s,

(United Nations photo/Bernard P. Wolff)

The role of the native woman in Latin America has been defined by centuries of tradition. This woman is spinning wool, in Chimburaso, Ecuador, just as her ancestors did.

they won the right to vote in local elections in Yucatán, Mexico, and San Juan, Argentina.

Here again, though, appearances can be deceiving. Many Latin American constitutions guarantee equality of treatment, but reality is burdensome for women in many parts of the region. They do not have the same kinds of access to jobs that men enjoy; they seldom receive equal pay for equal work; and family life, at times, can be brutalizing.

WORK AND LEISURE

Work, leisure, and concepts of time in Latin America correspond to an entirely different cultural mind-set than exists in Northern Europe and North America. The essential difference was demonstrated in a North American television commercial for a wine, in which two starry-eyed people were portrayed giving the Spanish toast *Salud, amor, y pesetas* ("Health, love, and money"). For a North American audience, the message was appropriate. But the full Spanish toast includes the tag line *y el tiempo para gozarlos* ("and the time to enjoy them").

In Latin America, leisure is viewed as a perfectly rational goal. It has nothing to do with being lazy or indolent. Indeed,

in *Ariel,* by writer José Enrique Rodo, leisure is described within the context of the culture: "To think, to dream, to admire—these are the ministrants that haunt my cell. The ancients ranked them under the word *otium,* well-employed leisure, which they deemed the highest use of being truly rational, liberty of thought emancipated of all ignoble chains. Such leisure meant that use of time which they opposed to mere economic activity as the expression of a higher life. Their concept of dignity was linked closely to this lofty conception of leisure." Work, by contrast, is often perceived as a necessary evil.

CONCEPTS OF TIME

Latin American attitudes toward time also reveal the inner workings of the culture. Exasperated North American businesspeople have for years complained about the *mañana, mañana* attitude of Latin Americans. People often are late for appointments; sometimes little *appears* to get done.

For the North American who believes that time is money, such behavior appears senseless. However, Glen Dealy, in his perceptive book *The Public Man,* argues that such behavior is

(United Nations photo/Jerry Frank)

Agriculture is the backbone of much of Latin America's cultures and economies. These workers are harvesting sugarcane on a plantation in the state of Pernambuco, Brazil.

perfectly rational. A Latin American man who spends hours over lunch or over coffee in a café is not wasting time. For here, with his friends, he is with the source of his power. Indeed, networks of friends and families are the glue of Latin American society. "Without spending time in this fashion he would, in fact, soon have fewer friends. Additionally, he knows that to leave a café precipitously for an 'appointment' would signify to all that he must not keep someone else waiting—which further indicates his lack of importance. If he had power and position the other person would wait upon his arrival. It is the powerless who wait." Therefore, friends and power relationships are more important than rushing to keep an appointment. The North American who wants the business deal will wait. In a sense, then, the North American is the client and the Latin American is the *patrón* (the "patron," or wielder of power).

Perceptions of time in Latin America also have a broader meaning. North American students who have been exposed to Latin American literature are almost always confused by the absence of a "logical," chronological development of the story. Time, for Latin Americans, tends to be circular rather than linear. That is, the past and the present are perceived as equally relevant—both are points on a circle. The past is as important as the present.

MYTH AND REALITY

The past that is exposed in works of Latin American literature as well as scholarly writings reflects wholly different attitudes toward what people from other cultures identify as reality. For example, in Nobel Prize–winning writer Gabriél García Márquez's classic novel *One Hundred Years of Solitude,*—a fictional history of the town of Macondo and its leading family—fantasy and tall tales abound. But García Márquez drew his inspiration from stories he heard on his grandmother's knee about Aracataca, Colombia, the real town in which he grew up. The point here is that the fanciful story of the town's origins constitutes that town's memory of its past. The stories give the town a common heritage and memory.

From a North American or Northern European perspective, the historical memory is faulty. From the Latin American perspective, however, it is the perception of the past that is important, regardless of its factual accuracy. Myth and reality, appearances and substance, merge.

POLITICAL CULTURE

The generalizations drawn here about Latin American society apply also to its political culture, which is essentially authoritarian and oriented toward power and power relationships. Ideology—be it liberalism, conservatism, or communism—is little more than window dressing. It is the means by which contenders for power can be separated. As Claudio Veliz has noted, regardless of the aims of revolutionary leaders, the great upheavals in Latin America in the twentieth century have without exception ended up by strengthening the political center, which is essentially authoritarian. This was true of the Mexican Revolution (1910), the Bolivian Revolution (1952), the Cuban Revolution (1958), and the Nicaraguan Revolution (1979).

Ideology has never been a decisive factor in the historical and social reality of Latin America. But charisma and the ability to lead are crucial ingredients. José Velasco Ibarra, five times the president of Ecuador in the twentieth century, once boasted: "Give me a balcony and I will be president!" He saw his personality, not his ideology, as the key to power.

In the realm of national and international relations, Latin America often appears to those outside the culture to be in a constant state of turmoil and chaos. It seems that every day there are reports that a prominent politician has fallen from power, border clashes have intensified, or guerrillas have taken over another section of a country. But the conclusion that chaos reigns in Latin America is most often based on the visible political and social violence, not on the general nature of a country. Political violence is often local in nature, and the social fabric of the country is bound together by the enduring social stability of the family. Again, there is the dualism of what *appears to be* and what *is*.

Much of this upheaval can be attributed to the division in Latin America between the people of Mediterranean background and the indigenous Indian populations. There may be several hundred minority groups within a single country. The problems that may arise from such intense internal differences, however, are not always necessarily detrimental, because they contribute to the texture and color of Latin American culture.

SEEING BEHIND THE MASK

In order to grasp the essence of Latin America, one must ignore the stereotypes, appreciate appearances for what they are, and attempt to see behind the mask. Latin America must be appreciated as a culture in its own right, as an essentially Mediterranean variant of Western civilization.

A Latin American world view tends to be dualistic. The family constitutes the basic unit; here one finds generosity, warmth, honor, and love. Beyond the walls of the home, in the world of business and politics, Latin Americans don their masks and enter "combat." It is a world of power relationships, of macho bravado, and of appearances. This dualism is deep-seated; scholars such as Richard Morse and Glen Dealy have traced its roots to the Middle Ages. For Latin Americans, one's activities are compartmentalized into those fitting for the City of God, which corresponds to religion, the home, and one's intimate circle of friends; and those appropriate for the City of Man, which is secular and often ruthless and corrupt. North Americans, who tend to measure their public and private lives by the same yardstick, often interpret Latin American dualism as hypocrisy. Nothing could be further from the truth.

(Photo Lisa Clyde)

Caracas, Venezuela, an ultra-modern city of 4 million exemplifying the extremes of poverty and wealth that exist in Latin America, sprawls for miles over mountains and valleys.

For the Latin American, life exists on several planes, has purpose, and is perfectly rational. Indeed, one is tempted to suggest that many Latin American institutions—particularly the supportive network of families and friends—are more in tune with a world that can alienate and isolate than are our own. As you will see in the following reports, the social structure and cultural diversity of Latin America add greatly to its character and, paradoxically, to its stability.

Mexico (United Mexican States)

GEOGRAPHY
Area in Square Kilometers (Miles): 1,978,000 (764,000) (about 3 times the size of Texas)
Capital (Population): Mexico City (approximately 20,000,000)
Climate: varies from tropical to desert

PEOPLE

Population
Total: 95,773,000
Annual Growth Rate: 1.87%
Rural/Urban Population Ratio: 29/71
Ethnic Makeup: 60% Mestizo; 30% Amerindian; 9% white; 1% others
Major Languages: Spanish; Amerindian languages

Health
Life Expectancy at Birth: 70 years (male); 77 years (female)
Infant Mortality Rate (Ratio): 25/1,000
Average Caloric Intake: 121% of FAO minimum
Physicians Available (Ratio): 1/885

Religions
89% Roman Catholic; 6% Protestant; 5% others

Education
Adult Literacy Rate: 90%

COMMUNICATION
Telephones: 11,890,900
Newspapers: 308 dailies; 10,360,000 circulation

TRANSPORTATION
Highways—Kilometers (Miles): 245,433 (153,150)
Railroads—Kilometers (Miles): 20,477 (12,778)
Usable Airfields: 1,411

America's First Cowboy

When Hernán Cortéz claimed Mexico for the king of Spain, in 1519, by his side was his friend and fellow *conquistador* ("conqueror"), Hernando Alonso. Eighty miles north of what is today Mexico City, Alonso established one of the first cattle ranches in Mexico and bred what may have been the first calves born in the Americas. Thus, Hernando Alonso may have been the first American cowboy.

GOVERNMENT
Type: federal republic
Independence Date: September 16, 1810
Head of State: President Ernesto Zedillo Ponce de León
Political Parties: Institutional Revolutionary Party; National Action Party; Popular Socialist Party; Party of the Democratic Revolution; Cardenist Front for the National Reconstruction; Authentic Party of the Mexican Revolution; others
Suffrage: universal and compulsory at 18

MILITARY
Number of Armed Forces: 148,500
Military Expenditures (% of Central Government Expenditures): 0.9%
Current Hostilities: none

ECONOMY
Currency ($ U.S. Equivalent): 7.77 pesos = $1 (floating rate)
Per Capita Income/GDP: $7,700/$721.4 billion
Inflation Rate: 52%
Total Foreign Debt: $155 billion
Natural Resources: petroleum; silver; copper; gold; lead; zinc; natural gas; timber
Agriculture: corn; beans; oilseeds; feed grains; fruit; cotton; coffee; sugarcane; winter vegetables
Industry: food processing; beverages; tobacco; chemicals; metals; petroleum products; mining; textiles; clothing; tourism

FOREIGN TRADE
Exports: $80.0 billion
Imports: $72.0 billion

Mexico
- ✪ Capital
- ○ State Capital
- ● City
- River
- Road

0   300   kilometers
0   300   miles

Mexico: On the Verge of Change?

There is a story that Hernán Cortéz, the conqueror of the Aztec Empire in the sixteenth century, when asked to describe the landscape of New Spain (Mexico), took a piece of paper in his hands and crumpled it. The analogy is apt. Mexico is a tortured land of mountains and valleys, of deserts in the north and rain forests in the south. Geography has helped to create an intense regionalism in Mexico, and the existence of hundreds of *patrias chicas* ("little countries") has hindered national integration for decades. Much of Mexico's territory is vulnerable to earthquakes and volcanic activity. In 1943, for example, a cornfield in one of Mexico's richest agricultural zones sprouted a volcano instead of maize. In 1982, a severe volcanic eruption in the south took several hundred lives, destroyed thousands of head of livestock, and buried crops under tons of ash. Thousands of people died when a series of earthquakes struck Mexico City in 1985.

Mexico is a nation of climatic extremes. Much-needed rains often fall so hard that most of the water runs off before it can be absorbed by the soil. When rains fail to materialize, crops die in the fields. The harsh face of the land, the unavailability of water, and erosion limit the agricultural potential of Mexico. Only 10 to 15 percent of Mexico's land can be planted with crops; but, because of unpredictable weather or natural disasters, good harvests can be expected from only 6 to 8 percent of the land in any given year.

MEXICO CITY

Mexico's central region has the best cropland. It was here that the Aztecs built their capital city, the foundations of which lie beneath the current Mexican capital, Mexico City. Given their agricultural potential as well as its focus as the commercial and administrative center of the nation, Mexico City and the surrounding region have always supported a large population. For decades, Mexico City has acted as a magnet for rural poor who have given up attempts to eke out a living from the soil. In the 1940s and 1950s, the city experienced a great population surge. In that era, however, it had the capacity to absorb the tens of thousands of migrants, and so a myth of plentiful money and employment was created. Even today, that myth exercises a strong influence in the countryside; it partially accounts for the tremendous growth of the city and its metropolitan area, now home to approximately 20 million people.

The size and location of Mexico City have spawned awesome problems. Because it lies in a valley surrounded by mountains, air pollution is trapped. Mexico City has the worst smog in the Western Hemisphere. Traffic congestion is among the worst in the world. And essential services—including the provision of drinkable water, electricity, and sewers—have failed to keep pace with the city's growth.

Social and Cultural Changes

Dramatic social and cultural changes have accompanied Mexico's population growth. These are particularly evident in Mexico City, which daily becomes less Mexican and more cosmopolitan and international.

As Mexico City has become more worldly, English words have become more common in everyday vocabulary. "Okay," "coffee break," and "happy hour" are some examples of English idioms that have slipped into popular usage. In urban centers, quick lunches and coffee breaks have replaced the traditional large meal that was once served at noon. For most people, the afternoon *siesta* ("nap") is a fondly remembered custom of bygone days.

Mass communication has had an incalculable impact on culture. Television commercials primarily use models who are European or North American in appearance—preferably white, blue-eyed, and blonde. As if in defiance of the overwhelmingly Mestizo (mixed Indian and white) character of the population, Mexican newspapers and magazines carry advertisements for products guaranteed to lighten one's skin. Success has become associated with light skin. Another symbol of success is ownership of a television. Antennas cover rooftops even in the poorest urban slums. Acute observers might note, however, that many of the antennas are not connected to anything; the residents of many hovels merely want to convey the impression that they can afford one.

Television, however, has helped to educate the illiterate. Some Mexican soap operas, for instance, incorporate educational materials. On a given day, a show's characters may attend an adult-education class that stresses basic reading and writing skills. Both the television characters and the home-viewing audience sit in on the class. Literacy is portrayed as being essential to one's success and well-being. Mexican *telenovelas*, or "soaps," have a special focus on teenagers and problems common to adolescents. Solutions are advanced within a traditional cultural context and reaffirm the central role of the family.

Cultural Survival: Compadrazgo

Despite these obvious signs of change, distinct Mexican traditions and customs have not only survived Mexico's transformation but have also flourished because of it. The chaos of city life, the hundreds of thousands of migrants uprooted from rural settings, and the sense of isolation and alienation common to city dwellers the world over are in part eased by the Hispanic institution of *compadrazgo* ("co-godparenthood" or "sponsorship").

Compadrazgo is found at all levels of Mexican society and in both rural and urban areas. It is a device for building economic and social alliances that are more enduring than simple friendship. Furthermore, it has a religious dimension as well as a secular, or everyday, application. In addition to basic religious occasions (such as baptism, confirmation, first communion, and marriage), Mexicans seek sponsors for minor religious occasions, such as the blessing of a business, and for events as common as a graduation or a boy's first haircut.

(United Nations photo/Claire Taplin)

Mexico City is now the world's largest city. More than 1,000 newcomers arrive daily. The city is no longer able to absorb them comfortably, as exemplified by this slum in the foothills of the volcanic mountains surrounding Mexico City.

Anthropologist Robert V. Kemper observes that the institution of compadrazgo reaches across class lines and knits the various strands of Mexican society into a whole cloth. Compadrazgo performs many functions, including providing assistance from the more powerful to the less powerful and, reciprocally, providing homage from the less powerful to the more powerful. The most common choices for *compadres* are neighbors, relatives, fellow migrants, coworkers, and employers. A remarkably flexible institution, compadrazgo is perfectly compatible with the tensions and anxieties of urban life.

Yet even compadrazgo—a form of patron/client relationship—has its limitations. As Mexico City has sprawled ever wider across the landscape, multitudes of new neighborhoods have been created. Many are the result of well-planned land seizures, orchestrated by groups of people attracted by the promise of the city. Technically, such land seizures are illegal; and a primary goal of the *colonos* (inhabitants of these low-income communities) is legitimization and consequent community participation.

Beginning in the 1970s, colonos forcefully pursued their demands for legitimization through protest movements and demonstrations, some of which revealed a surprising degree of radicalism. In response, the Mexican government adopted a two-track policy: It selectively repressed the best-organized and most radical groups of colonos and tried to co-opt the remainder through negotiation. In the early 1980s, the government created "Citizen Representation" bodies, official channels within Mexico City through which colonos could participate, within the system, in the articulation of their demands.

From the perspective of the colonos, the establishment of the citizen organizations afforded them an additional means to advance their demands for garbage collection; street paving; provision of potable water; sewage removal; and, most critically, the regularization of land tenure—that is, legitimization. In the government's view, representation for the colonos served to win supporters for the Mexican political structure, particularly the authority of the official ruling party, at a time of outspoken challenge from other political sectors.

Citizens are encouraged to work within the system; potential dissidents are transformed through the process of co-optation into collaborators. In today's Mexico City, then, patronage and clientage have two faces: the traditional one of compadrazgo, the other a form of state paternalism that promotes community participation.

THE BORDER

In the past few decades, driven by poverty, unemployment, and underemployment, many Mexicans have chosen not Mexico City but the United States as the place to improve their lives. Mexican workers in the United States are not a new phenomenon. During World War II, the presidents of both nations agreed to allow Mexican workers, called *braceros*, to enter the United States as agricultural workers. They were strictly regulated. In contrast, the new wave of migrants is largely unregulated. Each year, hundreds of thousands of undocumented Mexicans illegally cross the border in search of work. It has been estimated that, at any given time, between 4 million and 6 million Mexicans pursue an existence as illegal aliens in the United States.

Thousands of Mexicans are able to support families with the fruits of their labors, but, as undocumented workers, they are not protected by the law. Many are callously exploited by those who smuggle them across the border as well as by employers in the United States. For the Mexican government, however, such mass emigration has been a blessing in disguise. It has served as a kind of sociopolitical safety valve, and it has resulted in an inflow of dollars sent home by the workers.

In recent years, U.S. companies and the governments of Mexican states along the border have profited from the creation of assembly plants known as *maquiladoras*. Low wages and a docile labor force are attractive to employers, while the Mexican government reaps the benefits of employment and tax dollars. Despite the appearance of prosperity along the border, it must be emphasized that chronic unemployment in other parts of Mexico ensures the misery of millions of people. How these realities will be affected by the implementation of the North American Free Trade Agreement (NAFTA) remains to be seen.

THE INDIAN "PROBLEM"

Over the course of this century, urbanization and racial mixing have changed the demographic face of Mexico. A government official once commented: "A country predominately Mestizo, where Indian and white are now minorities, Mexico preserves the festivity and ceremonialism of the Indian civilizations and the religiosity and legalism of the Spanish Empire." The quotation is revealing, for it clearly identifies the Indian as a marginal member of society, as an object of curiosity.

In Mexico, as is the case with indigenous peoples in most of Latin America, Indians are viewed as obstacles to national integration and economic progress. There exist in Mexico more than 200 distinct Indian tribes or ethnic groups, who speak more than 50 languages or dialects. In the view of "progressive" Mexicans, the "sociocultural fragmentation" caused by the diversity of languages fosters political misunderstanding, insecurity, and regional incomprehension. Indians suffer from widespread discrimination. Language is not

(United Nations photo)

In many ways, the Mexican people have two separate identities: one public and one private. This carved door by artist Diego Rivera, located in Chapingo, depicts the dual identity that is so much a part of Mexican culture.

the only barrier to their economic progress. They have long endured the unequal practices of a ruling white and Mestizo elite. Indians may discover, for example, that they cannot expand a small industry, such as a furniture-making enterprise, because few financial institutions will lend a large amount of money to an Indian.

NATIONAL IDENTITY

Mexico's Mestizo face has had a profound impact on the attempts of intellectuals to understand the meaning of the term "Mexican." The question of national identity has always been an important theme in Mexican history; it became a particularly burning issue in the aftermath of the Revolution of 1910. Octavio Paz believes that most Mexicans have denied their origins: They do not want to be either Indian or Spaniard, but they also refuse to see themselves as a mixture of both. One result of this essential denial of one's ethnic roots is a collective inferiority complex. The Mexican, Paz writes, is insecure. To hide that insecurity, which stems from his sense of "inferiority," the Mexican wears a "mask." Machismo (the cult of manliness) is one example of such a mask. In Paz's estimation, aggressive behavior at a sporting event, while driving a car, or in relationships with women reflects a deep-seated identity crisis.

Perhaps an analogy can be drawn from Mexican domestic architecture. Traditional Mexican homes are surrounded by high, solid walls, often topped with shards of glass and devoid of windows looking out onto the street. From the outside, these abodes appear cold and inhospitable. Once inside (once behind the mask), however, the Mexican home is warm and comfortable. Here, appearances are set aside and Mexicans can relax and be themselves. By contrast, many homes in the United States have vast expanses of glass that allow every passerby to see within. That whole style of open architecture, at least for homes, is jolting for many Mexicans (as well as other Latin Americans).

THE FAILURE OF THE 1910 REVOLUTION

In addition to the elusive search for Mexican identity, one of Mexican intellectuals' favorite themes is the Revolution of 1910 and what they perceive as its shortcomings. That momentous struggle (1910–1917) cost more than 1 million lives, but it offered Mexico the promise of a new society, free from the abuses of past centuries. It began with a search for truth and honesty in government; it ended with an assertion of the dignity and equality of all men and women.

The goals of the 1910 Revolution were set forth in the Constitution of 1917, a remarkable document—not only in its own era, but also today. Article 123, for example, which concerns labor, includes the following provisions: an eight-hour workday, a general minimum wage, and a six-week leave with pay for pregnant women before the approximate birth date plus a six-week leave with pay following the birth. During the nursing period, the mother must be given extra rest periods each day for nursing the baby. Equal wages must be paid for equal work, regardless of sex or nationality. Workers are entitled to a participation in the profits of an enterprise (*i.e.,* profit sharing). Overtime work must carry double pay. Employers are responsible for and must pay appropriate compensation for injuries received by workers in the performance of their duties or for occupational diseases. In 1917, such provisions were viewed as astounding and revolutionary.

Unfulfilled Promises

Unfortunately, many of the goals of 1917 have yet to be achieved. A number of writers, frustrated by the slow pace of change, concluded long ago that the Mexican Revolution was dead. Leading thinkers and writers, such as the celebrated Carlos Fuentes, have bitterly criticized the failure of the Revolution to shape a more equitable society. Corruption, abuse of power, self-serving opportunism, and a general air of degeneration characterize Mexico today.

One of the failed goals of the Revolution, in the eyes of critics, was an agrarian reform program that fell short of achieving a wholesale change of land ownership or even of raising the standard of living in rural areas. Over the years, however, small-scale agriculture has sown the seeds of its own destruction. Plots of land that are barely adequate for subsistence farming have been further divided by peasant farmers anxious to satisfy the inheritance rights of their sons. More recently, government price controls on grain and corn have driven many marginal producers out of the market and off their lands.

Land Reform: One Story

Juan Rulfo, a major figure in the history of postrevolutionary literature, captured the frustration of peasants who have "benefited" from agrarian reform. "But sir," the peasant complained to the government official overseeing the land reform, "the earth is all washed away and hard. We don't think the plow will cut into the earth . . . that's like a rock quarry. You'd have to make with a pick-axe to plant the seed, and even then you can't be sure that anything will come up. . . ." The official, cold and indifferent, responded: "You can state that in writing. And now you can go. You should be attacking the large-estate owners and not the government that is giving you the land."

More frequently, landowners have attacked peasants. During the past several years in Mexico, insistent peasant demands for a new allocation of lands have been the occasion of a number of human-rights abuses—some of a very serious character. Some impatient peasants who have occupied lands in defiance of the law have been killed or have "disappeared." In one notorious case in 1982, 26 peasants were murdered in a dispute over land in the state of Puebla. The peasants, who claimed legal title to the land, were killed by mounted gunmen, reportedly hired by local ranchers. Political parties reacted to the massacre in characteristic fashion—all attempted to manipulate the event to their own advantage rather than to address the problem of land reform. Yet, years later, paramilitary bands and local police controlled by political bosses or landowners still routinely threatened and/or killed peasant activists. Indeed, access to the land was a major factor in the Mayan uprising in the southern state of Chiapas that began in 1994.

The Promise of the Revolution

While critics of the 1910 Revolution are correct in identifying its failures, the Constitution of 1917 represents more than dashed hopes. The very radical nature of the document allows governments (should they desire) to pursue aggressive egalitarian policies and still be within the law. For example, when addressing citizens, Mexican public officials often invoke the Constitution—issues tend to become less controversial if they are placed within the broad context of 1917. When President Adolfo López Mateos declared in 1960 that his government would be "extremely leftist," he quickly added that his position would be "within the Constitution." In 1982, with the Mexican economy bordering on collapse, outgoing president José López Portillo nationalized the banks. The nationalization, allowable under the Constitution, was of little practical value, but it demonstrated to Mexicans that the government was serious about tackling economic problems and that the spirit of the Revolution of 1910 was still alive.

Women's Rights

Although the Constitution made reference to the equality of women in Mexican society, it was not until World War II that the women's-rights movement gathered strength. Women won the right to vote in 1955; by the 1970s, they had challenged laws and social customs that were prejudicial to women. Some women have served on presidential cabinets, and one woman became governor of the state of Colima. The most important victory for women occurred in 1974, however, when the Mexican Congress passed legislation that, in effect, asked men to grant women full equality in society—including jobs, salaries, and legal standing.

But attitudes are difficult to change with legislation, and much social behavior in Mexico still has a sexist orientation. Many Mexican men feel that there are male and female roles in society, regardless of law. Government, public corpora-

(United Nations photo/Heidi Larson)

Mexican women won the right to vote in 1955. These women, at a political rally in Oaxaca, demonstrate their political consciousness.

tions, private businesses, the Roman Catholic Church, and the armed forces represent important areas of male activity. The home, private religious rituals, and secondary service roles represent areas of female activity. One is clearly dominant, the other subordinate.

The Role of the Church

Under the Constitution of 1917, no religious organization is allowed to administer or teach in Mexico's primary, secondary, or normal (higher education) schools; nor may clergy participate in the education of workers or peasants. Yet, between 1940 and 1979, private schools expanded to the point where they enrolled 1½ million of the country's 17 million pupils. Significantly, more than half of the private-school population attended Roman Catholic schools. Because they exist despite the fact that they are prohibited by law, the Catholic schools demonstrate the kinds of accommodation and flexibility that are possible in Mexico. It is in the best interests of the ruling party to satisfy as many interest groups as is possible, in order to achieve a certain societal balance.

From the perspective of politicians, the Roman Catholic Church has increasingly tilted the balance in the direction of social justice in recent years. Some Mexican bishops have been particularly outspoken on the issue; but, when liberal or radical elements in the Church embrace social change, they may cross into the jurisdiction of the state. Under the Constitution, the state is responsible for improving the welfare of its people. Some committed clergy, however, believe that religion must play an active role in the transformation of society; it must not only have compassion for the poor but must also act to relieve poverty and eliminate injustice.

In 1991, Mexican bishops openly expressed their concern about the torture and mistreatment of prisoners, political persecution, corruption, discrimination against indigenous peoples, mistreatment of Central American refugees, and electoral fraud. In previous years, the government would have reacted sharply against such charges emanating from the Church. But, in this case, there was a significant rapprochement between the Roman Catholic Church and the state in Mexico. Begun by President Manuel de la Madrid and further elaborated by President Carlos Salinas de Gortari, the new relationship culminated in 1990 with the exchange of diplomatic representatives and Pope John Paul II's successful and popular visit to Mexico in May. Some critics interpreted the new policy vis-à-vis the Church as another retreat from the goals of the Revolution. Others ascribed the move to pragmatic politics.

MEXICO'S STABILITY

The stability of the Mexican state, as has been suggested, depends on the ability of the ruling elite to maintain a state of relative equilibrium among the multiplicity of interests and demands in the nation. The whole political process is characterized by bargaining among elites with various views on politics, social injustice, economic policy, and the conduct of foreign relations.

It is the Institutional Revolutionary Party (PRI), in power since 1929, that sets policies and decides what is possible or desirable. All change is generated from above, from the president and presidential advisers. Although the Constitution provides for a federal system, power is effectively centralized. In the words of one authority, Mexico, with its one-party rule, is not a democracy but, rather, "qualified authoritarianism." Peruvian author Mario Vargas Llosa has referred to Mexico as a "perfect dictatorship." Indeed, the main role of the PRI in the political system is political domination, not power sharing. Paternalistic and all-powerful, the state controls the bureaucracies that direct the labor unions, peasant organizations, student groups, and virtually every other dimension of organized society.

Politicians tend to be more interested in building their careers than in responding to the demands of their constituents. According to political scientist Peter Smith, Mexican politicians are forever bargaining with one another, seeking favors from their superiors, and communicating in a language of "exaggerated deference." They have learned how to maximize power and success within the existing political structure. By following the "rules of the game," they move ahead. The net result is a consensus at the upper echelons of power.

In the past few decades, that consensus has been undermined. One of the great successes of the Revolution of 1910 was the rise to middle-class status of millions of people. But the current economic crisis has alienated that upwardly mobile sector from the PRI. People have registered their dissatisfaction at the polls; in 1988, in fact, the official party finished second in Mexico City and other urban centers. In 1989, the PRI's unbroken winning streak of 60 years, facilitated by widespread electoral corruption, was broken in the state of Baja California del Norte, where the right-wing National Action Party (PAN) won the governorship.

The most dramatic setback for the PRI occurred in the summer of 1997, when the left-of-center Party of the Democratic Revolution (PRD) scored stunning victories in legislative, gubernatorial, and municipal elections. For the first time, the PRI lost its stranglehold on the Chamber of Deputies, the lower house of Congress. Significantly, Cuauhtemoc Cardenas of the PRD was swept into power as mayor of Mexico City in the first direct vote for that position since 1928. In gubernatorial contests, the PAN won two elections and now controls an impressive seven of Mexico's 31 governorships.

Despite appearances, Mexico remains a one-party democracy—or, as some critics have phrased it, a "selective democracy." Change is still engineered from the top down and is designed to preserve the hegemony of the PRI. In the 1980s, to create an impression of broader participation in the workings of government, the authorities created an additional 200 seats in Congress. Half the new seats were reserved for minority parties. By 1990, the total number of seats in Con-

(Agence Franc Presse/Corbis-Bettmann)

The Institutional Revolutionary Party (PRI) has been in power since 1929, but the latest elections have given the National Action Party (PAN) substantial clout in Mexico. The presidency continues to be held by Ernesto Zedillo Ponce de León (pictured above in September 1997 presenting his third government report to members of Congress in Mexico City), but the PRI now must reform itself so that it may take its place as one party among others, not *the* party.

gress stood at 600. To channel discontent within the system, the registration of new political parties was fostered. (Electoral fraud, of course, would guarantee the PRI a comfortable majority in elections.)

Within the PRI, however, a new generation of leaders sees the need for political and economic change. Old-fashioned party and union bosses, on the other hand, see any change as threatening to their entrenched positions. Elections, to their way of thinking, were never meant to allow anyone but PRI candidates to win. In the words of political scientist George Grayson, "the *carro completo* or clean sweep enables labor chieftains and peasant leaders to reward their loyalists." Reform, in such instances, is difficult, but not impossible. Electoral results, even if rigged, could be used to foster change. Historically, the PRI could register its dissatisfaction with one of its own politicians by reducing the candidate's winning margin. This was a sign that, if the politician did not shape up, then he or she was in danger of being ousted.

Similarly, the PRI's poor showing in the presidential elections of 1988 gave the president-elect, Carlos Salinas de Gortari, all the justification he needed for reforming the party and for opening an unaccustomed dialogue with the opposition. Thus, in 1993, the PRI announced a broad range of proposals to reform the Mexican political process, in anticipation of the elections in 1994.

In the southern state of Chiapas, however, the rhetoric of change failed to ease the reality of abuses perpetrated by local landowners against Mayan Indians. Rebellion broke out in January 1994. The Mayan insurgents were led by Subcommandant Marcos, an articulate and shrewd activist who quickly became a hero not only in Chiapas but also in much of the rest of Mexico, where he symbolized the widespread dissatisfaction with the Salinas government. The Mayans were not intent on the destruction of the Mexican government, but they were insistent that their demands for justice be considered seriously. In an election year, a negotiated settlement seemed likely. Then, in March 1994, the PRI's presidential candidate, Luis Donaldo Colosio, was assassinated, further clouding Mexico's political future.

In other ways, President Salinas behaved traditionally, essentially as a *patrón* to his people. This was apparent on a political working trip that he took through northern Mexico in 1989. Mexicans felt that such trips were, in the words of *New York Times* reporter Larry Rohter, "essential to the functioning of the country's political system, which invests the President with an aura of omnipotence and consequently demands that he appear to have a hand in every decision made in his name." The primacy of the executive branch in the Mexican political system convinces people that only the president has both the authority and the credibility to correct injustices and to get things done. In the words of one of Salinas's cabinet ministers, "This is a presidential system par excellence. People want to see the President and to hear things from his own mouth." People wanted to get close to Salinas to deliver their letters and petitions.

ORGANIZED LABOR

Organized labor provides an excellent example of the ways in which power is wielded in Mexico and how social change occurs. Mexican trade unions have the right to organize, negotiate, and strike. Most unions, however, are not independent of the government. The major portion of the labor movement is affiliated with the PRI through an umbrella organization known as the Confederation of Mexican Workers (CTM). The Confederation, with a membership of $3\frac{1}{2}$ million, is one of the PRI's most ardent supporters. Union bosses truck in large crowds for campaign rallies, help PRI candidates win impressive victory margins at election time, and secure from union members approval of government policies. Union bosses are well rewarded by the system they help to support. Most become moderately wealthy and acquire status and prestige. Fully one third of Mexico's senators

and congressional representatives, as well as an occasional governor, come from the ranks of union leadership.

Such a relationship must be reciprocal if it is to function properly. The CTM has used an impressive array of left-wing slogans for years to win gains for its members. It has projected an aura of radicalism, when, in fact, it is not. The image is important to union members, however, for it gives them the feeling of independence from the government, and it gives a role to the true radicals in the movement.

Cracks have begun to appear in the foundation of union support for the government. The economic crisis has resulted in sharp cutbacks in government spending. Benefits and wage increases have fallen far behind the pace of inflation; layoffs and unemployment have led many union members to question the value of their special relationship with the government. Indeed, during the 1988 elections, the Mexican newspaper *El Norte* reported that Joaquín Hernández Galicia, the powerful leader of the Oil Workers' Union, was so upset with trends within the PRI that he directed his membership to vote for opposition candidates. Not surprisingly, President Salinas responded by naming a new leader to the Oil Workers' Union.

Independent unions outside the Confederation of Mexican Workers have capitalized on the crisis and increased their memberships. For the first time, these independent unions seem to possess sufficient power to challenge government policies. To negate the challenge from the independents, the CTM has invited them to join the larger organization. Incorporation of the dissidents into the system is seen as the only way in which the system's credibility can be maintained. It illustrates the state's power to neutralize opposing forces by absorbing them into its system. The demands of labor today are strong, and the government will have to make significant concessions. But, if the system is preserved and dissidents are transformed into supporters of the state, the costs will be worthwhile.

ECONOMIC CRISIS

As has been suggested, the primary threat to the consensus politics of the PRI has come from the economic crisis that began to build in Mexico and other Latin American countries (notably Brazil, Venezuela, and Argentina) in the early 1980s. In the 1970s, Mexico undertook economic policies designed to foster rapid and sustained industrial growth. Credit was readily available from international lending agencies and banks at low rates of interest. Initially, the development plan seemed to work, and Mexico achieved impressive economic growth rates, in the range of 8 percent per year. The government, confident in its ability to pay back its debts from revenues generated by the vast deposits of petroleum beneath Mexico, recklessly expanded its economic infrastructure.

A glut on the petroleum market in late 1981 and 1982 led to falling prices for Mexican oil. Suddenly, there was not enough money available to pay the interest on loans that were

| Hernán Cortés lands at Vera Cruz 1519 | Destruction of the Aztec Empire 1521 | Mexico proclaims its independence of Spain 1810 | War with the United States; Mexico loses four fifths of its territory 1846–1848 | The French take over the Mexican throne and install Emperor Maximillian 1862–1867 | Era of dictator Porfirio Díaz: modernization 1876–1910 | The Mexican Revolution 1910–1917 |

coming due, and the government had to borrow more money—at very high interest rates—to cover the unexpected shortfall. By the end of 1982, between 35 and 45 percent of Mexico's export earnings were devoured in interest payments on a debt of $80 billion. Before additional loans could be secured, foreign banks and lending organizations, such as the International Monetary Fund, demanded that the Mexican government drastically reduce state spending. This demand translated into layoffs, inadequate funding for social-welfare programs, and a general austerity that devastated the poor and undermined the high standard of living of the middle class.

Although political reform was important to President Salinas, he clearly recognized that economic reform was of more compelling concern. Under Salinas, the foreign debt was renegotiated and substantially reduced.

The North American Free Trade Agreement among Mexico, the United States, and Canada is seen as essential if these advances are to continue and jobs are to be generated. Opposition politicians on the left have generally opposed any free-trade agreement, which they see as binding Mexico to the imperialist designs of the United States and giving the United States control over Mexican oil.

In the meantime, there has been a high social cost to economic reform: standards of living continue a downward spiral. The minimum wage for workers since 1982 has not been adequate to sustain a family above the poverty line.

Many of those workers will continue to make their way to the U.S. border, which remains accessible despite the passage of immigration-reform legislation and the uncertain promise of free trade with the colossus of the north. Others will be absorbed by the so-called informal sector, or underground economy. When walking in the streets of Mexico City, one quickly becomes aware that there exists an economy that is not recognized, licensed, regulated, or "protected" by the government. Yet, in the 1980s, this informal sector of the economy produced 25 to 35 percent of Mexico's gross domestic product (GDP) and served as a shield for millions of Mexicans who might otherwise have been reduced to destitution. According to George Grayson, "Extended families, which often have several members working and others hawking lottery tickets or shining shoes, establish a safety net for upward of one third of the workforce in a country where social security coverage is limited and unemployment compensation is nonexistent."

FOREIGN POLICY

The problems created by Mexico's economic policy have been balanced by a visibly successful foreign policy. Histori-cally, Mexican foreign policy, which is noted for following an independent course of action, has been used by the government for domestic purposes. In the 1980s, President Miguel de la Madrid identified revolutionary nationalism as the historical synthesis, or melding, of the Mexican people. History, he argued, taught Mexicans to be nationalist in order to resist external aggression, and history made Mexico revolutionary in order to enable it to transform unequal social and economic structures. These beliefs, when tied to the formulation of foreign policy, have fashioned policies with a definite leftist bias.

The country has often been sympathetic to social change and has identified, at least in principle, with revolutionary causes all over the globe. The Mexican government opposed the economic and political isolation of Cuba that was so heartily endorsed by the United States. It supported the Marxist regime of Salvador Allende in Chile at a time when the United States was attempting to destabilize his government. Mexico was one of the first nations to break relations with President Anastasio Somoza of Nicaragua and to recognize the legitimacy of the struggle of the Sandinista guerrillas. In 1981, Mexico joined with France in recognizing the opposition front and guerrilla coalition in El Salvador. More recently, Mexico, together with several other Latin American countries, urged a negotiated solution to the armed conflict in Central America.

Mexico's leftist foreign policy balances conservative domestic policies. A foreign policy identified with change and social justice has the effect of softening the impact of leftist demands in Mexico for land reform or political change. Mexicans, if displeased with government domestic policies, are soothed by a vigorous foreign policy that places Mexico in a leadership role, often in opposition to the United States. As is the case in virtually every aspect of Mexican life, there is a sense of balance.

ECONOMIC AND POLITICAL CRISIS

Mexico's future is fraught with uncertainty. In December 1994, the economy collapsed after the government could no longer sustain an overvalued peso. In just a few months, the peso fell in value from 29 cents to 14 cents to the dollar, while the stock market, in terms of the peso, suffered a 38 percent drop. The crash was particularly acute because the Salinas government had not invested foreign aid in factories and job creation, but had instead put most of the money into Mexico's volatile stock market. It then proceeded to spend Mexico's reserves to prop up the peso when the decline gathered momentum. Salinas's successor, President Ernesto Zedillo Ponce de León, had to cut public spending, sell some state-

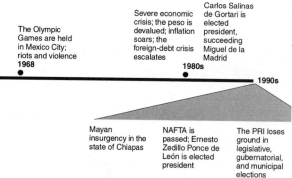

Land distribution under President Cárdenas
1934–1940

Nationalization of foreign petroleum companies
1938

Women win the right to vote
1955

The Olympic Games are held in Mexico City; riots and violence
1968

Severe economic crisis; the peso is devalued; inflation soars; the foreign-debt crisis escalates
1980s

Carlos Salinas de Gortari is elected president, succeeding Miguel de la Madrid

1990s

Mayan insurgency in the state of Chiapas

NAFTA is passed; Ernesto Zedillo Ponce de León is elected president

The PRI loses ground in legislative, gubernatorial, and municipal elections

owned industries, and place strict limits on wage and price increases.

To further confound the economic crisis, the Mayan insurgency in Chiapas succeeded in generating much antigovernment support in the rest of Mexico. President Zedillo has claimed that the rebels, who call themselves the Zapatista Army of National Liberation (EZLN, named for Emiliano Zapata, one of the peasant leaders of the Mexican Revolution), are "neither popular, nor indigenous, nor from Chiapas." Nobel laureate Octavio Paz condemned the uprising as an "interruption of Mexico's ongoing political and economic liberalization." The interests of the EZLN leadership, he said, are those of intellectuals rather than those of the peasantry. In other words, what happened in Chiapas is an old story of peasant Indians being used by urban intellectuals—in this instance, to challenge the PRI. Indeed, the real identity of "Subcomandante Marcos" was revealed as Rafael Sebastian Guillen Vicente, a 37-year-old former professor from a rich provincial family who had worked with Tzotzil and Tzeltal Mayan Indians since 1984.

George Collier, however, argues that the rebellion is a response to changing governmental policies, agricultural modernization, and cultural and economic isolation. While the peasants of central Chiapas profited from PRI policies, those in the eastern part of the state were ignored. Thus, the rebellion, in essence, was a demand to be included in the largesse of the state. The demands of the EZLN were instructive: democratic reform by the state, limited autonomy for indigenous communities, an antidiscrimination law, teachers, clinics, doctors, electricity, better housing, child-care centers, and a radio station for indigenous peoples. Only vague statements were made about subdivision of large ranches.

In summary, the insurgency can be seen to have several roots and to serve many purposes. It is far more complex than a "simple" uprising of an oppressed people.

THE FUTURE

Journalist Igor Fuser, writing in the Brazilian newsweekly *Veja,* observed: "For pessimists, the implosion of the PRI is the final ingredient needed to set off an apocalyptic bomb composed of economic recession, guerrilla war, and the desperation of millions of Mexicans facing poverty. For optimists, the unrest is a necessary evil needed to unmask the most carefully camouflaged dictatorship on the planet."

Be that as it may, the key to Mexico's immediate future lies in the state of the nation's economy. Although the political and social systems are remarkably durable and resilient, rampant corruption, persistent inflation, high domestic interest rates, the devaluation of the peso and collapse of the stock market, foreign debt, austerity in state spending and associated reductions in social programs, and high unemployment and underemployment have significantly undermined the PRI's consensus politics. If the government complies with new election laws to reduce corruption, brings inflation under control, and can secure further loans abroad, and if the North American Free Trade Agreement lives up to expectations in terms of foreign-exchange earnings and job creation, then Mexico will survive this latest challenge to its stability.

DEVELOPMENT

Mexico's stock market surged upward following PRI election defeats in 1997. Investors are confident that the PRI and PAN will support neo-liberal economic policies. And the leftist mayor of Mexico City stated that he "believed in freedom of the markets. . . and in the initiative to invest."

FREEDOM

Although the PRI has controlled Mexico's political life since 1929, opposition parties have made progress at the municipal and gubernatorial levels. Nevertheless, elections have continued to produce charges of electoral fraud, despite the government's stated commitment to the principle of political pluralism.

HEALTH/WELFARE

Violence against women in Mexico first became an issue of public policy when legislation was introduced in 1990 to amend the penal code with respect to sexual crimes. Among the provisions were specialized medical and social assistance for rape victims and penalties for sexual harassment.

ACHIEVEMENTS

Mexican authors and artists have won world acclaim. The works of novelists such as Carlos Fuentes, Mariano Azuela, and Juan Rulfo have been translated into many languages. The graphic-art styles of Posada and the mural art of Diego Rivera, José Clemente Orozco, and David Siqueiros are distinctively Mexican.

Central America

★ Capital cities

Much of Central America shares important historical milestones. In 1821, the states of Guatemala, Honduras, El Salvador, Costa Rica, and Nicaragua declared themselves independent of Spain. In 1822, they joined the Empire of Mexico and, in 1823, formed the United Provinces of Central America. This union lasted until 1838, when each member state severed its relations with the federation and went its own way. Since 1838, there have been more than 25 attempts to restore the union—but to no avail.

Central America: Lands in Turmoil

LIFE IN THE MOUTH OF THE VOLCANO

Sons of the Shaking Earth, a well-known study of Middle America by anthropologist Eric Wolf, captures in its title the critical interplay between people and the land in Central America. It asserts that the land is violent and that the inhabitants of the region live in an environment that is often shaken by natural disaster.

The dominant geographical feature of Central America is the impressive and forbidding range of volcanic mountains that runs from Mexico to Panama. These mountains have always been obstacles to communication, to the cultivation of the land, and to the national integration of the countries in which they lie. The volcanoes rest atop major fault lines; some are dormant, others are active, and new ones have appeared periodically. Over the centuries, eruptions and earthquakes have destroyed thousands of villages. Some have recovered, but others remain buried beneath lava and ash. Nearly every Central American city has been destroyed at one time or another; and some, such as Managua, Nicaragua, have suffered repeated devastation.

An ancient Indian philosophy speaks of five great periods of time, each doomed to end in disaster. The fifth period, which is the time in which we now live, is said to terminate with a world-destroying earthquake. "Thus," writes Wolf, "the people of Middle [Central] America live in the mouth of the volcano. Middle America ... is one of the proving grounds of humanity."

Earthquakes and eruptions are not the only natural disasters that plague the region. Rains fall heavily between May and October each year, and devastating floods are common. On the Caribbean coast, hurricanes often strike in the late summer and early autumn, threatening coastal cities and leveling crops.

The constant threat of natural disaster has had a deep impact on Central Americans' views of life and development. Death and tragedy have conditioned their attitudes toward the present and the future.

GEOGRAPHY

The land is not only violent but also diverse. In political terms, Central America consists of seven independent nations: Belize, Costa Rica, El Salvador, Guatemala, Honduras, Nicaragua, and Panama. With the exception of Costa Rica and Panama, where national borders coincide with geographical and human frontiers, political boundaries are artificial and were marked out in defiance of both the lay of the land and the cultural groupings of the region's peoples.

Geographically, Central America can be divided into four broad zones: Petén–Belize; the Caribbean coasts of Guatemala, Honduras, and Nicaragua; the Pacific volcanic region; and Costa Rica–Panama.

The northern Guatemalan territory of Petén and all of Belize are an extension of Mexico's Yucatán Peninsula. The region is heavily forested with stands of mahogany, cedar, and pine, whose products are a major source of revenue for Belize.

The Caribbean lowlands, steamy and disease-ridden, are sparsely settled. The inhabitants of the Caribbean coast in Nicaragua include Miskito Indians and English-speaking blacks whose ancestors have lived in the area since the seventeenth century. The Hispanic population there was small until recently. Coastal Honduras, however, presents a different picture. Because of heavy investments by foreign companies in the region's banana industry, it is a pocket of relative prosperity in the midst of a very poor country whose economy is based on agricultural production and textiles.

The Pacific volcanic highlands are the cultural heartland of Central America. Here, in highland valleys noted for their springlike climate, live more than 80 percent of the population of Central America; here are the largest cities. In cultural terms, the highlands are home to the whites, mixed bloods, Hispanicized Indians known as Ladinos, and pure-blooded Indians who are descended from the Maya. These highland groups form a striking ethnic contrast to the Indians (such as the Miskito), mulattos, and blacks of the coastlands. The

(United Nations photo/Sygma/J. P. Laffont)

The threat of earthquakes affects all Central Americans. Above, residents of Guatemala City, Guatemala, begin the long clean-up process after an earthquake.

entire country of El Salvador falls within this geographical zone. Unlike its neighbors, there is a uniformity to the land and people of El Salvador.

The fourth region, divided between the nations of Costa Rica and Panama, constitutes a single geographical unit. Mountains form the spine of the isthmus. In Costa Rica, the Central Mesa has attracted 70 percent of the nation's population, because of its climate.

CLIMATE AND CULTURE

The geographic and biological diversity of Central America—with its cool highlands and steaming lowlands, its incredible variety of microclimates and environments, its seemingly infinite types of flora and fauna, and its mineral wealth—has been a major factor in setting the course of the cultural history of Central America. Before the Spanish conquest, the environmental diversity favored the cultural cohesion of peoples. The products of one environmental niche could easily be exchanged for the products of another. In a sense, valley people and those living higher up in the mountains depended on one another. Here was one of the bases for the establishment of the advanced culture of the Maya.

The cultural history of Central America has focused on the densely populated highlands and Pacific plains—those areas most favorable for human occupation. Spaniards settled in the same regions, and centers of national life are located there today. But, if geography has been a factor in bringing peoples together on a local level, it has also contributed to the formation of regional differences, loyalties, interests, and jealousies. Neither Mayan rulers nor Spanish bureaucrats could triumph over the natural obstacles presented by the region's harsh geography. The mountains and rain forests have mocked numerous attempts to create a single Central American state.

CULTURES IN CONFLICT

Although geography has interacted with culture, the contact between Indians and Spaniards since the sixteenth century has profoundly shaped the cultural face of today's Central America. According to historian Ralph Woodward, the religious traditions of the Indians, with Christianity imperfectly superimposed over them, "together with the violence of the Conquest and the centuries of slavery or serfdom which followed, left clear impressions on the personality and mentality of the Central American Indian."

To outsiders, the Indians often appear docile and obedient to authority, but beneath this mask lie deeper emotions, including distrust and bitterness. The Indians' vision is usually local and oriented toward the village and family; they do not identify themselves as Guatemalan or Nicaraguan. When challenged, Indians have fought to defend their rights, and a long succession of rebellions from colonial days until the present attests to their sense of what is just and what is not. The Indians, firmly tied to their traditional beliefs and values,

(United Nations photo/Jerry Frank)

Central American Indians are firmly tied to their traditional beliefs and have strongly resisted the influence of European culture, as evidenced by this Cuna woman of Panama's Tubala Island.

have tried to resist modernization, despite government programs and policies designed to counter what urbanized whites perceive as backwardness and superstition.

Population growth, rather than government programs and policies, has had a great impact on the region's Indian peoples and has already resulted in the recasting of cultural traditions. Peasant villages in much of Central America have traditionally organized their ritual life around the principle of *mayordomía,* or sponsorship. Waldemar Smith, an anthropologist who has explored the relationship between the *fiesta* system and economic change, has shown the impact of changing circumstances on traditional systems. In any Central American community in any given year, certain families are appointed *mayordomos,* or stewards, of the village saints; they are responsible for organizing and paying for the celebrations in their names. This responsibility ordinarily lasts for a year. One of the outstanding features of the fiesta system is the phenomenal costs that the designated family must bear. An individual might have to expend the equivalent of a year's earnings or more to act as a sponsor in a community *fiesta,* or ceremony. Psychological and social burdens must also be borne by the mayordomos, for they represent their community before its saints. Mayordomos, who in essence are priests for a year, are commonly expected to refrain from sexual activity for long durations as well as to devote much time to ritual forms.

The office, while highly prestigious, can also be dangerous. Maya Indians, for example, believe that the saints use the weather as a weapon to punish transgressions, and extreme weather is often traced to ritual error or sins on the part of the mayordomo, who might on such occasions actually be jailed.

Since the late 1960s, the socioeconomic structure of much of the area heavily populated by Indians has changed, forcing changes in traditional cultural forms, including the fiesta system. Expansion of markets and educational opportunity, the absorption of much of the workforce in seasonal plantation labor, more efficient transportation systems, and population growth have precipitated change. Traditional festivals in honor of a community's saints have significantly diminished in importance in a number of towns. Costs have been reduced or several families have been made responsible for fiesta sponsorship. This reflects not only modernization but also crisis. Some communities have become too poor to support themselves, and the expensive fiestas have, naturally, suffered.

This increasing poverty is driven in part by population growth, which has exerted tremendous pressure on people's access to land. Families that cannot be sustained on traditional lands must now seek seasonal wage labor on sugarcane, coffee, or cotton plantations. Others emigrate. The net result is a culture under siege. Thus, while traditional festivals may not vanish, they are surely in the process of change.

The Ladino World

The word *Ladino* can be traced back to the Roman occupation of Spain. It referred to someone who had been "Latinized" and was therefore wise in the ways of the world. The word has several meanings in Central America. In Guatemala, it refers to a person of mixed blood, or *Mestizo*. In most of Central America, however, it refers to an Indian who has adopted white culture.

The Ladinos are caught between two cultures, both of which initially rejected them. The Ladinos attempted to compensate for their lack of cultural roots and cultural identity by aggressively carving out a place in Central American society.

Acutely status-conscious, Ladinos contrast sharply with the Indians they physically resemble. Ladinos congregate in the larger towns and cities, speak Spanish, and seek a livelihood as shopkeepers or landowners. They compose the local elite in Guatemala, Nicaragua, Honduras, and El Salvador (the latter country was almost entirely Ladinoized by the end of the nineteenth century), and they usually control regional politics. They are the most aggressive members of the community and are driven by the desire for self-advancement. Their vision is much broader than that of the Indian; they have

(United Nations photo)

Many Central Americans migrate from rural areas to the urban centers, but it is beyond the capacity of many urban areas to support them. The child pictured above has to get the family's water from a single, unsanitary community tap.

a perspective that includes the capital city and the nation. The vast majority of the population speak Spanish; few villages retain the use of their original, native tongues.

The Elite

For the elite, who are culturally "white," the city dominates their social and cultural horizons. For them, the world of the Indian is unimportant—save for the difficult questions of social integration and modernization. Businesspeople and bureaucrats, absentee landlords, and the professional class of doctors, lawyers, and engineers constitute an urban elite who are cosmopolitan and sophisticated. Wealth, status, and "good blood" are the keys to elite membership.

The Disadvantaged

The cities have also attracted disadvantaged people who have migrated from poverty-stricken rural regions in search of economic opportunity. Many are self-employed as peddlers, small-scale traders, or independent craftspeople. Others seek low-paying, unskilled positions in industry, construction work, and transportation. Most live on the edge of poverty and are the first to suffer in times of economic recession.

But there exist Hispanic institutions in this harsh world that help people of all classes to adjust. In each of the capital cities of Central America, lower-sector people seek help and sustenance from the more advantaged elements in society. They form economic and social alliances that are mutually beneficial. For example, a tradesman might approach a well-to-do merchant and seek advice or a small loan. In return, he can offer guaranteed service, a steady supply of crafts for the wholesaler, and a price that is right. It is a world built on mutual exchanges.

These networks, when they function, bind societies together and ease the alienation and isolation of the less advantaged inhabitants. Of course, networks that cut through class lines can effectively limit class action in pursuit of reforms; and, in many instances, the networks do not exist or are exploitive.

POPULATION MOVEMENT

For many years, Central America's peoples have been peoples in motion. Migrants who moved from rural areas into the cities were often driven from the lands they once owned, either because of the expansion of landed estates at the expense of the smaller landholdings, population pressure, or division of the land into plots so small that subsistence farming was no longer possible. Others moved to the cities in search of a better life.

Population pressure on the land is most intense in El Salvador. No other Latin American state utilizes the whole of its territory to the extent that El Salvador does. Most of the land

(World Bank photo/Jaime Martin-Escobal)

The migration of poor rural people to Central American urban centers has caused large numbers of squatters to take up residence in slums. The crowded conditions in urban El Salvador, as shown in this photograph, are typical results of this phenomenon.

is still privately owned and is devoted to cattle farming or to raising cotton and coffee crops for the export market. There is not enough land to provide crops for a population that has grown at one of the most rapid rates in the Western Hemisphere. There are no empty lands left to occupy. Agrarian reform, even if successful, will still leave hundreds of thousands of peasants without land.

Many Salvadorans have moved to the capital city of San Salvador in search of employment. Others have crossed into neighboring countries. In the 1960s, thousands moved to Honduras, where they settled on the land or were attracted to commerce and industry. By the end of that decade, more than 75 percent of all foreigners living in Honduras had crossed the border from El Salvador. Hondurans, increasingly concerned by the growing presence of Salvadorans, acted to stem the flow and passed restrictive and discriminatory legislation against the immigrants. The tension, an ill-defined border, and festering animosity ultimately brought about a brief war between Honduras and El Salvador in 1969.

Honduras, with a low population density of about 130 persons per square mile (as compared to El Salvador's 700), has attracted population not only from neighboring countries but also from the Caribbean. Black migrants from the "West Indian" Caribbean islands known as the Antilles have been particularly attracted to the north coast, where they have been able to find employment on the banana plantations or in the light industry that has increasingly been established in the area. The presence of these Caribbean peoples in moderate numbers has more sharply focused regional differences in Honduras. The coast, in many respects, is Caribbean in its peoples' identity and outlook; while peoples of the highlands of the interior identify with the capital city of Tegucigalpa, which is Hispanic in culture.

THE REFUGEE PROBLEM

Recent turmoil in Central America created yet another group of people on the move—refugees from the fighting in their own countries or from the persecution by extremists of the political left and right. For example, thousands of Salvadorans crowded into Honduras's western province. In the south, Miskito Indians, fleeing from Nicaragua's Sandinista government, crossed the Río Coco in large numbers. Additional thousands of armed Nicaraguan counterrevolutionaries camped along the border. Only in 1990–1991 did significant numbers of Salvadorans move back to their homeland. With the declared truce between Sandinistas and Contras and the election victory of Violeta Chamorro, Nicaraguan refugees were gradually repatriated. Guatemalan Indians sought refuge in southern Mexico, and Central Americans of all nationalities resettled in Costa Rica and Belize.

El Salvadorans, who began to emigrate to the United States in the 1960s, did so in much greater numbers with the onset of the El Salvadoran Civil War, which killed approximately 70,000 people and displaced about 25 percent of the nation's population. The Urban Institute, a Washington, D.C.–based research group, estimated in 1986 that there were then about 3/4 million El Salvadorans—of a total population of just over 5 million—living in the United States. Those emigrants became a major source of dollars for El Salvador; it is estimated that they now send home about $500 million a year.

While that money has undoubtedly helped to keep the nation's economy above water, it has also generated, paradoxically, a good deal of anti-U.S. sentiment in El Salvador. Lindsey Gruson, a reporter for *The New York Times*, studied the impact of expatriate dollars in Intipuca, a town 100 miles southwest of the capital, and concluded that they had a profound impact on Intipuqueño culture. The influx of money was an incentive not to work, and townspeople said that the "free" dollars "perverted cherished values" and were "breaking up many families."

THE ROOTS OF VIOLENCE

Central America still feels the effects of civil war and violence. Armies, guerrillas, and terrorists of the political left and right exacted a high toll on human lives and property. The civil wars and guerrilla movements that spread violence to the region sprang from each of the societies in question.

A critical societal factor was (and remains) the emergence of a middle class in Central America. In some respects, people of the middle class resemble the Mestizos or Ladinos, in that their wealth and position have placed them above the masses. But, like the Mestizos and Ladinos, they have been denied access to the upper reaches of power, which is the special preserve of the elite. Since World War II, it has been members of the middle class who have called for reform and a more equitable distribution of the national wealth. They have also attempted to forge alliances of opportunity with workers and peasants.

Nationalistic, assertive, restless, ambitious, and, to an extent, ruthless, people of the middle class (professionals, intellectuals, junior officers in the armed forces, office workers, businesspeople, teachers, students, and skilled workers) demand a greater voice in the political world. They want governments that are responsive to their interests and needs; and, when governments have proven unresponsive or hostile, elements of the middle class have chosen confrontation.

In the civil war that removed the Somoza family from power in Nicaragua in 1979, for example, the middle class played a critical leadership role. Guerrilla leaders in El Salvador were middle class in terms of their social origins, and there was significant middle-class participation in the unrest in Guatemala.

Indeed, Central America's middle class is among the most revolutionary groups in the region. Although middle-class people are well represented in antigovernment forces, they also resist changes that would tend to elevate those below them on the social scale. They are also significantly repre-

(United Nations photo/J. P. Laffont)

The problems incumbent with rapid population growth have put severe strains on many Central American nations. In Guatemala, government policy has driven Indians from their ancestral villages to crowded urban "resettlement" areas, such as the one pictured above.

sented among right-wing groups, whose reputation for conservative views is accompanied by systematic terror.

Other societal factors also figure prominently in the violence in Central America. The rapid growth of population since the 1960s has severely strained each nation's resources. Many rural areas have become overpopulated, poor agricultural practices have caused extensive erosion, the amount of land available to subsistence farmers is inadequate, and poverty and misery are pervasive. These problems have combined to compel rural peoples to migrate to the cities or to whatever frontier lands are still available. In Guatemala, government policy drove Indians from ancestral villages in the highlands to "resettlement" villages in the low-lying forested Petén to the north. Indians displaced in this manner often, not surprisingly, joined guerrilla movements. They were not attracted to insurgency by the allure of socialist or communist ideology; they simply responded to violence and the loss of their lands with violence against the governments that pursued such policies.

The conflict in this region does not always pit landless, impoverished peasants against an unyielding elite. Some members of the elite see the need for change. Most peasants have not taken up arms, and the vast majority wish to be left in peace. Others who desire change may be found in the ranks of the military or within the hierarchy of the Roman Catholic Church. Reformers are drawn from all sectors of society. It is thus more appropriate to view the conflict in Central America as a civil war rather than a class struggle, as civil wars cut through the entire fabric of a nation.

ECONOMIC PROBLEMS

Central American economies, always fragile, have in recent years been plagued by a combination of vexing problems. Foreign debt, inflation, currency devaluations, recession, and, in some instances, outside interference have had deleterious effects on the standard of living in all the countries. Civil war, insurgency, corruption and mismanagement, and population growth have added fuel to the crisis—not only in the region's economies but also in their societies.

Civil war in El Salvador brought unprecedented death and destruction and was largely responsible for economic deterioration and a decline of well over one third of per capita income from 1980 to 1992. Today, fully two thirds of the working-age population are either unemployed or underemployed. The struggle of the Sandinista government of Nicaragua against U.S.–sponsored rebels routinely consumed 60 percent of government spending; even with peace, much of the budget of the Chamorro regime was earmarked for economic recovery. In Guatemala, a savage civil war lasted more than a generation; took more than 140,000 lives; strained the economy; depressed wages; and left unaddressed pressing social problems in education, housing, and welfare. Although the violence has subsided, the lingering fears conditioned by that violence have not. U.S. efforts to force the ouster of

Panamanian strongman Manuel Antonio Noriega through the application of economic sanctions probably harmed middle-class businesspeople in Panama more than Noriega.

Against this backdrop of economic malaise there have been some creative attempts to solve, or at least to confront, pressing problems. In 1987, the Costa Rican government proposed a series of debt-for-nature swaps to international conservation groups, such as the Nature Conservancy. The first of the transactions took place in 1988, when several organizations purchased more than $3 million of Costa Rica's foreign debt at 17 percent of face value. The plan called for the government to exchange with the organizations part of Costa Rica's external debt for government bonds. The conservation groups would then invest the earnings of the bonds in the management and protection of Costa Rican national parks. According to the National Wildlife Federation, while debt-for-nature swaps are not a cure-all for the Latin American debt crisis, at least the swaps can go some distance toward protecting natural resources and encouraging ecologically sound long-term economic development.

INTERNAL AND EXTERNAL DIMENSIONS OF CONFLICT

The continuing violence in much of Central America suggests that internal dynamics are perhaps more important than the overweening roles formerly ascribed to Havana, Moscow, and Washington. The removal of foreign "actors" from the stage lays bare the real reasons for violence in the region: injustice, power, greed, revenge, and racial discrimination. Havana, Moscow, and Washington, among others, merely used Central American violence in pursuit of larger policy goals. And Central American governments and guerrilla groups were equally adept at using foreign powers to advance their own interests, be they revolutionary or reactionary.

Panama offers an interesting scenario in this regard. It, like the rest of Central America, is a poor nation consisting of subsistence farmers, rural laborers, urban workers, and unemployed and underemployed people dwelling in the shantytowns ringing the larger cities. For years, the pressures for reform in Panama were skillfully rechanneled by the ruling elite toward the issue of the Panama Canal. Frustration and anger were deflected from the government, and an outdated social structure was attributed to the presence of a foreign power—the United States—in what Panamanians regarded as their territory.

Central America, in summary, is a region of diverse geography and is home to peoples of many cultures. It is a region of strong local loyalties; its problems are profound and perplexing. The violence of the land is matched by the violence of its peoples as they fight for something as noble as justice or human rights, or as ignoble as political power or self-promotion.

Belize

GEOGRAPHY
Area in Square Kilometers (Miles):
22,963 (8,866) (slightly larger than
Massachusetts)
Capital (Population): Belmopan (5,300)
Climate: tropical

PEOPLE

Population
Total: 219,300
Annual Growth Rate: 2.4%
Rural/Urban Population Ratio: 48/52
Ethnic Makeup: 44% Mestizo; 30%
Creole; 11% Mayan; 7% Garifuna; 2%
East Indian; 6% others
Major Languages: English; Spanish;
Creole dialects

Health
Life Expectancy at Birth: 67 years
(male); 71 years (female)
Infant Mortality Rate (Ratio): 34/1,000
Average Caloric Intake: 111% of FAO
minimum
Physicians Available (Ratio): 1/2,021

Religions
62% Roman Catholic; 30% Protestant;
6% others; 2% none

Education
Adult Literacy Rate: 70%

COMMUNICATION
Telephones: 15,917
Newspapers: 4 weeklies

TRANSPORTATION
Highways—Kilometers (Miles): 2,560
(1,597)
Railroads—Kilometers (Miles): none
Usable Airfields: 35

Black Carib Customs

With the nation's independence, the Black Caribs of Belize have revived
many of their old customs and beliefs in an effort to recover their heritage.
For the Black Caribs, the *uribagabaga*, or butterfly, is a symbol of one's
fortune. A black butterfly connotes bad news, an illness in the family, or even
death. On the other hand, brightly colored butterflies, which abound in
Belize, are omens of good news.

GOVERNMENT
Type: parliamentary democracy
Independence Date: September 21, 1981
Head of State/Government: Governor
General Sir Colville Young; Prime
Minister Manuel Esquivel
Political Parties: People's United Party;
United Democratic Party; National
Alliance for Belizean Rights
Suffrage: universal at 18

MILITARY
Number of Armed Forces: n/a; Belize
Defense Force Air Wing, with RAF
Harrier detachment
*Military Expenditures (% of Central
Government Expenditures):* 2.2%
Current Hostilities: border dispute with
Guatemala

ECONOMY
Currency ($ U.S. Equivalent): 2 Belize
dollars = $1 (fixed rate)
Per Capita Income/GDP: $2,750/$575
million
Inflation Rate: 2.3%
Total Foreign Debt: $167.5 million
Natural Resources: arable land; timber;
fish
Agriculture: sugarcane; citrus fruits;
rice; beans; corn; cattle; bananas; honey
Industry: sugar refining; clothing;
construction materials; beverages;
cigarettes

FOREIGN TRADE
Exports: $115 million
Imports: $281 million

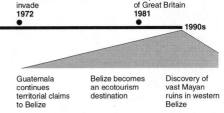

Belize is settled
by English
logwood cutters
1638

Belize is
declared an
independent
Crown colony
1884

Guatemala
threatens to
invade
1972

Independence
of Great Britain
1981

1990s

Guatemala
continues
territorial claims
to Belize

Belize becomes
an ecotourism
destination

Discovery of
vast Mayan
ruins in western
Belize

A LITTLE BIT OF ENGLAND

Belize was settled in the late 1630s by English woodcutters, who also indulged in occasional piracy at the expense of the Spanish crown. The loggers were interested primarily in dye-woods, which, in the days before chemical dyes, were essential to British textile industries. The country's name is derived from Peter Wallace, a notorious buccaneer who, from his base there, haunted the coast in search of Spanish shipping. The natives shortened and mispronounced Wallace's name until he became known as "Belize."

As a British colony (called "British Honduras"), Belize enjoyed relative prosperity as an important *entrepôt,* or storage depot for merchandise, until the completion of the Panama Railway in 1855. With the opening of a rail route to the Pacific, commerce shifted south, away from Caribbean ports. Belize entered an economic tailspin (from which it has never entirely recovered). Colonial governments attempted to diversify the colony's agricultural base and to attract foreign immigration to develop the land. But, except for some Mexican settlers and a few former Confederate soldiers who came to the colony after the U.S. Civil War, the immigration policy failed. Economically depressed, its population exposed to the ravages of yellow fever, malaria, and dengue (a tropical fever), Belize was once described by British novelist Aldous Huxley in the following terms: "If the world had ends, Belize would be one of them."

Living conditions improved markedly by the 1950s, and the colony began to move toward independence of Great Britain. Although self-governing by 1964, Belize did not become fully independent until 1981, because of Guatemalan threats to invade what it even today considers a lost province, stolen by Britain. British policy calls for a termination of its military presence, even though Guatemalan intentions toward Belize are ambivalent.

Culturally, Belize is English with Caribbean overtones. English common law is practiced in the courts, and politics are patterned on the English parliamentary system. About 30 percent of the people are Protestants. The Belizeans are primarily working-class poor and middle-class shopkeepers and merchants. There is no great difference between the well-to-do and the poor in Belize, and few people fall below the absolute poverty line.

Thirty percent of the population are Creole (black and English mixture), 7 percent Garifuna (black and Indian mixture). The Garifuna originally inhabited the Caribbean island of St. Vincent. In the eighteenth century, they joined with native Indians in an uprising against the English authorities. As punishment, virtually all the Garifuna were deported to Belize.

Despite a pervasive myth of racial democracy in Belize, discrimination exists. Belize is not a harmonious, multiethnic island in a sea of violence. For example, sociologist Bruce Ergood notes that it "is not uncommon to hear a light Creole badmouth 'blacks,' even though both are considered Creole. This reflects a vestige of English colonial attitude summed up in the saying, 'Best to be white, less good to be mulatto, worst to be black. . . .'"

A shift in population occurred in the 1980s because of the turmoil in neighboring Central American states. For years, well-educated, English-speaking Creoles had been leaving Belize in search of better economic opportunities in other countries; but this was more than made up for by the inflow of perhaps as many as 40,000 Latin American refugees fleeing the fighting in the region. Spanish is now the primary language of a significant percentage of the population, and some Belizeans are concerned about the "Hispanicization" of the country.

Women in Belize suffer discrimination that is rooted in the cultural, social, and economic structures of the society, even though the government promotes their participation in the nation's politics and development process. Great emphasis is placed on education (which is compulsory to age 16) and health care. Tropical diseases, once the primary cause of death in Belize, were brought under control by a government program of spraying. Health and nutritional awareness are emphasized in campaigns to encourage breastfeeding and the selection and preparation of meals using local produce.

DEVELOPMENT

Belize has combined its tourism and environmental-protection offices into one ministry, which holds great promise for ecotourism. Large tracts of land have been set aside to protect jaguars and other endangered species. But there is also pressure on the land from rapid population growth.

FREEDOM

The House and Senate established a Joint Select Committee to "canvass the views of the Belizean people and to make recommendations for bringing about political reform in the country."

HEALTH/WELFARE

A recent UNICEF study warns that teenage pregnancy is on the rise in Belize and, at the current rate, the level will double in 4 years. Officials cited the lack of "enough creative activities to curb the adolescent craving for sex" as well as peer pressure and alcohol consumption as reasons for the dramatic increase.

ACHIEVEMENTS

Recent digging by archaeologists has uncovered several Mayan sites that have convinced scholars that the indigenous civilization in the region was more extensive and refined than experts had previously believed.

Costa Rica (Republic of Costa Rica)

GEOGRAPHY
Area in Square Kilometers (Miles): 51,022 (19,700) (smaller than West Virginia)
Capital (Population): San José (1,000,000)
Climate: tropical and semitropical

PEOPLE

Population
Total: 3,463,100
Annual Growth Rate: 2.0%
Rural/Urban Population Ratio: 56/44
Ethnic Makeup: 96% white (including a few Mestizos); 2% black; 1% Indian; 1% Chinese
Major Language: Spanish

Health
Life Expectancy at Birth: 73 years (male); 78 years (female)
Infant Mortality Rate (Ratio): 13.5/1,000
Average Caloric Intake: 118% of FAO minimum
Physicians Available (Ratio): 1/981

Religions
95% Roman Catholic; 5% others

Education
Adult Literacy Rate: 95%

COMMUNICATION
Telephones: 281,000
Newspapers: 4 dailies

Costa Rica: Protecting Its Natural Resources

Costa Rica is not only a model democracy but also leads Central America in discouraging the soil-leaching deforestation that is ultimately so disastrous to agriculture. Costa Rica has 13 recently created national parks and six biological reserves. In these parks, some 2,000 native tree species are protected—twice the number of species found in the continental United States. New species are constantly being discovered as the lumber industry works virgin forest. To protect this important national resource further, the government has tightly controlled the number of permits it allows for the cutting and exporting of timber.

TRANSPORTATION
Highways—Kilometers (Miles): 35,560 (22,189)
Railroads—Kilometers (Miles): 950 (593)
Usable Airfields: 145

GOVERNMENT
Type: democratic republic
Independence Date: September 15, 1821
Head of State: President José María Figueres Olsen
Political Parties: National Liberation Party; Social Christian Unity Party; New Republic Movement; Progressive Party; People's Party of Costa Rica; Radical Democratic Party; Popular Vanguard Party
Suffrage: universal and compulsory at 18

MILITARY
Number of Armed Forces: about 4,700; army replaced by civil guard in 1948
Military Expenditures (% of Central Government Expenditures): 2.0%
Current Hostilities: none

ECONOMY
Currency ($ U.S. Equivalent): 200 colones = $1
Per Capita Income/GDP: $5,400/$18.4 billion
Inflation Rate: 22.5%
Total Foreign Debt: $4.0 billion
Natural Resources: hydroelectric power
Agriculture: coffee; bananas; sugarcane; rice; corn; cocoa; livestock products
Industry: food processing; textiles and clothing; construction materials; fertilizer; tourism

FOREIGN TRADE
Exports: $2.4 billion
Imports: $3.0 billion

Costa Rica
- ⊕ Capital
- • City
- ～ River
- - - - Road

0   40   kilometers
0   40 miles

COSTA RICA:
A DIFFERENT TRADITION?

Costa Rica has often been singled out as politically and socially unique in Latin America. It is true that the nation's historical development has not been as directly influenced by Spain as its neighbors' have, but this must not obscure the essential Hispanic character of the Costa Rican people and their institutions. Historian Ralph Woodward has observed that, historically, Costa Rica's "uniqueness was the product of her relative remoteness from the remainder of Central America, her slight economic importance to Spain, and her lack of a non-white subservient class and corresponding lack of a class of large landholders to exploit its labors." Indeed, in 1900, Costa Rica had a higher percentage of farmers with small- and medium-range operations than any other Latin American country.

The nature of Costa Rica's economy allowed a wider participation in politics and fostered the development of political institutions dedicated to the equality of all people, which existed only in theory in other Latin American countries. Costa Rican politicians, since the late nineteenth century, have endorsed programs that have been largely middle class in content. The government has consistently demonstrated a commitment to the social welfare of its citizens.

AN INTEGRATED SOCIETY

Despite the recent atmosphere of crisis and disintegration in Central America, Costa Rica's durable democracy has avoided the twin evils of oppressive authoritarianism and class warfare. But, what might be construed as good luck is actually a reflection of Costa Rica's history. In social, racial, linguistic, and educational terms, Costa Rica is an integrated country without the fractures and cleavages that typify the rest of the region.

Despite its apparent uniqueness, Costa Rica is culturally an integral part of Latin America and embodies what is most positive about Hispanic political culture. The government has long played the role of benevolent patron to the majority of its citizens. Opposition and antagonism have historically been defused by a process of accommodation, mutual cooperation, and participation. In the early 1940s, for example, modernizers who wanted to create a dynamic capitalist economy took care to pacify the emerging labor movement with appropriate social legislation and benefits. Moreover, to assure that development did not sacrifice social welfare, the state assumed a traditional role with respect to the economy—that is, it took an active role in

the production and distribution of income. After much discussion, in 1993, the Costa Rican Congress authorized the privatization of the state-owned cement and fertilizer companies. In both cases, according to *Latin American Regional Reports,* "a 30% stake [would] be reserved for employees, 20% [would] be offered to private investors, and the remainder [would] be shared out between trade unions . . . and cooperatives." Tight controls were retained on banking, insurance, oil refining, and public utilities.

Women, who were granted the right to vote in the 1940s, have participated freely in Costa Rica's elections. Women have served as a vice president, minister of foreign commerce, and president of the Legislative Assembly. Although in broader terms the role of women is primarily domestic, they are legally unrestricted. Equal work, in general, is rewarded by equal pay for men and women. But women also hold, as a rule, lower-paying jobs.

POLITICS OF CONSENSUS

Costa Rica's political stability is assured by the politics of consensus. Deals and compacts are the order of the day among various competing elites. Political competition is open, and participation by labor and peasants is expanding. Election campaigns provide a forum to air differing

viewpoints, to educate the voting public, and to keep politicians in touch with the population at large.

Costa Rica frequently has had strong, charismatic leaders who have been committed to social democracy and have rejected a brand of politics grounded in class differences. The country's democracy has always reflected the paternalism and personalities of its presidents.

This tradition was again endorsed when José María Figueres Olsen won the presidential election on February 6, 1994. Figueres is the son of the founder of the modern Costa Rican democracy, and he promised to return to a reduced version of the welfare state. But, by 1996, in the face of a sluggish economy, the populist champion adopted policies that were markedly pro-business. As a result, opinion polls rapidly turned against him; more than half the population felt that his performance was "bad or very bad."

Other oft-given reasons for Costa Rica's stability are the high levels of toleration exhibited by its people and the absence of a military establishment. Costa Rica has had no military establishment since a brief civil war in 1948. Government officials have long boasted that they rule over a country that has more teachers than soldiers. There is also a strong public tradition that favors demilitarization. Costa

(United Nations photo/Milton Grant)

The beauty of some Costa Rican mountains and forest is being sacrificed to development as more and more of the land is being turned to agricultural use.

Spain establishes its first settlements in Costa Rica **1522**	Independence of Spain **1821**	Costa Rica is part of the United Provinces of Central America **1823**	Costa Rica becomes independent as a separate state **1838**	Civil war; reforms; abolition of the army **1948**	Costa Rica takes steps to protect its tropical rain forests and dry forests **1980s**	**1990s**

Costa Rica experiences severe economic recession

Ecotourism to Costa Rica increases

Elections are scheduled for 1998

Rica's auxiliary forces, however, could form the nucleus of an army in a time of emergency.

The Costa Rican press is among the most unrestricted in Latin America, and differing opinions are openly expressed. Human-rights abuses are virtually nonexistent in the country, but there is a general suspicion of Communists in this overwhelmingly middle-class, white society. And some citizens are concerned about the antidemocratic ideas expressed by ultraconservatives.

The strain placed on the Costa Rican economy by the violence in the region and the press of refugees—at one time as high as 250,000—helped to create a climate of fear and uncertainty, especially with regard to the government's ability to deliver social services. (More than 80 percent of the population are covered by social-security programs, and approximately 60 percent are provided with pensions and medical benefits.)

With the dawn of peace in Central America, many refugees returned home, and the Costa Rican economy experienced a brief revival. But, by 1994 and 1995, signs of economic distress were common, and President Figueres was forced to reconsider many of his statist policies. While the export sector remained healthy, domestic industry languished and the internal debt ballooned. The Costa Rican–American Chamber of Commerce observed that "Costa Rica, with its tiny $8.6 billion GDP and 3.5 million people, can not afford a government that consistently overspends its budget by 5% or more and then sells short-term bonds,

mostly to state institutions, to finance the deficit." In 1997, there was a vigorous debate over the possible privatization of many state entities in an effort to reduce the debt quickly. But opponents of privatization noted that state institutions were important contributors to the high standard of living in the country. With presidential elections scheduled for 1998, the sluggish state of the economy will strain the politics of consensus.

THE ENVIRONMENT

At a time when tropical rain forests globally are under assault by developers, cattle barons, and land-hungry peasants, Costa Rica has taken concrete action to protect its environment. Minister of Natural Resources Álvaro Umaña was one of those responsible for engineering an imaginative debt-for-nature swap. In his words: "We would like to see debt relief support conservation ... a policy that everybody agrees is good." Since 1986, the Costa Rican government has authorized the conversion of $75 million in commercial debt into bonds. Interest generated by those bonds has supported a variety of projects, such as the enlargement and protection of La Amistad, a 1.7 million-acre reserve of tropical rain forest.

About 13 percent of Costa Rica's land is protected currently in a number of national parks. It is hoped that very soon about 25 percent of the country will be designated as national parkland in order to protect tropical rain forests as well as the even more endangered tropical dry forests.

Much of the assault on the forests typically has been dictated by economic ne-

cessity and/or greed. In one all-too-common scenario, a small- or middle-size cacao grower discovers that his crop has been decimated by a blight. Confronted by disaster, he will usually farm the forest surrounding his property for timber and then torch the remainder. Ultimately, he will likely sell his land to a cattle rancher, who will transform what had once been rain forest or dry forest into pasture.

In an effort to break this devastating pattern, at least one Costa Rican environmental organization has devised a workable plan to save the forests. Farmers are introduced to a variety of cash crops so that they will not be totally dependent on a single crop. Also, in the case of cacao, for example, the farmer will be provided with a disease- or blight-resistant strain to lessen further the chances of crop losses and subsequent conversion of land to cattle pasture.

Scientists in Costa Rica are concerned that tropical forests are being destroyed before their usefulness to humankind can be fully appreciated. Such forests contain a treasure-trove of medicinal herbs. In Costa Rica, for example, there is at least one plant common to the rain forests that might be beneficial in the struggle against AIDS.

DEVELOPMENT

Despite government claims that deforestation has been brought under control, environmentalists charge that more trees were cut in the last logging season than in previous years, according to a report in *The Tico Times.* Recent laws with regard to logging have loopholes that allow loggers to destroy the few forests remaining outside Costa Rica's national-park system.

FREEDOM

Despite a generally enviable human-rights record for the region, there is some de facto discrimination against blacks, Indians, and women (domestic violence against women is a serious problem). The press is free. A stringent libel law, however, makes the media cautious in reporting of personalities.

HEALTH/WELFARE

Costa Ricans enjoy the highest standard of living in Central America. But Costa Rica's indigenous peoples, in part because of their remote location, have inadequate schools, health care, and access to potable water. Moreover, because many lack citizenship papers, they cannot vote or hold office.

ACHIEVEMENTS

In a region torn by civil war and political chaos, Costa Rica's years of free and democratic elections stand as a remarkable achievement in political stability and civil rights. President Óscar Arias was awarded the Nobel Peace Prize in 1987; he remains an internationally recognized and respected world leader.

El Salvador (Republic of El Salvador)

GEOGRAPHY

Area in Square Kilometers (Miles):
21,476 (8,292) (about the size of
Massachusetts)
Capital (Population): San Salvador
(1,400,000)
Climate: semitropical; distinct wet and
dry seasons

PEOPLE

Population

Total: 5,829,000
Annual Growth Rate: 1.8%
Rural/Urban Population Ratio: 55/45
Ethnic Makeup: 94% Mestizo; 5%
Indian; 1% white
Major Language: Spanish

Health

Life Expectancy at Birth: 65 years
(male); 73 years (female)
Infant Mortality Rate (Ratio): 32/1,000
Average Caloric Intake: 94% of FAO
minimum
Physicians Available (Ratio): 1/1,322

Religions

75% Roman Catholic; 25% Protestant
groups

Education

Adult Literacy Rate: 72%

COMMUNICATION

Telephones: 116,000
Newspapers: 6 dailies

The Need to Flee

El Salvador has frequently been in a state of turmoil. Because revolution and
counterrevolution have historically been such a large element in their lives,
the people of El Salvador have had to decide which military or political
factions to back. Often the people of the villages have had to hide in the bush
to avoid soldiers—so often, in fact, that this occurrence has been called
aquinda, a word not found in any dictionary, which means "to flee in the
middle of the night with everything you've got." It is hoped that the lexicon
of El Salvador will become more life-affirming with the formal 1992 cease-fire
to the Civil War.

TRANSPORTATION

Highways—Kilometers (Miles): 12,251
(7,645)
Railroads—Kilometers (Miles): 602 (374)
Usable Airfields: 73

GOVERNMENT

Type: republic
Independence Date: September 15, 1821
Head of State: President Armando
Calderón Sol
Political Parties: Farabundo Martí
National Liberation Front; National
Republican Alliance Party; National
Conciliation Party; Christian
Democratic Party; Democratic
Convergence; Unity Movement; others
Suffrage: universal at 18

MILITARY

Number of Armed Forces: 31,500
Military Expenditures (% of Central
Government Expenditures): 1.0%
Current Hostilities: none

ECONOMY

Currency ($ U.S. Equivalent): 8.76
colones = $1
Per Capita Income/GDP: $1,950/$11.4
billion
Inflation Rate: 11.4%
Total Foreign Debt: $2.6 billion
Natural Resources: hydroelectric and
geothermal power
Agriculture: coffee; cotton; sugar;
livestock; corn; poultry; sorghum
Industry: food and beverages; textiles;
footwear and clothing; chemical
products; petroleum products

FOREIGN TRADE

Exports: $1.6 billion
Imports: $3.3 billion

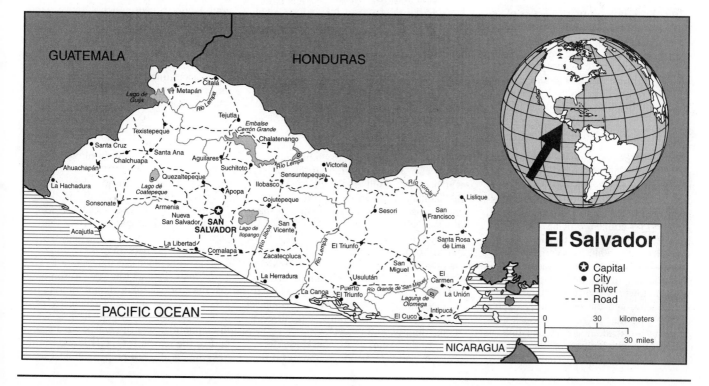

EL SALVADOR:
A TROUBLED LAND

El Salvador, a small country, was engaged until 1992 in a civil war that cut through class lines, divided the military and the Roman Catholic Church, and damaged the social and economic fabric of the nation. It was the latest in a long series of violent sociopolitical eruptions that have plagued the country since its independence in 1821.

In the last quarter of the nineteenth century, large plantation owners—spurred by the sharp increase in the world demand for coffee and other products of tropical agriculture—expanded their lands and estates. Most of the new land was purchased or taken from Indians and Mestizos (those of mixed white and Indian blood), who, on five occasions between 1872 and 1898, took up arms in futile attempts to preserve their land. The once-independent Indians and Mestizos were reduced to becoming tenant farmers, sharecroppers, day laborers, or peons on the large estates. Indians, when deprived of their lands, also lost much of their cultural and ethnic distinctiveness. Today, El Salvador is an overwhelmingly Mestizo society.

The uprooted peasantry was controlled in a variety of ways. Some landowners played the role of *patrón* and assured workers the basic necessities of life in return for their labor. Laws against "vagabonds" (those who, when stopped by rural police, did not have a certain amount of money in their pockets) assured plantation owners a workforce and discouraged peasant mobility.

To enforce order further, a series of security organizations—the National Guard, the National Police, and the Treasury Police—were created by the central government. Many of these security personnel actually lived on the plantations and estates and followed the orders of the owner. Although protection of the economic system was their primary function, over time, elements of these organizations became private armies.

This phenomenon lay at the heart of much of the "unofficial" violence in El Salvador in recent years. In Salvadoran society, personal loyalties to relatives or local strongmen competed with and often superseded loyalty to government officials. Because of this, the government was unable to control some elements within its security forces.

In an analysis of the Salvadoran Civil War, it is tempting to place the rich, right-wing landowners and their military allies on one side; and the poor, the peasantry, and the guerrillas on the other. Such a division is artificial, however, and fails to reflect the complexities of the conflict. Granted, the military and landowners had

enjoyed a mutually beneficial partnership since 1945. But there were liberal and conservative factions within the armed forces, and, since the 1940s, there had been some movement toward needed social and economic reforms. It was a military regime in 1949 that put into effect the country's first social-security legislation. In 1950, a Constitution was established that provided for public-health programs, women's suffrage, and extended social-security coverage. The reformist impulse continued in the 1960s, when it became legal to organize opposition political parties.

A TIME FOR CHANGE

Food production increased in the 1970s by 44 percent, a growth that was second in Latin America only to Brazil's. Although much of the food grown was exported to world markets, some of the revenue generated was used for social programs in El Salvador. Life expectancy increased; the death rate fell; illiteracy declined; and the percentage of government expenditures on public health, housing, and education was among the highest in Latin America.

The programs and reforms, in classic Hispanic form, were generated by the upper classes. The elite believed that state-sponsored changes could be controlled in such a way that traditional balances in society would remain intact and elite domination of the government would be assured.

El Salvador's Civil War may be traced to 1972, when the Christian Democratic candidate for president, José Napoleón Duarte, is believed to have won the popular vote but deprived of his victory when the army declared the results false and handed the victory to its own candidate. Impatient and frustrated, middle-class politicians and student leaders from the opposition began to consider more forceful ways to oust the ruling class.

By 1979, guerrilla groups had become well established in rural El Salvador, and some younger army officers grew concerned that a successful left-wing popular revolt was a distinct possibility. Rather than wait for revolution from below, which might result in the destruction of the military as an institution, the officers chose to seize power in a coup and manipulate change from above. Once in power, this *junta,* or ruling body, moved quickly to transform the structure of Salvadoran society. A land-reform program, originally developed by civilian reformers and Roman Catholic clergy, was adopted by the military. It would give the *campesinos* ("peasants") not only land but also status, dignity, and respect.

In its first year, 1980, the land-reform program had a tremendous impact on the

landowning elite—37 percent of the lands producing cotton and 34 percent of the coffee-growing lands were confiscated by the government and redistributed. The junta also nationalized the banks and assumed control of the sale of coffee and sugar. Within months, however, several peasant members of the new cooperatives and the government agricultural advisers sent to help them were gunned down. The violence spread. Some of the killings were attributed to government security men in the pay of dispossessed landowners, but most of the killings may have been committed by the army.

In the opinion of a land-reform program official, the army was corrupt and had returned to the cooperatives that it had helped to establish in order to demand money for protection and bribes. When the peasants refused, elements within the army initiated a reign of terror against them.

In 1989, further deterioration of the land-reform program was brought about by Supreme Court decisions and by policies adopted by the newly elected right-wing government of President Alfredo Cristiani. Former landowners who had had property taken for redistribution to peasants successfully argued that seizures under the land reform were illegal. Subsequently, five successive land-reform cases were decided by the Supreme Court in favor of former property owners.

Cristiani, whose right-wing National Republican Alliance Party (ARENA) fought hard against land reform, would not directly attack the land-reform program—only because such a move would further alienate rural peasants and drive them into the arms of left-wing guerrillas. Instead, Cristiani favored the reconstitution of collective farms as private plots. Such a move, according to the government, would improve productivity and put an end to what authorities perceived as a form of U.S.–imposed "socialism." Critics of the government's policy charged that the privatization plan would ultimately result in the demise of land reform altogether.

Yet another problem was that many of the collectives established under the reform were (and remain) badly in debt. A 1986 study by the U.S. Agency for International Development reported that 95 percent of the cooperatives could not pay interest on the debt they were forced to acquire to compensate the landlords. *New York Times* reporter Lindsey Gruson noted that the world surplus of agricultural products as well as mismanagement by peasants who suddenly found themselves in the unfamiliar role of owners were a large part of the reason for the failures. But the government did not help. Technical assistance was not provided, and the tremendous debt gave the cooperatives a poor credit rating, which made it difficult for them to secure needed fertilizer and pesticides.

Declining yields and, for many families, lives of increasing desperation have been the result. Some peasants must leave the land and sell their plots to the highest bidder. This will ultimately bring about a reconcentration of land in the hands of former landlords.

Other prime farmland lay untended because of the Civil War. Violence drove many peasants from the land to the slums of the larger cities. And free-fire zones established by the military (in an effort to destroy the guerrillas' popular base) and guerrilla attacks against cooperatives (in an effort to sabotage the economy and further destabilize the country) had a common victim: the peasantry.

Some cooperatives and individual families failed to bring the land to flower because of the poor quality of the soil they inherited. Reporter Gruson told the story of one family, which was, unfortunately, all too common:

José . . . received 1.7 acres on a rock-pocked slope an hour's walk from his small shack. José . . . used to sell some of his beans and rice to raise a little

cash. But year after year his yields have declined. Since he cannot afford fertilizers or insecticides, the corn that survives the torrential rainy season produces pest-infested ears the size of a baby's foot. Now, he has trouble feeding his wife and seven children.

"The land is no good," he said. "I've been working it for 12 years and my life has gotten worse every year. I don't have anywhere to go, but I'll have to leave soon."

After the coup, several governments came and went. The original reformers retired, went into exile, or went over to the guerrillas. The Civil War continued into 1992, when a United Nations–mediated cease-fire took effect. The extreme right and left regularly utilized assassination to eliminate or terrorize both each other and the voices of moderation who still dared to speak out. The death squads and guerrillas claimed their victims from all social classes. Some leaders, such as former president Duarte, described a culture of violence in El Salvador that had become part of the national character.

HUMAN-RIGHTS ISSUES

Through 1992, human-rights abuses still occurred on a wide scale in El Salvador.

Public order was constantly disrupted by military operations, guerrilla raids, factional hatreds, acts of revenge, personal grudges, pervasive fear, and a sense of uncertainty about the future. State-of-siege decrees suspended all constitutional rights to freedom of speech and press. However, self-censorship, both in the media and by individuals, out of fear of violent reprisals, was the leading constraint on free expression in El Salvador.

Release of the report in 1993 by the UN's "Truth Commission," a special body entrusted with the investigation of human-rights violations in El Salvador, prompted the right wing–dominated Congress to approve an amnesty for those named. But progress has been made in other areas. The National Police have been separated from the Defense Ministry; and the National Guard, Civil Defense forces, and the notorious Treasury Police have been abolished. A new National Civilian Police, comprised of 20 percent of National Police, 20 percent former Farabundo Martí National Liberation Front (FMLN) guerrillas, and 60 percent with no involvement on either side in the Civil War, was instituted in 1994.

In El Salvador, as elsewhere in Latin America, the Roman Catholic Church was divided. The majority of Church officials

(Y. Nagata/PAS United Nations photo)

The need for self-sufficient food production has gone through a number of challenges in El Salvador. Civil strife disrupted much of the agrarian production, and lack of developed fishery planning necessitated importing from other parts of the world. With a new and efficient program to take advantage of available fish in domestic waters, El Salvador has been able to develop an effective food industry from the sea.

backed government policy and supported the United States' contention that the violence in El Salvador was due to Cuban-backed subversion. Other clergy strongly disagreed and argued convincingly that the violence was deeply rooted in historical social injustice.

GOVERNANCE

The election to the presidency of José Napoleón Duarte in 1984 was an important first step in establishing the legitimacy of government in El Salvador, as were municipal elections in 1985. The United States supported Duarte as a representative of the "democratic" middle ground between the guerrillas of the FMLN and the right-wing ARENA party. Ironically, U.S. policy in fact undermined Duarte's claims to legitimacy and created a widespread impression that he was little more than a tool for U.S. interests.

Yet, while the transfer of power to President Cristiani via the electoral process in 1989 reflected the will of those who voted, it did not augur well for the lessening of human-rights abuses. With respect to the guerrillas of the FMLN, Cristiani made it clear that the government would set the terms for any talks about ending the Civil War. For its part, the FMLN warned that it would make the country "ungovernable." In effect, then, the 1989 election results polarized the country's political life even more.

After several unsuccessful efforts to bring the government and the guerrillas to the negotiating table, the two sides reached a tentative agreement in April 1991 on constitutional reforms at a UN-sponsored meeting in Mexico City. The military, judicial system, and electoral process were all singled out for sweeping changes. By October, the FMLN had promised to lay down its arms; and near midnight on December 31, the final points of a peace accord were agreed upon. Final refinements of the agreement were drawn up in New York, and a formal signing ceremony was staged in Mexico City on January 16, 1992. The official cease-fire took effect February 1, thus ending the 12-year Civil War that had claimed more than 70,000 lives and given El Salvador the reputation of a bloody and abusive country.

Implementation of the agreement reached between the government and the FMLN has proven contentious. "But," according to *Boston Globe* correspondent Pamela Constable, "a combination of war-weariness and growing pragmatism among leaders of all persuasions suggests that once-bitter adversaries have begun to develop a modus vivendi."

President Cristiani reduced the strength of the army from 63,000 to 31,500 by February 1993, earlier than provided for by the agreement; and the class of officers known as the *tondona*, who had long dominated the military and were likely responsible for human-rights abuses, were forcibly retired by the president on June 30, 1993. Land, judicial, and electoral reforms followed. Despite perhaps inevitable setbacks because of the legacy of violence and bitterness, editor Juan Comas wrote that "most analysts are inclined to believe that El Salvador's hour of madness has passed and the country is now on the road to hope."

In 1994, Armando Calderón Sol of the ARENA party swept elections at the local and national levels by a two-to-one majority. Calderón has proven to date to be an indecisive leader. Political scientist Tommie Sue Montgomery notes that his "reputation for espousing as policy the last viewpoint he has heard has produced in civil society both heartburn and black humor." But the former guerrillas of the FMLN have not been able to take advantage of ARENA's weak leadership. In legislative elections in 1997, neither ARENA nor the former guerrillas gained a majority in the 84-seat Legislature.

ECONOMIC PROSPECTS

El Salvador has always been an inherently rich country, in terms of its resources. Recovery from the Civil War has been impressive, although the 7 percent growth rates of the early 1990s had fallen to about 4 percent by 1997. Inflation is relatively low, the level of foreign indebtedness modest, and the gross domestic product has grown steadily since 1990. But a UN–sponsored program of reconstruction and reconciliation was short on funds and, in 1995, was in danger of losing momentum.

DEVELOPMENT

Since 1991, the government has been able to attract substantial investment in a new industry of low-wage, duty-free assembly plants patterned after the *maquiladora* industries along Mexico's border with the United States. Advantageous tax laws and a free-market climate favorable to business are central to the government's development policy.

FREEDOM

The end of the Civil War brought an overall improvement in human rights in El Salvador. The number of extrajudicial killings fell significantly, and politically motivated killings seem to be on the wane. News from across the political spectrum, often critical of the government, is reported in El Salvador, although foreign journalists seem to be the target of an unusually high level of muggings, robberies, and burglaries.

HEALTH/WELFARE

Many Salvadorans suffer from parasites and malnutrition. El Salvador has one of the highest infant mortality rates in the Western Hemisphere, largely because of polluted water. Potable water is readily available to only 10% of the population. Violence against women is widespread. Judges often dismiss rape cases on the pretext that the victim provoked the crime.

ACHIEVEMENTS

Despite the violence of war, political power has been transferred via elections at both the municipal and national levels. Elections have helped to establish the legitimacy of civilian leaders in a region usually dominated by military regimes.

Guatemala (Republic of Guatemala)

GEOGRAPHY

Area in Square Kilometers (Miles):
108,780 (42,000) (about the size of Tennessee)
Capital (Population): Guatemala City (1,100,000)
Climate: temperate in highlands; semitropical on coasts

PEOPLE

Population

Total: 11,278,000
Annual Growth Rate: 2.5%
Rural/Urban Population Ratio: 62/38
Ethnic Makeup: 56% Ladino (Mestizo and Westernized Indian); 44% Amerindian
Major Languages: Spanish; Mayan languages

Health

Life Expectancy at Birth: 63 years (male); 68 years (female); 44 years (Indian population)
Infant Mortality Rate (Ratio): 51/1,000
Average Caloric Intake: 93% of FAO minimum
Physicians Available (Ratio): 1/2,356

Religions

predominantly Roman Catholic; also Protestant and traditional Mayan

Education

Adult Literacy Rate: 55%

COMMUNICATION

Telephones: 210,000
Newspapers: 4 dailies

TRANSPORTATION

Highways—Kilometers (Miles): 12,033 (7,509)
Railroads—Kilometers (Miles): 884 (552)
Usable Airfields: 463

GOVERNMENT

Type: republic
Independence Date: September 15, 1821
Head of State: President Alvaro Arzu Irigoyen
Political Parties: National Centrist Union; Solidarity Action Movement; Christian Democratic Party; National Advancement Party; National Liberation Movement; Social Democratic Party; Revolutionary Democratic Party; Guatemalan Republican Front; Democratic Union
Suffrage: universal at 18

MILITARY

Number of Armed Forces: 43,500
Military Expenditures (% of Central Government Expenditures): 13.3%
Current Hostilities: civil war

ECONOMY

Currency ($ U.S. Equivalent): 5.93 quetzals = $1
Per Capita Income/GDP: $3,300/$36.7 billion
Inflation Rate: 9%
Total Foreign Debt: $3.1 billion
Natural Resources: oil; nickel; timber
Agriculture: corn; beans; coffee; cotton; cattle; sugarcane; bananas; timber; rice; cardamom
Industry: food processing; textiles; construction materials; pharmaceuticals; furniture; tires

FOREIGN TRADE

Exports: $2.3 billion
Imports: $2.9 billion

Miguel Ángel Asturias

For many years, the infamous United Fruit Company, based in Boston, Massachusetts, played an important role in Guatemala's economy and political life. The Guatemalan Nobel Prize–winning author Miguel Ángel Asturias bitterly criticized the excesses of this company in a famous trilogy of novels: *Strong Wind, The Green Pope,* and *The Eyes of the Interred.* For these and other novels—notably, *El Señor Presidente,* which is the story of one of Guatemala's most ruthless dictators—Asturias has been called "the conscience of his country."

Guatemala map

GUATEMALA:
PEOPLES IN CONFLICT

Ethnic relations between the descendants of Mayan Indians, who comprise 44 percent of Guatemala's population, and whites and Ladinos (Hispanicized Indians) have always been unfriendly and have contributed significantly to the nation's turbulent history. During the colonial period and since independence, Spaniards, Creoles (in Guatemala, whites born in the New World—as opposed to in Nicaragua, where Creoles are native-born blacks), and Ladinos have repeatedly sought to dominate the Guatemalan Indian population, largely contained in the highlands, by controlling the Indians' land and their labor.

The process of domination was accelerated between 1870 and 1920, as Guatemala's entry into world markets hungry for tropical produce such as coffee resulted in the purchase or extensive seizures of land from Indians. Denied sufficient lands of their own, Indians were forced onto the expanding plantations as debt peons. Others were forced to labor as seasonal workers on coastal plantations; many died there because of the sharp climatic differences.

THE INDIAN AND INTEGRATION

Assaulted by the Ladino world, highland Indians withdrew into their own culture and built social barriers between themselves and the changing world outside their villages. Those barriers have persisted until the present.

For the Guatemalan governments that have thought in terms of economic progress and national unity, the Indians have always presented a problem. (In 1964, the Guatemalan national census separated the population into two social categories: whites and Ladinos, and Indians.) Traditionally, the white world has perceived them as a burden. "Backward," "custom-bound," "superstitious," "uneducated," and "unassimilable" is how the Indians were described in the late nineteenth century. Those same descriptions are often used today.

According to anthropologist Leslie Dow, Jr., Guatemalan governments too easily explain the Indian's lack of material prosperity in terms of the "deficiencies" of Indian culture. Indian "backwardness" is better explained by elite policies calculated to keep Indians subordinate. Social, political, and economic deprivations have consistently and consciously been utilized by governments anxious to maintain the Indian in an inferior status.

Between 1945 and 1954, however, there was a period of remarkable social reform in Guatemala. Before the reforms were cut short by the resistance of landowners, fac-

tions within the military, and a U.S. Central Intelligence Agency–sponsored invasion, Guatemalan governments made a concerted effort to integrate the Indian into national life. Some Indians who lived in close proximity to large urban centers such as the capital, Guatemala City, learned that their vote had the power to effect changes to their benefit. They also realized that they were unequal not because of their illiteracy, "backwardness," poverty, or inability to converse in Spanish, but because of governments that refused to reform their political, social, and economic structures.

In theory, indigenous peoples in Guatemala enjoy equal legal rights under the Constitution. In fact, however, they remain largely outside the national culture, do not speak Spanish, and are not integrated into the national economy. Indian males are far more likely to be impressed into the army or guerrilla units. Indigenous peoples in Guatemala have suffered most of the combat-related casualties and repeated abuses of their basic human rights. There remains a pervasive discrimination against Indians in white society.

Indians have on occasion challenged state policies that they have considered inequitable and repressive. But, if they become too insistent on change, threaten violence or societal upheaval, or support and/or join guerrilla groups, government repression is usually swift and merciless.

GUERRILLA WARFARE

A civil war, which was to last for 36 years, developed in 1960. Guatemala was plagued by violence, attributed both to left-wing insurgencies in rural areas and to armed forces' counterinsurgency operations. Led by youthful middle-class rebels, guerrillas gained strength because of several factors: the radical beliefs of some Roman Catholic priests in rural areas; the ability of the guerrillas to mobilize Indians for the first time; and the "demonstration effect" of events elsewhere in Central America. Some of the success is explained by the guerrilla leaders' ability to converse in Indian languages. Radical clergy increased the recruitment of Indians into the guerrilla forces by suggesting that revolution was an acceptable path to social justice. The excesses of the armed forces in their search for subversives drove other Indians into the arms of the guerrillas. In some parts of the highlands, the loss of ancestral lands to speculators or army officers was sufficient to inspire the Indians to join the radical cause.

According to the *Latin American Regional Report* for Mexico and Central America, government massacres of guer-

rillas and their actual or suspected supporters were frequent and "characterized by clinical savagery." At times, the killing was selective, with community leaders and their families singled out. In other instances, entire villages were destroyed and all the inhabitants slaughtered. "Everything depends on the army's perception of the local level of support for the guerrillas," according to the report.

To counterbalance the violence, once guerrillas were cleared from an area, the government implemented an "Aid Program to Areas in Conflict." Credit was offered to small farmers to boost food production in order to meet local demand, and displaced and jobless people were enrolled in food-for-work units to build roads or other public projects.

By the mid-1980s, most of the guerrillas' military organizations had been destroyed. This was the result not only of successful counterinsurgency tactics by the Guatemalan military but also of serious errors of judgment by guerrilla leaders. Impatient and anxious for change, the guerrillas overestimated the willingness of the Guatemalan people to rebel. They also underestimated the power of the military establishment. Surviving guerrilla units maintained an essentially defensive posture for the remainder of the decade. In 1989, however, the guerrillas regrouped. The subsequent intensification of human-rights abuses and the climate of violence were indicative of the military's response.

There was some hope for improvement in 1993, in the wake of the ouster of President Jorge Serrano, whose attempt to emulate the "self-coup" of Peru's Alberto Fujimori failed. Guatemala's next president, Ramiro de León Carpio, was a human-rights activist who was sharply critical of security forces in their war against the guerrillas of the Guatemalan National Revolutionary Unity (URNG). Peace talks between the government and guerrillas had been pursued with the Roman Catholic Church as intermediary for several years, with sparks of promise but no real change. In July 1993, de León announced a new set of proposals to bring to an end the decades of bloodshed that had resulted in 140,000 deaths. Those proposals were the basis for the realization of a peace agreement worked out under the auspices of the United Nations in December 1996.

But the underlying causes of the violence still must be addressed. Colin Woodard, writing in *The Chronicle of Higher Education,* reported that the peace accords promise to "reshape Guatemala as a democratic, multicultural society." But an estimated 70 percent of the Maya Indians live in poverty, and more than 80 percent are illiterate. Estuardo Zapeta, Guatemala's first Mayan newspaper columnist, wrote: "This is a multicultural, multilingual society. . . . As long as we leave the Maya illiterate, we're condemning them to being peasants. And if that happens, their need to acquire farmland will lead us to another civil war." This, however, is only one facet of a multifaceted set of issues. The very complexity of Guatemalan society, according to political scientist Rachel McCleary, "make[s] it extremely difficult to attain a consensus at the national level on the nature of the problems confronting society." But the new ability of leaders from many sectors of society to work together to shape a meaningful peace is a hopeful sign.

Although the fighting has ended, the fear persists. Journalist Woodard wrote in July 1997, "In many neighborhoods [in Guatemala City,] private property is protected by razor wire and patrolled by guards with pump-action shotguns." One professor at the University of San Carlos observed, "It is good that the war is over, but I am pessimistic about the peace. . . . There is intellectual freedom now, but we are very unsure of the permanence of that freedom. It makes us very cautious."

URBAN VIOLENCE

Although most of the violence occurred in rural areas, urban Guatemala did not escape the horrors of the Civil War. The following characterization of Guatemalan politics, written by an English traveler in 1839, is still relevant today: "There is but one side to the politics in Guatemala. Both

(United Nations photo/152/271/Antoinette Jongen)

This elderly Indian woman of San Mateo looks back on a life of economic and social prejudice. In recent years, Indians in Guatemala have pursued their rights by exercising their voting power. On occasion, they have resorted to violence, which has been repressed swiftly and mercilessly by the government. But the power of the ballot box has finally begun to reap gains.

Guatemala is conquered by Spanish forces from Mexico
1523

Independence
1821

Guatemala is part of the United Provinces of Central America
1822–1838

Guatemala becomes independent as a separate state
1838

Revolution; many reforms
1944

A CIA–sponsored coup deposes the reformist government
1954

Miguel Ángel Asturias wins the Nobel Prize
1967

An earthquake leaves 22,000 dead
1976

Human-rights abuses lead to the termination of U.S. aid
1977

1990s

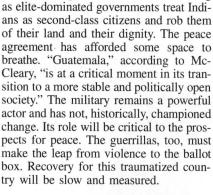

Human-rights activist Ramiro de León Carpio is named to the presidency

Alvaro Arzu Irigoyen is elected president in 1995

Talks between the government and guerrillas end 36 years of violence

parties have a beautiful way of producing unanimity of opinion, by driving out of the country all who do not agree with them."

During the Civil War, right-wing killers murdered dozens of leaders of the moderate political left to prevent them from organizing viable political parties that might challenge the ruling elite. These killers also assassinated labor leaders if their unions were considered leftist or antigovernment. Leaders among university students and professors "disappeared" because the national university had a reputation as a center of leftist subversion. Media people were gunned down if they were critical of the government or the right wing. Left-wing extremists also assassinated political leaders associated with "repressive" policies, civil servants (whose only "crime" was government employment), military personnel and police, foreign diplomats, peasant informers, and businesspeople and industrialists associated with the government.

Common crime rose to epidemic proportions in Guatemala City (as well as in the capitals of other Central American republics). Many of the weapons that once armed the Nicaraguan militias and El Salvador's civil-defense patrols found their way onto the black market, where, according to the Managua newspaper *Pensamiento Propio,* they were purchased by the Guatemalan Army, the guerrillas of the URNG, and criminals.

The fear of official or unofficial violence has always inhibited freedom of the press in Guatemala. Early in the 1980s, the Conference on Hemispheric Affairs

noted that restrictions on the print media and the indiscriminate brutality of the death squads "turned Guatemala into a virtual no-man's land for journalists." Lingering fears and memories of past violence tend to limit the exercise of press freedoms guaranteed by the Constitution. The U.S. State Department's *Country Reports* notes that "the media continues to exercise a degree of self-censorship on certain topics. . . . The lack of aggressive investigative reporting dealing with the military and human rights violations apparently is due to self-censorship."

HEALTH CARE AND NUTRITION

In rural Guatemala, half the population have a diet that is well below the minimum daily caloric intake established by the Food and Agricultural Organization. Growth in the staple food crops (corn, rice, beans, wheat) has failed to keep pace with population growth. Marginal malnutrition is endemic.

Health services vary, depending on location, but are uniformly poor in rural Guatemala. The government has begun pilot programs in three departments to provide basic primary health care on a wide scale. But some of these well-intentioned policies have failed because of a lack of sensitivity to cultural differences. Anthropologist Linda Greenberg has observed that the Ministry of Health, as part of its campaign to bring basic health-care services to the hinterlands, introduced midwives ignorant of Indian traditions. For Guatemalan Indians, pregnancy is considered an illness and demands specific care,

calling for certain foods, herbs, body positions, and interpersonal relations between expectant mother and Indian midwife. In the Mayan culture, traditional medicine has spiritual, psychological, physical, social, and symbolic dimensions. Ministry of Health workers too often dismiss traditional practices as superstitious and unscientific. This insensitivity and ignorance creates ineffectual health-care programs.

THE FUTURE

Turmoil will persist in Guatemala as long as elite-dominated governments treat Indians as second-class citizens and rob them of their land and their dignity. The peace agreement has afforded some space to breathe. "Guatemala," according to McCleary, "is at a critical moment in its transition to a more stable and politically open society." The military remains a powerful actor and has not, historically, championed change. Its role will be critical to the prospects for peace. The guerrillas, too, must make the leap from violence to the ballot box. Recovery for this traumatized country will be slow and measured.

DEVELOPMENT

The Guatemalan economy has grown at a modest 4% rate over the past 2 years, and inflation has stabilized at about 9%. Since 185, the government has taken steps to open the economy in an effort to combat high unemployment and underemployment (estimated to be as high as 45%) and poverty. Good international prices for coffee, sugar, and cardamom have stimulated export earnings.

FREEDOM

Former president Ramiro de León Carpio warned those who would violate human rights, saying that the law would punish those guilty of abuses, "whether or not they are civilians or members of the armed forces." The moment has come, he continued, "to change things and improve the image of the army and of Guatemala."

HEALTH/WELFARE

While constitutional bars on child labor in the industrial sector are not difficult to enforce, in the informal and agricultural sectors, such labor is common. It is estimated that 5,000 Guatemalan children live on the streets and survive as best they can. They are often targeted for elimination by police and death squads.

ACHIEVEMENTS

Guatemalan novelist Miguel Ángel Asturias gained an international reputation for his works about political oppression. In 1967, he was awarded the Nobel Prize for Literature. Rigoberta Menchú Tum won the Nobel Peace Prize in 1992 for her passionate support of the Maya peoples of Guatemala.

Honduras (Republic of Honduras)

GEOGRAPHY

Area in Square Kilometers (Miles):
109,560 (42,300) (slightly larger than
Tennessee)
Capital (Population): Tegucigalpa
(738,500)
Climate: subtropical, but varies with
elevation (temperate highlands)

PEOPLE

Population

Total: 5,605,000
Annual Growth Rate: 2.7% (estimates
vary)
Rural/Urban Population Ratio: 53/47
Ethnic Makeup: 90% Mestizo
(European and Indian mix); 7% Indian;
2% African; 1% European, Arab, and
Oriental
Major Language: Spanish

Health

Life Expectancy at Birth: 66 years
(male); 71 years (female)
Infant Mortality Rate (Ratio): 43/1,000
Average Caloric Intake: 96% of FAO
minimum
Physicians Available (Ratio): 1/1,586

Religions

about 97% Roman Catholic; a small
Protestant minority

Education

Adult Literacy Rate: 73%

Antonio Velázquez

Honduras's most important twentieth-century artist, Antonio Velázquez,
was self-taught. He won international acclaim and fame for his renditions of
his hometown of San Antonio de Oriente, a sixteenth-century mining town.
Detailed without being photographic, his style has been classified as an
example of the primitive school. Velázquez was also able to serve simultaneously as mayor and town barber.

COMMUNICATION

Telephones: 38,000
Newspapers: 4 dailies

TRANSPORTATION

Highways—Kilometers (Miles): 8,950
(5,585)
Railroads—Kilometers (Miles): 735 (490)
Usable Airfields: 159

GOVERNMENT

Type: republic
Independence Date: September 15, 1821
Head of State: President Carlos
Roberto Reina Idiaquez
Political Parties: Liberal Party;
National Party of Honduras; National
Innovation and Unity Party; Christian
Democratic Party; others
Suffrage: universal and compulsory at 18

MILITARY

Number of Armed Forces: 18,900
Military Expenditures (% of Central

Government Expenditures): 7%
Current Hostilities: border skirmishes
with Nicaragua

ECONOMY

Currency ($ U.S. Equivalent): 11.16
lempira = $1
Per Capita Income/GDP: $1,820/$9.7
billion
Inflation Rate: 30%
Total Foreign Debt: $4 billion
Natural Resources: forest products;
minerals; fish
Agriculture: coffee; bananas; corn;
beans; livestock; cotton; sugarcane;
tobacco
Industry: textiles; wood products;
cement; cigars

FOREIGN TRADE

Exports: $850 million
Imports: $990 million

HONDURAS:
PEACEABLE KINGDOM?

In political terms, Honduras resembles much of the rest of Central America. Frequent changes of government, numerous constitutions, authoritarian presidents, widespread corruption, and an inability to solve basic problems are common to Honduras and to the region. A historian of Honduras once wrote that his country's history could be "written in a tear."

In terms of social policy, however, Honduras stands somewhat apart from its neighbors. It was slower to modernize, there were no great extremes of wealth between landowners and the rest of the population, and society appeared more paternalistic and less exploitive than was the case in other Central American states.

Honduras is a poor country. It has serious social problems—widespread illiteracy, malnutrition, and inadequate health care. "Ironically," noted journalist Loren Jenkins, "the land's precarious existence as a poor and unstable backwater has proven almost as much a blessing as a curse." Honduras lacks the sharp social divisions that helped to plunge Nicaragua, El Salvador, and Guatemala into rebellion and civil war. And Honduran governments have seemed somewhat more responsive to demands for change.

A WILLINGNESS TO CHANGE

In 1962 and 1975, agrarian-reform laws were passed and put into effect with relative success. The Honduran government, with the aid of peasant organizations and organized labor, was able to resettle 30,000 families on their own land. Today, two thirds of the people who use the land either own it or have the legal right to its use. Labor legislation and social-security laws were enacted in the early 1960s. Even the Honduran military, usually corrupt, has at times brought about reform. An alliance of the military and organized labor in the early 1970s produced a series of reforms in response to pressure from the less advantaged sectors of the population; in 1974, the military government developed a 5-year plan to integrate the rural poor into the national economy and to increase social services in the area. The state has often shown a paternalistic face rather than a brutal, repressive one. The capacity for reform led one candidate in the 1981 presidential campaign to comment: "We Hondurans are different. There is no room for violence here."

There are now many signs of change. Agrarian reform slowed after 1976, prompting a peasant-association leader to remark: "In order to maintain social peace in the countryside, the peasants' needs will have to be satisfied to avoid revolt." In 1984, the Honduran government initiated a land-titling program and issued about 1,000 titles per month to landless peasants. The government's agrarian-reform program, which is under the control of the National Agrarian Institute, has always been characterized by the carrot and the stick. While some *campesinos* ("peasants") have been granted titles to land, others have been jailed or killed.

Honduran campesinos, according to *Central America Report*, "have had a long and combative history of struggling for land rights." In 1987, hundreds of peasants were jailed as "terrorists" as a result of land invasions. Occupation of privately owned lands has become increasingly common in Honduras and reflects both population pressure on and land hunger of the peasantry. Land seizures by squatters are sometimes recognized by the National Agrarian Institute. In other cases, the government has promoted the relocation of people to sparsely populated regions of the country. Unfortunately, the chosen regions are tropical rain forests, which are already endangered throughout the region. The government wishes to transform the forests into rubber and citrus plantations or into farms to raise rice, corn, and other crops.

Peasants who fail to gain access to land usually migrate to urban centers in search of a better life. What they find in cities such as the capital, Tegucigalpa, are inadequate social services, a miserable standard of living, and a municipal government without the resources to help. In 1989, Tegucigalpa was deeply in debt, mortgaged to the limit, months behind in wage payments to city workers, and plagued by garbage piling up in the streets.

The nation's economy as a whole fared badly in the late 1980s. But by 1992, the economy, following painful adjustments occasioned by the reforms of the government of President Rafael Callejas, again showed signs of growth. Real gross domestic product reached 3.5 percent, and inflation was held in check. Unemployment remained a persistent problem; some agencies calculated that two thirds of the workforce lacked steady employment. A union leader warned: "Unemployment leads to desperation and becomes a time bomb that could explode at any moment."

In addition to internal problems, pressure has been put on Honduras by the International Monetary Fund. According to the *Caribbean & Central America Report,* the first phase of a reform program agreed to with the International Monetary Fund succeeded in stabilizing the economy through devaluation of the lempira (the Honduran currency), public-spending cuts, and increased taxes. But economic growth declined, and international agencies urged a reduction in the number of state employees as well as an accelerated campaign to privatize state-owned enterprises. The government admitted that there was much room for reform, but one official complained: "As far as they [the IMF] are concerned, the Honduran state should make gigantic strides, but our position is that this country cannot turn into General Motors overnight."

Opposition to the demands of international agencies was quick to materialize. One newspaper warned that cuts in social programs would result in violence. Trade-union and Church leaders condemned the social costs of the stabilization program despite the gains recorded in the credit-worthiness of Honduras.

HUMAN AND CIVIL RIGHTS

In theory, despite the continuing violence in the region, basic freedoms in Honduras are still intact. The press is privately owned and free of government censorship. There is, however, a quietly expressed concern about offending the government, and self-censorship is considered prudent. Moreover, it is an accepted practice in Honduras for government ministries and other agencies to have journalists on their payrolls.

Honduran labor unions are free to organize and have a tradition of providing their rank-and-file certain benefits. They are allowed to bargain, but labor laws guard against "excessive" activity. A complex procedure of negotiation and arbitration must be followed before a legal strike can be called. If a government proves unyielding, labor will likely pass into the ranks of the opposition.

In 1992, Honduras's three major workers' confederations convinced the private sector to raise the minimum wage by 13.7 percent, the third consecutive year of increases. Nevertheless, the minimum wage, which varies by occupation and location, is not adequate to provide a decent standard of living, especially in view of inflation. One labor leader pointed out that the minimum wage will "not even buy tortillas." To compound workers' problems, the labor minister admitted that about 30 percent of the enterprises under the supervision of his office paid wages *below* the minimum. To survive, families must pool the resources of all their working members. Predictably, health and safety laws are usually ignored. As is the case in the rural sector, the government has listened to the complaints of workers—but union leaders have also on occasion been jailed.

The government is also confronted by the problem of an increasing flow of rural

Honduras is
settled by
Spaniards from
Guatemala
1524

Independence
of Spain
1821

Honduras is part
of the United
Provinces of
Central America
1822–1838

Honduras
becomes
independent as a
separate country
1838

Brief border war
with El Salvador
1969

Tensions with
Nicaragua grow
1980s

1990s

Honduras joins
the Central
American Free
Trade Zone

President Reina
declares a "moral
revolution"
against
corruption and
human-rights
abuses

Presidential
elections are
scheduled for
November 1997

poor into the cities. Employment opportunities in rural areas have declined as landowners convert cropland into pasture for beef cattle. Because livestock raising requires less labor than growing crops, the surplus rural workers seek to better their opportunities in the cities. But the new migrants have discovered that Honduras's commercial and industrial sectors are deep in recession and cannot provide jobs.

Fortunately, many of the 300,000 refugees from Nicaragua and El Salvador have returned home. With the election of President Violeta Chamorro in Nicaragua, most of the 20,000 rebel Contras laid down their arms and returned home, thus eliminating—from the perspective of the Honduran government—a source of much violence in its border regions.

To the credit of the Honduran government, which is under strong pressure from conservative politicians and businesspeople as well as elements within the armed forces for tough policies against dissent, allegations vis-à-vis human-rights abuses are taken seriously. (In one celebrated case, the Inter-American Court of Human Rights, established in 1979, found the government culpable in at least one person's "disappearance" and ordered the payment of an indemnification to the man's family. While not accepting any premise of guilt, the government agreed to pay. More important, according to the COHA *Washington Report*, the decision sharply criticized "prolonged isolation" and "incommunicado detention" of prisoners and equated such abuses with "cruel and inhuman punishment.") President Carlos Roberto Reina is a strong advocate of human rights as part of his "moral revolution." In 1995, he took three steps in this direction: a special prosecutor was created

to investigate human-rights violations, human-rights inquiries were taken out of the hands of the military and given to a new civilian Department of Criminal Investigation, and promises were made to follow up on cases of disappearances during previous administrations. While Honduras may no longer be characterized as "the peaceable kingdom," the government has not lost touch with its people and still acts out a traditional role of patron.

From the mid-1980s to the mid-1990s, the most serious threat to civilian government came from the military. The United States' Central American policy boosted the prestige, status, and power of the Honduran military, which grew confident in its ability to forge the nation's destiny. With the end of the Contra–Sandinista armed struggle in Nicaragua, there has been a dramatic decline in military assistance from the United States. This has allowed President Reina to assert civilian control over the military establishment.

The sharp drop in U.S. economic assistance to Honduras—it fell from $229 million in 1985 to about $50 million in 1997—has revealed deep problems with the character of that aid. *Wall Street Journal* reporter Carla Anne Robbins wrote that "Honduras's experience suggests that massive, politically motivated cash transfers . . . can buy social peace, at least temporarily, but can't guarantee lasting economic growth or social development." Rather, such unconditional aid "may have slowed development by making it possible for the government to put off economic reform." On the other hand, some of the aid that found its way to programs that were not politically motivated has also been lost. One program provided access

to potable water and was credited with cutting the infant mortality rate by half. Other programs funded vaccinations and primary-education projects. In the words of newspaperman and development expert Juan Ramón Martínez: "Just when you [the United States] started getting it right, you walked away."

President Reina's "moral revolution" also moved to confront the problem of endemic official corruption. In June 1995, Reina alluded to the enormity of the task when he said that, if the government went after all of the guilty, "there would not be enough room for them in the prisons." One of those who agreed to appear in court was former president Callejas; but he insisted that he would not surrender his immunity as a member of the Central American Parliament because, as reported by *Caribbean & Central America Report,* he feared that the "political persecution" to which he was subjected by Reina's government would deny him justice. Other Callejas officials under investigation included the former cabinet ministers of interior, planning and budget, and education. Reina's campaign against corruption and in defense of human rights has won him much admiration. But military involvement in corruption and the abuse of human rights present a danger to Reina that cannot be ignored.

DEVELOPMENT

The Central American Free Trade Zone, of which Honduras is a member, will reduce tariffs by 5% to 20% on more than 5,000 products traded within the region. In the coming years, more products will be included and tariffs will be progressively lowered.

FREEDOM

President Reina has reduced the power of the Honduran military. Constitutional reforms in 1994–1995 replaced obligatory military service and the press-gang recruitment system with voluntary service. As a result, the size of army declined.

HEALTH/WELFARE

Honduras remains one of the region's poorest countries. Serious shortcomings are evident in education and health care, and economic growth is essentially erased by population growth. In 1997, 67% of the population lived in poverty.

ACHIEVEMENTS

The small size of Honduras, in terms of territory and population, has produced a distinctive literary style that is a combination of folklore and legend.

Nicaragua (Republic of Nicaragua)

GEOGRAPHY
Area in Square Kilometers (Miles): 148,000 (57,143) (about the size of Iowa)
Capital (Population): Managua (1,200,000)
Climate: subtropical, but varies with elevation (temperate highlands)

PEOPLE

Population
Total: 4,272,400
Annual Growth Rate: 2.6%
Rural/Urban Population Ratio: 39/61
Ethnic Makeup: 69% Mestizo; 17% white; 9% black; 5% Indian
Major Language: Spanish

Health
Life Expectancy at Birth: 62 years (male); 68 years (female)
Infant Mortality Rate (Ratio): 50/1,000
Average Caloric Intake: 99% of FAO minimum
Physicians Available (Ratio): 1/1,258

Religions
95% Roman Catholic; 5% Protestant

Education
Adult Literacy Rate: 66%

COMMUNICATION
Telephones: 60,000
Newspapers: 3 dailies; 105,000 circulation

TRANSPORTATION
Highways—Kilometers (Miles): 15,286 (9,538)
Railroads—Kilometers (Miles): 373 (233)
Usable Airfields: 198

GOVERNMENT
Type: republic
Independence Date: September 15, 1821
Head of State: President Arnoldo Alemán
Political Parties: Liberal Constitutionalist Party; Neoliberal Party; Conservative Popular Alliance Party; National Action Party; Sandinista National Liberation Front; many others
Suffrage: universal at 16

MILITARY
Number of Armed Forces: 60,600
Military Expenditures (% of Central Government Expenditures): 8.1%
Current Hostilities: border skirmishes with Honduras

ECONOMY
Currency ($ U.S. Equivalent): 8.4 gold córdobas = $1
Per Capita Income/GDP: $1,570/$6.4 billion
Inflation Rate: 19.5%
Total Foreign Debt: $11 billion
Natural Resources: arable land; livestock; timber; fisheries
Agriculture: cotton; coffee; sugarcane; cattle
Industry: food processing; chemicals; metals; textiles; petroleum; beverages

FOREIGN TRADE
Exports: $329 million
Imports: $786 million

Filibusters

A U.S. adventurer named William Walker, known to his admirers as the "grey-eyed man of destiny," led 58 armed men called filibusters (from the Spanish word *filibustero*, or "freebooter") in a coup against the government of Nicaragua in 1855. After capturing the city of Granada, he arranged for Patricio Rivas to become provisional president. Effective power was held by Walker, however, as he was commander-in-chief of the army. The government was recognized by the United States in 1856. Walker was forced to flee Nicaragua in 1857 after he confiscated interests belonging to Cornelius Vanderbilt, who supported and financed a Central American force that drove Walker from power. William Walker was executed in Honduras in 1860, following an abortive coup against the Honduran government.

NICARAGUA:
A NATION IN RECOVERY

Nicaraguan society, culture, and history have been molded to a great extent by the country's geography. A land of volcanoes and earthquakes, the frequency of natural disasters in Nicaragua has profoundly influenced its peoples' perceptions of life, death, and fate. What historian Ralph Woodward has written about Central America is particularly apt for Nicaraguans: Fatalism may be said to be a "part of their national mentality, tempering their attitudes toward the future. Death and tragedy always seem close in Central America. The primitive states of communication, transportation, and production, and the insecurity of human life, have been the major determinants in the region's history. . . ."

Nicaragua is a divided land, with distinct geographic, cultural, racial, ethnic, and religious zones. The west-coast region, which contains about 90 percent of the total population, is overwhelmingly white or Mestizo (mixed blood), Catholic, and Hispanic. The east coast is a sharp contrast, with its scattered population and multiplicity of Indian, Creole (in Nicaragua, native-born blacks), and Hispanic ethnic groups.

The east coast's geography, economy, and isolation from Managua, the nation's capital city, have created a distinct identity among its people. Many east-coast citizens think of themselves as *costeños* ("coast dwellers") rather than Nicaraguans. Religion reinforces this common identity. About 70 percent of the east-coast population, regardless of ethnic group, are members of the Protestant Moravian Church. After more than 135 years of missionary work, the Moravian Church has become "native," with locally recruited clergy. Among the Miskito Indians, Moravian pastors commonly replace tribal elders as community leaders. The Creoles speak English and originally arrived either as shipwrecked or escaped slaves or as slave labor introduced by the British to work in the lumber camps and plantations in the seventeenth century. Many Creoles and Miskitos feel a greater sense of allegiance to the British than to Nicaraguans from the west coast, who are regarded as foreigners.

SANDINISTA POLICIES

Before the successful 1979 Revolution that drove the dictator Anastasio Somoza from power, Nicaraguan governments generally ignored the east coast. Revolutionary Sandinistas—who took their name from a guerrilla, Augusto César Sandino, who fought against occupying U.S. forces in the late 1920s and early 1930s—adopted a new policy toward the neglected region. The Sandinistas were concerned with the east coast's history of rebelliousness and separatism, and they were attracted by the economic potential of the region (palm oil and rubber). Accordingly, they hastily devised a bold campaign to unify the region with the rest of the nation. Roads, communications, health clinics, economic development, and a literacy campaign for local inhabitants were planned. The Sandinistas, in defiance of local customs, also tried to organize the local population into mass formations—that is, organizations for youth, peasants, women, wage earners, and the like. It was believed in Managua that such groups would unite the people behind the government and the Revolution and facilitate the economic, political, and social unification of the region.

In general, the attempt failed, and regional tensions within Nicaragua persist to this day. Historically, costeños were unimpressed with the exploits of the guerrilla Sandino, who raided U.S. companies along the east coast in the 1930s. When the companies left or cut back on operations, workers who lost their jobs blamed Sandino rather than the worldwide economic crisis of the 1930s. Consequently, there was a reluctance to accept Sandino as the national hero of the new Nicaragua. Race and class differences increased due to an influx of Sandinistas from the west. Many of the new arrivals exhibited old attitudes and looked down on the east-coast peoples as "uncivilized" or "second class."

The Miskito Question

In 1982, the government forced 10,000 Indians from their ancestral homes along the Río Coco because of concern with border security. As a result, many Indians joined the Contras, U.S.–supported guerrillas who fought against the Sandinista regime.

In an attempt to win back the Miskito and associated Indian groups, the government decided on a plan of regional autonomy. In 1985, Interior Minister Tomás Borge finished a draft plan whose main proposals included the following features: a regional assembly for the east coast, with each of the six ethnic groups (Miskito, Sumo, Rama, Garifuna, Creole, Mestizo) having the same number of representatives; regional control over Sandinista federal officials working in the region; natural resources under the control of regional governments; and bilingual-education programs. Defense of the east-coast region remained in the hands of Managua, in coordination with the autonomous governments. The Sandinista government initiated a "repatriation" scheme in 1984, allowing 1,000 Miskitos to return to their homes.

The significance of the Sandinista policy was that the government finally appreciated how crucial regional differences are in Nicaragua. Cultural and ethnic differences must be respected if Managua expects to rule its peoples effectively. The lesson learned by the Sandinistas was taken to heart by the subsequent Chamorro government, which was the first in history to appoint a Nicaraguan of Indian background to a ministerial-level position. The limited self-government granted to the east-coast region by the Sandinistas in 1987 has been maintained; local leaders were elected to office in 1990.

A Mixed Record

The record of the Sandinista government was mixed. When the rebels seized power in 1979, they were confronted by an economy in shambles. Nineteen years of civil war had taken an estimated 50,000 lives and destroyed half a billion dollars' worth of factories, businesses, medical facilities, and dwellings. Living standards had tumbled to 1962 levels, and unemployment had reached an estimated 25 percent.

Despite such economic difficulties, the government made great strides in the areas of health and nutrition. A central goal of official policy was to provide equal access to health services. The plan had more success in urban areas than in rural ones. The government emphasized preventive, rather than curative, medicine. Preventive medicine included the provision of clean water, sanitation, immunization, nutrition, and maternal and child care. People were also taught basic preventive medical techniques. National campaigns to wipe out malaria, measles, and polio had reasonable success. But because of restricted budgets, the health system was overloaded, and there was a shortage of medical supplies. In the area of nutrition, basic foodstuffs such as grains, oil, eggs, and milk were paid for in part by the government in an effort to improve the general nutritional level of Nicaraguans.

By 1987, the Sandinista government was experiencing severe economic problems that badly affected all social programs. In 1989, the economy, for all intents and purposes, collapsed. Hyperinflation ran well over 100 percent a month; and in June 1989, following a series of mini-devaluations, the nation's currency was devalued by an incredible 100 percent. Commerce was virtually paralyzed.

The revolutionary Sandinista government, in an attempt to explain the economic debacle, with some justice argued that the Nicaragua that it had inherited in 1979 had been savaged and looted by former dictator Somoza. The long-term costs of economic reconstruction; the restructuring of the economy to redistribute wealth; the trade embargo erected by the United States and North American diplomatic pressure designed to discourage lending or aid from international institutions such as the International Monetary Fund; and the high cost of fighting a war against the U.S.–supported Contra rebels formed the backdrop to the crisis. Opposition leaders added to this list various Sandinista economic policies that discouraged private business.

The impact of the economic crisis on average Nicaraguans was devastating. Overnight, prices of basic consumer goods such as meat, rice, beans, milk, sugar, and cooking oil were increased 40 to 80 percent. Gasoline prices doubled. Schoolteachers engaged in work stoppages in an effort to increase their monthly wages of about $15, equal to the pay of a domestic servant. (To put the teachers' plight into perspective, note that the cost of a liter of milk absorbed fully 36 percent of a day's pay.)

As a hedge against inflation, other Nicaraguans purchased dollars on the black market. *Regionews,* published in Managua, noted that conversion of córdobas into dollars was "seen as a better proposition than depositing them in savings accounts."

Economic travail inevitably produces dissatisfaction; opinion polls taken in July 1989 signaled political trouble for the Sandinistas. The surveys reflected an electorate with mixed feelings. While nearly 30 percent favored the Sandinistas, 57 percent indicated that they would not vote for President Daniel Ortega.

The results of the election of 1990 were not surprising, for the Sandinistas had lost control of the economy. They failed to survive a strong challenge from the opposition, led by the popular Violeta Chamorro.

Sandinista land reform, for the most part, consisted of the government's confiscation of the huge estates of the ousted Somoza family. These lands amounted to more than 2 million acres, including about 40 percent of the nation's best farmland. Some peasants were given land, but the government preferred to create cooperatives. This policy prompted the criticism that the state had simply become an old-style landowner. The Sandinistas replied that "the state is not the same state as before; it is a state of producers; we organized production and placed it at the disposal of the people." In 1990, there were several reports of violence between Sandinista security forces and peasants

and former Contras who petitioned for private ownership of state land.

The Role of the Church

The Revolution created a sharp division within the Roman Catholic Church in Nicaragua. Radical priests, who believed that Christianity and Marxism share similar goals and that the Church should play a leading role in social change and revolution, were at odds with traditional priests fearful of "godless communism." Since 1979, many radical Catholics had become involved in social and political projects; several held high posts in the Sandinista government.

One priest of the theology of liberation was interviewed by *Regionews.* The interviewer stated that an "atheist could say, 'These Catholics found a just revolution opposed by the Church hierarchy. They can't renounce their religion and are searching for a more convenient theology. But it's their sense of natural justice that motivates them.'" The priest replied: "I think that's evident and that Jesus was also an 'atheist,' an atheist of the religion as practiced in his time. He didn't believe in the God of the priests in the temples who

were allied with Caesar. Jesus told of a new life. And the 'atheist' that exists in our people doesn't believe in the God that the hierarchy often offers us. He believes in life, in man, in development. God manifests Himself there. A person who believes in life and justice in favor of the poor is not an atheist." The movement, he noted, would continue "with or without approval from the hierarchy."

The Drift to the Left

As has historically been the case in revolutions, after a brief period of unity and excitement, the victors begin to disagree over policies and power. For a while in Nicaragua, there was a perceptible drift to the left, and the Revolution lost its image of moderation. While radicalization was a dynamic inherent in the Revolution, it was also pushed in a leftward direction by a hostile U.S. foreign policy that attempted to bring down the Sandinista regime through its support of the Contras. In 1987, however, following the peace initiatives of Latin American governments, the Sandinista government made significant efforts to project a more moderate image in the region. *La Prensa,* the main oppo-

(United Nations photo/Jerry Frank)

A lakeside section of Managua, Nicaragua, was destroyed by an earthquake. The region is often shaken by both large and small earthquakes.

Nicaragua is explored by Gil González **1522**	Independence of Spain **1821**	Nicaragua joins the United Provinces of Central America **1823**	Nicaragua becomes independent as a separate state **1838**	William Walker and filibusters (U.S. insurgents) invade Nicaragua **1855**	Augusto César Sandino leads guerrillas against occupying U.S. forces **1928–1934**	Domination of Nicaragua by the Somoza family **1934–1979**	Sandinista guerrillas oust the Somoza family **1979**	Sharp deterioration of relations with the United States **1980s**

1990s

A cease-fire allows an opening for political dialogue

Political instability and rural violence plague reconstruction

Former Managua mayor Arnoldo Alemán wins the presidential election in 1996

sition newspaper, which the Sandinistas had shut down in 1986, was again allowed to publish. Radio Católica, another source of opposition to the government, was given permission to broadcast after its closure the year before. And antigovernment demonstrations were permitted in the streets of Managua.

Significantly, President Ortega proposed reforms in the country's election laws in April 1989, to take effect before the national elections in 1990. Although the Bush administration was not convinced that the changes would ensure free elections, a report prepared by the Hispanic Division of the Library of Congress was generally favorable. The new Nicaraguan legislation was based on Costa Rican and Venezuelan models and in some instances was even more forward-looking.

An important result of the laws was the enhancement of political pluralism, which allowed the National Opposition Union (UNO) victory in 1990. Rules for organizing political parties, once stringent, were loosened; opposition parties were granted access to the media; foreign funding of political parties was allowed; the system of proportional representation permitted minority parties to maintain a presence; and the opposition was allowed to monitor the elections closely.

The Sandinistas realized that, to survive, they had to make compromises. In need of breathing space, the government embraced the Central American Peace Plan designed by Costa Rican president Óscar Arias and designed moderate policies to isolate the United States.

On the battlefield, the cease-fire unilaterally declared by the Sandinistas was eventually embraced by the Contras as well, and both sides moved toward a political solution of their differences. Armed conflict formally ended on June 27, 1990, although sporadic violence continued in rural areas.

A PEACEFUL TRANSITION

It was the critical state of the Nicaraguan economy that in large measure brought the Sandinistas down in the elections of 1990. Even though the government of Violeta Chamorro made great progress in the demilitarization of the country and national reconciliation, the economy remained a time bomb.

The continuing economic crisis and disagreements over policy directions destroyed the original base of Chamorro's political support. Battles between the legislative and executive branches of government virtually paralyzed the country. At the end of 1992, President Chamorro closed the Assembly building and called for new elections. But, by July 1995, an accord had been reached between the two contending branches of government. Congress passed a "framework law" that created the language necessary to implement changes in the Sandinista Constitution of 1987. The Legislative Assembly, together with the executive branch, are pledged to the passage of laws on matters such as property rights, agrarian reform, consumer protection, and taxation. The July agreement also provided for the election of the five-member Consejo Supremo Electoral (Supreme Electoral Council), which oversaw the presidential elections in November 1996.

The election marked something of a watershed in Nicaraguan political history. Outgoing president Chamorro told reporters at the inauguration of Arnoldo Alemán: "For the first time in more than 100 years . . . one civilian, democratically elected president will hand over power to another." But the election did not mask the fact that Nicaragua was still deeply polarized and that the Sandinistas only grudgingly accepted their defeat.

President Alemán sought a dialogue with the Sandinistas, and both sides agreed to participate in discussions to study poverty, property disputes occasioned by the Sandinista policy of confiscation, and the need to attract foreign investment. While defeated Sandinista candidate Daniel Ortega agreed to talk, he also intimated that Nicaragua could return to violence if the new government followed policies detrimental to the poor.

The new administration faces a host of difficult problems. Only Haiti is poorer in the hemisphere. Perhaps 80 percent of the population are unemployed or underemployed, and more than 70 percent of the population live below the poverty line. On the other hand, the nation has begun to emerge from the economic chaos of the 1980s. In 1996, the economy grew at a rate of 5.5 percent, and there were expectations that this rate could rise to 7 percent in 1997. Economic stability would immeasurably enhance Nicaragua's fragile democracy.

DEVELOPMENT

The possibility of the construction of a "dry canal" across Nicaragua has raised the hopes of thousands for a better future. A group of Asian investors are actively investigating the construction of a 234-mile-long rail link between the oceans to carry container cargo.

FREEDOM

Diverse points of view have been freely and openly discussed in the media. Radio, the most important medium for news distribution in Nicaragua, has conveyed a broad range of opinion.

HEALTH/WELFARE

Almost 60% of the households in Nicaragua are headed by women. Of these, 72% live in poverty. Of the unemployed, 57% are women; 75% of these are single mothers. Nicaragua's housing deficit stands at 500,000 units and is growing at a rate of 20,000 units per year.

ACHIEVEMENTS

The Nicaraguan poet Rubén Darío was the most influential representative of the Modernist Movement, which swept Latin America in the late nineteenth century. Darío was strongly critical of injustice and oppression.

Panama (Republic of Panama)

GEOGRAPHY
Area in Square Kilometers (Miles): 75,650 (29,208) (slightly larger than West Virginia)
Capital (Population): Panama City (413,000)
Climate: tropical

PEOPLE

Population
Total: 2,681,000
Annual Growth Rate: 1.9%
Rural/Urban Population Ratio: 45/55
Ethnic Makeup: 70% Mestizo; 14% West Indian; 10% white; 6% Indian and others
Major Languages: Spanish; English

Health
Life Expectancy at Birth: 73 years (male); 78 years (female)
Infant Mortality Rate (Ratio): 16/1,000
Average Caloric Intake: 103% of FAO minimum
Physicians Available (Ratio): 1/800

Religions
85% Roman Catholic; 15% Protestant and others

Education
Adult Literacy Rate: 89%

COMMUNICATION
Telephones: 220,000
Newspapers: 5 Spanish dailies; 1 English

The Great "South Sea"

In 1502, on his fourth voyage to the New World, Christopher Columbus visited the north coast of what today is Panama. As a result, the first colonies of this area were settled along the Caribbean coast. The first head of the European colony, Vasco Nuñez de Balboa, ruled the natives through friendship rather than by force. After listening to an Indian chief's son talk about the "South Sea," Balboa set out on an expedition in 1513 and became the first white man to view the Pacific Ocean.

TRANSPORTATION
Highways—Kilometers (Miles): 8,530 (5,297)
Railroads—Kilometers (Miles): 238 (149)
Usable Airfields: 115

GOVERNMENT
Type: constitutional republic
Independence Date: November 3, 1903
Head of State: President Ernesto Pérez Balladares Gonzalez Revilla
Political Parties: Nationalist Republican Liberal Movement; Solidarity Party; Authentic Liberal Republican Party; Arnulfista Party; Christian Democratic Party; Democratic Revolutionary Party; Independent Democratic Union; Liberal Party; Labor Party; others
Suffrage: universal and compulsory at 18

MILITARY
Number of Armed Forces: all armed forces were disbanded in 1990

Military Expenditures (% of Central Government Expenditures): 1.0%
Current Hostilities: none

ECONOMY
Currency ($ U.S. Equivalent): 1 balboa = $1 (fixed rate)
Per Capita Income/GDP: $4,670/$12.3 billion
Inflation Rate: 1.8%
Total Foreign Debt: $6.7 billion
Natural Resources: geographic location; copper ore; timber
Agriculture: bananas; rice; sugarcane; corn; coffee
Industry: food processing; beverages; petroleum products; construction materials; clothing

FOREIGN TRADE
Exports: $520 million
Imports: $2.2 billion

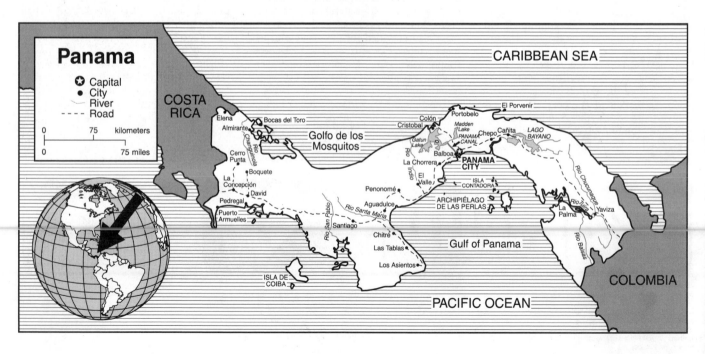

PANAMA:
A NATION AND A CANAL

The Panama Canal, opened to shipping in 1914, has had a sharp impact on Panamanian political life, foreign policy, economy, and society. Panama is a country of minorities and includes blacks, Mestizos (mixed Indian and white), Indians, and Chinese. Many of the blacks and Chinese are the children or grandchildren of the thousands of workers who were brought to Panama to build the canal. Unable to return home, they remained behind, an impoverished people, ignored for decades by a succession of Panamanian governments.

The government has usually been dominated by whites, although all of the country's minorities are politically active. In areas where Indians comprise a majority of the population, they play significant roles in provincial political life. Some, such as the San Blas islanders—famous for the art form known as Mola, which consists of different colored fabrics that are cut away to make designs—live in self-governing districts. Although Indians are not restricted to tribal areas, most remain by choice, reflecting a long tradition of resistance to assimilation and defense of their cultural integrity.

Panama's economy has both profited and suffered from the presence of the canal. Because governments traditionally placed too much reliance on the direct and indirect revenues generated by the canal tolls, they tended to ignore other types of national development. Much of Panama's economic success in the 1980s, however, was the result of a strong service sector associated with the presence of a large number of banks, the Panama Canal, and the Colón Free Zone. Agriculture and industry, on the other hand, usually experienced slow growth rates.

Because of U.S. control of the canal and the Canal Zone, this path between the seas continuously stoked the fires of Panamanian nationalism. The high standard of living and the privileges enjoyed by U.S. citizens residing in the zone contrasted sharply with the poverty of Panamanians. President Omar Torrijos became a national hero in 1977 when he signed the Panama Canal Treaties with U.S. president Jimmy Carter. The treaties provide for full Panamanian control over the canal and its revenues by the end of this century.

Panamanian officials speak optimistically of their plans for the bases they will soon inherit, citing universities, modern container ports, luxury resorts, and retirement communities. But there is much concern over the loss of an estimated $500 million that tens of thousands of American troops, civilians, and their dependents

pump into the Panamanian economy. Moreover, while all agree that the canal itself will be well run because Panamanians have been phased into its operation, there is pessimism about the lack of planning for ancillary facilities. In 1995, more than 300 poor, landless people a day were moving into the Zone and were clearing forest for crops. The rain forest in the Canal Basin supplies not only the water essential to the canal but also the drinking water for about 40 percent of Panama's population. Loss of the rain forest could prove catastrophic. One official noted: "If we lose the Canal Basin we do not lose only our water supply, it will also be the end of the Canal itself."

A RETURN TO CIVILIAN GOVERNMENT

President Torrijos, who died in a suspicious plane crash in 1981, left behind a legacy that included much more than the treaties. He elevated the National Guard to a position of supreme power in the state and ruled through a National Assembly of community representatives.

The 1984 elections appeared to bring to fruition the process of political liberalization initiated in 1978. But, even though civilian rule was officially restored, the

armed forces remained the real power behind the throne. Indeed, spectacular revelations in 1987 strongly suggested that Defense Forces chief general Manuel Antonio Noriega had rigged the 1984 elections. He was also accused of drug trafficking, gun running, and money laundering.

Indeed, in February 1988, Noriega was indicted by two U.S. grand juries and charged with using his position to turn Panama into a center for the money-laundering activities of the Medellín, Colombia, drug cartel and providing protection for cartel members living temporarily in Panama.

Attempts by Panamanian president Eric Arturo Delvalle to oust the military strongman failed, and Delvalle himself was forced into hiding. Concerted efforts by the United States to remove Noriega from power—which included an economic boycott, plans to kidnap the general and have the CIA engineer a coup, and saber-rattling by the dispatch of thousands of U.S. troops to the Canal Zone—proved fruitless.

The fraud and violence that accompanied an election called by Noriega in 1989 to legitimize his government and the failure of a coup attempt in October ultimately resulted in the invasion of Panama by U.S. troops in December. Noriega was

(Library of Congress photo)

The Panama Canal has been of continuing importance to the country since it opened in 1914. Full control of the canal will be turned over to Panama in 1999, marking the end of U.S. involvement and representing a source of Panamanian nationalism.

Panama City is
established
1518

Panama is a
department of
Colombia
1821–1903

Independence
of Colombia
1903

The signing of
the Panama
Canal Treaties
1977

The death of
President Omar
Torrijos creates
a political
vacuum
1980s

American
troops invade
Panama;
Noriega
surrenders to
face drug
charges in the
United States

1990s

Ernesto Pérez
Balladares is
elected president

The Panama
Canal is to pass
to local control in
1999

Presidential
elections are
scheduled for
1999

arrested, brought to the United States for trial, and eventually was convicted on drug-trafficking charges.

The U.S. economic sanctions succeeded in harming the wrong people. Noriega and his cronies were shielded from the economic crisis by their profits from money laundering. But many other Panamanians were devastated by the U.S. policy.

Members of Panama's electoral commission declared Guillermo Endara president (although his victory in the election of 1989 was annulled on Noriega's orders). Among the major problems faced by the Endara government were reconstruction of the economy, the restoration of law and order, and elimination of endemic corruption in the government.

Nearly a decade after the invasion by U.S. troops to restore democracy and halt drug trafficking, the situation in Panama remains problematic. The country is characterized by extremes of wealth and poverty, and corruption is pervasive. The economy is still closely tied to drug-money laundering, which has reached levels higher than during the Noriega years.

Elections in 1994 reflected the depth of popular dissatisfaction with the Endara regime. Three quarters of the voters supported political movements that had risen in opposition to the policies and politics imposed on Panama by the U.S. invasion. The new president, Ernesto Pérez Balladares, a 48-year-old economist and businessman and a former supporter of Noriega, promised "to close the Noriega chapter" in Panama's history. Unfortunately, Pérez's first months in office witnessed the systematic rehabilitation of

numbers of people identified with Noriega and the military that had ruled for 20 years. Former lower-ranking officers in the military are now in command of the police force.

The Panamanian economy, on the other hand, has recovered from the crisis induced by the anti-Noriega policies of the Reagan and Bush administrations. In 1992, real gross domestic product growth reached an impressive 8 percent; and most sectors of the economy, led by the Canal, banking, and the Colón Free Zone, moved forward. Pérez continued the privatization policies of Endara and introduced a plan to sell shares in state-owned industries. Lower import tariffs were ordered, and the revision of labor laws inhibiting foreign investment were put in place. It is still necessary to diversify the Panamanian economy, which is overly dependent on canal revenues and traditional agricultural exports. Unemployment hovers around the 15 percent mark, which fuels the fires of discontent.

SOCIAL POLICIES

As is the case in most Latin American nations, Panama's Constitution authorizes the state to direct, regulate, replace, or create economic activities designed to increase the nation's wealth and to distribute the benefits of the economy to the greatest number of people. In reality, the income of 35 to 40 percent of Panama's population frequently fails to provide for families' basic needs. One fifth of the population are extremely poor and cannot provide for basic necessities. On the positive side, however, the government has made moderately suc-

cessful attempts to improve health care in both urban and rural areas.

Women, who won the right to vote in the 1940s, are accorded equal political rights under the law and hold a number of important government positions. But, as in all of Latin America, women do not enjoy the same opportunities for advancement as men. There are also profound domestic constraints to their freedom. Panamanian law, for example, does not recognize community property; divorced or deserted women have no protection and can be left destitute, if that is the will of their former spouses. Many female heads-of-household from poor areas are obliged to work for the government, often as street cleaners, in order to receive support funds from the authorities.

With respect to human rights, Panama's record is mixed. The press and electronic media, while theoretically free, have experienced some harassment. In 1983, the Supreme Court ruled that journalists need not be licensed by the government. Nevertheless, both reporters and editors still exercise a calculated self-censorship, and press conduct in general is regulated by an official "Morality and Ethics Commission," whose powers are broad and vague.

DEVELOPMENT

President Pérez Balladares seeks to implement an economic strategy similar to that of Taiwan, Singapore, Hong Kong, and South Korea: export-led growth. Tariff barriers were dramatically reduced—as were domestic wages—in an effort to increase the country's international competitiveness.

FREEDOM

Panama's indigenous population of 194,000 have the same political rights as other citizens. In 1992, Cuna Indians asked for the creation of an additional reserve to prohibit incursions by squatters into areas traditionally considered their own.

HEALTH/WELFARE

Deforestation and other environmental damage have reached such a point, according to *Latin American Regional Report,* that, unless a halt is called now, "Panama could be without drinking water within 20 years." Climatic changes accelerated by deforestation have already significantly reduced average rainfall.

ACHIEVEMENTS

The Panama Canal, which will pass wholly to Panamanian control in 1999, is one of the greatest engineering achievements of the twentieth century. A maze of locks and gates, it cuts through 50 miles of the most difficult terrain on Earth.

South America

CARIBBEAN SEA

ATLANTIC OCEAN

★ Caracas
VENEZUELA

GUYANA
SURINAME
Georgetown ★
Paramaribo ★
Cayenne ★
FRENCH GUIANA (FR.)

COLOMBIA
Bogotá ★

ECUADOR
Quito ★

PERU

Lima ★

PACIFIC OCEAN

BRAZIL

BOLIVIA

★ Brasília

La Paz (de facto) ★
Sucre (legal) ★

PARAGUAY

Asunción ★

CHILE

Santiago ★

URUGUAY

Buenos Aires ★   ★ Montevideo

ARGENTINA

N
W   E
S

South America is the fourth largest of the world's seven continents. It has a land area of approximately 6,875,000 square miles. The land area consists of some of the highest mountains in the world (the Andes) and the largest rain forest in the world (the Amazon Basin). It was the land of some of the oldest developed civilizations in the world. The diversity of South America's geography is complemented by its many cultures.

★ Capital cities

49

South America: An Imperfect Prism

Any overview of South America must first confront the incredible geographic and climatic diversity of the region. Equatorial rain forests are found in Brazil, Ecuador, Colombia, and Venezuela, and other countries; and the coastal deserts in Peru and northern Chile are among the driest and most forbidding in the world (naturalist Charles Darwin described the area as "a complete and utter desert"). More hospitable are the undulating pampas and plains of Argentina, Uruguay, central Venezuela, eastern Colombia, and southeastern Brazil. The spine of the continent is formed by the Andes Mountains, majestic and snowcapped. Because of its topography and the many degrees of latitude in which it lies, South America also has extremes of temperatures, ranging from desert heat to the steaming humidity of the tropics to the cold gales of Tierra del Fuego, which lies close to the Antarctic Circle. To add further to the perils of generalization, wide-ranging differences often occur *within* a country. Geography has played a critical role in the evolution of each of the nations of South America; it has been one of several major influences in their histories and their cultures.

(United Nations photo)

In many parts of South America, producing enough food to feed the people has been a constant problem. The geographic diversity, extremes of weather, and unpredictable natural disasters have made food production difficult.

NATURE'S CHALLENGE

Nature has presented the inhabitants of South America with an unrelenting challenge. On the west coast, most of the major cities are located in geologically active zones. All too frequently, earthquakes, tidal waves, volcanic activity, and landslides have taken a staggering toll of human life. And throughout the region, floods and droughts make agriculture a risky business. In 1982–1983, for example, the worst drought in living memory struck Peru and Bolivia. With food supplies dwindling, thousands of farmers and their families were forced to migrate to the cities.

REGIONALISM

South America's diverse topography has also helped to foster a deep-seated regionalism that has spawned innumerable civil wars and made national integration an extremely difficult task. In Colombia, for instance, the Andes fan out into three distinct ranges, separated by deep valleys. Each of the nation's three major cities—Bogotá, Medellín, and Cali—dominates a valley and is effectively isolated from the others by the mountains. The broad plains to the east have remained largely undeveloped because of the difficulty of access from the centers of population. Troubling to Colombian governments is the fact that, in terms of topography, the eastern plains are tied to Venezuela and not to the Colombian cities to the west.

Similarly, mountains divide Ecuador, Peru, Bolivia, and Venezuela. In all of these nations, there is a permanent tension between the capital cities and the hinterlands. As is the case in those republics that have large Indian populations, the tension often is as much cultural as it is a matter of geography. But in the entire region, geography interacts with culture, society, politics, and economics. Regionalism has been a persistent theme in the history of Ecuador, where there has been an often bitter rivalry between the capital city of Quito, located high in the central mountains, and the port city of Guayaquil. Commonly, port cities, with their window on the world outside, tend to be more cosmopolitan, liberal, and dynamic than cities that are more isolated. Such is the case with freewheeling Guayaquil, which stands in marked contrast to conservative, traditional, deeply Catholic Quito.

Venezuela boasts six distinct geographical regions, which include mountains and valleys, plains and deserts, rivers and jungles, and a coastline. Historian John Lombardi has observed that each of these regions has had an important role in identifying and defining the character of Venezuela's past and present: "Over the centuries the geographical focus has shifted from one region to another in response to internal arrangements and external demands."

THE SOUTHERN CONE

The cultures of the countries of the so-called Southern Cone—Argentina, Uruguay, Paraguay, and Chile—have also been shaped by the geographical environment. Argentina,

(United Nations photo)

The countries of the Southern Cone—Argentina, Uruguay, Paraguay, and Chile—have had their cultures influenced by the geography of their vast, fertile plains. These latter-day gauchos herd their animals to the auction pens.

Uruguay, and Brazil's southern state of Rio Grande do Sul developed subcultures that reflected life on the vast, fertile plains, where cattle grazed by the millions. The *gaucho* ("cowboy") became symbolic of the "civilization of leather." Fierce, independent, a law unto himself, the gaucho was mythologized by the end of the nineteenth century. At a time when millions of European immigrants were flooding into the region, the gaucho emerged as a nationalist symbol of Argentina and Uruguay, standing firm in the face of whatever natives viewed as "foreign."

Landlocked Paraguay, surrounded by powerful neighbors, has for most of its history been an introspective nation, little known to the outside world. Because of its geography, most of Paraguay's population is concentrated near the capital city of Asunción. A third of the nation is tropical and swampy—not suitable for settlement. To the west, the desolate Chaco region, with its lack of adequate sources of drinkable water, is virtually uninhabitable.

Chile, with a coastline 2,600 miles long, is a country of topographic and climatic extremes. If superimposed on a map of North America, Chile would stretch from Baja California to the Yukon in Alaska. It is on Chile's border with Argentina that the Andes soar to their greatest heights. Several peaks, including Aconcagua, reach to nearly 23,000 feet in elevation. That mountain barrier has historically isolated Chile

from eastern South America and from Europe. The central valley of Chile is the political, industrial, social, and cultural heart of the nation. With the capital city of Santiago and the large port of Valparaíso, the valley holds about 70 percent of Chile's population. The valley's Mediterranean climate and fertile soil have long acted as a magnet for Chileans from other, less hospitable, parts of the country.

BRAZIL

Historian Rollie Poppino has noted that the "major miracle of Brazil is its existence as a single nation." What he implies is that Brazil embraces regions that are so distinct that they could well be separate countries. "There are actually many Brazils within the broad expanse of the national territory, and the implication of uniformity conveyed by their common flag and language is often deceptive." In Brazil, there exists a tremendous range of geographical, racial, cultural, and economic contrasts. But part of the Brazilian "miracle" lies in the ability of its people to accept the diversity as normal. Many Brazilians were unaware of the great differences within their country for years, until the improvement of transportation and communications as well as the impact of the mass media informed them not only of their common heritage but also of their profound regional differences.

DIVERSE PEOPLES

In many respects, the peoples of South America are as diverse as its geography. While the populations of Argentina and Uruguay are essentially European, with virtually no Indian intermixture, Chilean society is descended from Spanish conquerors and the Indians they dominated. The Indian presence is strongest in the Andean republics of Bolivia, Peru, and Ecuador—the heart of the ancient Inca civilization. Bolivia is the most Indian, with well over half its population classified as such. Mestizos (mixed white and Indian) constitute about a quarter of the population, and whites make up only about 10 percent.

Three ethnic groups are found among the populations of Colombia and Venezuela: Spanish and Indian predominate, and there are small black minorities. About 60 percent of the populations of both countries are of Mestizo or *pardo* (mixed blood) origin. One of Brazil's distinctive features is the rich racial mixture of its population. Peoples of Indian, European, African, and Japanese heritage live in an atmosphere largely free of racial enmity.

Taken as a whole, the predominant culture is Iberian (that is, Spanish or Portuguese), although many mountain areas are overwhelmingly Indian in terms of ethnic makeup. With the conquest and colonization of South America in the sixteenth century, Spain and Portugal attempted to fasten their cultures, languages, and institutions on the land and its peoples. Spanish cities in South America—laid out in the familiar grid pattern consisting of a large central plaza bordered by a Catholic church, government buildings, and the dwellings of the ruling elite—represented the conscious intention of the conquerors to impose their will, not only on the defeated Indian civilizations but also on nature itself.

By way of contrast, the Brazilian cities that were laid out by early Portuguese settlers tended to be less formally structured, suggesting that their planners and builders were more flexible and adaptable to the new world around them. Roman Catholicism was imposed on all citizens by the central authority. Government, conforming to Hispanic political culture, was authoritarian in the colonial period and continues to be so today. The conquerors created a stratified society of essentially two sectors: a ruling white elite and a ruled majority. But Spain and Portugal also introduced institutions that knit society together. Paternalistic patron–client relationships that bound the weak to the strong were common; they continue to be so today.

INDIAN CULTURE
Among the isolated Indian groups of Ecuador, Peru, and Bolivia, Spanish cultural forms were strongly and, for the most part, successfully resisted. Suspicious and occasionally hostile, the Indians refused integration into the white world outside their highland villages. By avoiding integration, in the words of historian Frederick Pike, "they maintain the freedom to live almost exclusively in the domain of their own language, social habits, dress and eating styles, beliefs, prejudices, and myths."

Only the Catholic religion was able to make some inroads, and that was (and still is) imperfect. The Catholicism practiced by Quechua- and Aymara-speaking Indians is a blend of Catholic teachings and ancient folk religion. For example, in an isolated region in Peru where eight journalists were massacred by Indians, a writer who investigated the incident reported in *The New York Times* that, while Catholicism was "deeply rooted" among the Indians, "it has not displaced old beliefs like the worship of the *Apus,* or god mountains." When threatened, the Indians are "zealous defenders of their customs and mores." The societies' two cultures have had a profound impact on the literature of Ecuador, Peru, and Bolivia. The plight of the Indian, social injustice, and economic exploitation are favorite themes of these nations' authors.

Other Indian groups more vulnerable to the steady encroachment of "progress" did not survive. In the late nineteenth century, pampas Indians were virtually destroyed by Argentine cavalry armed with repeating rifles. Across the Andes, in Chile, the Araucanian Indians met a similar fate in the 1880s. Unfortunately, relations between the "civilized" world and the "primitive" peoples clinging to existence in the rain forests of Brazil, Peru, Bolivia, and Venezuela have generally improved little. Events in Brazil, Ecuador, and Venezuela in the early 1990s, however, may signal a significant shift toward greater Indian rights. Indigenous peoples throughout the Amazon Basin, however, are still under almost daily assault from settlers hungry for land, road builders,

(United Nations photo/Bruno J. Zehnder)

The region's Indian cultures and modern development have never really mixed. The native cultures persist in many areas, as exemplified by this Indian woman at a market in Ecuador.

developers, and speculators—most of whom care little about the cultures they are annihilating.

AFRICAN-AMERICAN CULTURE
In those South American countries where slavery was widespread, the presence of a large black population has contributed yet another dimension to Hispanic culture (or, in the case of Guyana and Suriname, English and Dutch culture). Slaves, brutally uprooted from their cultures in Africa, developed new cultural forms that were often a combination of Christian and pagan. To insulate themselves against the rigors of forced labor and to forge some kind of common identity, slaves embraced folk religions that were heavily oriented toward magic. Magic helped blacks to face an uncertain destiny, and folk religions built bridges between peoples facing a similar, horrible fate. Folk religions not only survived the emancipation of slaves but have remained a common point of focus for millions of Brazilian blacks.

This phenomenon had become so widespread that in the 1970s, the Roman Catholic Church made a concerted effort to win Afro-Brazilians to a religion that was more Christian and less pagan. This effort was partly negated by the development of close relations between Brazil and Africa, which occurred at the same time as the Church's campaign. Brazilian blacks became more acutely aware of their African origins and began a movement of "re-Africanization." So pervasive had the folk religions become that one authority stated that

Umbada (one of the folk religions) was now the religion of Brazil. The festival of *Carnaval* ("Carnival") in Rio de Janeiro, Brazil, is perhaps the best-known example of the blending of Christianity with spiritism. Even the samba, a sensuous dance form that is central to the Carnaval celebration, had its origins in black folk religions.

IMMIGRATION AND CULTURE

Italians, Eastern and Northern Europeans, Chinese, and Japanese have also contributed to the cultural, social, and economic development of several South American nations. The great outpouring of Europe's peoples that brought millions of immigrants to the shores of the United States also brought millions to South America. From the mid-1800s to the outbreak of World War I in 1914, great numbers of Italians and Spaniards and much smaller numbers of Germans, Russians, Welsh, Scots, Irish, and English boarded ships that would carry them to South America.

Many were successful in the New World. Indeed, immigrants were largely responsible for the social restructuring of Argentina, Uruguay, and southern Brazil, as they created a large and dynamic middle class where none had existed before.

Italians

Many of the new arrivals came from urban areas, were literate, and possessed a broad range of skills. Argentina received the greatest proportion of immigrants. So great was the influx that an Argentine political scientist labeled the years 1890–1914 the "alluvial era" (flood). His analogy was apt, for by 1914, half the population of the capital city of Buenos Aires were foreign-born. Indeed, 30 percent of the total Argentine population were of foreign extraction. Hundreds of thousands of immigrants also flocked into Uruguay.

In both countries, they were able to move quickly into middle-class occupations in business and commerce. Others found work on the docks or on the railroads that carried the produce of the countryside to the ports for export to foreign markets. Some settled in the interior of Argentina, where they usually became sharecroppers or tenant farmers, although a sizable number were able to purchase land in the northern province of Santa Fe or became truck farmers in the immediate vicinity of Buenos Aires. Argentina's wine industry underwent a rapid transformation and expansion with the arrival of Italians in the western provinces of Mendoza and San Juan. In the major cities of Argentina, Uruguay, Chile, Peru, and Brazil, Italians built hospitals and established newspapers; they formed mutual aid societies and helped to found the first labor unions. Their presence is still strong today, and Italian words have entered into everyday discourse in Argentina and Uruguay.

Other Groups

Other immigrant groups also made their contributions to the formation of South America's societies and cultures. Germans colonized much of southern Chile and were instrumental in creating the nation's dairy industry. In the wilds of Patagonia, Welsh settlers established sheep ranches and planted apple, pear, and cherry trees in the Río Negro Valley.

In Buenos Aires, despite the 1982 conflict over the Falkland Islands, there remains a distinct British imprint. Harrod's is the largest department store in the city, and one can board a train on a railroad built with English capital and journey to suburbs with names such as Hurlingham, Temperley, and Thames. In both Brazil and Argentina, soccer was introduced by the English, and two Argentine teams still bear the names "Newell's Old Boys" and "River Plate." Collectively, the immigrants who flooded into South America in the late nineteenth and early twentieth centuries introduced a host of new ideas, methods, and skills. They were especially important in stimulating and shaping the modernization of Argentina, Uruguay, Chile, and southern Brazil.

In other countries that were bypassed earlier in the century, immigration has become a new phenomenon. Venezuela—torn by political warfare, its best lands long appropriated by the elite, and its economy only slowly developing—was far less attractive than the lands of opportunity to its north (the United States) and south (Argentina, Uruguay, and Brazil). In the early 1950s, however, Venezuela embarked on a broad-scale development program that included an attempt to attract European immigrants. Thousands of Spaniards, Portuguese, and Italians responded to the economic opportunity. Most of the immigrants settled in the capital city of Caracas, where many eventually became important in the construction business, retail trade, and the transportation industry.

INTERNAL MIGRATION

Paralleling the movement of peoples from across the oceans to parts of South America has been the movement of populations from rural areas to urban centers. In every nation, cities have been gaining in population for years. What prompts people to leave their homes and strike out for the unknown? In the cases of Bolivia and Peru, the very real prospect of famine has driven people out of the highlands and into the larger cities. Frequently, families will plan the move carefully. Vacant lands around the larger cities will be scouted in advance, and suddenly, in the middle of the night, the new "settlers" will move in and erect a shantytown. With time, the seizure of the land is usually recognized by city officials and the new neighborhood is provided with urban services. Where the land seizure is resisted, however, violence and loss of life are common.

Factors other than famine also force people to leave their ancestral homes. Population pressure and division of the land into parcels too small to sustain families compel people to migrate. Others move to the cities in search of economic opportunities or chances for social advancement that do not exist in rural regions. Tens of thousands of Colombians illegally crossed into Venezuela in the 1970s and 1980s in search of employment. As is the case with Mexicans who enter the United States, Colombians experienced discrimination and remained on the margins of urban society, mired in low-paying, unskilled jobs. Those who succeeded in finding work in industry were a source of anger and frustration to labor-union members, who resented Colombians who accepted low rates of pay. Other migrants sought employment in the agricultural sector on coffee plantations or the hundreds of cattle ranches that dot the *Ilanos,* or plains. In summary, a combination of push and pull factors are involved in a family's decision to begin a new life.

Since World War II, indigenous migration in South America has rapidly increased urban populations and has forced cities to reorganize. Rural people have been exposed to a broad range of push–pull pressures to move to the cities. Land hunger, extreme poverty, and rural violence might be included among the push factors; while the hope of a better job, upward social mobility, and a more satisfying life help to explain the attraction of a city. The phenomenon can be infinitely complex.

In Lima, Peru, there has been a twofold movement of people. While the unskilled and illiterate, the desperately poor and unemployed, the newly arrived migrant, and the delinquent have moved to or remained in inner-city slums, former slum dwellers have in turn moved to the city's perimeter. Although less centrally located, they have settled in more spacious and socially desirable shantytowns. In this way, some 16,000 families created a squatter settlement practically overnight in the south of Lima. Author Hernando DeSoto, in his groundbreaking and controversial book *The Other Path,* captures the essence of the shantytowns. "Modest homes cramped together on city perimeters, a myriad of workshops in their midst, armies of vendors hawking their wares on the street, and countless minibus lines crisscrossing them—all seem to have sprung from nowhere, pushing the city's boundaries ever outward."

Significantly, DeSoto notes, collective effort has increasingly been replaced by individual effort, upward mobility exists even for the inner-city slum dwellers, and urban culture and patterns of consumption have been transformed. Opera, theater, and *zarzuela* (comic opera) have gradually been replaced by movies, soccer, folk festivals, and television. Beer, rice, and table salt are now within the reach of much of the population; consumption of more expensive items, however, such as wine and meat, has declined.

On the outskirts of Buenos Aires there exists a *villa miseria* (slum) built on the bottom and sides of an old clay pit. Appropriately, the *barrio,* or neighborhood, is called La Cava (literally "The Digging"). The people of La Cava are very poor; most have moved there from rural Argentina or from Paraguay. Shacks seem to be thrown together from whatever is available—scraps of wood, packing crates, sheets of tin, and cardboard. There is no source of potable water, garbage litters the narrow alleyways, and there are no sewers. Because

of the concave character of the barrio, the heat is unbearable in the summer. Rats and flies are legion. At times, the smells are repulsive. The visitor to La Cava experiences an assault on the senses; this is Latin America at its worst.

But there is another side to the slums of Buenos Aires, Lima, and Santiago. A closer look at La Cava, for example, reveals a community in transition. Some of the housing is more substantial, with adobe replacing the scraps of wood and tin; other homes double as places of business and sell general merchandise, food, and bottled drinks. One advertises itself as a food store, bar, and butcher shop. Another sells watches and repairs radios. Several promote their merchandise or services in a weekly newspaper that circulates in La Cava and two other *barrios de emergencia* ("emergency"— that is, temporary—neighborhoods). The newspaper addresses items of concern to the inhabitants. There are articles on hygiene and infant diarrhea; letters and editorials plead with people not to throw their garbage in the streets; births and deaths are recorded. The newspaper is a chronicle of progress as well as frustration: people are working together to create a viable neighborhood; drainage ditches are constructed with donated time and equipment; collections and raffles are held to provide materials to build sewers and, in some cases, to provide minimal street lighting; and men and women who have contributed their labor are singled out for special praise.

The newspaper also reproduces municipal decrees that affect the lives of the residents. The land on which the barrio sits was illegally occupied, the stores that service the neighborhood were opened without the necessary authorization, and the housing was built without regard to municipal codes, so city ordinances such as the following aimed at the barrios de emergencia are usually restrictive: "The sale, renting or transfer of *casillas* [homes] within the boundaries of the barrio de emergencia is prohibited; casillas can not be inhabited by single men, women or children; the opening of businesses within the barrio is strictly prohibited, unless authorized by the Municipality; dances and festivals may not be held without the express authorization of the Municipality." But there are also signs of accommodation: "The Municipality is studying the problem of refuse removal." For migrants, authority and the legal system are not helpful; instead, they are hindrances.

Hernando DeSoto found this situation to be true also of Peru, where "the greatest hostility the migrants encountered was from the legal system." Until the end of World War II, the system had either absorbed or ignored the migrants "because the small groups who came were hardly likely to upset the status quo." But when the rural-to-urban flow became a flood, the system could no longer remain disinterested. Housing and education were barred to them, businesses would not hire them. The migrants discovered over time that they would have to fight for every right and every service from an unwilling establishment. Thus, to survive, they became part of the

(Photo Lisa Clyde)

The northern Andes Mountains meet the Caribbean Sea in Venezuela.

informal sector, otherwise known as the underground or parallel economy.

On occasion, however, municipal laws can work to the advantage of newly arrived migrants. In the sprawling new communities that sprang up between Lima and its port city of Callao, there are thousands of what appear to be unfinished homes. In almost every instance, a second floor was begun but, curiously, construction ceased. The reason for the uncomplete projects relates to taxes—they are not assessed until a building is complete.

These circumstances are true not only of the squatter settlements on the fringes of South America's great cities but also of the inner-city slums. Slum dwellers *have* been able to improve their market opportunities and *have* been able to acquire better housing and some urban services, because they have organized on their own, outside formal political channels. In the words of sociologist Susan Eckstein, "They refused to allow dominant class and state interests to determine and restrict their fate. Defiance and resistance won them concessions which quiescence would not."

DeSoto found this to be the case with Lima: Migrants, "if they were to live, trade, manufacture, or even consume . . . had to do so illegally. Such illegality was not antisocial in intent, like trafficking in drugs, theft, or abduction, but was designed to achieve such essentially legal objectives as building a house, providing a service, or developing a business."

This is also the story of Buenos Aires' La Cava. To open a shop in the barrio with municipal approval, an aspiring busi-

nessperson must be a paragon of patience. Various levels of bureaucracy, with their plethora of paperwork and fees, insensitive municipal officials, inefficiency, and interminable waiting, drive people outside the system where the laws do not seem to conform to social need.

AN ECCLESIASTICAL REVOLUTION
During the past 20 years, there have been important changes in the religious habits of many South Americans. Virtually everywhere, Roman Catholicism, long identified with the traditional order, has been challenged by newer movements such as Evangelical Protestantism and the Charismatics. Within the Catholic Church, the theology of liberation once gained ground. The creation of Christian communities in the barrios, people who bond together to discuss their beliefs and act as agents of change, has become a common phenomenon throughout the region. Base communities from the Catholic perspective instill Christian values in the lives of ordinary people. But it is an active form of religion that pushes for change and social justice. Hundreds of these communities exist in Peru, thousands in Brazil.

NATIONAL MYTHOLOGIES
In the midst of geographical and cultural diversity, the nations of South America have created national mythologies designed to unite people behind their rulers. Part of that mythology is rooted in the wars of independence that tore through much of the region between 1810 and 1830. Liberation from

European colonialism imparted to South Americans a sense of their own national histories, replete with military heroes such as José de San Martín, Simón Bolívar, Bernardo O'Higgins, and Antonio José de Sucre, as well as a host of revolutionary myths. This coming to nationhood paralleled what the United States experienced when it won its independence from Britain. South Americans, at least those with a stake in the new society, began to think of themselves as Venezuelans, Chileans, Peruvians, or Brazilians. The architects of Chilean national mythology proclaimed the emergence of a new and superior being who was the result of the symbolic and physical union of Spaniards and the tough, heroic Araucanian Indians. The legacy of Simón Bolívar lives on in particular in Venezuela, his homeland; even today, the nation's foreign policymakers speak in Bolivarian terms about Venezuela's rightful role as a leader in Latin American affairs. In some instances, the mythology generated by the wars for independence became a shield against foreign ideas and customs and was used to force immigrants to become "Argentines" or "Chileans." It was an attempt to bring national unity out of diversity.

Argentines have never solved the question of their identity. Many consider themselves European and hold much of the rest of Latin America in contempt. Following the unsuccessful conclusion of the Falklands War with Britain, one scholar suggested that perhaps Argentines should no longer consider themselves as "a forlorn corner of Europe" but should wake up to the reality that they are Latin Americans. Much of Argentine literature reflects this uncertain identity and may help to explain author Jorge Luis Borges's affinity for English gardens and Icelandic sagas. It was also an Argentine military government that invoked Western Catholic civilization in its fight against a "foreign" and "godless" communism in the 1970s.

THE ARTIST AND SOCIETY

There is a strongly cultured and humane side of South America. Jeane Franco, an authority on Latin American cultural movements, has observed that to "declare oneself an artist in Latin America has frequently involved conflict with society." The art and literature of South America in particular, and Latin America in general, represent a distinct tradition within the panorama of Western civilization.

The art of South America has as its focus social questions and ideals. It expresses love for one's fellow human beings and "has kept alive the vision of a more just and humane form of society." It rises above purely personal relationships and addresses humanity.

Much change is also evident at the level of popular culture. Andean folk music, for example, is being replaced by the more urban and upbeat *chicha* music in Peru; and in Argentina, the traditional *tango* has lost much of its early appeal. Radio and television programs are more and more in the form of soap operas, adventure programs, or popular entertainment, once considered vulgar by cosmopolitan city dwellers.

South America is rather like a prism. It can be treated as a single object or region. Yet when exposed to a shaft of sunlight of understanding, it throws off a brilliant spectrum of colors that exposes the diversity of its lands and peoples.

Argentina (Republic of Argentina)

GEOGRAPHY

Area in Square Kilometers (Miles): 2,771,300 (1,100,000) (about 4 times the size of Texas)
Capital (Population): Buenos Aires (metropolitan area, 12,582,000)
Climate: varied; predominantly temperate

PEOPLE

Population

Total: 34,628,000
Annual Growth Rate: 1.1%
Rural/Urban Population Ratio: 14/86
Ethnic Makeup: 85% white; 15% Mestizo, Indian, and others
Major Languages: Spanish; Italian

Health

Life Expectancy at Birth: 68 years (male); 75 years (female)
Infant Mortality Rate (Ratio): 29/1,000
Average Caloric Intake: 125% of FAO minimum
Physicians Available (Ratio): 1/376

Religions

90% Roman Catholic (fewer than 20% practicing); 2% Protestant; 2% Jewish; 6% others

Education

Adult Literacy Rate: 95%

COMMUNICATION

Telephones: 2,650,000
Newspapers: 227

TRANSPORTATION

Highways—Kilometers (Miles): 208,350 (129,385)

Railroads—Kilometers (Miles): 34,572 (21,573)
Usable Airfields: 1,602

GOVERNMENT

Type: republic
Independence Date: July 9, 1816
Head of State: President Carlos Saul Menem
Political Parties: Radical Civic Union Party; Justicialist Party (Peronist); Intransigent Party; Union of the Democratic Center; others
Suffrage: universal at 18

MILITARY

Number of Armed Forces: 20,000
Military Expenditures (% of Central Government Expenditures): 8.6%
Current Hostilities: none

ECONOMY

Currency ($ U.S. Equivalent): 1.0 new peso = $1
Per Capita Income/GDP: $7,990/$271 billion
Inflation Rate: 3.9%
Total Foreign Debt: $73 billion
Natural Resources: fertile plains (pampas); minerals
Agriculture: grains; oilseeds; livestock products
Industry: food processing; motor vehicles; consumer durables; textiles; metallurgy; chemicals

FOREIGN TRADE

Exports: $15.7 billion
Imports: $21.4 billion

THE TANGO

The dance known as the tango had its origins in the outskirts of Argentina's capital city of Buenos Aires in the closing decades of the nineteenth century. It initially lacked respectability and social acceptance, but around the turn of the century, the tango became popular in Paris, where it gained respectability. By 1910 the tango had returned to Buenos Aires. Eventually, it became a national symbol of Argentina. That which had been shunned by "proper society" was now warmly embraced by all.

ARGENTINA:
THE DIVIDED LAND

Writers as far back as the mid-1800s have perceived two Argentinas. Domingo F. Sarmiento, the president of Argentina in the 1860s, entitled his classic work about his country *Civilization and Barbarism.* More contemporary writers speak of Argentina as a divided land or as a city and a nation. All address the relationship of the capital city, Buenos Aires, to the rest of the country. Buenos Aires is cultured, cosmopolitan, modern, and dynamic. The rural interior is in striking contrast in terms of living standards, the pace of life, and, perhaps, expectations as well. For many years, Buenos Aires and other urban centers have drawn population away from the countryside: Today, Argentina is 86 percent urban.

There are other contrasts. The land is extremely rich and produces a large share of the world's grains and beef. Few Argentines are malnourished, and the annual per capita consumption of beef is comparable to that of the United States. Yet this land of promise, which seemed in the 1890s to have a limitless future, has slowly decayed. Its greatness is now more mythical than real. Since the Great Depression of the 1930s, the Argentine economy has, save for brief spurts, never been able to return to the sustained growth of the late nineteenth and early twentieth centuries.

Today, the Argentine economy is more stable than it has been for years. Inflation has dropped from 200 percent per year to about 4 percent; inefficient and costly state enterprises have been privatized, including petroleum, traditionally a strategic sector reserved to the state; the foreign debt is under control; and the pace of business activity, employment, and (especially before the collapse of the Mexican peso sent shock waves through the Argentine economy) foreign investment has quickened.

Whether the economy can recover and the turnaround can be sustained is problematical, however, for Argentine economic history has been typified by unrealized potential and unfulfilled promises. Much depends on the continued confidence of the Argentine people in the leadership and policies of President Carlos Menem.

AUTHORITARIAN GOVERNMENT

In political terms, Argentina has revealed a curious inability to bring about the kind of stable democratic institutions that seemed assured in the 1920s. Since 1930, the military has seized power at least half a dozen times. It must be noted, however, that it has been civilians who have encouraged the generals to play an active role in politics. Historian Robert Potash writes: "The notion that Argentine political parties or other important civilian groups have consistently opposed military takeovers bears little relation to reality."

Argentina has enjoyed civilian rule since 1983, but the military is still a presence. Indeed, one right-wing faction, the *carapintadas* ("painted faces"), responsible for mutinies against President Raúl Alfonsín in 1987 and 1988, have organized a nationwide party and have attracted enough votes to rank as an important political force. An authoritarian tradition is very much alive in Argentina, as is the bitter legacy of the so-called Dirty War.

THE DIRTY WAR

What made the most recent period of military rule different is the climate of political violence that gripped Argentina starting in the late 1960s and early 1970s. The most recent period of violence began with the murder of former president Pedro Aramburu by left-wing guerrillas (Montoneros) who claimed to be fighting on behalf of the exiled popular leader Juan Perón (president from 1946 to 1955 and from 1973 to 1974). The military responded to what it saw as an armed challenge from the left with tough antisubversion laws and official violence against suspects. Guerrillas increased their activities and intensified their campaign to win popular support.

Worried by the possibility of a major popular uprising and divided over policy, the military called for national elections in 1973, hoping that a civilian government would calm passions. The generals could then concentrate their efforts on destroying the armed left. The violence continued, however, and even the brief restoration of Juan Perón to power failed to bring peace.

In March 1976, with the nation on the verge of economic collapse and guerrilla warfare spreading, the military seized power once again and declared a state of internal war, popularly called the Dirty War. Between 1976 and 1982, approximately 6,000 Argentine citizens "disappeared." Torture, the denial of basic human rights, harsh press censorship, officially directed death squads, and widespread fear came to characterize Argentina.

The labor movement—the largest, most effective, and most politically active on the continent—was, in effect, crippled by the military. Identified as a source of leftist subversion, the union movement was destroyed as an independent entity. Collective-bargaining agreements were dismantled, pension plans were cut back, and social-security and public-health programs were eliminated. The military's intent was to destroy a labor movement capable of operating on a national level.

The press was one of the immediate victims of the 1976 coup. A law was decreed warning that anyone spreading information derived from organizations "dedicated to subversive activities or terrorism"

(United Nations photo/P. Teuscher)

Few people are malnourished in Argentina. Well known for its abundant grains and beef, Argentina also has a large fishing industry. These fishing boats are in the bay of the Plata River in Buenos Aires.

would be subject to an indefinite sentence. To speak out against the military was punishable by a 10-year jail term. The state also directed its terrorism tactics against the media, and approximately 100 journalists disappeared. Hundreds more received death threats, were tortured and jailed, or fled into exile. Numerous newspapers and magazines were shut down, and one, *La Opinión,* passed to government control.

The ruling junta justified these excesses by portraying the conflict as the opening battle of "World War III," in which Argentina was valiantly defending Western Christian values and cultures against hordes of Communist, "godless" subversives. It was a "holy war," with all of the unavoidable horrors of such strife.

By 1981, leftist guerrilla groups had been annihilated. Argentines slowly began to recover from the shock of internal war and talked of a return to civilian government. The military had completed its task; the nation needed to rebuild. Organized labor attempted to re-create its structure and threw the first tentative challenges at the regime's handling of the economy. The press carefully criticized both the economic policies of the government and the official silence over the fate of *los desaparecidos* ("the disappeared ones"). Human-rights groups pressured the generals with redoubled efforts.

OPPOSITION TO THE MILITARY

Against this backdrop of growing popular dissatisfaction with the regime's record, together with the approaching 150th anniversary of Great Britain's occupation of Las Islas Malvinas (Falkland Islands), President Leopoldo Galtieri decided in 1982 to regain Argentine sovereignty and attack the Falklands. A successful assault, the military reasoned, would capture the popular imagination with its appeal to Argentine nationalism. The military's tarnished image would regain its luster. Forgiven would be the excesses of the Dirty War. But the attack ultimately failed.

In the wake of the fiasco, which cost thousands of Argentine and British lives, the military lost its grip on labor, the press, and the general population. Military and national humiliation, the continuing economic crisis made even worse by war costs, and the swelling chorus of discontent lessened the military's control over the flow of information and ideas. Previously forbidden subjects—such as the responsibility for the disappearances during the Dirty War—were raised in the newspapers.

The labor movement made a rapid and striking recovery and is now in the forefront of renewed political activity. Even though the movement is bitterly divided into moderate and militant wings, it is a force that cannot be ignored by political parties on the rebound.

The Falklands War may well prove to be a watershed in recent Argentine history. A respected Argentine observer, Torcuato DiTella, argues that the Falklands crisis was a "godsend," for it allowed Argentines to break with "foreign" economic models that had failed in Argentina. Disappointed with the United States and Europe over their support of Great Britain, he concludes: "We belong in Latin America and it is better to be a part of this strife-torn continent than a forlorn province of Europe."

Popularly elected in 1983, President Raúl Alfonsín's economic policies initially struck in bold new directions. He forced the International Monetary Fund to renegotiate Argentina's huge multi-billion-dollar debt in a context more favorable to Argentina, and he was determined to bring order out of chaos.

One of his most difficult problems centered on the trials for human-rights abuses against the nation's former military rulers. According to *Latin American Regional Reports,* Alfonsín chose to "distinguish degrees of responsibility" in taking court action against those who conducted the Dirty War. Impressively, Alfonsín put on trial the highest authorities, to be followed by action against those identified as responsible for major excesses.

Almost immediately, however, extreme right-wing nationalist officers in the armed forces opposed the trials and engineered a series of mutinies that undermined the stability of the administration. In 1987, during the Easter holiday, a rebellion of dissident soldiers made its point, and the Argentine Congress passed legislation that limited the prosecution of officers who killed civilians during the Dirty War to those only at the highest levels. Mini-mutinies in 1988 resulted in further concessions to the mutineers by the Alfonsín government, including reorganization of the army high command and higher wages.

Political scientist Gary Wynia aptly observed: "The army's leadership is divided between right-wing officers willing to challenge civilian authorities with force and more romantic officers who derive gratification from doing so. Many of the latter refuse to accept the contention that they are 'equal' to civilians, claiming that they have a special role that prevents their subordination to civilian authorities." To this day, the Argentine military has come to terms neither with itself nor with democratic government.

Argentina's current president, Carlos Menem, was supported by the military in the elections of May 1989, with perhaps 80 percent of the officer corps casting their votes for the Peronist Party. Menem adopted a policy of rapprochement with the military, which included the 1990 pardon of former junta members convicted of human-rights abuses. Historian Peter Calvert argues that Menem chose the path of amnesty because elements in the armed forces "would not be content until they got it." Rebellious middle-rank officers were well disposed toward Peronists, and Menem's pardon was "a positive gain in terms of the acceptance of the Peronists among the military themselves." In essence, then, Menem's military policy is consistent with other policies in terms of its pragmatic core.

On the other hand, significant progress has been made with regard to "disappeared" people. In 1992, President Menem agreed to create a commission to deal with the problem of children of the disappeared who were adopted by other families. Many have had their true identities established as a result of the patient work of "The Grandmothers of the Plaza de Mayo" and by the technique of cross-generational genetic analysis. In 1995, the names of an additional 1,000 people were added to the official list of the missing. Also, a retired military officer revealed his part in pushing drugged prisoners out of planes over the South Atlantic Ocean.

ECONOMIC TRAVAIL AND RECOVERY

President Alfonsín was fond of telling the following story of the frustrations of high office. George Bush, praying in the White House, asked God, "Will the hostages in the Middle East ever be released?" The reply came from above: "Yes, but not during your term in office." Similarly, Mikhail Gorbachev, alone in his library in the Kremlin, looked heavenward and asked: "Will perestroika succeed?" Once again the reply was heard: "Yes, but not during your time in office." And then, Alfonsín continued, "I myself looked up to God and asked, 'Will Argentina's economic, military and political crises ever be solved?'" Once more comes God's answer: "Yes, but not in *my* time in office." The humor is bitter and suggests the intractable character of crisis in Argentina. Indeed, Argentina's runaway inflation forced President Alfonsín to hand over power to Carlos Menem 6 months early.

Menem's government has worked a bit of an economic miracle, despite an administration nagged by corruption and early policy indecision, which witnessed

| Pedro de Mendoza establishes the first settlement at Buenos Aires **1536** | Independence of Spain **1816** | War with Paraguay **1865–1870** | Electoral reform: compulsory male suffrage **1912** | Juan Perón is in power **1946–1955 and 1973–1974** | The Dirty War **1976–1982** | War with Great Britain over the Falkland Islands; military mutinies and economic chaos **1980s** |

1990s

Privatization of the economy accelerates

Constitutional reform allows President Carlos Menem to serve a second consecutive term

Presidential elections are scheduled for 1999

the appointment of 21 ministers to 9 cabinet positions during his first 18 months in office. In Menem's favor, he is not an ideologue but, rather, an adept politician whose acceptance by the average voter is equaled by his ability to do business with almost anyone. He quickly identified the source of much of Argentina's chronic inflation: the state-owned enterprises. From the time of Perón, these industries were regarded as wellsprings of employment and cronyism rather than as instruments for the production of goods or the delivery of services such as electric power and telephone service. "Ironically," says Luigi Manzetti, writing in *North-South FOCUS,* "it took a Peronist like Menem to dismantle Perón's legacy." While Menem's presidential campaign stressed "traditional Peronist themes like social justice and government investments" to revive the depressed economy, once in power, "having inherited a bankrupt state and under pressure from foreign banks and domestic business circles to enact a stiff adjustment program, Menem reversed his stand." He embraced the market-oriented policies of his political adversaries, "only in a much harsher fashion." State-owned enterprises were sold off in rapid-fire order. Argentina thus underwent a rapid transformation, from one of the world's most closed economies to one of the most open.

Economic growth began again in 1991, but the social costs were high. Thousands of public-sector workers lost their jobs; a third of Argentina's population lived below the poverty line, and the gap between the rich and poor tended to increase. But both inflation and the debt were eventu-

ally contained, foreign investment increased, and confidence began to return to Argentina.

Menem has turned his economic success into political promise. Early in 1993, he announced a $1.5 billion antipoverty initiative, which set the stage for machinations aimed at securing a second term despite a constitutional prohibition against consecutive terms in office.

In November 1993, former president Alfonsín supported a constitutional reform that allowed Menem to serve another term. Menem accepted some checks on executive power, including reshuffling the Supreme Court, placing members of the political opposition in charge of certain state offices, creating a post similar to that of prime minister, awarding a third senator to each province, and shortening the presidential term from 6 to 4 years. With these reforms in place, Menem easily won another term in 1995.

FOREIGN POLICY

The Argentine government's foreign policy has usually been determined by realistic appraisals of the nation's best interests. Since 1946, the country has moved between the two poles of pro-West and nonaligned. President Menem has firmly supported the foreign-policy initiatives of the United States and the United Nations. Argentine participation in the Persian Gulf War and the presence of Argentine troops under United Nations command in Croatia, Somalia, and other trouble spots have paid dividends: Washington has agreed to supply Argentina with military supplies for the first time

since the Falklands War in 1982. Such a policy obviously wins points for Menem with the Argentine military.

ARGENTINA'S FUTURE

The Argentine economy, despite recent successes, still remains volatile. Although the growth rate since 1991 has averaged 6 percent a year, unemployment surged from 6 percent in 1991 to 17 percent in 1996. Unemployment and underemployment trouble 30 percent of the workforce and have multiple causes—according to the *Buenos Aires Herald,* the increasing entry of women into the workforce; advances in technology and productivity; and, most important, the lack of training, not only for the post-40 generation but also for youths. Education and training are critical for the future health of the economy. Politically, however, Argentina's experiment with constitutional reform must be judged a success. And the military seems to have been contained; military spending has been halved, the army has been reduced from 100,000 to 20,000 soldiers, military enterprises have been divested, and mandatory service has been abandoned in favor of a professional force.

DEVELOPMENT

Argentina, in its rapid pursuit of privatization of state-owned industries, was the first Latin American country to sell its energy company. The remarkable economic progress made between 1991 and 1997, saw economic growth of 6% per year.

FREEDOM

In 1995, Argentines were again reminded of the horrors of the "Dirty War" as retired navy commander Adolfo Francisco Scilingo described the "disposal" of victims of the military's campaign against subversion in the 1970s.

HEALTH/WELFARE

Argentina's inflation rate of about 4%, although appreciably lower than past years, still has an adverse impact on the amount of state spending on social services. Moreover, the official minimum wage falls significantly lower than the $12,000 per year necessary to support a family of four.

ACHIEVEMENTS

Argentine citizens have won four Nobel Prizes—two for peace and one each for chemistry and medicine. The nation's authors— Jorge Luis Borges, Julio Cortazar, Manuel Puig, and Ricardo Guiraldes, to name only a few—are world-famous.

Bolivia (Republic of Bolivia)

GEOGRAPHY

Area in Square Kilometers (Miles): 1,098,160 (424,162) (about the size of California and Texas combined)
Capitals (Population): La Paz (de facto) (711,000); Sucre (legal) (105,800)
Climate: varies from humid and tropical to semiarid and cold

PEOPLE

Population

Total: 7,896,300
Annual Growth Rate: 2.3%
Rural/Urban Population Ratio: 42/58
Ethnic Makeup: 30% Quechua; 25% Aymara; 30% Mestizo; 15% white
Major Languages: Spanish; Quechua; Aymara

Health

Life Expectancy at Birth: 61 years (male); 66 years (female)
Infant Mortality Rate (Ratio): 71/1,000
Average Caloric Intake: 91% of FAO minimum
Physicians Available (Ratio): 1/3,518

La Diablada

Each year in Bolivia's city of Oruro, there occurs a remarkable ceremony known as *La Diablada*. Dating from colonial times, La Diablada combines Catholic and indigenous religious themes in processions and short plays that depict the ageless conflict between good and evil. In one play, the Spanish conquest is re-created; the Inca, sad but noble, are defeated. There is little doubt left in the minds of the native audience as to which side is "good" and which side "evil."

Religions

95% Roman Catholic; also Methodist and other Protestants

Education

Adult Literacy Rate: 80%

COMMUNICATION

Telephones: 150,000
Newspapers: 14 dailies

TRANSPORTATION

Highways—Kilometers (Miles): 42,815 (26,717)

Railroads—Kilometers (Miles): 3,684 (2,288)
Usable Airfields: 1,382

GOVERNMENT

Type: republic
Independence Date: August 6, 1825
Head of State: President Hugo Banzer Suárez
Political Parties: Free Bolivia Movement; Revolutionary Front of the Left; Nationalist Revolutionary Movement; Christian Democratic Party; Nationalist Democratic Action; Popular Patriotic Movement; Unity and Progress Movement; others
Suffrage: universal and compulsory at 18 if married, 21 if single

MILITARY

Number of Armed Forces: 29,800
Military Expenditures (% of Central Government Expenditures): 14.1%
Current Hostilities: dispute with Chile regarding sovereign access to the sea for Bolivia

ECONOMY

Currency ($ U.S. Equivalent): 5.08 bolivianos = $1
Per Capita Income/GDP: $2,370/$18.3 billion
Inflation Rate: 8.5%
Total Foreign Debt: $4.2 billion
Natural Resources: tin; natural gas; petroleum; zinc; tungsten; antimony; silver; iron ore
Agriculture: potatoes; corn; sugarcane; rice; wheat; coffee; coca; bananas
Industry: textiles; mining; food processing; chemicals; plastics

FOREIGN TRADE

Exports: $1.1 billion
Imports: $1.2 billion

BOLIVIA: AN INDIAN NATION

Until recently, the images of Bolivia captured by the world's press were uniformly negative. Human-rights abuses were rampant, a corrupt and brutal military government was deeply involved in cocaine trafficking, and the nation was approaching bankruptcy.

Other images might include Bolivia's complex society. So intermixed has this multiethnic culture become that one's race is defined by one's social status. So-called whites, who look very much like the Indians with whom their ancestors intermarried, form the upper classes only because of their economic, social, and cultural positions—that is, the degree to which they have embraced European culture.

Another enduring image fixed in the literature is Bolivia's political instability. The actual number of governments over the past 200 years is 80, however, and not the 200 commonly noted. Indeed, elected governments have been in power for nearly the past 2 decades. What outsiders perceive as typical Latin American political behavior clouds what is unusual and positive about Bolivia.

One nineteenth-century leader, Manuel Belzu, played an extremely complex role that combined the forces of populism, nationalism, and revolution. Belzu encouraged the organization of the first trade unions, abolished slavery, promoted land reform, and praised Bolivia's Indian past.

In 1952, a middle-class–led and popularly supported revolution swept the country. The ensuing social, economic, and political reforms, while not erasing an essentially dual society of "whites" and Indians, did significantly ease the level of exploitation. Most of the export industries, including those involved with natural resources, were nationalized. Bolivia's evolution—at times progressive, at times regressive—continues to reflect the impulse for change.

THE SOCIETY: POSITIVE AND NEGATIVE ASPECTS

Bolivia, despite the rapid and startling changes that have occurred in the recent past, remains an extremely poor society. In terms of poverty, life expectancy, death rates, and per capita income, the country ranks among the worst in the Western Hemisphere.

Rights for women have made slow progress, even in urban areas. In 1975, a woman was appointed to the Bolivian Supreme Court; and in 1979, Congress elected Lidia Gueiler Tejada, leader of the lower house, as president. Long a supporter of women's rights, Tejada earlier had drafted and pushed through Congress a bill that created a ministry to provide social benefits for women and children. That remarkably advanced legislation has not guaranteed that women enjoy a social status equal to that of men, however. Furthermore, many women are likely unaware of their rights under the law.

Bolivia's press is reasonably free, although many journalists are reportedly paid by politicians, drug traffickers, and officials to increase their exposure or suppress negative stories. A few journalists who experienced repression under previous governments still practice self-censorship.

URBANIZATION

Santa Cruz, commonly known as "the other capital" of Bolivia, has been transformed in the last 40 years from an isolated backwater into a modern city with links to the other parts of the country and to the rest of South America. From a population of 42,000 in 1950, the number of inhabitants quickly rose to half a million in the mid-1980s and is now growing at the rate of about 8 percent a year. Bolivia's second-largest city, its population is expected to surpass that of the capital, La Paz, in this decade.

The city's political and economic strength has kept pace with the population growth. Politically, Santa Cruz represents the interests of lowland regionalism against the traditional hegemony of the highlands. Santa Cruz is also a growing commercial center; much of its wealth derives from the production and export of cocaine.

Most of the city's population growth has been the result of rural-to-urban migration, a phenomenon closely studied by geographer Gil Green. On paper, Santa Cruz is a planned city, but, since the 1950s, there has been a running battle between city planners and new settlers wanting land. "Due to the very high demand for cheap land and the large amount of flat, empty, nonvaluable land surrounding it, the city has tended to expand by a process of land invasion and squatting. Such invasions are generally overtly or covertly organized by political parties seeking electoral support of the low-income population." In the wake of a successful "invasion," the land is divided into plots that are allocated to the squatters, who then

(United Nations photo)

Bolivia has a complex society, tremendously affected by the continued interplay of multiethnic cultures. The influence of indigenous peoples on Bolivia remains strong.

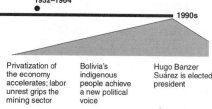

Spanish settle
the altiplano
(high plain)
1538

Bolivian
declaration of
independence
of Spain
1825

The War of the
Pacific with Chile;
Bolivia loses
access to the sea
1879–1880

The Chaco War
with Paraguay
1932–1935

Reforms:
nationalization of
mines, land
reform, universal
suffrage, creation
of labor federation
1952–1964

1990s

Privatization of
the economy
accelerates; labor
unrest grips the
mining sector

Bolivia's
indigenous
people achieve
a new political
voice

Hugo Banzer
Suárez is elected
president

build houses from whatever materials are at hand. Then begins the lengthy process of settlement consolidation and regularization of land tenure. Once again the new land is subdivided and sold cheaply to the low-income population.

Mass migration to Santa Cruz has drawn people from different geographical regions in Bolivia who are also different from one another in terms of their ethnicity. Once they arrive in Santa Cruz, they are labeled either as *Cambas* or *Kollas*. Cambas, from the tropical lowlands, are of European stock and speak Spanish. They are the politically dominant ethnic group in Santa Cruz, and discriminate against the Kollas. Kollas are Aymara- or Quechua-speaking Indians from the Andean highlands.

The labels are used by the city dwellers to determine how one should behave in social interactions and reflect profound differences in language, dress, food, and music. Racial differences reinforce the tensions between the two groups. Kollas are particularly unwilling to adopt the lowland culture of the city, for the Indians' cultural heritage is an important part of their identity. The constant infusion of highland culture into Santa Cruz is resisted by Cambas, who use racial and cultural differences to retain their own "elite" status in the city. In Green's words: "What may in fact be happening, is that whilst some cultural divisions are becoming less marked, the ideology of difference is maintained in order that city residents born in certain areas of the country are excluded from local positions of power."

One's migrant status usually determines housing status in Santa Cruz. Kollas, who are long-distance migrants and the most recent arrivals in the city, lack information about Santa Cruz and have the fewest contacts to offer them help with accommodations. Thus, they are forced to rent. Cambas, who are city natives or long-term residents, for the most part have well-developed support networks of interdependence with other Camba residents. They know the city and can best take advantage of land invasions and sales of cheap property. Kin and acquaintances are a critical part of the process.

FOREIGN POLICY AND DRUGS
Nonalignment has characterized Bolivian foreign policy since the 1952 Revolution. Relations with the United States have been strained occasionally because of official involvement in drug trafficking. Bolivian politicians have repeatedly promised to put an end to the trade and substitute other crops, a policy that most Bolivians view with suspicion.

Estimates suggested that illegal exports of coca paste and cocaine contributed the equivalent of 13 to 15 percent of Bolivia's gross domestic product in 1991 and that coca by-products accounted for about 40 percent of total exports, legal and illegal, in 1990. About 400,000 Bolivians are estimated to live off coca and cocaine production. U.S. wishes run afoul of the multifaceted heritage of coca, the sacred plant of the Incas. There is virtually no activity in domestic, social, or religious life in which coca does not play a role; thus, attempts to limit its cultivation would have profound repercussions among the peasantry.

CHALLENGES
Bolivia's problems are formidable. Although the economic horizon is less threatening and the country is blessed with substantial natural resources, Bolivia's people remain the poorest, most malnourished, and least educated in the Andean region; and extensive drug trafficking and the widespread corruption associated with it may prove resistant to any action the Bolivian government may choose to take.

The 1997 presidential election was won by Hugo Banzer Suárez, with only 22.3 percent of the votes cast. His victory may in part be explained by a campaign strategy that negotiated agreements with other major parties as well as the new image he projected as a populist leader. In a previous political incarnation, Banzer seized power in 1971 in a coup d'etat and ruled with an iron fist until 1978. In a recent interview with the Argentine newspaper *La Nación,* he said that he wants "to humanize the neoliberal model" and that privatization was behind the increase in poverty and unemployment. Some critics claim that he has ties to narcotraffickers, but his vice president announced that the new administration would eradicate drug production by the end of Banzer's term in 2002.

DEVELOPMENT

Under President Sánchez de Lozada, Bolivia turned to privatization in an attempt to escape from poverty. Plans called for selling up to 50% of the state-owned airline, telephone, oil, railroad, and tin-smelting operations. The 50% remaining in Bolivian hands would be transformed into shares and distributed to all Bolivians over age 21 and used to fund pension plans.

FREEDOM

A corrupt judicial system, overcrowded prisons, and violence and discrimination against women and indigenous peoples are perennial problems in Bolivia, despite protective legislation. A government campaign against narcotics traffickers has resulted not only in abuses by the police but also the further corruption of law enforcement.

HEALTH/WELFARE

Provisions against child labor in Bolivia are frequently ignored; many children may be found shining shoes, selling lottery tickets, and as street vendors. Although urban children generally attend school through the elementary level, more than half of rural children do not. Taken together, fewer than 30% of children are educated beyond elementary school.

ACHIEVEMENTS

The Bolivian author Armando Chirveches, in his political novel *La Candidatura de Rojas* (1909), produced one of the best examples of this genre in all of Latin America. The book captures the politics of the late nineteenth century extraordinarily well.

Brazil (Federal Republic of Brazil)

GEOGRAPHY

Area in Square Kilometers (Miles): 8,512,100 (3,285,670) (larger than the 48 contiguous U.S. states)
Capital (Population): Brasília (1,600,000)
Climate: mostly tropical or semitropical; temperate zone in the south

PEOPLE

Population

Total: 162,661,000
Annual Growth Rate: 1.2%
Rural/Urban Population Ratio: 24/76
Ethnic Makeup: 55% white; 38% mixed; 6% black; 1% others
Major Languages: Portuguese; English; German; Italian

Health

Life Expectancy at Birth: 57 years (male); 67 years (female)
Infant Mortality Rate (Ratio): 57/1,000
Average Caloric Intake: 107% of FAO minimum
Physicians Available (Ratio): 1/715

> ## Carnaval: A Form of Social Control?
>
> Every year, just before the Lenten season, the wild celebrations of Carnaval ("Carnival") take place in Brazil. These days are a time to release pent-up frustrations and to immerse oneself in song and dance. Brazilian social critics have long accused the government of using Carnaval as an emotional safety valve for the disadvantaged, saying that the celebrations are little more than psychological therapy. But Carnaval is also a popular mass art form that allows Brazil's subcultures to express themselves through music and dance. In this sense, it has become central to the complex culture of Brazil.

Religions

90% Roman Catholic; 10% others

Education

Adult Literacy Rate: 80%

COMMUNICATION

Telephones: 9,860,000
Newspapers: 322 dailies

TRANSPORTATION

Highways—Kilometers (Miles): 1,670,148 (1,042,172)
Railroads—Kilometers (Miles): 30,612

(19,102)
Usable Airfields: 3,476

GOVERNMENT

Type: federal republic; democratically elected president since 1985
Independence Date: September 7, 1822
Head of State: President Fernando Henrique Cardoso
Political Parties: National Reconstruction Party; Brazilian Democratic Movement Party; Liberal Front Party; Workers' Party; Brazilian Labor Party; Democratic Labor Party; Brazilian Social Democratic Party; Popular Socialist Party; Communist Party of Brazil; Liberal Party; others
Suffrage: voluntary at 16; compulsory between 18 and 70; voluntary at 70

MILITARY

Number of Armed Forces: 324,200
Military Expenditures (% of Central Government Expenditures): 3.0%
Current Hostilities: none

ECONOMY

Currency ($ U.S. Equivalent): 0.62 real = $1 (changes frequently)
Per Capita Income/GDP: $5,580/$886.3 billion
Inflation Rate: about 1,094%
Total Foreign Debt: $134 billion
Natural Resources: iron ore; manganese; bauxite; nickel; uranium; gemstones; petroleum
Agriculture: coffee; rice; corn; sugarcane; soybeans; cotton; manioc; oranges
Industry: textiles; chemicals; cement; lumber; steel; motor vehicles; metalwork; capital goods

FOREIGN TRADE

Exports: $43.6 billion
Imports: $33.2 billion

BRAZIL:
A TROUBLED GIANT

In 1977, Brazilian president Ernesto Geisel stated that progress was based on "an integrated process of political, social, and economic development." Democracy, he argued, was the first necessity in the political arena. But democracy could only be achieved "if we also further social development. . . , if we raise the standard of living of Brazilians." The standard of living, he continued, "can only be raised through economic development."

It was clear from his remarks that the three broad objectives of democratization, social progress, and economic development were interconnected. He could not conceive of democracy in a poor country or in a country where there were "gaps, defects, and inadequacies in the social realm."

CONCEPTS OF PROGRESS

Geisel's comments offer a framework within which to consider not only the current situation in Brazil but also historical trends that reach back to the late nineteenth century—and, in some instances, to Portugal. Historically, most Brazilians have believed that progress would take place within the context of a strong, authoritarian state. In the nineteenth century, for example, a reform-minded elite adapted European theories of modernization that called for government-sponsored changes. The masses would receive benefits from the state; in this way, the elite reasoned, pressure for change from the poorer sectors of society would be eliminated. There would be progress with order. *Ordem e Progresso* ("Order and Progress") is the motto that graces the Brazilian flag; the motto is as appropriate today as it was in 1889, when the flag first flew over the new republic.

The tension among modernization, social equity, and order and liberty was first obvious in the early 1920s, when politically isolated middle-class groups united with junior military officers (*tenentes*) to challenge an entrenched ruling class of coffee-plantation owners. By the mid-1920s, the tenentes, bent on far-reaching reforms, conceived a new role for themselves. With a faith that bordered at times on the mystical and a philosophy that embraced change in the vaguest of terms, they felt that only the military could shake Brazil from its lethargy and force it to modernize. Their program demanded the ouster of conservative, tradition-minded politicians, an economic transformation of the nation, and, eventually, a return to strong, centralized constitutional rule. The tenentes also proposed labor reforms that

included official recognition of trade unions, a minimum wage and maximum work week, restraints on child labor, land reform, nationalization of natural resources, and a radical expansion of educational facilities. Although the tenentes were frustrated in their attempts to mold policy, many of their reforms were taken up by Getulio Vargas, who seized power in 1930 and imposed a strong, authoritarian state on Brazil.

THE 1964 REVOLUTION

In some respects, the goals of the tenentes were echoed in 1964 when a broad coalition of civilians—frustrated by an economy that seemed to be disintegrating, concerned with the "leftist" slant of the government of João Goulart, and worried about a social revolution that might well challenge the status and prestige of the

wealthy and the middle classes—called on the military to impose order on the country.

The military leaders did not see their intervention as just another coup but, rather, as a revolution. They foresaw change but believed that it would be dictated from above. Government was highly centralized, the traditional parties were virtually frozen out of the political process, and the military and police ruthlessly purged Brazil of elements considered "leftist" or "subversive." (The terms were used interchangeably.) Order and authority triumphed over liberty and freedom. The press was muzzled, and human-rights abuses were rampant.

Brazil's economic recovery eventually began to receive attention. The military gave economic growth and national security priority over social programs and political liberalization. Until the effects of

Certain areas of Brazil attract enormous numbers of visitors from all over the world. This beach in Rio de Janeiro has one of the most famous skylines in South America.

the oil crisis generated by the Organization of Petroleum Exporting Countries (OPEC) in 1973 began to be felt, the recovery of the Brazilian economy was dubbed a "miracle," with growth rates averaging 10 percent a year.

The benefits of that growth went primarily to the upper and middle classes, who enjoyed the development of industries based largely on consumer goods. Moreover, Brazil's industrialization was flawed. It was heavily dependent on foreign investment, foreign technology, and foreign markets. It required large investments in machinery and equipment but needed little labor, and it damaged the environment through pollution of the rivers and air around industrial centers. Agriculture was neglected to the point that even basic foodstuffs had to be imported.

THE IMPACT OF
RURAL–URBAN MIGRATION
The stress on industrialization tremendously increased rural-to-urban migration and complicated the government's ability to keep up with the expanded need for public health and social services. In 1970, nearly 56 percent of the population were concentrated in urban areas; by the mid-1990s, 76 percent of the population were so classified. These figures also illustrate the inadequacies of an agrarian program based essentially on a "moving frontier." Peasants evicted from their plots have run out of new lands to exploit, unless they move to the inhospitable Amazon region. As a result, many have been attracted by the cities.

The pressure of the poor on the cities, severe shortages of staple foods, and growing tension in rural areas over access to the land forced the government to act. In 1985, the civilian government of José Sarney announced an agrarian-reform plan to distribute millions of acres of unused private land to peasants. Implementation of the reform was not easy, and confrontations between peasants and landowners occurred.

MILITARY RULE
IS CHALLENGED
Nineteen seventy-four was a crucial year for the military government of Brazil. The virtual elimination of the urban-guerrilla threat challenged the argument that democratic institutions could not be restored because of national security concerns.

Pressure grew from other quarters as well. Many middle- and upper-class Brazilians were frightened by the huge state-controlled sector in the economy that had been carved out by the generals. The military's determination to promote the rapid development of the nation's resources, to

control all industries deemed vital to the nation's security, and to compete with multinational corporations concerned Brazilian businesspeople, who saw their role in the economy decreasing.

Challenges to the military regime also came from the Roman Catholic Church, which attacked the government for its brutal violations of human rights and constantly called for economic and social justice. One Brazilian bishop publicly called the government "sinful" and in "opposition to the plans of God" and noted that it was the Church's moral and religious obligation to fight it. After 1974, as Brazil's economic difficulties mounted, the chorus of complaints grew insistent.

THE RETURN OF DEMOCRACY
The relaxation of political repression was heralded by two laws passed in 1979. The Amnesty Bill allowed for the return of hundreds of political exiles; the Party Reform Bill in essence reconstructed Brazilian politics. Under the provisions of the Party Reform Bill, new political parties could be established—provided they were represented in nine states and in 20 percent of the counties of those states. The new parties were granted the freedom to formulate political platforms, as long as they were not ideological and did not favor any one economic class. The Communist Party was outlawed, and the creation of a workers' party was expressly forbidden. (Communist parties were legalized again in 1985.)

The law against the establishment of a workers' party reflected the regime's concern that labor, increasingly anxious about the state of the economy, might withdraw its traditional support for the state. Organized labor had willingly cooperated with the state since the populist regime of Getulio Vargas (1937–1945). For Brazilian workers in the 1930s, the state was their "patron," the source of benefits. This dependence on the government, deeply rooted in Portuguese political culture, replaced the formation of a more independent labor movement and minimized industrial conflict. The state played the role of mediator between workers and management. President Vargas led the workers to believe that the state was the best protector of their interests. (Polls have indicated that workers still cling to that belief.)

If workers expect benefits from the state, however, the state must then honor those expectations and allocate sufficient resources to assure labor's loyalty. A deep economic crisis, such as the one that occurred in the early 1960s and again in the early 1990s, endangered the state's control

of labor. In 1964, organized labor supported the coup, because workers felt that the civilian regime had failed to perform its protective function. This phenomenon also reveals the extremely shallow soil in which Brazilian democracy has taken root.

Organized labor tends not to measure Brazilian governments in political terms, but within the context of the state's ability to address labor's needs. For the rank-and-file worker, it is not a question of democracy or military authoritarianism, but of bread and butter. Former president Sarney, in an effort to keep labor loyal to the government, sought the support of union leaders for a proposal to create a national pact with businesspeople, workers, and his government. But pervasive corruption, inefficient government, and a continuing economic crisis eventually eroded the legitimacy of the elites and favored nontraditional parties in the 1989 election. The candidacy of Luís Inácio da Silva, popularly known as "Lula" and leader of the Workers' Party, "was stunning evidence of the Brazilian electorate's dissatisfaction with the conduct of the country's transition to democracy and with the political class in general." He lost the election by a very narrow margin.

Yet workers continue to regard the state as the source of benefits, as do other Brazilians. Many social reformers, upset with the generals for their neglect of social welfare, believe that social reform should be dispensed from above by a strong and paternalistic state. Change is possible, even welcome—but it must be the result of compromise and conciliation, not confrontation or non-negotiable demands.

THE NEW CONSTITUTION
The *abertura* (political liberalization) climaxed in January 1985 with the election of President Sarney, a civilian, following 21 years of military rule. Importantly, the military promised to respect the Constitution and promised a policy of nonintervention in the political process. In 1987, however, with the draft of a new constitution under discussion, the military strongly protested language that removed its responsibility for internal law and order and restricted its role to that of defense of the nation against external threats. According to *Latin American Regional Reports: Brazil,* the military characterized the draft constitution as "confused, inappropriate, at best a parody of a constitution, just as Frankenstein was a gross and deformed imitation of a human being."

Military posturing aside, the new Constitution went into effect in October 1988. It reflects the input of a wide range of interests: The Constituent Assembly—which also served as Brazil's Congress—heard testimony and suggestions from Amazonian Indians, peasants, and urban poor as well as from rich landowners and the military. The 1988 Constitution is a document that captures the byzantine character of Brazilian politics and influence peddling and reveals compromises made by conservative and liberal vested interests.

The military's fears about its role in internal security were removed when the Constituent Assembly voted constitutional provisions to grant the right of the military independently to ensure law and order, a responsibility it historically has claimed. But Congress also arrogated to itself the responsibility for appropriating federal monies. This is important, because it gives

Congress a powerful check on both the military and the executive office.

Nationalists won several key victories. The Constituent Assembly created the concept of "a Brazilian company of national capital" that can prevent foreigners from engaging in mining, oil-exploration risk contracts, and biotechnology. Brazilian-controlled companies were also given preference in the supply of goods and services to local, state, and national governments. Legislation re-affirmed and strengthened the principle of government intervention in the economy should national security or the collective interest be at issue.

Conservative congressional representatives were able to prevail in matters of land reform. They defeated a proposal that would have allowed the compulsory appropriation of property for land reform. Although a clause that addressed the "social function" of land was included in the Constitution, it was clear that powerful landowners and agricultural interests had triumphed over Brazil's landless peasantry.

In other areas, however, the Constitution is remarkably progressive on social and economic issues. The workweek was reduced to a maximum of 44 hours, profit sharing was established for all employees, time-and-a-half was promised for overtime work, and paid vacations were to include a bonus of 30 percent of one's monthly salary. Day-care facilities were to be established for all children under age 6, maternity leave of 4 months and paternity leave of 5 days were envisaged, and workers were protected against "arbitrary dismissal." The Constitution also introduced a series of innovations that would increase significantly the ability of Brazilians to claim their guaranteed rights before the nation's courts and ensure the protection of human rights, particularly the rights of Indians and peasants involved in land disputes.

Despite the ratification of the 1988 Constitution, a functioning Congress, and an independent judiciary, the focus of power in Brazil is still the president. A legislative majority in the hands of the opposition in no way erodes the executive's ability to govern as he or she chooses. Any measure introduced by the president automatically becomes law after 40 days, even without congressional action. Foreign observers perceive "weaknesses" in the new parties, which in actuality are but further examples of well-established political practices. The parties are based on personalities rather than issues, platforms are vague, goals are so broad that they are almost illusions, and party organization conforms to traditional alliances and the

(United Nations photo)

By the late 1980s, agrarian reforms that were designed to establish peasants in plots of workable land had caused the depletion of Brazilian jungle and, as space and opportunities diminished, a large movement of these people to the cities. The urban crowding in Brazil is illustrated by this photo of a section of Rio de Janeiro.

"rules" of patronage. Democratic *forms* are in place in Brazil; the *substance* remains to be realized.

The election of President Fernando Collor de Mello, who assumed office in March 1990, proves the point. As political scientist Margaret Keck explains, Collor fit well into a "traditional conception of elite politics, characterized by fluid party identifications, the predominance of personal relations, a distrust of political institutions, and reliance on charismatic and populist appeals to *o povo,* the people." Unfortunately, such a system is open to abuse; revelations of widespread corruption that reached all the way to the presidency brought down Collor's government in 1992 and gave Brazilian democracy its most difficult challenge to date. The scandal brought to light a range of strengths and weaknesses that presents insights into the Brazilian political system.

THE PRESS AND
THE PRESIDENCY
Brazil's press was severely censored and harassed from the time of the military coup of 1964 until 1982. Not until passage of the Constitution of 1988 was the right of free speech and a free press guaranteed. It was the press, and in particular the news magazine *Veja* that opened the door to President Collor's impeachment. In the words of *World Press Review,* "Despite government pressure to ease off, the magazine continued to uncover the president's malfeasance, tugging hard at the threads of Collor's unraveling administration. As others in the media followed suit, Congress was forced to begin an investigation and, in the end, indict Collor." The importance of the event to Brazil's press, according to *Veja* editor Mario Sergio Conti, is that "It will emerge with fewer illusions about power and be more rigorous. Reporting has been elevated to a higher plane. . . ."

While the failure of Brazil's first directly elected president in 29 years was tragic, it should not be interpreted as the demise of Brazilian democracy. Importantly, according to Brazilian journalist Carlos Eduardo Lins da Silva, writing in *Current History,* many "Brazilians and outside observers saw the workings of the impeachment process as a sign of the renewed strength of democratic values in Brazilian society. They were also seen as a healthy indicator of growing intolerance to corruption in public officials."

The military, despite persistent rumors of a possible coup, has to date allowed the constitutional process to dictate events. For the first time, most civilians do not see the generals as part of the solution to

political shortcomings. And Congress, to its credit, chose to act responsibly and not be "bought off" by the executive office.

THE RIGHTS OF WOMEN
AND CHILDREN
Major changes in Brazilian households have occurred over the last decade as the number of women in the workforce has dramatically increased. In 1990, just over 35 percent of women were in the workforce, and the number was expected to grow. As a result, many women are limiting the size of their families. More than 20 percent use birth-control pills, and Brazil is second only to China in the percentage of women who have been sterilized. The traditional family of 5.0 or more children has shrunk to an average of 3.4. With two wage earners, the standard of living has risen slightly for some families. Many homes now have electricity and running water. Television sales increased by more than 1,000 percent in the last decade.

In relatively affluent, economically and politically dynamic urban areas, women are more obvious in the professions, education, industry, the arts, media, and political life. In rural areas, especially in the northeast, traditional cultural attitudes, which call upon women to be submissive, are still well entrenched.

Women are routinely subjected to physical abuse in Brazil. Americas Watch, an international human-rights group, reports that more than 70 percent of assault,

(United Nations photo/Shelley Rotner)

The status of blacks in Brazil is considered better than in most other multiracial societies. The class structure is determined by a number of factors: income, family history, education, social behavior, cultural tastes, and talent. Still, the upper class remains mainly white, and the lower class principally of color.

rape, and murder cases take place in the home and that many incidents are unreported. Even though Brazil's Supreme Court struck down the outmoded concept of a man's "defense of honor," local courts routinely acquit men who kill unfaithful wives. Brazil, for all intents and purposes, is still a patriarchy.

Children are also in many cases denied basic rights. According to official statistics, almost 18 percent of children between the ages of 10 and 14 are in the labor force, and often work in unhealthy or dangerous environments. Violence against urban street children has reached frightening proportions. Between January and June 1992, 167 minors were killed in Rio de Janeiro; 306 were murdered in São Paulo over the first 7 months of the year. In July 1993, the massacre in a single night of seven street children in Rio de Janeiro resulted, for a time, in cries for an investigation of the matter. In February 1997, however, five children were murdered on the streets of Rio.

THE STATUS OF BLACKS
Scholars continue to debate the actual status of blacks in Brazil. Not long ago, an elected black member of Brazil's federal Congress blasted Brazilians for their racism. However, argues historian Bradford Burns, Brazil probably has less racial tension and prejudice than other multiracial societies.

A more formidable barrier, Burns says, may well be class. "Class membership depends on a wide variety of factors and their combination: income, family history and/or connections, education, social behavior, tastes in housing, food and dress, as well as appearance, personality and talent." But, he notes, "The upper class traditionally has been and still remains mainly white, the lower class principally colored." Upward mobility exists and barriers can be breached. But if such advancement depends upon a symbolic "whitening out," does not racism still exist?

This point is underscored by the 1988 celebration of the centennial of the abolition of slavery in Brazil. In sharp contrast to the government and Church emphasis on racial harmony and equality were the public protests by militant black groups claiming that Brazil's much-heralded "racial democracy" was a myth. In 1990, blacks earned 40 percent less than whites in the same professions.

THE INDIAN QUESTION
Brazil's estimated 200,000 Indians have suffered greatly in recent decades from the gradual encroachment of migrants from the heavily populated coastal regions and from government efforts to open the Amazon region to economic development. Highways have penetrated Indian lands, diseases for which the Indians have little or no immunity have killed thousands, and additional thousands have experienced a profound culture shock. Government efforts to protect the Indians have been largely ineffectual.

The two poles in the debate over the Indians are captured in the following excerpts from *Latin American Regional Reports: Brazil:* A Brazilian Army officer observed that the "United States solved the problem with its army. They killed a lot of Indians. Today everything is quiet there, and the country is respected throughout the world." And in the words of a Kaingang Indian woman: "Today my people see their lands invaded, their forests destroyed, their animals exterminated and their hearts lacerated by this brutal weapon that is civilization."

Sadly, the assault against Brazil's Indian peoples has accelerated, and disputes over land have become more violent. One case speaks for itself. In the aftermath of a shooting incident in which several Yanomamö Indians were killed by prospectors, the Brazilian federal government declared that all outsiders would be removed from Yanomamö lands, ostensibly to protect the Indians. Those expelled by the government included anthropologists, missionaries, doctors, and nurses. A large number of prospectors remained behind. By the end of 1988, while medical personnel had not been allowed back in, the number of prospectors had swelled to 50,000 in an area peopled by 9,000 Yanomamö. Evidence suggests that the Indians have been devastated by diseases, particularly malaria, and by mercury poisoning as a result of prospecting activities upriver from Yanomamö settlements. In 1991, cholera began to spread among indigenous Amazon peoples, due to medical waste dumped into rivers in cholera-ridden Peru and Ecuador.

The new Constitution devotes an entire chapter to the rights of Indians. For the first time in the country's history, Indians have the authority to bring suits in court to defend their rights and interests. In all such cases, they will be assisted by a public prosecutor. Even though the government established a large protected zone for Brazil's Yanomamö Indians in 1991, reports of confrontations between Indians and prospectors have persisted. There are also Brazilian nationalists who insist that a 150-mile-wide strip along the border with Venezuela be excluded from the reserve as a matter of national security. The Yanomamö cultural area extends well into Venezuela; such a security zone would bisect Yanomamö lands.

THE BURNING OF BRAZIL
Closely related to the destruction of Brazil's Indians is the destruction of the tropical rain forests. The burning of the forests by peasants clearing land in the traditional slash-and-burn method, or by developers and landowners constructing dams or converting forest to pasture, has become a source of worldwide concern and controversy.

Ecologists are horrified by the mass extinction of species of plants, animals, and insects, most of which have not even been catalogued. The massive annual burning (equivalent in 1987 to the size of Kansas) also fuels the debate on the greenhouse effect and global warming. The problem of the burning of Brazil is indeed global, because we are all linked to the tropics by climate and the migratory patterns of birds and animals.

World condemnation of the destruction of the Amazon basin has produced a strong xenophobic reaction in Brazil. Foreign Ministry Secretary-General Paulo Tarso Flecha de Lima informed a 24-nation conference on the protection of the environment that the "international community cannot try to strangle the development of Brazil in the name of false ecological theories." He further noted that foreign criticism of his government in this regard was "arrogant, presumptuous and aggressive." The Brazilian military, according to *Latin American Regional Reports: Brazil,* has adopted a high-profile posture on the issue. The military sees the Amazon as "a kind of strategic reserve vital to national security interests." Any talk of transforming the rain forests into an international nature reserve is rejected out of hand.

Over the next decade, however, Brazilian and foreign investors will create a 2.5 million-acre "green belt" in an already devastated area of the Amazon rain forest. Fifty million seedlings have been planted in a combination of natural and commercial zones. It is hoped that responsible forestry will generate jobs to maintain and study the native forest and to log the commercial zones. Steady employment would help to stem the flow of migrants to cities and to untouched portions of the rain forest.

FOREIGN POLICY
If Brazil's Indian and environmental policies leave much to be desired, its foreign policy has won it respect throughout much of Latin America and the developing world. Cuba, Central America, Angola, and Mozambique seemed far less threat-

Pedro Alvares
Cabral discovers
and claims Brazil
for Portugal
1500

Declaration of
Brazil's
independence
1822

The Golden Law
abolishes slavery
1888

The republic is
proclaimed
1889

The Brazilian
Expeditionary
Force
participates in
the Italian
campaign
1944

The military
seizes power
1964

Economic, social,
and ecological
crises
1980s

1990s

President
Fernando Collor
de Mello is
convicted on
impeachment
charges; he is
replaced by Vice
President Itamar
Franco

Fernando
Henrique
Cardoso is
elected president
in an impressive
victory

Economic
reforms restore
a measure of
stability

ening during the cold war to the Brazilian government than they did to Washington. Brazil is more concerned about its energy needs, capital requirements, and trade opportunities. Its foreign policy, in short, is one of pragmatism.

ECONOMIC POLICY

In mid-1993, Finance Minister Fernando Henrique Cardoso announced a plan to restore life to an economy in shambles. The so-called Real Plan, which pegged the new Brazilian currency (the real) to the dollar, brought an end to hyperinflation and won Cardoso enough popularity to carry him to the presidency. Inflation, which had raged at a rate of 45 percent per month in July 1994, was only 2 percent per month in February 1995. His two-to-one victory in elections in October 1994 was the most one-sided win since 1945.

President Cardoso has transformed the economy thorugh carefully conceived and brilliantly executed constitutional reforms. A renovated tax system, an overhauled social security program, and extensive privatization of state-owned enterprises were supported by a new generation of legislators pledged to support broad-based reform.

But, as was the case in much of Latin America in 1995, Mexico's financial crisis spread quickly to affect Brazil's economy, in large measure because foreign investors were unable to distinguish between Mexico and other Latin American nations. Their moment of panic hurt Cardoso's abilities to carry through his reforms in a

timely fashion. Capital flight resulted in a 6 percent devaluation of the currency and forced the president to delay his plans to address problems that involved state subsidies, pension programs, and tax evasion.

A fundamental problem is the state of Brazilian industry. According to reports in *World Press Review,* Brazil is 15 to 20 years behind the economies of the Northern Hemisphere in the modernization of machinery and products. In the 1980s, the nation's industries "went into hibernation" and stopped investing in themselves. As a result, there was no increase in productive capacity. The steel industry is characterized as "lazy and rusty," and the automotive industry is described as the "least productive in the world and among the worst for quality." Electricity generation is stagnant. However, the scope of Brazilian industry is impressive; it "produces virtually everything."

Cardoso's laudable economic reforms have not as yet transformed the quality of Brazilian democracy. The lament of Brazilian journalist Lins da Silva is still accurate: "Brazilian elites have once again shown how capable they are of solving political crises in a creative and peaceful manner but also how unwilling to promote change in inequitable social structures." The wealth of the nation still remains in the hands of a few, and the educational system has failed to absorb and train as many citizens as it should. Police continue routinely to abuse their power.

On a positive note, though, Brazilians in record numbers have joined voluntary

associations devoted to helping the less fortunate. This reflects a level of confidence in the government and an ability to transform society that augers well for the future. At a broader level, Brazil hopes to prosper from its membership in Mercosul, a regional trade organization that consists of Argentina, Brazil, Paraguay, and Uruguay. The success of Mercosul has expanded relations with other countries, especially Chile, which became an "associate" member of sorts in 1997. Tariffs will be ended on 95 percent of goods traded among member nations. Brazilian manufacturers are pleased by the prospect of a 50 percent expansion of the duty-free area open to their products.

The military—which to its credit has remained aloof from recent political agonies—has spoken out about the dangers posed by poverty, unemployment, and inflation. In 1993, it identified the "struggle against misery" as a priority. Cardoso's economic successes together with a new style of politics that eschews self-interest for meaningful change should keep the military in the barracks.

DEVELOPMENT

Brazil's economy has refocused outward to the rest of South America and the world. The success of Mercosul has been instrumental in Brazil's "discovery" of its neighbors. Inflation has been cut back dramatically and has put more money into the hands of consumers. But Brazil, according to the World Bank, still has the world's worst distribution of income.

FREEDOM

Violence against street children, indigenous peoples, homosexuals, and common criminals at the hands of the police, landowners, vigilante groups, gangs, and hired thugs is commonplace. Homicide committed by police is the third-leading cause of death among children and adolescents. Investigation of such crimes is lax and prosecution of the perpetrators sporadic. Indians continue to clash with miners and landowners.

HEALTH/WELFARE

One *favela* (slum) in Rio de Janeiro is the largest in South America, with over 300,000 inhabitants. According to sociologist Fábio L. S. Petrarolha, the "lack of housing and high rates of unemployment has created a new form of violence—the *arrastões*, mobs of poor who leave the slums as a group and literally overrun a neighborhood or a beach and steal everything they can."

ACHIEVEMENTS

Brazil's cultural contributions to the world are many. Authors such as Joaquim Maria Machado de Assis, Jorge Amado, and Graciliano Ramos are evidence of Brazil's high rank in terms of important literary works. Brazilian music has won millions of devotees throughout the world, and Brazil's *Cinema Novo* (New Cinema) has won many awards.

Chile (Republic of Chile)

GEOGRAPHY
Area in Square Kilometers (Miles): 756,945 (292,180) (nearly 2 times the size of California)
Capital (Population): Santiago (5,100,000)
Climate: mild; desert in north; Mediterranean in center; cool and damp in south

PEOPLE

Population
Total: 14,333,300
Annual Growth Rate: 1.5%
Rural/Urban Population Ratio: 15/85
Ethnic Makeup: 95% European and Mestizo; 3% Indian; 2% others
Major Language: Spanish

Health
Life Expectancy at Birth: 72 years (male); 78 years (female)
Infant Mortality Rate (Ratio): 14/1,000
Average Caloric Intake: 114% of FAO minimum
Physicians Available (Ratio): 1/889

Religions
89% Roman Catholic; 11% Protestant; small Jewish population

Education
Adult Literacy Rate: 94%

COMMUNICATION
Telephones: 768,000
Newspapers: 65 dailies

TRANSPORTATION
Highways—Kilometers (Miles): 79,599 (49,670)
Railroads—Kilometers (Miles): 7,766 (4,823)
Usable Airfields: 390

"A Synthesis of the Planet"

In "My Country," *United Nations World* (May 1950), Gabriela Mistrál, the Nobel Prize-winning Chilean poet and writer, described her nation in the following terms:

> Something like a synthesis of the planet is fulfilled in the geography of Chile. It starts in the desert, which is like beginning with sterility that loves no man. It is humanized in the valleys. It creates a home for living beings in the ample fertile agricultural zone, it takes on a grandiose sylvan beauty at the end of the continent as if to finish with dignity, and finally crumbles, offering half life, half death, in the sea.

GOVERNMENT
Type: republic
Independence Date: September 18, 1818
Head of State: President Eduardo Frei Ruiz-Tagle
Political Parties: Christian Democratic Party; Party for Democracy; Radical Party; Social Democratic Party; Socialist Party; National Revolution; Independent Democratic Union; others
Suffrage: universal and compulsory at 18

MILITARY
Number of Armed Forces: 95,800
Military Expenditures (% of Central Government Expenditures): 3.4%
Current Hostilities: none

ECONOMY
Currency ($ U.S. Equivalent): 414 pesos = $1
Per Capita Income/GDP: $7,010/$97.7 billion
Inflation Rate: 8.7%
Total Foreign Debt: $20 billion
Natural Resources: copper; timber; iron ore; nitrates; precious metals; molybdenum
Agriculture: wheat; potatoes; sugar beets; onions; beans; fruits; livestock
Industry: mineral refining; metal manufacturing; food processing; fish processing; wood products

FOREIGN TRADE
Exports: $11.5 billion
Imports: $10.9 billion

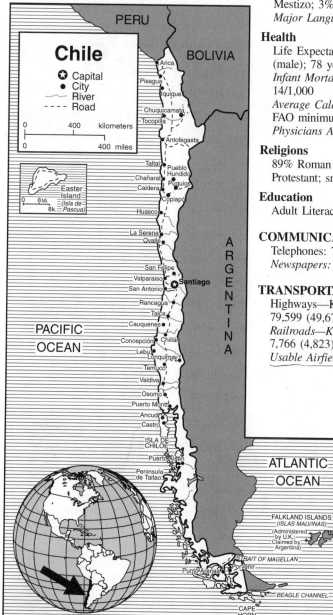

CHILE: A NATION
ON THE REBOUND — отскок

In September 1973, the Chilean military, with the secret support of the U.S. Central Intelligence Agency (CIA), seized power from the constitutionally elected government of President Salvador Allende. Chile, with its longstanding traditions of free and honest elections, respect for human rights, and freedom of the press, was quickly transformed into a brutal dictatorship that arrested, tortured, and killed thousands of its own citizens. In the larger sweep of Chilean history, however, the coup seemed to be the most recent and severe manifestation of a lengthy conflict between social justice, on the one hand, and the requirements of order dictated by the nation's ruling elite, on the other. This was true in the colonial period, when there was conflict over Indian rights between the Roman Catholic Church and landowners. It was also apparent in later confrontations among Marxists, reformers, and conservatives.

FORM, NOT SUBSTANCE — He cоличност

Form, as opposed to substance, had characterized the rule of the Christian Democrats in the 1960s, when they created many separate rural unions, supposedly to address the needs of *campensinos* ("peasants"). A divided union movement in effect became a form of government control that prevented the emergence of a single powerful rural organization.

In the early 1970s, President Allende—despite his talk of socialism and his genuine attempt to destroy the institutions and values of an old social order—used a centralized bureaucracy that would have been recognized by sixteenth-century viceroys and nineteenth-century presidents as his weapon of transformation. Allende's attempts to institute far-reaching social change led to a strong reaction from powerful sectors of Chilean society who felt threatened.

THE 1973 COUP D'ETAT

When the military ousted Allende, it had the support of many Chileans, including the majority of the middle classes, who had been hurt by the government's economic policies, troubled by continuous political turmoil, and infuriated by official mismanagement. The military, led by General Augusto Pinochet, began a new experiment with another form of centrist rule: military authoritarianism. The generals made it clear that they had not restored order merely to return it to the "discredited" constitutional practices of the past. They spoke of regeneration, of a new Chile, and of an end to the immorality,

(Reuters/Bettmann)

On October 5, 1988, the voters of Chile denied the brutal dictator General Augusto Pinochet an additional 8-year term as president. To his credit, his military regime accepted defeat peacefully.

corruption, and incompetence of all civilian politics. The military announced in 1974 that, "guided by the inspiration of [Diego] Portales,"—one of nineteenth-century Chile's greatest civilian leaders—"the government of Chile will energetically apply the principle of authority and drastically punish any outburst of disorder and anarchy."

The political, economic, and social reforms proposed by the military aimed at restructuring Chile to such an extent that there would no longer be a need for traditional political parties. Economic policy favored free and open competition as the main regulator of economic and social life. The Chilean state rid itself of hundreds of state-owned corporations, struck down tariffs designed to protect Chilean industry from foreign competition, and opened the economy to widespread foreign investment. The changes struck deeply at the structure of the Chilean economy and produced a temporary but sharp recession, high unemployment, and hundreds of bankruptcies. A steep decline in the standard of living for most Chileans was the result of the government's anti-inflation policy.

Social-welfare programs were reduced to a minimum. The private sector was encouraged to assume many functions and services once provided by the state. Pen-

sions were moved entirely to the private sector as all state programs were phased out. In this instance, the state calculated that workers tied through pensions and other benefits to the success of private enterprise would be less likely to be attracted to "non-Chilean" ideologies such as Marxism, socialism, and even Christian democracy. State-sponsored health programs were also cut to the bone, and many of the poor now paid for services once provided by the government.

THE DEFEAT OF A DICTATOR

To attain a measure of legitimacy, Chileans expected the military government to produce economic achievement. By 1987, and continuing into 1989, the regime's economic policies seemed successful: the economic growth rate for 1988 was an impressive 7.4 percent. However, it masked critical weaknesses in the Chilean economy. For example, much of the growth was overdependent on exports of raw materials—notably copper, pulp, timber, and fishmeal.

Modest economic success and an inflation rate of less than 20 percent convinced General Pinochet that he could take his political scenario for Chile's future to the voters for their ratification. But, in the October 5, 1988, plebiscite, Chile's voters upset the general's plans and decisively denied him an additional 8-year term. (He did, however, continue in office until the next presidential election determined his successor.) Importantly, the military regime (albeit reluctantly) accepted defeat at the polls, which signifies the reemergence of a deep-rooted civic culture and long democratic tradition.

Where had Pinochet miscalculated? Public-opinion surveys on the eve of the election showed a sharply divided electorate. Some political scientists even spoke of the existence of "two Chiles." In the words of government professor Arturo Valenzuela and *Boston Globe* correspondent Pamela Constable, one Chile "embraced those who had benefited from the competitive economic policies and welfare subsidies instituted by the regime and who had been persuaded that power was best entrusted to the armed forces." The second Chile "consisted of those who had been victimized by the regime, who did not identify with Pinochet's anti-Communist cause, and who had quietly nurtured a belief in democracy." Polling data from the respected Center for Public Policy Studies showed that 72 percent of those who voted against the regime were motivated by economic factors. These were people who had lost skilled jobs or who had suffered a decrease in real wages. While Pinochet's economic reforms had helped some, it had also created a disgruntled mass of downwardly mobile wage earners.

Valenzuela and Constable explain how a dictator allowed himself to be voted out of power. "To a large extent Pinochet had been trapped by his own mythology. He was convinced that he would be able to win and was anxious to prove that his regime was not a pariah but a legitimate government. He and other officials came to believe their own propaganda about the dynamic new Chile they had created." The closed character of the regime, with all lines of authority flowing to the hands of one man, made it "impossible for them to accept the possibility that they could lose." And when the impossible occurred and the dictator lost an election played by his own rules, neither civilians on the right nor the military were willing to override the constitutional contract they had forged with the Chilean people.

In March 1990, Chile returned to civilian rule for the first time in almost 17 years, with the assumption of the presidency by Patricio Aylwin. His years in power revealed that tensions still existed between civilian politicians and the military. In 1993, for example, General Pinochet mobilized elements of the army in Santiago—a move that, in the words of the independent newspaper *La Época,* "marked the crystallization of long-standing hostility" between the Aylwin government and the army. The military had reacted both to investigations into human-rights abuses during the Pinochet dictatorship and proposed legislation that would have subordinated the military to civilian control. On the other hand, the commanders of the navy and air force as well as

the two right-wing political parties refused to sanction the actions of the army.

President Aylwin regained the initiative when he publicly chastised General Pinochet. Congress, in a separate action, affirmed its supremacy over the judiciary in 1993, when it successfully impeached a Supreme Court justice for "notable dereliction of duty." The court system had been notorious for transferring human-rights cases from civil to military courts, where they were quickly dismissed. The impeachment augured well for further reform of the judicial branch.

Further resistance to the legacy of General Pinochet was expressed by the people when, on December 11, 1993, the center-left coalition candidate Eduardo Frei Ruiz-Tagle won the Chilean presidential election with 58 percent of the vote. As part of his platform, Frei had promised to bring the military under civilian rule. The parliamentary vote, however, did not give him the two-thirds majority needed to push through such a reform. The trend toward civilian government, though, seemed to be continuing.

In 1997, the Chilean economy grew for the 13th consecutive year, with a gross domestic product growth of 7 percent. Foreign investment for the first 6 months of 1997 rose by nearly 33 percent over the same period in 1996. Most of the investments were in the mining sector, followed closely by services. Heavy industry attracted about 14 percent of foreign investment. Great Britain accounted for more

(United Nations photo)

The rural areas of Chile have presented challenges for community development. Here, volunteers work on a road that will link the village of Tincnamar to a main road.

The founding of
Santiago de Chile
1541

Independence
of Spain is
proclaimed
1818

The
administration of
Eduardo Frei;
Revolution in
Liberty
dramatically
alters Chilean
society
1964–1970

A military coup
ousts President
Salvador Allende;
General Augusto
Pinochet
becomes
president
1973

1990s

Chile returns to
civilian rule with
the election of
Patricio Aylwin

Economic
growth in Chile
surpasses all
modern records

Eduardo Frei
Ruiz-Tagle is
elected president

than 40 percent of foreign investment, followed by 26 percent from Japan and about 15 percent from the United States. Unemployment stood at an official level of 5.8 percent in 1996. Even if this figure seems improbably low and fails to consider underemployment, Chile still enjoys the lowest unemployment rate in South America. The foreign debt has been reduced to $20 billion from a high of $30 billion at the beginning of economic restructuring, during the dictatorship of Pinochet.

Planning Minister Roberto Pizarro, as reported in *El Mercurio* and *La Nación*, noted that poverty in Chile declined by 4 percent between 1994 and 1996. However, more than 23 percent of the population—some 3 million people—still live in poverty. Pizarro credited the country's social programs and an economic policy that promoted growth while simultaneously reducing unemployment and inflation. Despite these positive signs, Chilean income distribution remains badly skewed in favor of the wealthy. Between 1994 and 1996, the lowest-income groups experienced an increase in their incomes of a meager 0.1 percent. The average per capita income of the poor was about $120 a month, while the top 10 percent averaged a monthly income of more than $4,000. Pizarro identified educational reform as critical to the future of the nation and said that the government must create more jobs, raise wages, support small- and medium-size companies, and promote labor reforms designed to give workers more bargaining power.

Novelist and politician Mario Vargas Llosa observed that, while Chile "is not paradise," it does have a "stability and economic dynamism unparalled in Latin America." Indeed, "Chile is moving closer to Spain and Australia and farther from Peru or Haiti." He suggests that there has been a shift in Chile's political culture. "The ideas of economic liberty, a free market open to the world, and private initiative as the motor of progress have become embedded in the people of Chile."

In part, the change was the product of the harsh policies of the Pinochet regime. To quote Vargas Llosa, "For many people it is difficult to admit that Chile's extraordinarily successful economic programs were carried out under a brutally repressive dictatorship." The results do not justify the regime's crimes; neither do they invalidate the crimes.

SIGNS OF CHANGE
Although the Chilean Constitution was essentially imposed on the nation by the military in 1980, there are signs of change. The term for president was reduced from 8 to 6 years in 1993; and in 1997 the Chamber of Deputies, the lower house of the Legislature, approved legislation to further reduce the term of a president to 4 years, with a prohibition on reelection. Military courts, which have broader peacetime jurisdiction than most other countries in the Western Hemisphere, have also come under scrutiny by politicians. According to the *Revista Hoy*, as summarized by *CHIP News,* military justice reaches far beyond the ranks. If, for example, several people are involved in the commission of a crime and one of the perpetrators happens to be a member of the military, all are tried in a military court.

Another abuse noted by politicians is that the military routinely uses the charge of sedition against civilians who criticize it. Although the Frei government has no intention to pursue reform of the military, a group of Christian Democrats wants to limit the jurisdiction of the military to military crimes committed by military personnel; eliminate the participation of the army prosecutor in the Supreme Court, where he sits on the bench in cases related to the military; grant civilian courts the authority to investigate military premises; and accord civilian courts jurisdiction over military personnel accused of civilian-related crimes. The military disagrees. One prosecutor noted: "The country needs the Armed Forces and needs them to function well."

Another healthy sign of change is a concerted effort by the Chilean and Argentine governments to discuss issues that have been a historical source of friction between the two nations. Arms escalation, mining exploration and exploitation in border areas, and trade and investment concerns were on the agenda. The Chilean Foreign Relations minister and the Defense minister sat down with their Argentine counterparts in the first meeting of its kind in the history of Argentine–Chilean relations.

DEVELOPMENT

Chile, with an average gross domestic product growth of 6% over the last decade, has become a model for other Latin American nations. Bilateral trade agreements have continued with Mexico, Venezuela, and Bolivia. Chile eventually hopes to join NAFTA but, in the meantime, has become an associate member of Mercosur.

FREEDOM

Chile's human-rights record has improved significantly in recent years. There is still the need to address hundreds of abuses committed during the years of military rule, however. The military pursues obstructionist tactics in this regard, but the Frei government, with its careful and methodical rule, continues to make progress in this area.

HEALTH/WELFARE

Since 1981, all new members of Chile's labor force have been required to contribute 10% of their monthly gross earnings to private pension-fund accounts, which they own. By 1995, more than 93% of the labor force were enrolled in 20 separate and competing private pension funds. The reforms increased the domestic savings rate to 26% of GDP.

ACHIEVEMENTS

Chile's great literary figures, such as Gabriela Mistrál and Pablo Neruda, have a great sympathy for the poor and oppressed. This places Chilean authors in the mainstream of Latin American literature. Another major Chilean writer, Isabel Allende, has won worldwide acclaim.

Colombia (Republic of Colombia)

GEOGRAPHY

Area in Square Kilometers (Miles):
1,139,600 (440,000) (about the size of
Texas and New Mexico combined)
Capital (Population): Bogotá
(5,000,000)
Climate: tropical on coast and eastern
plains; cooler in highlands

PEOPLE

Population

Total: 36,813,000
Annual Growth Rate: 1.7%
Rural/Urban Population Ratio: 32/68
Ethnic Makeup: 58% Mestizo; 20%
white; 14% mulatto; 4% African; 3%
African-Indian; 1% Indian
Major Language: Spanish

Health

Life Expectancy at Birth: 70 years
(male); 75 years (female)
Infant Mortality Rate (Ratio): 27/1,000;
Indians 233/1,000
Average Caloric Intake: 108% of FAO
minimum
Physicians Available (Ratio): 1/1,078

Religions

95% Roman Catholic; 5% others

Education

Adult Literacy Rate: 87% (Indians 40%)

COMMUNICATION

Telephones: 1,890,000
Newspapers: 31 dailies

TRANSPORTATION

Highways—Kilometers (Miles):
107,377 (67,033)
Railroads—Kilometers (Miles): 3,386

(2,103)
Usable Airfields: 1,307

GOVERNMENT

Type: republic
Independence Date: July 20, 1810
Head of State: President Ernesto
Samper Pizano
Political Parties: Liberal Party; Social
Conservative Party; National Salvation
Movement; Democratic Alliance M-19;
Patriotic Union; Communist Party;
others
Suffrage: universal at 18

MILITARY

Number of Armed Forces: 130,400 plus
50,000 national police
*Military Expenditures (% of Central
Government Expenditures):* 7%
Current Hostilities: territorial dispute
with Venezuela

ECONOMY

Currency ($ U.S. Equivalent): 1,238
pesos = $1
Per Capita Income/GDP: $4,850/$172.4
billion
Inflation Rate: 22.6%
Total Foreign Debt: $12.6 billion
Natural Resources: petroleum; natural
gas; coal; iron ore; nickel; gold;
copper; emeralds
Agriculture: coffee; bananas; rice; corn;
sugarcane; marijuana; coca; plantains;
cotton; tobacco
Industry: textiles; food processing;
clothing and footwear; beverages;
chemicals; metal products; cement

FOREIGN TRADE

Exports: $8.3 billion
Imports: $10.6 billion

The Stone Monuments of San Agustín

The archaeological site of San Agustín is an important testimony to the artistic
and cultural achievements of the Indians who inhabited the southwestern
region of Colombia more than 2,000 years ago. Impressive contributions of
this culture include the imposing, larger-than-life stone monuments with
part-human, part-jaguar features. The jaguar played an important role in the
people's religious system and persisted as a popular symbol for centuries.
The jaguar theme also links the inhabitants of San Agustín with other cultures
in the Americas.

Colombia

⊛ Capital
• City
〜 River
- - - - Road

0   150   kilometers
0   150   miles

COLOMBIA:
THE VIOLENT LAND

Colombia has long been noted for its violent political history. The division of political beliefs in the mid-nineteenth century into conservative and liberal factions produced not only debate but also civil war. To the winner went the presidency and the spoils of office. That competition for office came to a head during the savage War of the Thousand Days (1899–1902). Nearly half a century later, Colombia was again plagued by political violence, which took perhaps 200,000 lives. Although on the surface it is distinct from the nineteenth-century civil wars, *La Violencia* ("The Violence," 1946–1958) offers striking parallels to the violence of the last century. Competing factions were again led by conservatives and liberals, and the presidency was the prize. Explanations for this phenomenon have tended to be at once simple and powerful. Colombian writers blame a Spanish heritage and its legacy of lust for political power.

Gabriel García Márquez, in his classic novel *One Hundred Years of Solitude*, spoofed the differences between liberals and conservatives. "The Liberals," said Aureliano Buendia's father-in-law, "were Freemasons, bad people, wanting to hang priests, to institute civil marriage and divorce, to recognize the rights of illegitimate children as equal to those of legitimate ones, and to cut the country up into a federal system that would take power away from the supreme authority." On the other hand, "the Conservatives, who had received their power directly from God, proposed the establishment of public order and family morality. They were the defenders of the faith of Christ, of the principle of authority, and were not prepared to permit the country to be broken down into autonomous entities." Aureliano, when later asked if he was a Liberal or a Conservative, quickly replied: "If I have to be something I'll be a Liberal, because the Conservatives are tricky."

THE ROOTS OF VIOLENCE

The roots of the violence are far more complex than a simple quest for spoils caused by a flaw in national character. Historian Charles Bergquist has shown that "divisions within the upper class and the systematic philosophical and programmatic positions that define them are not merely political manifestations of cultural traits; they reflect diverging economic interests within the upper class." These opposing interests developed in both the nineteenth and twentieth centuries. Moreover, to see Colombian politics solely as a violent quest for office ignores long periods of relative peace (1902–1935). But, whatever the underlying causes of the violence, it has profoundly influenced contemporary Colombians.

La Violencia was the largest armed conflict in the Western Hemisphere since the Mexican Revolution (1910–1917). It was a civil war of ferocious intensity that cut through class lines and mobilized people from all levels of society behind the banners of either liberalism or conservatism. That elite-led parties were able to win popular support was evidence of their strong organization rather than their opponents' political weakness.

These multiclass parties still dominate Colombian political life, although the fierce interparty rivalry that characterized the civil wars of the nineteenth century as well as La Violencia has been stilled. In 1957, Colombia's social elite decided to bury partisan differences and devised a

(United Nations photo/M. Grant)

Colombia, as is the case with many other Latin American nations, has experienced rapid urbanization. Large numbers of migrants from rural areas spread into slums on the outskirts of cities, as exemplified by this picture of a section of Colombia's capital, Bogotá. Most of the migrants are poorly paid, and the struggle to meet basic needs precludes political activism.

plan to end the widespread strife. Under this National Front agreement, the two parties agreed to divide legislative and bureaucratic positions equally and to alternate the presidency every 4 years from 1958 to 1974. This form of coalition government proved a highly successful means of elite compromise.

THE IMPACT OF LA VIOLENCIA

The violence has left its imprint on Colombia in other ways. Some scholars have suggested that peasants now shun political action because of fear of renewed violence. Refugees from La Violencia generally experienced confusion and a loss of values. Usually, rising literacy rates, improved transportation and communications, and integration into the nation's life produce an upsurge of activism as people clamor for more rapid change. This has not been the case in rural Colombia. Despite guerrilla activity in the countryside—some of which is a spin-off from La Violencia, some of which until recently had a Marxist orientation, and some of which is banditry—the guerrillas have not been able to win significant rural support.

La Violencia also led to the professionalization and enlargement of the Colombian armed forces in the late 1950s and early 1960s. Never a serious participant in the nation's civil wars, the military has acquired a new prestige and status unusual for Colombia. It must be considered an important factor in any discussion of Colombian politics today.

A standoff between guerrillas and the military prompted the government of Virgilio Barco to engage reluctantly in a dialogue with the insurgents, with the ultimate goal of peace. In 1988, he announced a three-phase peace plan to end the violence, to talk about needed reforms, and ultimately to re-incorporate guerrillas into society. This effort came to fruition in 1991, when the guerrilla movement M-19 laid down its arms after 16 years of fighting and engaged in political dialogue. Other guerrilla groups, notably the long-lived (since 1961) Colombian Revolutionary Armed Forces (FARC) and the National Liberation Army (ELN), led by a Spanish priest, have chosen to remain in the field.

Numbering perhaps 10,000, the guerrillas claim that their armed insurgency is

about social change, but, as *The Economist* has observed, lines between revolution and crime are increasingly blurred. Guerrillas ambush army units, attack oil pipelines, engage in blackmail, and kidnap rich ranchers and foreign oil executives for ransom. Some guerrillas are also apparently in the pay of the drug traffickers and collect a bounty for each helicopter they shoot down in the government's campaign to eradicate coca-leaf and poppy fields.

The government of President Ernesto Samper Pizano has pledged to end guerrilla warfare and has urged direct talks. But reality has overwhelmed good intentions. Widespread conflict and multiple levels of violence continue to exact a horrible human toll. Guerrillas-cum-bandits are organized into as many as 100 groups and exercise a permanent influence in more than half of the country's towns and cities.

In addition to the deaths attributed to guerrilla warfare, literally hundreds of politicians, judges, and police officers have been murdered in Colombia. It has been estimated that 10 percent of the nation's homicides are politically motivated. Murder is the major cause of death for men between ages 15 and 45. While para-

(United Nations photo/J. Sailas)

Drugs have been an enormous destabilizing factor in the society and economy of Colombia for many years. As part of a cocoa-substitution project, the United Nations Drug Control Program has helped to establish shops run by local peasants.

military violence accounts for many deaths, drug trafficking and the unraveling of Colombia's fabric of law are responsible for most. As political scientist John D. Martz has written: "Whatever the responsibility of the military or the rhetoric of government, the penetration of Colombia's social and economic life by the drug industry [is] proving progressively destructive of law, security and the integrity of the political system."

DRUGS AND DEATH

Drug traffickers, according to *Latin American Update*, "represent a new economic class in Colombia; since 1981 'narcodollars' have been invested in real estate and large cattle ranches." The Colombian weekly newsmagazine *Semana* noted that drug cartels had purchased 2.5 million acres of land since 1984 and now own one twelfth of the nation's productive farmland in the Magdalena River Basin. More than 100,000 acres of forest have been cut down to grow marijuana, coca, and opium poppies. Of particular concern to environmentalists is the fact that opium poppies are usually planted in the forests of the Andes at elevations above 6,000 feet. "These forests," according to *Semana,* "do not have great commercial value, but their tree cover is vital to the conservation of the sources of the water supply." The cartels have also bought up factories, newspapers, radio stations, shopping centers, soccer teams, and bullfighters. The emergence of Medellín as a modern city of gleaming skyscrapers and expensive cars also reflects the enormous profits of the drug business. In rural Colombia, drug traffickers have utilized paramilitary groups to clear areas of guerrillas who had themselves forced traditional landowners to leave. The drug traffickers have taken possession of the land and defend it with private "armies."

Drug warfare among rival drug cartels contributes to the climate of violence. The high level of drug-related killings in Medellín and Cali and attempts by the Cali cartel to purchase 550-pound bombs from the Salvadoran military testify to the horrific character of the competition.

Political scientist Francisco Leal Buitrago argues that, while trafficking in narcotics in the 1970s was economically motivated, it had evolved into a social phenomenon by the 1980s. "The traffickers represent a new social force that wants to participate like other groups—new urban groups, guerrillas and peasant movements. Like the guerrillas, they have not been able to participate politically. . . ." Constitutional reforms that prevent the extradition of drug traffickers to the United

States convinced several of the more notorious drug barons to surrender in return for lenient sentences. That policy shifted abruptly when the head of the Medellín cartel, Pablo Escobar, escaped from jail and when it was shown that the levels of violence between the cartels had not diminished despite a softer government line. In June 1996, President Samper was absolved by the House of Representatives with regard to accusations that he had accepted $6 million in campaign contributions from the Cali cocaine cartel. However, despite the vote, drug-related allegations and demands that he resign continued to dog Samper. He promised to complete his term of office, which ends in August 1998.

In 1994 and 1995, the Samper regime, despite allegations of financial support from drug traffickers, pursued a much tougher policy against the leadership of the cartels. The death of Escobar and the capture of Gilberto Rodriguez Orejuela, one of the kingpins of the Cali cocaine and heroin cartel, disrupted, if not destroyed, the cartels' organizational structure.

Domestic drug consumption has also emerged as a serious problem in Colombia's cities. *Latin American Regional Reports* noted that the increase in consumption of the Colombian form of crack, known as bazuko, "has prompted the growth of gangs of youths in slum areas running the bazuko business for small distributors." In Bogotá, police reported that more than 1,500 gangs operated from the city's slums.

URBANIZATION

As is the case in other Andean nations, urbanization has been rapid in Colombia. But the constantly spreading slums on the outskirts of the larger cities have not produced significant urban unrest or activism. Most of the migrants to the cities are first generation and are less frustrated and demanding than the general urban population. The new migrants perceive an improvement in their status and opportunities simply because they have moved into a more hopeful urban environment. Also, since most of the migrants are poorly paid, their focus tends to be on daily survival, not political activism.

Migrants make a significant contribution to the parallel Colombian economy. As is the case in Peru and other South American countries, the informal sector amounts to approximately 30 percent of gross domestic product.

The Roman Catholic Church in Colombia has also tended to take advantage of rapid urbanization. Depending on the individual beliefs of local bishops, the Church has to a greater or lesser extent

embraced the migrants, brought them into the Church, and created or instilled a sense of community where none existed before. The Church has generally identified with the expansion and change taking place and has played an active social role.

Marginalized city dwellers are often the targets of violence. Hired killers, called *sicarios*, have murdered hundreds of petty thieves, beggars, prostitutes, indigents, and street children. Such "clean-up" campaigns are reminiscent of the activities of the Brazilian death squads since the 1960s. An overloaded judicial system and interminable delays have contributed to Colombia's high homicide rate. According to government reports, lawbreakers have not been brought to justice in 97 to 99 percent of *reported* crimes. (Perhaps three quarters of all crimes remain unreported to the authorities.) Increasingly, violence and murder have replaced the law as a way to settle disputes; private justice is now commonly resorted to for a variety of disputes. Debts, for example, are more easily and quickly resolved through murder than by lengthy court proceedings.

SOCIAL CHANGE

Government has responded to calls for social change and reform. President Virgilio Barco sincerely believed that the eradication of poverty would help to eliminate guerrilla warfare and reduce the escalating scale of violence in the countryside. Unfortunately, his policies lacked substance, and he was widely criticized for his indecisiveness.

President César Gaviria felt that political reform must precede social and economic change and was confident that Colombia's new Constitution would set the process of national reconciliation in motion. The constitutional debate generated some optimism about the future of liberal democracy in Colombia. As Christopher Abel wrote, it afforded a forum for groups ordinarily denied a voice in policy formulation—"to civic and community movements in the 40 and more intermediate cities angry at the poor quality of basic public services; to indigenous movements. . . ; and to cooperatives, blacks, women, pensioners, small businesses, consumer and sports groups."

Unfortunately, the debates have not been transformed into a viable social policy. The distribution of income in Colombia has been deteriorating since 1983, and the significant improvement in the incomes of the poor in the 1970s has not been sustained. Successful social policy springs from committed politicians. But Colombia's political parties are in disarray,

The first Spanish settlement at Santa Marta 1525	Independence of Spain 1810	The creation of Gran Colombia (including Venezuela, Panama, and Ecuador) 1822	Independence as a separate country 1830	War of the Thousand Days 1899–1902	La Violencia; nearly 200,000 lose their lives 1946–1958	Women's suffrage 1957	The drug trade becomes big business 1980s

1990s

Government offensive against guerrillas, narcotraffickers, and organized crime	Drug lord Pablo Escobar is killed; leaders of the Cali cartel are captured	Ernesto Samper Pizano is elected president; Samper is accused of receiving financial support from drug traffickers

which in turn weakens the confidence of people in the ability of the state to govern.

ECONOMIC POLICIES

Colombia has a mixed economy. While state enterprises control domestic participation in the coal and oil industries and play a commanding role in the provision of electricity and communications, most of the economy is dominated by private business. At this point, Colombia is a moderate oil producer. (Recent attacks on pipelines and storage facilities by guerrillas have cut into export earnings from this growing sector.) A third of the nation's legal exports comes from the coffee industry, while exports of coal, cut flowers, seafood, and other nontraditional exports have experienced significant growth. In that Colombia is not saddled with an onerous foreign debt, its economy is relatively prosperous.

Contributing to economic success is the large informal sector. Also of tremendous importance are the profits from the illegal-drug industry. *The Economist* estimated that Colombia grossed perhaps $1.5 billion in drug sales in 1987, as compared to official export earnings of $5.5 billion. Drugs contributed an estimated 4 percent of gross domestic product in 1989. Perhaps half the profits are repatriated—that is, converted from dollars into local currency. An unfortunate side effect of the inflow of cash is an increase in the inflation rate.

FOREIGN POLICY

In the foreign-policy arena, President Barco's policies were attacked as low-profile, shallow, and too closely aligned to the policies of the United States. Presidents Gaviria and Samper both adopted a more independent line, especially in terms of the drug trade.

With an uneasy peace reigning in Central America, Colombia's focus has turned increasingly toward its neighbors and a festering territorial dispute with Venezuela over waters adjacent to the Guajira Peninsula. Colombia has proposed a multilateral solution to the problem, perhaps under the auspices of the International Court of Justice. Venezuela continues to reject a multilateral approach and seeks to limit any talks to the two countries concerned. It is likely that a sustained deterioration of internal conditions in either Venezuela or Colombia will keep the territorial dispute in the forefront. A further detriment to better relations with Venezuela is the justified Venezuelan fears that Colombian violence as a result of guerrilla activity, military sweeps, and drugs, will cross the border. As it is, thousands of Colombians have fled to Venezuela to escape their violent homeland.

More positively, the government's support of free trade initiatives has stimulated bilateral trade with Venezuela. Mexico and Chile have also been targeted by the Colombian government for similar bilateral agreements to liberalize import policies, stimulate exports, and attract foreign capital.

THE CLOUDED FUTURE

Francisco Leal Buitrago, a respected Colombian academic, argues forcefully that his nation's crisis is, above all, "political":

"It is the lack of public confidence in the political regime. It is not a crisis of the state itself. . . , but in the way in which the state sets the norms—the rules for participation—for the representation of public opinion. . . ."

Constitutional reforms are considered a step in the right direction and, once completed, will be tested in new congressional elections. Significant changes include, in addition to no extradition to the United States, a ban on those currently holding public office from seeking election unless they resigned before the middle of June 1991; a reduction in the number of senators; and the granting to the president of extraordinary special powers to be overseen by a commission chosen proportionally from parties represented in the next Congress. The Supreme Court's Office of the Constitution will be replaced by a Constitutional Court to guard the integrity of the Constitution. Endemic violence and lawlessness, the continued operation of guerrilla groups, the emergence of mini-cartels in the wake of the eclipse of drug kingpins, and the attitude of the military toward conditions in Colombia all threaten the new constitutional accord.

DEVELOPMENT

In 1996, the government continued its economic liberalization program and the privatization of selected public industries. Exports of crude petroleum have increased to the point that they almost equaled coffee exports. Two new oil fields will likely increase the importance of petroleum to the Colombian economy.

FREEDOM

Colombia continues to have the highest rate of violent deaths in Latin America. Guerrillas, the armed forces, right-wing vigilante groups and drug traffickers are responsible for many deaths. On the positive side, a 1993 law that accorded equal rights to black Colombians resulted in the 1995 election of Piedad de Castro, the first black female, to the Senate.

HEALTH/WELFARE

Rape and other acts of violence against women are pervasive but seldom prosecuted. Spousal abuse was not considered a crime until 1996. Law 294 on family violence identifies as crimes violent acts committed within families, including spousal rape. Although the Constitution of 1991 prohibits it, discrimination against women persists in terms of access to employment and equal pay for equal work.

ACHIEVEMENTS

Colombia has a long tradition in the arts and humanities and has produced international figures such as the Nobel Prize–winning author Gabriel García Márquez; the painters and sculptors Alejandro Obregón, Fernando Botero, and Edgar Negret; the poet León de Greiff; and many others well known in music, art, and literature.

Ecuador (Republic of Ecuador)

GEOGRAPHY

Area in Square Kilometers (Miles): 276,840 (106,860) (about the size of Colorado)
Capital (Population): Quito (1,500,000)
Climate: varied; tropical on coast and inland jungle; springlike year-round on Andean plateau

PEOPLE

Population
Total: 11,466,300
Annual Growth Rate: 1.9%
Rural/Urban Population Ratio: 41/59
Ethnic Makeup: 55% Mestizo; 25% Indian; 10% Spanish; 10% black
Major Languages: Spanish; Quechua; Jivaroan

Health
Life Expectancy at Birth: 68 years (male); 73 years (female)
Infant Mortality Rate (Ratio): 38/1,000
Average Caloric Intake: 97% of FAO minimum
Physicians Available (Ratio): 1/836

THE NECESSARY INDIAN

Galo Plaza Lasso, the president of Ecuador from 1948 to 1952, once remarked:

Indians raise most of the food we eat in Ecuador. What nonsense it is to say that Indians are a drag on the economies of our Andean countries. Forty percent of Ecuadorians are Indians. Most of the rest are Mestizos. With love and understanding, the Indians are ready to forget four centuries of abuse and increase their stature in our society. We need their common sense—and their colorful dress.

Religions
95% Roman Catholic; 5% indigenous and others

Education
Adult Literacy Rate: 87%

COMMUNICATION
Telephones: 318,000
Newspapers: 22 dailies

TRANSPORTATION
Highways—Kilometers (Miles): 43,709 (27,274)
Railroads—Kilometers (Miles): 965 (602)
Usable Airfields: 175

GOVERNMENT
Type: republic
Independence Date: May 24, 1822
Head of State: President Abdalá Bucaram
Political Parties: Republican Unity Party; Democratic Left; Social Christian Party; Popular Democracy; Popular Democratic Movement; Socialist Party; Communist Party; others
Suffrage: universal at 18; compulsory for literate people ages 18–65

MILITARY
Number of Armed Forces: 57,800
Military Expenditures (% of Central Government Expenditures): 12.9%
Current Hostilities: unresolved, long-smoldering dispute with Peru over a 49-mile stretch of border

ECONOMY
Currency ($ U.S. Equivalent): 4,110 sucres = $1
Per Capita Income/GDP: $3,840/$41.1 billion
Inflation Rate: 25%
Total Foreign Debt: $13.2 billion
Natural Resources: petroleum; fish; timber
Agriculture: bananas; coffee; cocoa; seafood; sugarcane; rice; corn; livestock
Industry: food processing; wood products; textiles; chemicals; fishing; petroleum

FOREIGN TRADE
Exports: $3.3 billion
Imports: $3.0 billion

ECUADOR: A LAND OF CONTRASTS

Several of Ecuador's great novelists have had as the focus of their works the exploitation of the Indians. Jorge Icaza's classic *Huasipungo* (1934) describes the actions of a brutal landowner who first forces Indians to work on a road so that the region might be "developed" and then forces them, violently, from their plots of land so that a foreign company's operations will not be impeded by a troublesome Indian population.

That scenario, while possible in some isolated regions, is for the most part unlikely in today's Ecuador. In recent years, Ecuador has apparently made great strides forward in health care, literacy, human rights, press freedom, and representative government. Conaie, an organization of Ecuadoran Indians, has become increasingly assertive in national politics since 1990 and reflects developments in other Latin American countries with significant indigenous populations. Nobel Peace Prize–winner Rigoberta Menchú, a Quiché–Mayan from Guatemala, has used her position to intervene in favor of indigenous peoples in countries like Ecuador. Conaie, which has from time to time aligned itself with urban unions, pressed for an agrarian-reform law from the center-right government of President Sixto Durán-Ballén.

Although Ecuador is still a conservative, traditional society, it has recently shown an increasing concern for the plight of its rural inhabitants, including the various endangered Indian groups inhabiting the Amazonian region. The new attention showered on rural Ecuador—traditionally neglected by policymakers in Quito, the capital city—reflects in part the government's concern with patterns of internal migration. Even though rural regions have won more attention from the state, social programs continue to be implemented only sporadically.

Two types of migration are currently taking place: the move from the highlands to the coastal lowlands and the move from the countryside to the cities. In the early 1960s, most of Ecuador's population was concentrated in the mountainous central highlands. Today, the population is about equally divided between that area and the coast, with more than half the nation's people crowded into the cities. So striking and rapid has the population shift been that the director of the National Institute of Statistics commented that it had assumed "alarming proportions" and that the government had to develop appropriate policies if spreading urban slums were not to develop into "potential focal points for insurgency."

Despite the large-scale movement of people in Ecuador, it still remains a nation of regions. Political rivalry has always characterized relations between Quito, in the sierras, and cosmopolitan Guayaquíl, on the coast. The presidential elections of 1988 illustrated the distinctive styles of the country. Rodrigo Borja's victory was regionally based, in that he won wide support in Ecuador's interior provinces. Usually conservative in its politics, the interior voted for the candidate of the Democratic Left, in part because of the extreme populist campaign waged by a former mayor of Guayaquíl, Abdalá Bucaram. Bucaram claimed to be a man of the people who was persecuted by the oligarchy. He spoke of his lower-class followers as the "humble ones," or, borrowing a phrase from former Argentine president Juan Perón, *los descamisados* ("the shirtless ones"). Bucaram, in the words of political scientist Catherine M. Conaghan, "honed a political style in the classic tradition of coastal populism. He combined promises of concrete benefits to the urban poor with a colorful anti-oligarchic style." Bucaram's style triumphed in 1996, when he won the presidential election.

EDUCATION AND HEALTH

Central to the government's policy of development is education. Twenty-nine percent of the national budget was set aside for education in the early 1980s, with increases proposed for the following years. Adult literacy improved from 74 percent in 1974 to 87 percent by 1995. In the central highlands, however, illiteracy rates of more than 35 percent are still common, largely because Quechua is still the preferred language among the Indian peasants.

The government has approached this problem with an unusual sensitivity to indigenous culture. Local Quechua speakers have been enlisted to teach reading and writing both in Quechua and Spanish. This approach has won the support of Indian leaders who are closely involved in planning local literacy programs built around indigenous values.

Health care has also shown steady improvement, but the total statistics hide sharp regional variations. Infant mortality and malnutrition are still severe problems in rural areas. In this sense, Ecuador suffers from a duality found in other Latin American nations with large Indian populations: Social and racial differences persist between the elite-dominated capitals and the Indian hinterlands. Income, services, and resources tend to be concentrated in the capital cities. Ecuador, at least, is attempting to correct the imbalance.

The profound differences between Ecuador's highland Indian and its European cultures is illustrated by the story of an Indian peasant who, when brought to a clinic, claimed that he was dying as the result of a spell. He told the doctor, trained

(United Nations photo)

The migration of the poor to the urban areas of Ecuador has been very rapid and of great concern to the government. The increase in inner-city population can easily lead to political unrest. The graffito in this photo says, "We don't want a dictatorship."

First Spanish
contact
1528

Ecuador is part
of Gran
Colombia (with
Panama,
Venezuela, and
Colombia);
independence as
a separate state
1822

Women's suffrage
1929

A border war
with Peru
1941

1990s

Modernization
laws aim to
speed the
privatization of
the economy

Renewed fighting
with Peru over
Ecuador's
southern
boundary

Abdalá Bucaram
wins the
presidency

in Western medicine, that, while traveling a path from his highland village down to a valley, he passed by a sacred place, where a witch cast a spell on him. The man began to deteriorate, convinced that this had happened. The doctor, upon examination of the patient, could find no physical reason for the man's condition. Medicine produced no improvements. The doctor finally managed to save his patient, but only after a good deal of compromise with Indian culture. "Yes," he told the peasant, "a witch has apparently cast a spell on you and you are indeed dying." And then the doctor announced: "Here is a potion that will remove the spell." The patient's recovery was rapid and complete. Thus, though modern medicine can work miracles, health-care workers must also be sensitive to cultural differences.

THE ECONOMY

The high expectations of the León Febres-Cordero administration were dashed by poor and self-serving economic policies, compounded by the deterioration of Ecuador's export performance and a growing debt. Revenue fall-off from declining oil prices hurt the economy badly; to offset the lost revenues, the government was forced to contract more debt. Other export sectors, notably coffee, cocoa, and shrimp, could not compensate for the lost income. Rather than pursue a policy of fiscal restraint, Febres-Cordero, anxious to win a place in his nation's history as a man of accomplishment, pushed expensive public-works programs, which also pushed up the rate of inflation.

Febres-Cordero's successor, Rodrigo Borja, confronted with a weakened economy, was forced to introduce an unpopular austerity program, including currency devaluation in the range of 75 percent, tax increases, import restrictions, higher fuel and electricity prices, and controls on banks on hard-currency transactions. A modest increase in the minimum wage temporarily prevented the United Workers' Front, the country's most powerful union confederation, from organizing serious opposition to the measures.

The government attempted to balance its unpopular economic measures with a show of nationalism, and announced that the state would assume control of 4 petroleum operations. The Trans-Ecuadoran pipeline became state-operated as of October 1989; oil fields managed by Texaco passed to full state control in July 1990.

On the other hand, Borja made some changes in the nation's policy that reflected the new impetus toward free-market economics. The government announced that foreign investors would enjoy the same rights and treatment as national investors.

President Sixto Durán-Ballén Cordovez then accelerated the pace of economic change and pushed a modernization law that resulted in the privatization of 160 state-owned enterprises and a reduction in the number of public employees from 400,000 to 280,000. President Bucaram, despite his populist leanings, moved to assure the business community that he would not abandon the free-market reforms introduced by his predecessor.

BITTER NEIGHBORS

A long legacy of boundary disputes that reached back to the wars for independence created a strained relationship between Ecuador and Peru that erupted in violence in July 1941. Ecuador initiated an undeclared war against Peru in an attempt to win territory along its southeastern border, in the Marañón River region, and, in the southwest, around the town of Zaramilla. In the 1942 Pact of Peace, Amity, and Limits, which followed a stunning Peruvian victory, Ecuador lost about 120,000 square miles of territory. The peace accord was guaranteed by Argentina, Brazil, Chile, and the United States. In January 1995, the usual tensions that grew each year as the anniversary of the conflict approached were given foundation when fighting again broke out between Peru and Ecuador; Peruvian soldiers patrolling the region had stumbled upon well-prepared and waiting Ecuadoran soldiers. Three weeks later, with the intervention of the guarantors of the original pact, the conflict ended. The Peruvian armed forces were shaken from their smug sense of superiority over the Ecuadorans, and the Ecuadoran defense minister used the fight to support his political pretensions. The border war sent waves of alarm through the rest of Latin America, in that it reminded more than a dozen nations of boundary problems with their neighbors. President Bucaram has announced his intention to seek a resolution of the border issue with Peru.

DEVELOPMENT

Ecuador's development problems have been exacerbated by problems with debt negotiations with and interest payments to foreign creditors. Further complicating the picture is the uncertain future of petroleum revenues, which have fallen below expectations.

FREEDOM

Ecuador's media, with the exception of two government-owned radio stations, are in private hands and represent a broad range of opinion. They are often critical of government policies, but they practice a degree of self-censorship in coverage involving corruption among high-level military personnel.

HEALTH/WELFARE

Educational and economic opportunities in Ecuador are often not made available to women, blacks, and indigenous peoples. Most of the nation's peasantry, overwhelmingly Indian or Mestizo, are poor. Infant mortality, malnutrition, and epidemic disease are common among these people.

ACHIEVEMENTS

Ecuadoran poets have often made their poetry an expression of social criticism. The so-called Tzántzicos group has combined avant-garde techniques with social commitment and has won a measure of attention from literary circles.

Guyana (Cooperative Republic of Guyana)

GEOGRAPHY
Area in Square Kilometers (Miles): 215,000 (82,990) (about the size of Idaho)
Capital (Population): Georgetown (248,500)
Climate: tropical; two rainy seasons (May to mid-August and mid-November to mid-January)

PEOPLE

Population
Total: 712,100
Annual Growth Rate: -0.8%
Rural/Urban Population Ratio: 75/35
Ethnic Makeup: 51% East Indian; 43% African and mixed African; 4% Amerindian; 2% European and Chinese
Major Languages: English; indigenous dialects

Health
Life Expectancy at Birth: 62 years (male); 69 years (female)
Infant Mortality Rate (Ratio): 48/1,000
Average Caloric Intake: 110% of FAO minimum
Physicians Available (Ratio): 1/5,314

The Jungle Falls
Deep in the jungles of Guyana, the Potaro River cascades over the Kaieteur Falls. After a sheer drop of 741 feet over the edge of a sandstone plateau, the rushing water has gouged out a chasm 5 miles long. The falls are the central attraction of the Kaieteur National Park, which was established in 1930. Getting to the falls can be accomplished by car or boat, but the trip is easier by using a chartered aircraft out of the capital city of Georgetown.

Religions
57% Christian; 33% Hindu; 9% Muslim; 1% others

Education
Adult Literacy Rate: 96%

COMMUNICATION
Telephones: 27,000
Newspapers: 1 daily

TRANSPORTATION
Highways—Kilometers (Miles): 7,665 (4,760)

Railroads—Kilometers (Miles): 100 (62)
Usable Airfields: 54

GOVERNMENT
Type: republic
Independence Date: May 26, 1966
Head of State: President Samuel Hinds
Political Parties: People's National Congress; Working People's Alliance; People's Progressive Party; United Force; Democratic Labor Movement; People's Democratic Movement; National Democratic Front; others
Suffrage: universal at 18

MILITARY
Number of Armed Forces: 5,550
Military Expenditures (% of Central Government Expenditures): 6%
Current Hostilities: border disputes with Venezuela and Suriname

ECONOMY
Currency ($ U.S. Equivalent): 139 Guyana dollars = $1
Per Capita Income/GDP: $1,950/$1.4 billion
Inflation Rate: 15.5%
Total Foreign Debt: $2.2 billion
Natural Resources: bauxite; gold; diamonds; hardwood timber; shrimp; fish
Agriculture: sugarcane; rice
Industry: bauxite mining; alumina production; sugar and rice milling

FOREIGN TRADE
Exports: $475 million
Imports: $456 million

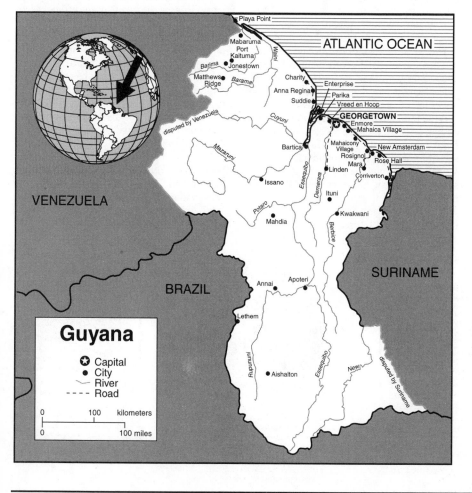

The first permanent Dutch settlements on Essequibo River
1616

The Netherlands cedes the territory to Britain
1815

Independence
1966

President Forbes Burnham dies
1985

1990s

Territorial disputes with Suriname and Venezuela persist

The government promises to end racial and ethnic discrimination

Cheddi Jagan's death elevates Prime Minister Samuel Hinds to the presidency

GUYANA: RACIAL AND ETHNIC TENSIONS

Christopher Columbus, who cruised along what are now Guyana's shores in 1498, named the region *Guiana*. The first European settlers were the Dutch, who settled in Guyana late in the sixteenth century, after they had been ousted from Brazil by a resurgent Portuguese Crown. Dutch control ended in 1796, when the British gained control of the area. In 1815, as part of the treaty arrangements that brought the Napoleonic Wars to a close, the Dutch colonies of Essequibo, Demerera, and Berbice were officially ceded to the British. In 1831, the former Dutch colonies were consolidated as the Crown Colony of British Guiana.

Guyana is a society deeply divided along racial and ethnic lines. East Indians make up the majority of the population. They predominate in rural areas, constituting the bulk of the labor force on the sugar plantations, and they comprise nearly all of the rice-growing peasantry. They also dominate local businesses and are prominent in the professions. Blacks are concentrated in urban areas, where they are employed in clerical and secretarial positions in the public bureaucracy, in teaching, and in semiprofessional jobs. A black elite dominates the state bureaucratic structure.

Before Guyana's independence in 1966, plantation owners, large merchants, and British colonial administrators consciously favored some ethnic groups over others, providing them with a variety of economic and political advantages. The regime of President Forbes Burnham revived old patterns of discrimination for political gain.

Burnham, after ousting the old elite when he nationalized the sugar plantations and the bauxite mines, built a new regime that simultaneously catered to lower-class blacks and discriminated against East Indians. In an attempt to address the blacks' basic human needs, the Burnham government greatly expanded the number of blacks holding positions in public administration. To demonstrate his largely contrived black-power ideology, Burnham spoke out strongly in support of African liberation movements. The government played to the fear of communal strife in order to justify its increasingly authoritarian rule.

In the mid-1970s, a faltering economy and political mismanagement generated an increasing opposition to Burnham that cut across ethnic lines. The government increased the size of the military, packed Parliament through rigged elections, and amended the Constitution so that the president held virtually imperial power.

There has been some improvement since Burnham's death in 1985. The appearance of newspapers other than the government-controlled *Guyana Chronicle* and the public's dramatically increased access to television have served to curtail official control of the media. In politics, the election of Indo-Guyanese leader Cheddi Jagan to the presidency reflected deep-seated disfavor with the behavior and economic policies of the previous government of Desmond Hoyte. President Jagan identified the nation's foreign debt of $2 billion as a "colossally big problem, because the debt overhang impedes human development."

While president, Hoyte once pledged to continue the socialist policies of the late Forbes Burnham; but, in the same breath, he talked about the need for privatization of the crucial sugar and bauxite industries. Jagan's economic policies, according to *Latin American Regional Reports,* outlined an uncertain course. During his campaign, Jagan stated that government should not be involved in sectors of the economy where private or cooperative ownership would be more efficient. In 1993, however, he backed away from the sale of the Guyana Electric Company and had some doubts about selling off the sugar industry. In Jagan's words: "Privatisation and divestment must be approached with due care. I was not elected president to preside over the liquidation of Guyana. I was mandated by the Guyanese people to rebuild the national economy and to restore a decent standard of living." Jagan's policies stimulated rapid socioeconomic progress as Guyana embarked on the road to economic recovery. Samuel Hinds, the prime minister, assumed the presidency in 1997, upon the death of Jagan, and promised to continue his policies.

DEVELOPMENT

At the Canadian-owned Omai mine, the largest open-pit gold mine in the Americas, significant amounts of proven and probable reserves have been discovered. At the same time, the company's environmental policies have been brought into question, as large amounts of cyanide escaped from containment lakes, spilled into local rivers, and killed large numbers of fish and game.

FREEDOM

One of the priorities of the Jagan/Hinds government is the elimination of all forms of ethnic and racial discrimination, a difficult task in a country where political parties are organized along racial lines. Not to be ignored are Guyana's indigenous peoples, who will be offered accelerated development programs to enhance their health and welfare.

HEALTH/WELFARE

The government has initiated policies designed to lower the cost of living for Guyanese. Prices for essentials have been cut. Money has been allocated for school lunch programs and for a "food-for-work" plan. Pensions have been raised for the first time in years. The minimum wage, however, will not sustain an average Guyanese family.

ACHIEVEMENTS

The American Historical Association selected Walter Rodney for the 1982 Beveridge Award for his study of the Guyanese working people. The award is for the best book in English on the history of the United States, Canada, or Latin America. Rodney, the leader of the Working People's Alliance, was assassinated in 1980.

Paraguay

GEOGRAPHY
Area in Square Kilometers (Miles): 406,752 (157,048) (about the size of California)
Capital (Population): Asunción (607,000)
Climate: temperate east of the Paraguay River; semiarid to the west

PEOPLE

Population
Total: 5,504,200
Annual Growth Rate: 2.7%
Rural/Urban Population Ratio: 50/50
Ethnic Makeup: 95% Mestizo; 5% white and Indian
Major Languages: Spanish; Guaraní; Portuguese

Health
Life Expectancy at Birth: 72 years (male); 75 years (female)
Infant Mortality Rate (Ratio): 24/1,000
Average Caloric Intake: 126% of FAO minimum
Physicians Available (Ratio): 1/1,406

Religions
90% Roman Catholic; 10% Mennonite and other Protestant denominations

Education
Adult Literacy Rate: 90%

COMMUNICATION
Telephones: 78,300
Newspapers: 5 dailies

Selling Power

The government of Paraguay is authoritarian but welcomes development by outsiders. This atmosphere may well allow Paraguay to realize its great potential as an exporter of electric power. In fact, by the year 2000, it could be the world's largest producer of electric power. The first hydroturbine is at the Itaipú Dam project on the Paraná River. This dam was jointly constructed by Paraguay and Brazil, and there has been international interest in the project.

TRANSPORTATION
Highways—Kilometers (Miles): 28,300 (17,659)
Railroads—Kilometers (Miles): 970 (602)
Usable Airfields: 929

GOVERNMENT
Type: constitutional republic with a powerful executive branch
Independence Date: May 14, 1811
Head of State: President Juan Carlos Wasmosy
Political Parties: Colorado Party; Liberal Party; Radical Liberal Party; Christian Democratic Party; Febrerist Revolutionary Party; Popular Democratic Party; National Encounter
Suffrage: universal and compulsory from 18 to 60

MILITARY
Number of Armed Forces: 16,000
Military Expenditures (% of Central Government Expenditures): 13.3%
Current Hostilities: none

ECONOMY
Currency ($ U.S. Equivalent): 2,050 guaranis = $1 (fixed rate)
Per Capita Income/GDP: $2,950/$15.4 billion
Inflation Rate: 18%
Total Foreign Debt: $1.4 billion
Natural Resources: hydroelectric sites; forests
Agriculture: meat; corn; sugarcane; soybeans; lumber; cotton
Industry: sugar; cement; textiles; beverages; wood products

FOREIGN TRADE
Exports: $728 million
Imports: $1.4 billion

The Spanish found Asunción **1537**	Independence is declared **1811**	War against the "Triple Alliance": Argentina, Brazil, and Uruguay **1865–1870**	General Alfredo Stroessner begins his rule **1954**	Women win the right to vote **1961**	Stroessner is ousted in a coup **1989**

1990s

A new Constitution is promulgated in 1993

Juan Carlos Wasmosy is elected president

Presidential elections are scheduled for May 1998

A COUNTRY OF PARADOX

Paraguay is a country of paradox. Although there is little threat of foreign invasion and guerrilla activity is insignificant, a state of siege was in effect for 35 years, ending only in 1989 with the ouster of President (General) Alfredo Stroessner, who had held the reins of power since 1954. Government expenditures on health care in Paraguay are among the lowest in the Western Hemisphere, yet life expectancy is impressive, and infant mortality reportedly has fallen to levels comparable to more advanced developing countries. On the other hand, nearly a third of all reported deaths are of children under 5 years of age. Educational achievement, especially in rural areas, is low.

Paraguayan politics, economic development, society, and even its statistical base are comprehensible only within the context of its geography and Indo–Hispanic culture. Its geographic isolation in the midst of powerful neighbors has encouraged Paraguay's tradition of militarism and self-reliance—of strongmen who tolerate little opposition. There is no tradition of constitutional government or liberal democratic procedures upon which to draw. Social values influence politics to the extent that politics is an all-or-nothing struggle for power and its accompanying prestige and access to wealth. These political values, in combination with a population that is poor and politically ignorant, contribute to the type of paternalistic, personal rule characteristic of a dictator such as Stroessner.

The paradoxical behavior of the Acuerdo Nacional, a block of opposition parties under Stroessner, was understandable within the context of a quest for power or at least a share of power. Stroessner, always eager to divide and conquer, identified the Acuerdo Nacional as a fruitful field for new alliances. Leaping at the chance for patronage positions but anxious to demonstrate to Stroessner that they were a credible political force worthy of becoming allies, Acuerdo members tried to win the support of unions and the peasantry. At the same time, the party purged its youth wing of leftist influences.

Just when it seemed that Stroessner would rule until his death, Paraguayans were surprised in February 1989 when General Andrés Rodríguez—second-in-command of the armed forces, a member of the Traditionalist faction of the Colorado Party, which was in disfavor with the president, and a relative of Stroessner—seized power. Rodríguez's postcoup statements promised the democratization of Paraguay, respect for human rights, repudiation of drug trafficking, and the scheduling of presidential elections. Not surprisingly, General Rodríguez emerged as President Rodríguez. When asked about voting irregularities, Rodríguez indicated that "real" democracy would begin with elections in 1993 and that his rule was a necessary "transition."

"Real" democracy, following the 1993 victory of President Juan Carlos Wasmosy, had a distinct Paraguayan flavor. Wasmosy won the election with 40 percent of the vote; and the Colorado Party, which won most of the seats in Congress, was badly divided. When an opposition victory seemed possible, the military persuaded the outgoing government to push through legislation to reorganize the armed forces. In effect, they were made autonomous. Unsettling were remarks made just days before the election, when army strongman General Lino Oviedo said, according to *Latin American Regional Reports,* that "the military would not stomach an opposition victory [and] . . . that the military would 'co-govern' with the Colorado Party forever, 'whether anyone likes it or not, no matter who dislikes it, and no matter who squeals.' " What was clear was that the military is still the arbiter of Paraguayan politics. Wasmosy's difficulties with the generals have continued.

It is difficult to acquire accurate statistics about the Paraguayan economy, in part because of the large informal sector and in part because of large-scale smuggling and drug trafficking. From the government's perspective, the economic problems are manageable. Wasmosy has promised to push ahead with plans to privatize the Paraguayan economy, but the military may stand in his way—the generals control the most important state-owned enterprises. There is also concern about the "Brazilianization" of the eastern part of Paraguay, which has developed to the point at which Portuguese is heard as frequently as Spanish or Guaraní, the most common Indian language.

DEVELOPMENT

Monies earned from the sale of state-owned companies, according to President Juan Carlos Wasmosy, will be used, together with profits from the Itaipú hydroelectric facility, to create a national development fund. But, he emphasized, economic development should be led by the private sector.

FREEDOM

Monolingual Guaraní speakers suffer from a marked disadvantage in the labor market. Where Guaraní speakers are employed, their wages are much lower than monolingual Spanish speakers. This differential is accounted for by the educational deficiencies of the Guaraní speakers as opposed to those who speak Spanish.

HEALTH/WELFARE

The Paraguayan government spends very little on human services and welfare. As a result, its population is plagued by health problems— including poor levels of nutrition, lack of drinkable water, absence of sanitation, and a prevalence of fatal childhood diseases.

ACHIEVEMENTS

Paraguay has produced several notable authors, including Gabriel Casaccia and Augusto Roa Bastos. Roa Bastos makes extensive use of religious symbolism in his novels as a means of establishing true humanity and justice.

Peru (Peruvian Republic)

GEOGRAPHY
Area in Square Kilometers (Miles): 1,280,000 (496,222) (about ⅚ the size of Alaska
Capital (Population): Lima (5,659,000)
Climate: coast area, arid and mild; Andes, temperate to frigid; eastern lowlands, tropically warm and humid

PEOPLE

Population
Total: 24,524,000
Annual Growth Rate: 1.8%
Rural/Urban Population Ratio: 30/70
Ethnic Makeup: 45% Indian; 37% Mestizo; 15% white; 3% black, Asian, and others
Major Languages: Spanish; Quechua; Aymara

Health
Life Expectancy at Birth: 64 years (male); 68 years (female)
Infant Mortality Rate (Ratio): 52/1,000
Average Caloric Intake: 98% of FAO minimum
Physicians Available (Ratio): 1/1,116

Religions
more than 90% Roman Catholic; others

Education
Adult Literacy Rate: 82%

COMMUNICATION
Telephones: 544,000
Newspapers: 12 dailies

TRANSPORTATION
Highways—Kilometers (Miles): 69,942 (43,364)
Railroads—Kilometers (Miles): 1,801

A Lost Kingdom

Peru has an exciting and rich cultural history, as evidenced most dramatically by Machu Picchu and other influences and tangible remains of the Incas. In 1985, explorer Gene Savoy discovered another "lost kingdom," Gran Vilaya, in the rain forest of Peru, north of Lima. Because of the inaccessibility of the region, archaeologists are just beginning to learn about this ancient culture. They had an exciting start: Savoy's expedition found stone complexes and terracing, indications of a well-organized and complex society.

(1,118)
Usable Airfields: 236

GOVERNMENT
Type: constitutional republic
Independence Date: July 28, 1821
Head of State: President Alberto Fujimori
Political Parties: Change 90–New Majority; Union for Peru; Popular Action Party; American Popular Revolutionary Alliance; Popular Christian Party; United Left; Civic Works Movement; Independent Moralizing Front; Socialist Left; Democratic Coordinator; Renovacion; others
Suffrage: universal at 18

MILITARY
Number of Armed Forces: 120,000
Military Expenditures (% of Central Government Expenditures): 11.2%
Current Hostilities: none

ECONOMY
Currency ($ U.S. Equivalent): 2.62 soles = $1
Per Capita Income/GDP: $3,110/$73.6 billion
Inflation Rate: 15% (est.)
Total Foreign Debt: $22.4 billion
Natural Resources: minerals; metals; petroleum; forests; fish
Agriculture: coffee; cotton; cocoa; sugar; wool; corn
Industry: mineral processing; oil refining; textiles; food processing; light manufacturing; automobile assembly

FOREIGN TRADE
Exports: $4.1 billion
Imports: $5.1 billion

Peru
⊗ Capital
● City
⌇ River
- - - Road
0   100   kilometers
0   100 miles

PERU: HEIR TO THE INCAS

The culture of Peru, from pre-Hispanic days to the present, has in many ways reflected the nation's variegated geography and climate. While 55 percent of the nation is covered with jungle, coastal Peru boasts one of the world's driest deserts. Despite its forbidding character, irrigation of the desert is made possible by run-offs from the Andes. This allows for the growing of a variety of crops in fertile oases that comprise about 5.5 percent of the land area.

Similarly, in the highlands, or sierra, there is little land available for cultivation. Because of the difficulty of the terrain, only about 7 percent of the land can produce crops. Indeed, Peru contains the lowest per capita amount of arable land in South America. The lack of good land has had—and continues to have—profound social and political repercussions, especially in the southern highlands near the city of Ayacucho.

THE SUPREMACY OF LIMA

Historically, coastal Peru and its capital city of Lima have attempted to dominate the sierra, politically, economically, and, at times, culturally. Long a bureaucratic and political center, Lima in the twentieth century has presided over the economic expansion of the coast. Economic opportunity in combination with severe population pressure in the sierra have caused Lima and its port of Callao to grow tremendously in population, if not in services. Ironically, the capital city has one of the worst climates for dense human settlement. Thermal inversions are common; between May and September, they produce a cloud ceiling and a pervasive cool fog.

Middle- and upper-class city dwellers have always been ignorant of the people of the highlands. Very few are knowledgeable of either Quechua or Aymara, the Indian languages spoken daily by millions of Peruvians. Yet this ignorance of the languages—and, by extension, of the cultures—has not prevented government planners or well-meaning intellectuals from trying to impose a variety of developmental models on the inhabitants of the sierra. In the late nineteenth century, for example, modernizers known collectively in Latin America as Positivists sought in vain to transform indigenous cultures by Europeanizing them. Other reformers sought to identify with the indigenous peoples. In the 1920s, a young intellectual named Victor Raúl Haya de la Torre fashioned a political ideology called APRISMO, which embraced the idea of an alliance of Indoamerica to recover the American states for their original inhabitants. While his broader vision proved to be too idealistic,

the specific reforms he recommended for Peru were put into effect by reform-minded governments in the 1960s and 1970s. Sadly, reform continued to be developed and imposed from Lima, without an understanding of the rationale behind existing agrarian systems or an appreciation of a peasant logic that was based not on production of a surplus but on attaining a satisfying level of well-being. Much of the turmoil in rural Peru today stems from the agrarian reform of 1968–1979.

AGRARIAN REFORM

From the mid-1950s, rural laborers in the central and southern highlands and on the coastal plantations demonstrated an increasingly insistent desire for agrarian reform. Peasant communities in the sierra staged a series of land invasions and challenged the domination of the large estate, or *hacienda,* from outside. Simultaneously, tenants living on the estates pressured the hacienda system from within. In both cases, peasants wanted land.

The Peruvian government responded with both the carrot and the stick. A military regime, on the one hand, tried to crush peasant insurgency in 1962 and, on the other, passed agrarian reform legislation. The laws had no practical effect, but they did give legal recognition to the problem of land reform. In the face of continued peasant unrest in the south, the military enacted more substantial land laws in 1963, confiscating some property and redistributing it to peasants. The trend toward reform continued with the election of Francisco Belaunde Terry as president of a civilian government.

In the face of continued peasant militancy, Belaunde promised far-ranging reforms, but a hostile Congress refused to provide sufficient funds to implement the proposed reforms. Peasant unrest increased, and the government feared the development of widespread rural guerrilla warfare.

Against this backdrop of rural violence, the Peruvian military again seized power in 1968. To the astonishment of most observers, the military chose not to crush popular unrest but, rather, to embrace reforms. Clearly, the military had become sensitive to the political, social, and economic inequalities in Peru that had bred unrest. The military was intent on revolutionizing Peru from the top down rather than waiting for revolution from below.

In addition to land reform, the military placed new emphasis on Peru's Indian heritage. Tupac Amaru, an Incan who had rebelled against Spanish rule in 1780–1781, became a national symbol. In 1975, Quechua, the ancient language of the Inca,

became Peru's second official language (along with Spanish). School curricula were revised and approached Peru's Indian heritage in a new and positive light.

NATIONALIZATION AND INTEGRATION

Behind the reforms, which were extended to industry and commerce and included the nationalization of foreign enterprises, lay the military's desire to provide for Peru a stable social and political order. The military leaders felt that they could provide better leadership in the quest for national integration and economic development than could "inefficient" civilians. Their ultimate goal was to construct a new society based on citizen participation at all levels.

As is so often the case, however, the reform model was not based on the realities of the society. It was naively assumed by planners that the Indians of the sierra were primitive socialists and wanted collectivized ownership of the land. In reality, each family's interests tended to make it competitive, rather than cooperative, with every other peasant family. Collectivization in the highlands failed because peasant communities outside the old hacienda structure clamored for the return of traditional lands that had been taken from them over the years. The Peruvian government found itself, awkwardly, attempting to defend the integrity of the newly reformed units from peasants who wanted their own land.

THE PATRON

Further difficulties were caused by the disruption of the patron–client relationship in the more traditional parts of the sierra. Hacienda owners, although members of the ruling elite, often enjoyed a tight bond with their tenants. Rather than a boss–worker relationship, the patron–client tie came close to kinship. Hacienda owners, for example, were often godparents to the children of their workers. A certain reciprocity was expected and given. But, with the departure of the hacienda owners, a host of government bureaucrats arrived on the scene, most of whom had been trained on the coast and were ignorant of the customs and languages of the sierra. The peasants who benefited from the agrarian reform looked upon the administrators with a good deal of suspicion. The agrarian laws and decrees, which were all written in Spanish, proved impossible for the peasants to understand. Not surprisingly, fewer than half of the sierra peasants chose to join the collectives; and, in a few places, peasants actually asked for the return of the hacienda owner, someone to

(United Nations photo)

Machu Picchu, a famous Inca ruin, stands atop a 6,750-foot mountain in the Peruvian Andes.

whom they could relate. On the coast, the cooperatives did not benefit all agricultural workers equally, since permanent workers won the largest share of the benefits. In sum, the reforms had little impact on existing trends in agricultural production, failed to reverse income inequalities within the peasant population, and did not ease poverty.

The shortcomings of the reforms—in combination with drought, subsequent crop failures, rising food prices, and population pressure—created very difficult and tense situations in the sierra. The infant mortality rate rose 35 percent between 1978 and 1980, and caloric intake dropped well below the recommended minimum. More than half of the children under age 6 suffered from some form of malnutrition. Rural unrest continued.

RETURN TO CIVILIAN RULE
Unable to solve Peru's problems and torn by divisions within its ranks, the military stepped aside in 1980, and Belaunde was again elected as Peru's constitutional president. Despite the transition to civilian government, unrest continued in the highlands, and the appearance of a left-wing guerrilla organization known as Sendero Luminoso (Shining Path) led the government to declare repeated states of emergency and to lift civil guarantees.

In an attempt to control the situation, the Ministry of Agriculture won the power to restructure and, in some cases, to liquidate the cooperatives and collectives established by the agrarian reform. Land

was divided into small individual plots and given to the peasants. Because the plots can be bought, sold, and mortgaged, some critics argue that the undoing of the reform may hasten the return of most of the land into the hands of a new landed elite.

Civilian rule, however, has not necessarily meant democratic rule for Peru's citizens. This helps to explain the spread of Sendero Luminoso despite its radical strategy and tactics of violence. By 1992, according to Diego García-Sayán, the executive director of the Andean Commission of Jurists, the Sendero Luminoso controlled "many parts of Peruvian territory. Through its sabotage, political assassinations, and terrorist actions, Sendero Luminoso has helped to make political violence, which used to be rather infrequent, one of the main characteristics of Peruvian society."

Violence was not confined to the guerrillas of Sendero Luminoso or of the Tupac Amaru Revolutionary Movement (MRTA). Economist Javier Iguíñiz, of the Catholic University of Lima, argued that a solution to the violence requires an understanding that it flows from disparate, autonomous, and competing sources, including guerrillas, right-wing paramilitary groups, the Peruvian military and police forces, and cocaine traffickers, "particularly the well-armed Colombians active in the Huallaga Valley." Sendero Luminoso, until recently, was also active in the Huallaga Valley and profited from taxing drug traffickers. Raúl González, of Lima's Center for Development Studies, observed

that, as both the drug traffickers and the guerrillas "operate[d] outside the law, there has evolved a relationship of mutual convenience in certain parts of Huallaga to combat their common enemy, the state."

President Alan García vacillated on a policy toward the Sendero Luminoso insurgency. But ultimately, he authorized the launching of a major military offensive against Sendero Luminoso bases thought to be linked to drug trafficking. Later, determined to confront an insurgency that has claimed 29,000 victims over the past decade and a half, President Alberto Fujimori armed rural farmers, known as *rondas campesinas,* to fight off guerrilla incursions. (The arming of peasants is not new to Peru; it is a practice that dates to the colonial period.) Critics correctly feared that the accelerated war against insurgents and drug traffickers would only strengthen the Peruvian military's political power.

A BUREAUCRATIC REVOLUTION?
Peruvian author Hernando DeSoto's best-selling and controversial book, *The Other Path* (as opposed to Sendero Luminoso, or Shining Path), argues convincingly that both left- and right-wing governments in Latin America in general and in Peru in particular are neo-mercantile—that is, both intervene in the economy and promote the expansion of state activities. "Both strengthened the role of the government's bureaucracy until they made it the main obstacle, rather than the main incentive, to progress, and together they produced, without consulting the electorate, almost 99 percent of the laws governing us." There are differences between left- and right-wing approaches: The left governs with an eye to redistributing wealth and well-being to the neediest groups, and the right tends to govern to serve foreign investors or national business interests. "Both, however, will do so with bad laws which explicitly benefit some and harm others. Although their aims may seem to differ, the result is that in Peru one wins or loses by political decisions. Of course, there is a big difference between a fox and a wolf but, for the rabbit, it is the similarity that counts."

DeSoto attacked the bureaucracy head-on when his private research center, the Institute for Liberty and Democracy, drafted legislation to abolish a collection of requirements built on the assumption that citizens are liars until proven otherwise. The law, which took effect in April 1989, reflected a growing rebellion against bureaucracy in Peru. Another law, which took effect in October 1989, radically simplified the process of gaining title

					A military coup: far-reaching reforms are pursued **1968**	Debureaucratization campaign begins **1989**	
The Inca Empire is at its height **1500**	The Spanish found Lima **1535**		Independence is proclaimed **1821**	Women gain the right to vote **1955**			**1990s**

President Alberto
Fujimori executes
a "self-coup"

Fujimori easily
wins reelection

Guerrillas seize
the Japanese
Embassy;
Fujimori's
popularity
plummets

to land. (DeSoto discovered that, to purchase a parcel of state-owned land in Peru, one had to invest 56 months of effort and 207 visits to 48 different offices). The legislation will have an important impact on the slum dwellers of Lima, for it will take much less time to regularize land titles as the result of invasions and seizures. Slum dwellers with land titles, according to DeSoto, invest in home improvements at a rate 9 times greater than that of slum dwellers without titles. Slum dwellers who own property will be less inclined to turn to violent solutions to their problems.

The debureaucratization campaign has been paralleled by grassroots social movements that grew in response to a state that no longer could or would respond to the needs of its citizenry. Cataline Romero, director of the Bartolome de Las Cases Institute of Lima, said that "grass-roots social movements have blossomed into political participants that allow historically marginalized people to feel a sense of their own dignity and rights as citizens." Poor people have developed different strategies for survival as the government has failed to meet even their most basic needs. Most have entered the informal sector and have learned to work together through the formation of unions, mothers' clubs, and cooperatives. Concluded Romero: "As crisis tears institutions down, these communities are preparing the ground for building new institutions that are more responsive to the needs of the majority." DeSoto concurs and adds: "No one has ever considered that most poor Peruvians are a step ahead of the revolutionaries and are already changing the country's structures, and

what politicians should be doing is guiding the change and giving it an appropriate institutional framework so that it can be properly used and governed."

DEMOCRACY AND THE "SELF-COUP"

In April 1992, President Fujimori, increasingly isolated and unable to effect economic and political reforms, suspended the Constitution, arrested a number of opposition leaders, shut down Congress, and openly challenged the power of the judiciary. The military, Fujimori's staunch ally, openly supported the *autogolpe,* or "self-coup," as did business leaders and about 80 percent of the Peruvian people. In the words of political scientist Cynthia McClintock, writing in *Current History,* "Fujimori emerged a new caudillo, destroying the conventional wisdom that institutions, whether civilian or military, had become more important than individual leaders in Peru and elsewhere in Latin America." In 1993, a constitutional amendment allowed Fujimori to run for a second consecutive term.

In April 1995, Fujimori won a comfortable victory, with 64 percent of the vote. This was attributable to his successful economic policies, which saw the Peruvian economy grow by 12 percent—the highest in the world for 1994—and the campaign against Sendero Luminoso.

To everyone's surprise, however, the guerrillas of MRTA openly challenged the government with their seizure of the Japanese Embassy in Lima in December 1996. The siege continued for months and was a source of embarrassment for the Fujimori administration. None of the guerril-

las survived the assault on the embassy by the Peruvian military, although all but one of the hostages was rescued. Despite the apparent success of the operation, serious damage had been done to the prestige of the government. Public-opinion polls in July 1997 revealed that Fujimori's approval rate had fallen to only 19 percent, the lowest in his 7 years of rule. More than three quarters of the respondents felt that Fujimori's government was "dictatorial," and about half of Peruvians surveyed asserted that the government was essentially in the hands of the military. Others felt that the government lacked direction.

The presence of the military has had economic as well as political ramifications. Many higher-ranking officers are not convinced that a liberal economic model is best for Peru. Not surprisingly, foreign investment has slowed. Recent developments have overshadowed an overall record of success with regard to the economy. In Peru, pessimism has replaced optimism—the future is indeed clouded.

DEVELOPMENT

In 1994, as a result of the privatization policy of the government, foreign investment in Peru doubled. The revenues from privatization amounted to $1.2 billion in 1995, which gave President Fujimori the money needed to wage war against poverty.

FREEDOM

President Fujimori's increasing centralization of power poses a threat to the civil and political rights of Peruvians. Amendments to the Constitution allow the president to dissolve Congress without cause, veto legislation, rule by emergency decree, and be eligible for immediate re-election.

HEALTH/WELFARE

The newsweekly *Caretas* of Lima said that one of the keys to Fujimori's success has been a vast public-works program. In rural areas, jobs, health care, and a higher standard of living are issues of great concern. The president convinced rural dwellers that he could deliver on his promises.

ACHIEVEMENTS

Peru has produced a number of literary giants, including José Maria Mariategui, who believed that the "socialism" of the Indians should be a model for the rest of Peru; and Mario Vargas Llosa, always concerned with the complexity of human relationships.

Suriname (Republic of Suriname)

GEOGRAPHY

Area in Square Kilometers (Miles):
163,265 (63,037) (about the size of
Georgia)
Capital (Population): Paramaribo
(201,000)
Climate: tropical

PEOPLE

Population

Total: 436,500
Annual Growth Rate: 1.6%
Rural/Urban Population Ratio: 51/49
Ethnic Makeup: 37% Hindustani
(locally called East Indian); 31%
Creole; 15% Javanese; 10% Bush
Negro; 3% Amerindian; 3% Chinese
Major Languages: Dutch; Sranantonga;
English

Health

Life Expectancy at Birth: 67 years
(male); 72 years (female)
Infant Mortality Rate (Ratio): 30/1,000
Average Caloric Intake: 108% of FAO
minimum
Physicians Available (Ratio): 1/1,903

The First American Synagogue

Suriname (once known as Guiana) was pretty much left alone by the early
Spanish and Portuguese explorers because of its lack of gold. The first
successful settlement was established by Britain's Lord Willoughby in 1651.
Willoughby welcomed people from unsuccessful West Indian and other
South American colonies, who brought capital and skills to the new settlement. Because of his policy, the first synagogue in the Western Hemisphere
was erected in Suriname in 1665 by Jewish immigrants from Brazil.

Religions

27% Hindu; 25% Protestants; 23%
Roman Catholic; 20% Muslim; 5%
others

Education

Adult Literacy Rate: 95%

COMMUNICATION

Telephones: 27,500
Newspapers: 2 dailies

TRANSPORTATION

Highways—Kilometers (Miles): 8,800
(5,491)

Railroads—Kilometers (Miles): 166
(103)
Usable Airfields: 46

GOVERNMENT

Type: republic
Independence Date: November 25, 1975
Head of State: President Ronald
Venetiaan
Political Parties: New Front;
Progressive Reform Party; National
Democratic Party; National Party; others
Suffrage: universal at 18

MILITARY

Number of Armed Forces: 2,950
*Military Expenditures (% of Central
Government Expenditures):* 9%
Current Hostilities: none

ECONOMY

Currency ($ U.S. Equivalent): 401
Suriname guilders = $1
Per Capita Income/GDP: $2,800/$1.2
billion
Inflation Rate: 225%
Total Foreign Debt: $180 million
Natural Resources: bauxite; iron ore;
minerals; forests; hydroelectric
potential; fish
Agriculture: rice; sugarcane; bananas;
timber
Industry: aluminum; alumina; food
processing; lumber; bricks; cigarettes

FOREIGN TRADE

Exports: $443 million
Imports: $521 million

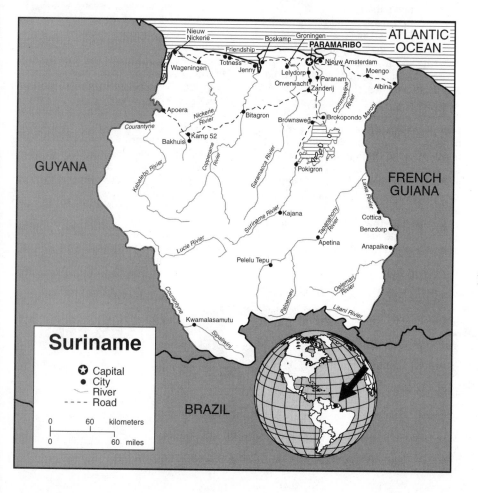

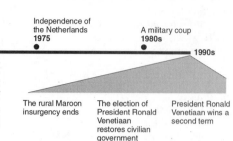

British
colonization
efforts
1651

The Dutch
receive Suriname
from the British in
exchange for
New Amsterdam
1667

Independence of
the Netherlands
1975

A military coup
1980s

1990s

The rural Maroon
insurgency ends

The election of
President Ronald
Venetiaan
restores civilian
government

President Ronald
Venetiaan wins a
second term

SURINAME:
A SMALL-TOWN STATE

Settled by the British in 1651, Suriname, a small colony on the coast of Guiana, prospered with a plantation economy based on cocoa, sugar, coffee, and cotton. The colony came under Dutch control in 1667; in exchange, the British were given New Amsterdam (Manhattan, New York). The colony was often in turmoil because of Indian and slave uprisings, which took advantage of a weak Dutch power. When slavery was finally abolished, in 1863, plantation owners brought contract workers from China, India, and Java.

Suriname, on the eve of independence of the Netherlands in 1975, was a complex multiracial society. Although existing ethnic tensions were heightened as communal groups jockeyed for power in the new state, other factors cut across racial lines. Even though Creoles (native-born whites) were dominant in the bureaucracy as well as in the mining and industrial sectors, there was sufficient economic opportunity for all ethnic groups, so acute socioeconomic conflict was avoided.

THE POLITICAL FABRIC

Until 1980, Suriname enjoyed a parliamentary democracy that, because of the size of the nation, more closely resembled a small town or extended family in terms of its organization and operation. The various ethnic, political, and economic groups that comprised Surinamese society were united in what sociologist Rob Kroes describes as an "oligarchic web of patron-client relations" that found its expression in government. Through the interplay of the various groups, integration in the political process and accommodation of their needs were achieved. Despite the fact that most interests had access to the center of power, and despite the spirit of accommodation and cooperation, the military seized power early in 1980.

THE ROOTS OF MILITARY RULE

In Kroes's opinion, the coup originated in the army among noncommissioned officers, because they were essentially outside the established social and political system—they were denied their "rightful" place in the patronage network. The officers had a high opinion of themselves and resented what they perceived as discrimination by a wasteful and corrupt government. Their demands for reforms, including recognition of an officers' union, were ignored. In January 1980, one government official talked of disbanding the army altogether.

The coup, masterminded and led by Sergeant Desire Bouterse, had a vague, undefined ideology. It claimed to be nationalist; and it revealed itself to be puritanical, in that it lashed out at corruption and demanded that citizens embrace civic duty and a work ethic. Ideological purity was maintained by government control or censorship of a once-free media. Wavering between left-wing radicalism and middle-of-the-road moderation, the rapid shifts in Bouterse's ideological declarations suggest that this was a policy designed to keep the opposition off guard and to appease factions within the military.

The military rule of Bouterse seemed to come to an end early in 1988, when President Ramsewak Shankar was inaugurated. However, in December 1990, Bouterse masterminded another military coup. The military and Bouterse remained above the rule of law, and the judiciary was not able to investigate or prosecute serious cases involving military personnel.

With regard to Suriname's economic policy, most politicians see integration into Latin American and Caribbean markets as critical. The Dutch, who suspended economic aid after the 1990 coup, restored their assistance with the election of President Ronald Venetiaan in 1991. But civilian authorities were well aware of the roots of military rule and pragmatically allowed officers a role in government befitting their self-perceived status.

In 1993, Venetiaan confronted the military when it refused to accept his choice of officers to command the army. Army reform was still high on the agenda in 1995 and was identified by President Venetiaan as one of his government's three great tasks. The others were economic reform necessary to ensure Dutch aid and establish the country's eligibility for international credit; and the need to reestablish ties with the interior to consolidate an Organization of American States–brokered peace, after almost a decade of insurgency.

Bouterse ran against Venetiaan in presidential elections in 1996. Venetiaan won, but the close vote indicated profound discontent with the economic and social policies of his government.

DEVELOPMENT

Although Suriname is one of the world's largest bauxite producers, its economy has been in decline for a decade and a half. To compensate, logging rights in tropical rain forests have been signed over to Asian investors, raising merited fears of deforestation.

FREEDOM

The Venetiaan government successfully brought to an end the Maroon insurgency of 8 years' duration. Under the auspices of the OAS, the rebels turned in their weapons, and an amnesty for both sides in the conflict was declared.

HEALTH/WELFARE

Amerindians and Maroons (the descendants of escaped African slaves) who live in the interior have suffered from the lack of educational and social services, partly from their isolation and partly from insurgency. With peace, however, it is hoped that the health, education, and general welfare of these peoples will improve.

ACHIEVEMENTS

Suriname, unlike most developing countries, has a small foreign debt and a relatively strong repayment capacity based on its export industry.

Uruguay (Oriental Republic of Uruguay)

GEOGRAPHY

Area in Square Kilometers (Miles): 176,215 (68,037) (about the size of Washington State)
Capital (Population): Montevideo (1,400,000)
Climate: temperate

PEOPLE

Population

Total: 3,239,000
Annual Growth Rate: 0.7%
Rural/Urban Population Ratio: 10/90
Ethnic Makeup: 88% white; 8% Mestizo; 4% black
Major Language: Spanish

Health

Life Expectancy at Birth: 71 years (male); 78 years (female)
Infant Mortality Rate (Ratio): 16/1,000
Average Caloric Intake: 110% of FAO minimum
Physicians Available (Ratio): 1/286

Religions

66% Roman Catholic; 2% Protestant; 2% Jewish; 30% nonprofessing or others

---

Cultural Life

Uruguayan literary figures and artists have won worldwide acclaim. The essayist José Enrique Rodo (1872–1917) has been called the "greatest modernist prose writer." Another luminary was the short-story writer Horacio Quiroga (1878–1937), whose jungle stories from the Argentine province of Misiones made the outdoors a popular subject for story material. The artist Joaquín Torres García (1874–1949) went to Spain as an art student and studied under Joan Miró and Pablo Picasso. It was Torres who introduced Picasso's style to South America.

Education

Adult Literacy Rate: 96%

COMMUNICATION

Telephones: 337,000
Newspapers: 5 dailies; 210,000 circulation

TRANSPORTATION

Highways—Kilometers (Miles): 49,900 (30,988)
Railroads—Kilometers (Miles): 3,000 (1,872)
Usable Airfields: 85

GOVERNMENT

Type: republic
Independence Date: August 25, 1828
Head of State: President Julio Maria Sanguinetti
Political Parties: National (Blanco) Party; Colorado Party; Broad Front Coalition; New Sector Coalition
Suffrage: universal and compulsory at 18

MILITARY

Number of Armed Forces: 25,200
Military Expenditures (% of Central Government Expenditures): 9.2%
Current Hostilities: none

ECONOMY

Currency ($ U.S. Equivalent): 7.92 pesos = $1
Per Capita Income/GDP: $7,200/$23.0 billion
Inflation Rate: 44%
Total Foreign Debt: $4.2 billion
Natural Resources: soil; hydroelectric potential; minerals (minor)
Agriculture: beef; wool; wheat; rice; corn; sorghum; fish
Industry: meat processing; wool and hides; textiles; footwear; leather apparel; tires; cement; fishing; petroleum refining

FOREIGN TRADE

Exports: $1.8 billion
Imports: $2.5 billion

Voters reject a
government
privatization plan

President Julio
Maria Sanguinetti
returns the
Colorado Party
to power

The government
endorses
sweeping
economic and
social reforms

URUGUAY: ONCE A PARADISE

The modern history of Uruguay begins with the administration of President José Batlle y Ordoñez. Between 1903 and 1929, Batlle's Uruguay became one of the world's foremost testing grounds for social change, and it eventually became known as the "Switzerland of Latin America." Batlle's Colorado Party supported a progressive role for organized labor and formed coalitions with the workers to challenge the traditional elite and win benefits. Other reforms included the formal separation of church and state, nationalization of key sectors of the economy, and the emergence of mass-based political parties. Batlle's masterful leadership was facilitated by a nation that was compact in size; had a small, educated, and homogeneous population; and had rich soil and a geography that facilitated easy communication and national integration.

Although the spirit of Batllismo eventually faded after his death in 1929, Batlle's legacy is still reflected in many ways. Reports on income distribution reveal an evenness that is uncommon in developing countries. Extreme poverty is unusual in Uruguay, and most of the population enjoy an adequate diet and minimal standards of living. Health care is within the reach of all citizens. And women in Uruguay are granted equality before the law, are present in large numbers at the national university, and have access to professional careers.

But this model state fell on bad times beginning in the 1960s. Runaway inflation, declining agricultural production, a swollen bureaucracy, official corruption, and bleak prospects for the future led to the appearance of youthful middle-class urban guerrillas. Known as Tupamaros, they first attempted to jar the nation to its senses with a Robin Hood–style approach to reform. When that failed, they turned increasingly to violence and terrorism in an effort to destroy a state that resisted reform. The Uruguayan government was unable to quell the rising violence. It eventually called on the military, which crushed the Tupamaros and then drove the civilians from power in 1973.

RETURN TO CIVILIAN RULE

In 1980, the military held a referendum to try to gain approval for a new constitution. Despite extensive propaganda, 60 percent of Uruguay's population rejected the military's proposals and forced the armed forces to move toward a return to civilian government. Elections in 1984 returned the Colorado Party to power, with Julio Maria Sanguinetti as president.

By 1989, Uruguay was again a country of laws, and its citizens were anxious to heal the wounds of the 1970s. A test of the nation's democratic will involved the highly controversial 1986 Law of Expiration, which effectively exempted military and police personnel from prosecution for alleged human-rights abuses committed under orders during the military regime. Many Uruguayans objected and created a pro-referendum commission. They invoked a provision in the Constitution that is unique to Latin America: Article 79 states that, if 25 percent of eligible voters sign a petition, it will initiate a referendum, which, if passed, will implicitly annul the Law of Expiration. Despite official pressure, the signatures were gathered.

The referendum was held on April 16, 1989. It was defeated by a margin of 57 to 43 percent.

The winds of free-market enterprise and privatization are starting to blow through the country. President Luis Alberto Lacalle failed in 1992 to open the economy and sell off state-owned enterprises. About 9 percent of the population were on the state payroll, and they were resistant to reform. As Lacalle stated at the time, "We were brought up in a country where the ethics of security overrode the ethics of change." When Julio Maria Sanguinetti won the presidential election in 1994, he was expected, as the leader of the Colorado Party—the party of Batlle—to maintain the economic status quo. But in 1995, he said that his first priority would be to reform the social-security system, which cannot pay for itself, in large part because people are allowed to retire years earlier than in other countries. Reform has also begun in other sectors of the economy. Government employees have been laid off, tariffs have been reduced, and a program to privatize state industries has been inaugurated. The new policies, according to officials, will produce "a change of mentality and culture" in public administration.

DEVELOPMENT

President Sanguinetti inaugurated his reform program with a series of measures designed to reduce the size of Uruguay's public administration. The key provision would reduce personnel in ministries and government agencies by 40%. The object of the downsizing is to reduce the fiscal deficit.

FREEDOM

Uruguay's military is constitutionally prohibited from involvement in issues of domestic security unless ordered to do so by civilian authorities. The press is free and unrestricted, as is speech. The political process is open, and academic freedom is the norm in the national university.

HEALTH/WELFARE

Uruguay compares favorably with all of Latin America in terms of health and welfare. Medical care is outstanding, and the quality of public sanitation equals or exceeds that of other developing countries. Women, however, still experience discrimination in the workplace.

ACHIEVEMENTS

Uruguay, of all the small countries in Latin America, has been the most successful in creating a distinct culture. High levels of literacy and a large middle class have allowed Uruguay an intellectual climate that is superior to many much-larger nations.

Venezuela (Republic of Venezuela)

GEOGRAPHY
Area in Square Kilometers (Miles): 912,050 (352,143) (about the size of Texas and Oklahoma combined)
Capital (Population): Caracas (4,000,000)
Climate: varies from tropical to temperate

PEOPLE

Population
Total: 21,983,000
Annual Growth Rate: 2.1%
Rural/Urban Population Ratio: 16/84
Ethnic Makeup: 67% Mestizo; 21% white; 10% black; 2% Indian
Major Language: Spanish

Health
Life Expectancy at Birth: 70 years (male); 76 years (female)
Infant Mortality Rate (Ratio): 27/1,000
Average Caloric Intake: 107% of FAO minimum
Physicians Available (Ratio): 1/626

Religions
96% Roman Catholic; 4% Protestant and others

The Kinetic School of Modern Art

Venezuela, perhaps as a reflection of the rapid modernization and industrialization of the country, has produced a large number of artists devoted to the kinetic school. Kinetic art, exemplified by the Venezuelan artist Jesús Soto, is an art of movement and symbolizes modern technology. It grew from the futurist school, which at the turn of the century predicted the coming of the industrial age. Venezuelan kinetic artists play optical games with the viewer. The artist thus forces the viewer to become a participant, to relate to the painting or sculpture.

Education
Adult Literacy Rate: 91%

COMMUNICATION
Telephones: 1,440,000
Newspapers: 25 dailies

TRANSPORTATION
Highways—Kilometers (Miles): 81,000 (50,544)
Railroads—Kilometers (Miles): 542 (336)
Usable Airfields: 431

GOVERNMENT
Type: federal republic
Independence Date: July 5, 1811
Head of State: President Rafael Caldera
Political Parties: Social Christian Party; Democratic Action; Movement Toward Socialism; National Convergence; Radical Cause; others
Suffrage: universal at 18

MILITARY
Number of Armed Forces: 51,000
Military Expenditures (% of Central Government Expenditures): n/a
Current Hostilities: border conflicts with Colombia and Guyana

ECONOMY
Currency ($ U.S. Equivalent): 499 bolívars = $1 (losing value rapidly)
Per Capita Income/GDP: $8,670/$178.3 billion
Inflation Rate: 71%
Total Foreign Debt: $40.1 billion
Natural Resources: petroleum; natural gas; iron ore; gold; hydroelectric power; bauxite
Agriculture: rice; coffee; corn; sugar; bananas; dairy; meat; poultry products
Industry: oil refining; iron-ore mining; petrochemicals; textiles; transport equipment; food processing

FOREIGN TRADE
Exports: $15.2 billion
Imports: $7.6 billion

VENEZUELA: CHANGING TIMES

Venezuela is a country in transition. After decades of rule by a succession of *caudillos* (strong, authoritarian rulers), national leaders can now point to nearly 4 decades of unbroken civilian rule and peaceful transfers of presidential power. Economic growth—stimulated by mining, industry, and petroleum—has, until recently, been steady and, at times, stunning. With the availability of better transportation; access to radio, television, newspapers, and material goods; and the presence of the national government in once-isolated towns, regional diversity is less striking now than a decade ago. Fresh lifestyles and perspectives, dress and music, and literacy and health care are changing the face of rural Venezuela.

THE PROBLEMS OF CHANGE

Such changes have not been without problems—significant ones. Venezuela, despite its petroleum-generated wealth, remains a nation plagued by imbalances, inequalities, contradictions, and often bitter debate over the meaning and direction of national development. Some critics note the danger of the massive rural-to-urban population shift and the influx of illegal immigrants (from Colombia and other countries), both the result of Venezuela's rapid economic development. Others warn of the excessive dependence on petroleum as the means of development and are concerned about the agricultural output at levels insufficient to satisfy domestic requirements. Venezuela, once a food exporter, periodically has had to import large amounts of basic commodities—such as milk, eggs, and meat—to feed the expanding urban populations. Years of easy, abundant money also promoted undisciplined borrowing abroad to promote industrial expansion and has saddled the nation with a serious foreign-debt problem. Government corruption is rampant and, in fact, led to the impeachment of President Carlos Andrés Pérez in 1993.

THE CHARACTER OF MODERNIZATION

The rapid changes in Venezuelan society have produced a host of generalizations as to the nature of modernization in this Andean republic. Commentators who speak of a revolutionary break with the past—of a "new" Venezuela completely severed from its historic roots reaching back to the sixteenth century—ignore what is enduring about Venezuela's Hispanic culture.

Even before it began producing petroleum, Venezuela was not a sleepy backwater. Its Andean region had always been the most prosperous area in the South American continent and was a refuge from the civil wars that swept other parts of the country. There were both opportunity and wealth in the coffee-growing trade. With the oil boom and the collapse of coffee prices in 1929, the Andean region experienced depopulation as migrants left the farms for other regions or for the growing Andean cities. In short, Venezuela's rural economy should not be seen as a static point from which change began but as a part of a dynamic process of continuing change, which now has the production of petroleum as its focus.

CULTURAL IDENTITY

Historian John Lombardi has identified language, culture, and an urban network centered on the capital city of Caracas as primary forces in the consolidation of the nation. "Across the discontinuities of civil war and political transformation, agricultural and industrial economies, rural life styles and urban agglomerations, Venezuela has functioned through the stable network of towns and cities whose interconnections defined the patterns of control, the directions of resource distribution, and the country's identity."

One example of the country's cultural continuity can be seen by looking into one dimension of Venezuelan politics. Political parties are not organized along class lines but tend to cut across class divisions. This is not to deny the existence of class consciousness—which is certainly ubiquitous in Venezuela—but it is not a major *political* force. Surprisingly, popular support for elections and strong party affiliations are more characteristic of rural areas than of

(United Nations photo/H. Null)

When oil was discovered in Venezuela, rapid economic growth caused many problems in national development. By depending on petroleum as the major source of wealth, Venezuela was at the mercy of the often fickle world energy market.

cities. The phenomenon cannot be explained as a by-product of modernization. Party membership and electoral participation are closely linked to party organization, personal ties and loyalties, and charismatic leadership. The party, in a sense, becomes a surrogate *patrón* that has power and is able to deliver benefits to the party faithful.

IMPACTS OF URBANIZATION

Another insight into Hispanic political culture can be found in the rural-to-urban shift in population that has often resulted in large-scale seizures of land in urban areas by peasants. Despite the illegality of the seizures, such actions are frequently encouraged by officials because, they argue, it provides the poor with enough land to maintain political stability and to prevent peasants from encroaching on richer neighborhoods. Pressure by the new urban dwellers at election time usually results in their receiving essential services from government officials. In other words, municipal governments channel resources in return for expected electoral support from the migrants. Here is a classic Hispanic response to challenge from below—to bend, to cooperate.

Cultural values also underlie both the phenomenon of internal migration and the difficulty of providing adequate skilled labor for Venezuela's increasingly technological economy. While the attraction of the city and its many opportunities is one reason for the movement of population out of rural areas, so too is the Venezuelan culture, which belittles the peasant and rural life in general. Similarly, the shortage of skilled labor is the result not only of inadequate training but also of social values that neither reward nor dignify skilled labor.

THE SOCIETY

The rapid pace of change has contributed to a reexamination of the roles and rights of women in Venezuela. In recent years, women have occupied positions in the cabinet and in the Chamber of Deputies; several women deputies have held important posts in political parties.

Yet, while educated women are becoming more prominent in the professions, there is a reluctance to employ women in traditional "men's" jobs, and blatant inequality still blemishes the workplace. Women, for example, are paid less than men for similar work. And, although modern feminist goals have become somewhat of a social and economic force, at least in urban centers, the traditional roles of wife

(United Nations photo)

From the rain forest to the Caribbean, from the Andes to vast inland plains, from peasant villages to large cities, Venezuela is an interesting and diversified country. This photo shows the modern capital city of Caracas, nestled in the northern coastal mountain range.

and mother continue to hold the most prestige, and physical beauty is still often viewed as a woman's most precious asset. In addition, many men seek deference from women rather than embracing social equality. Nevertheless, the younger generations of Venezuelans are experiencing the social and cultural changes that have tended to follow women's liberation in Western industrialized nations: higher levels of education and career skills; broadened intellectualism; increasing freedom and equality for both men and women; relaxed social mores; and the accompanying personal turmoil, such as rising divorce and single-parenthood rates.

Venezuelans generally enjoy a high degree of individual liberty. Civil, personal, and political rights are protected by a strong and independent judiciary. Citizens generally enjoy a free press. There exists the potential for governmental abuse of press freedom, however. Several laws leave journalists vulnerable to criminal charges, especially in the area of libel. Journalists must be certified to work, and certification may be withdrawn by the government if journalists stray from the "truth," misquote sources, or refuse to correct "errors." But, as a rule, radio, television, and newspapers are free and are often highly critical of the government.

The civil and human rights enjoyed by most Venezuelans have not necessarily extended to the nation's Indian population in the Orinoco Basin. For years, extra-regional forces—in the form of rubber gatherers, missionaries, and developers—have, to varying degrees, undermined the economic self-sufficiency, demographic viability, and tribal integrity of indigenous peoples. A government policy that stresses the existence of only one Venezuelan culture poses additional problems for Indians.

In 1991, however, President Pérez signed a decree granting a permanent homeland, encompassing some 32,000 square miles in the Venezuelan Amazon forest, to the country's 14,000 Yanomamö Indians. Venezuela will permit no mining or farming in the territory and will impose controls on existing religious missions. President Pérez stated that "the primary use will be to preserve and to learn the traditional ways of the Indians." As James Brooke reported in *The New York Times,* "Venezuela's move has left anthropologists euphoric."

Race relations are outwardly tranquil in Venezuela, but there exists an underlying racism in nearly all arenas. People are commonly categorized by the color of their skin, with white being the most prized. Indeed, race, not economic level, is still the major social-level determinant.

This unfortunate reality imparts a sense of frustration and a measure of hopelessness to many of Venezuela's people, in that even those who acquire a good education and career training may be discriminated against in the workplace because they are "of color." Considering that only one fifth of the population are of white extraction, with 67 percent Mestizos and 10 percent blacks, this is indeed a widespread and debilitating problem.

A VIGOROUS FOREIGN POLICY
Venezuela has always pursued a vigorous foreign policy. In the words of former president Luis Herrera Campins: "Effective action by Venezuela in the area of international affairs must take certain key facts into account: economics—we are a producer-exporter of oil; politics—we have a stable, consolidated democracy; and geopolitics—we are at one and the same time a Caribbean, Andean, Atlantic, and Amazonian country." Venezuela has long assumed that it should be the guardian of Simón Bolívar's ideal of creating an independent and united Latin America. The nation's memory of its continental leadership, which developed during the Wars for Independence (1810–1826), has been rekindled in Venezuela's desire to promote the political and economic integration of both the continent and the Caribbean. Venezuela's foreign policy remains true to the Bolivarian ideal of an independent Latin America. It also suggests a prominent role for Venezuela in Central America. In the Caribbean, Venezuela has emerged as a source of revenue for the many microstates in the region; the United States is not without competitors for its Caribbean Basin Initiative.

PROMISING PROSPECTS
TURN TO DISILLUSIONMENT
The 1980s brought severe turmoil to Venezuela's economy. The boom times of the 1970s turned to hard times as world oil prices dropped. Venezuela became unable to service its massive foreign debt (currently $40.1 billion) and to subsidize the "common good," in the form of low gas and transportation prices and other amenities. In 1983, the currency, the bolívar, which had remained stable and strong for many years at 4.3 to the U.S. dollar, was devalued, to an official rate of 14.5 bolívars to the dollar. This was a boon to foreign visitors to the country, which became known as one of the world's greatest travel bargains, but a catastrophe for Venezuelans. (In 1998, the exchange rate was about 500 bolívars to the dollar on the free market.)

President Jaime Lusinchi of the Democratic Action Party, who took office early in 1984, had the unenviable job of trying to cope with the results of the preceding years of free spending, high expectations, dependence on oil, and spiraling foreign debt. Although the country's gross national product grew during his tenure (agriculture growth contributed significantly, rising from 0.4 percent of GNP in 1983 to 6.8 percent in 1986), austerity measures were in order. The Lusinchi government was not up to the challenge. Indeed, his major legacy was a corruption scandal at the government agency Recadi, which was responsible for allocating foreign currency to importers at the official rate of 14.5 bolívars to the dollar. It was alleged that billions of dollars were skimmed, with a number of high-level government officials, including three finance ministers, implicated. Meanwhile, the distraught and economically pinched Venezuelans watched inflation and the devalued bolívar eat up their savings; the once-blooming middle class started getting squeezed out.

In the December 1988 national elections, another Democratic Action president, Carlos Andrés Pérez, was elected. Pérez, who had served as president from 1974 to 1979 (presidents may not serve consecutive terms), was widely rumored to have stolen liberally from Venezuela's coffers during that tenure. Venezuelans joked at first that "Carlos Andrés is coming back to get what he left behind," but as the campaign wore on, some political observers were dismayed to hear the preponderance of the naive sentiment that "now he has enough and will really work for Venezuela this time."

One of Pérez's first acts upon re-entering office was to raise the prices of government-subsidized gasoline and public transportation. Although he had warned that tough austerity measures would be implemented, the much-beleaguered and disgruntled urban populace took to the streets in February 1989 in the most serious rioting to have occurred in Venezuela since it became a democracy. Army tanks rolled down the major thoroughfares of Caracas, the capital; skirmishes between the residents and police and military forces were common; looting was widespread. The government announced that 287 people had been killed. Unofficial hospital sources charge that the death toll was closer to 2,000. A stunned Venezuela quickly settled down in the face of the violence, mortified that such a debacle, widely reported in the international press, should take place in this advanced and peaceable country. But tourism, a newly vigorous and promising industry as a re-

The first Spanish settlement at Cumaná **1520**	Venezuela is part of Gran Colombia **1822–1829**	Venezuela achieves independence as a separate country **1829**	The first productive oil well **1922**	Women win the right to vote **1947**	Foreign oil companies are nationalized **1976**	Booming public investment fuels inflation; Venezuela seeks renegotiation of foreign debt **1980s**

1990s

President Carlos Andres Pérez is suspended from office; Rafael Caldera is elected president | Social and economic crisis grips the nation | Presidential elections are scheduled for 1998

sult of favorable currency-exchange rates, subsided immediately; it has yet to recover fully.

On February 4, 1992, another ominous event highlighted Venezuela's continuing political and economic weaknesses. Rebel military paratroopers attacked the presidential palace in Caracas and government sites in several other major cities. The coup attempt, the first in Venezuela since 1962, was rapidly put down by forces loyal to President Pérez, who escaped what he described as an assassination attempt. Reaction within Venezuela was mixed, reflecting widespread discontent with Pérez's tough economic policies, government corruption, and declining living standards. A second unsuccessful coup attempt, on November 27, 1992, followed months of public demonstrations against Pérez's government.

Perhaps the low point was reached in May 1993, when President Pérez was suspended from office and impeachment proceedings initiated. Allegedly the president had embezzled more than $17 million and had facilitated other irregularities. Against a backdrop of military unrest, Ramón José Velásquez was named interim president. (Interestingly, Pérez resurfaced in 1997 with a new political "movement" to solve Venezuela's woes—just in time, perhaps, to make another bid for the presidency in national elections scheduled for 1998. Whether Venezuelan voters would be gullible enough to re-elect him yet again, as they did in 1988, is a topic of lively and humorous debate.)

In December 1993, Venezuelans elected as president Rafael Caldera, who had been president in a more prosperous and promising era (1969–1974). Caldera's presidency too has been fraught with problems. In his first year, he had to confront widespread corruption in official circles, the devaluation of the bolívar, drug trafficking, a banking structure in disarray, and a high rate of violent crime in Caracas. Indeed, in 1997, a relative of President Caldera was mugged and a Spanish diplomat who had traveled to Caracas to negotiate a trade agreement with Venezuela was robbed in broad daylight.

In 1994 and 1995, the collapse of nearly 20 banks forced the government to divert the equivalent of 13 percent of the nation's economic output in 1994 to the banking sector. The problem began in 1989, when the government freed interest rates and deregulated the industry. Without supervision, banks expanded wildly and, when the economy experienced a deep recession in 1993, lacked the assets to survive. A shrinking economy also dried up international sources of credit. Larger government deficits then led the state to print more money to cover the growing debts. As a result, inflation doubled to 71 percent in 1994, a trend that continued in 1995 and 1996. For the first half of 1997, however, the economy showed some signs of recovery with a very modest growth rate of 2.8 percent.

Economic crisis in turn has exacerbated political and social tensions; pressure exists within the military for decisive action. Perhaps to forestall any move by the military, the army has been assigned the task of monitoring the nation's border with Colombia. In 1995, Venezuelan soldiers moved through border areas and rounded up more than 1,000 illegal Colombian aliens, burned some of their homes and crops, and expelled them. At the same time, the government arrested 150 "leftists" across the country and alleged that they were plotting an uprising.

The Venezuelan people have good reason to be anxious about how they will fare in the future. The country is blessed with an extraordinary amount and diversity of geographic beauty and natural resources—including the versatile Venezuelans themselves. Whether or not Venezuela can retain its reputation as a model of democracy in Latin America will depend on the restraint of the military, a future-directed improvement in the economy, politicians willing to enact meaningful change that includes the elimination of corruption, and dedicated efforts to address widespread social problems. Because of its exceptional political, social, and economic history and its potential, the decisions that Venezuela makes in the next few years will be of acute interest not only to Latin America but to the entire world.

DEVELOPMENT

President Caldera moved away from some of the free market reforms of his predecessors. Critics have charged that he is oblivious to the dangers of exchange controls, price controls, and planned economies and that the government is using "discredited economic formulas" to "undo market reforms that are modernizing the rest of the region."

FREEDOM

Venezuela has a free and vigorous daily press, numerous weekly news magazines, 3 nationwide television networks, and nearly 200 radio stations. Censorship or interference with the media on political grounds is rare. Venezuela has traditionally been a haven for refugees and displaced persons. "Justice" in the justice system remains elusive for the poor.

HEALTH/WELFARE

A 1997 survey of children working in the informal sector revealed that 25% were between ages 5 and 12; that they worked more than 7 hours a day and earned about $2; and that their "jobs" included garbage collection, lotteries and gambling, and selling drugs. Fewer than half attended school.

ACHIEVEMENTS

Venezuela's great novelists, such as Rómulo Gallegos and Artúro Uslar Pietri, have been attracted by the barbarism of the backlands and the lawlessness native to rural regions. Gallegos's classic *Doña Barbara*, the story of a female regional chieftain, has become world-famous.

The Caribbean

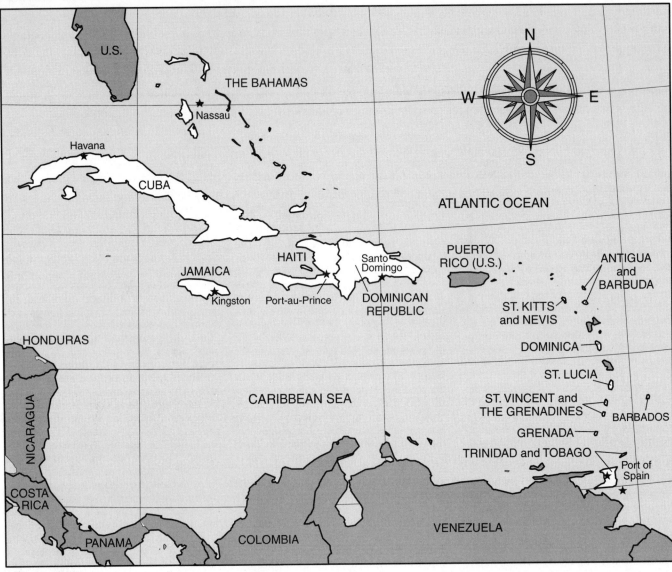

★ Capital cities

The Caribbean region consists of hundreds of islands stretching from northern South America to the southern part of Florida. Many of the islands cover just a few square miles and are dominated by a central range of mountains; only Cuba has any extensive lowlands. Almost every island has a ring of coral, making approaches very dangerous for ships. The land that can be used for agriculture is extremely fertile; but many islands grow only a single crop, making them vulnerable to fluctuations in the world market in that particular commodity.

The Caribbean: Sea of Diversity

To construct a coherent overview of the Caribbean is an extremely difficult task because of the region's profound geographical and cultural diversity. "The history of the Caribbean is the examination of fragments, which, like looking at a broken vase, still provides clues to the form, beauty, and value of the past." So writes historian Franklin W. Knight in his study of the Caribbean. Other authors have drawn different analogies: geographer David Lowenthal and anthropologist Lambros Comitas note that the West Indies "is a set of mirrors in which the lives of black, brown, and white, of American Indian and East Indian, and a score of other minorities continually interact."

For the geographer, the pieces fall into a different pattern, consisting of four distinct geographical regions. The first contains the Bahamas as well as the Turks and Caicos Islands. The Greater Antilles—consisting of Cuba, Hispaniola (Haiti and the Dominican Republic), Jamaica, the Cayman Islands, Puerto Rico, and the Virgin Islands—make up the second region. Comprising the third region are the Lesser Antilles—Antigua and Barbuda, Dominica, St. Lucia, St. Vincent and the Grenadines, Grenada, and St. Kitts and Nevis as well as various French departments and British and Dutch territories.

The fourth group consists of islands that are part of the South American continental shelf: Trinidad and Tobago, Barbados, and the Dutch islands of Aruba, Curaçao, and Bonaire. Within these broad geographical regions, each nation is different. On each island there often is a firmly rooted parochialism—a devotion to a parish or a village, a mountain valley or a coastal lowland.

CULTURAL DIVERSITY

To break down the Caribbean region into culture groups presents its own set of problems. The term "West Indian" inadequately describes the culturally Hispanic nations of Cuba and the Dominican Republic. On the other hand, "West Indian" does capture the essence of the cultures of Belize, the Caribbean coast of Central America, and Guyana, Suriname, and Cayenne (French Guiana). In Lowenthal's view: "Alike in not being Iberian [Hispanic], the West Indies are not North American either, nor indeed do they fit any ordinary regional pattern. Not so much undeveloped as overdeveloped, exotic without being traditional, they are part of the Third World yet ardent emulators of the West."

(United Nations photo/King)

These Jamaican agricultural workers, who reflect the strong African heritage of the Caribbean, contribute to the ethnic and cultural diversity of the region.

EFFORTS AT INTEGRATION

To complicate matters further, few West Indians would identify themselves as such. They are Jamaicans, or Bajans (people from Barbados), or Grenadans. Their economic, political, and social worlds are usually confined to the islands on which they live and work. In the eyes of its inhabitants, each island, no matter how small, is—or should be—sovereign.

Communications by air, sea, and telephone with the rest of the world are ordinarily better than communications within the Caribbean region itself. Trade, even between neighboring islands, has always been minimal. Economic ties with the United States or Europe, and in some cases with Venezuela, are more important.

A British attempt to create a "West Indies Federation" in 1958 was reduced to a shambles by 1962. Member states had the same historical background; spoke the same languages; had similar economies; and were interested in the same kinds of food, music, and sports. But their spirit of independence triumphed over any kind of regional federation that "threatened" their individuality. In the words of a former Bajan prime minister, "We live together very well, but we don't like to live together *together*." A Trinidadian explanation for the failure of the federation is found in a popular calypso verse from the early 1960s:

Plans was moving fine
When Jamaica stab we from behind
Federation bust wide open
But they want Trinidad to bear the burden.

Recently, however, the Windward Islands (Dominica, Grenada, St. Lucia, and St. Vincent and the Grenadines) have discussed political union. While each jealously guards its sovereignty, leaders are nevertheless aware that some integration is necessary if they are to survive in a changing world. The division of the world into giant economic blocs points to political union and the creation of a Caribbean state with a combined population of nearly half a million. Antigua and Barbuda resist because, in the words of former prime minister Vere Bird, "political union would be a new form of colonialism and undermine sovereignty."

While political union remains problematic, the 15 members of the Caribbean Community and Common Market (CARICOM, a regional body created in 1973) began long-term negotiations with Cuba in 1995 with regard to a free-trade agreement. CARICOM leaders informed Cuba that "it needs to open up its economy more." The free-market economies of CARICOM are profoundly different from Cuba's rigid state controls. "We need to assure that trade and investment will be mutually beneficial." Caribbean leaders have pursued trade with Cuba in the face of strong opposition from the United States. In general, CARICOM countries are convinced that "constructive engagement" rather than a policy of isolation is the best way to transform Cuba.

Political problems also plague the Dutch Caribbean. Caribbean specialist Aaron Segal notes that the six-island Netherlands Antilles Federation has encountered severe internal difficulties. Aruba never had a good relationship with the larger island of Curaçao and, in 1986, became a self-governing entity, with its own flag, Parliament, and currency, within the Netherlands. "The other Netherlands Antillean states have few complaints about their largely autonomous relations with the Netherlands but find it hard to get along with one another."

Interestingly, islands that are still colonial possessions generally have a better relationship with their "mother" countries than with one another. Over the past few decades, smaller islands, with populations of less than 50,000, have learned that there are advantages to a continued colonial connection. The extensive subsidies paid by Great Britain, France, or the Netherlands have turned dependency into an asset. Tax-free offshore sites for banks and companies as well as tourism and hotel investments have led to modest economic growth.

CULTURAL IDENTIFICATION

Yet, despite the local focus of the islanders, there do exist some broad cultural similarities. To the horror of nationalists, who are in search of a Caribbean identity that is distinct from Western civilization, most West Indians identify themselves as English or French in terms of culture. Bajans, for example, take a special pride in identifying their country as the "Little England of the Caribbean." English or French dialects are the languages spoken in common.

Nationalists argue that the islands will not be wholly free until they shatter the European connection. In the nationalists' eyes, that connection is a bitter reminder of slavery. After World War II, several Caribbean intellectuals attacked the strong European orientation of the islands and urged the islanders to be proud of their black African heritage. The shift in focus was most noticeable in the French Caribbean, although this new ethnic consciousness was echoed in the English-speaking islands as well in the form of a black-power movement during the 1960s and 1970s. It was during those years, when the islands were in transition from colonies to associated states to independent nations, that the Caribbean's black majorities seized political power by utilizing the power of their votes.

It is interesting to note that, at the height of the black-power and black-awareness movements, sugar production was actually halted on the islands of St. Vincent, Antigua, and Barbuda—not because world market prices were low, but because sugar cultivation was associated with the slavery of the past.

African Influences

The peoples of the West Indies are predominantly black, with lesser numbers of "mixed bloods" and small numbers of whites. Culturally, the blacks fall into a number of groups. In

Haiti, blacks, throughout the nineteenth century, strove to realize an African-Caribbean identity. African influences have remained strong on the island, although they have been blended with European Christianity and French civilization. Mulattos, traditionally the elite in Haiti, have strongly identified with French culture in an obvious attempt to distance themselves from the black majority, who comprise about 95 percent of the population. African-Creoles, as blacks of the English-speaking islands prefer to be called, are manifestly less "African" than the mass of Haitians. An exception to this generalization is the Rastafarians, common in Jamaica and found in lesser numbers on some of the other islands. Convinced that they are Ethiopians, the Rastafarians hope to return to Africa.

Racial Tension

The Caribbean has for years presented an image of racial harmony to the outside world. Yet, in actuality, racial tensions are not only present but also have tended to become sharper during the past few decades. Racial unrest broke to the surface in Jamaica in 1960 with riots in the capital city of Kingston. Tensions heightened again in 1980–1981 and in 1984, to the point that the nation's tourist industry drastically declined. The recent slogan of the Jamaican tourist industry, "Make It Jamaica Again," was a conscious attempt to downplay racial antagonism. The black-power movement in the 1960s on most of the islands also put to the test notions of racial harmony.

Most people of the Caribbean, however, believe in the myth of racial harmony. It is essential to the development of nationalism, which must embrace all citizens. Much racial tension is officially explained as class difference rather than racial prejudice. There is some merit to the class argument. A black politician on Barbuda, for example, enjoys much more status and prestige than a poor white "Redleg" from the island's interior. Yet if a black and a Redleg competed for the job of plantation manager, the white would likely win out over the black. In sum, race does make a difference, but so too does one's economic or political status.

East Indians

The race issue is more complex in Trinidad and Tobago, where there is a large East Indian (i.e., originally from India) minority. The East Indians, for the most part, are agricultural workers. They were originally introduced by the British between 1845 and 1916 to replace slave labor on the plantations. While numbers of East Indians have moved to the cities, they still feel that they have little in common with urban blacks. Because of their large numbers, East Indians are able to preserve a distinctive, healthy culture and community and to compete with other groups for political office and status.

East Indian culture has also adapted, but not yielded, to the West Indian world. In the words of Trinidadian-East Indian author V. S. Naipaul: "We were steadily adopting the food

(United Nations photo/Milton Grant)

The African influence on the population of the Caribbean is substantial; a large majority of African descendants are represented on just about every island.

styles of others: The Portuguese stew of tomato and onions . . . the Negro way with yams, plantains, breadfruit, and bananas," but "everything we adopted became our own; the outside was still to be dreaded. . . ." The East Indians in Jamaica, who make up about 3 percent of the population, have made even more accommodations to the cultures around them. Most Jamaican-East Indians have become Protestant (the East Indians of Trinidad have maintained their Hindu or Islamic faith).

East Indian conformity and internalization, and their strong cultural identification, have often made them the targets of the black majority. Black stereotypes of the East Indians describe them in the following terms: "secretive," "greedy," and "stingy." And East Indian stereotypes describing blacks as "childish," "vain," "pompous," and "promiscuous" certainly do not help to ease ethnic tensions.

REVOLUTIONARY CUBA

In terms of culture, the Commonwealth Caribbean (former British possessions) has little in common with Cuba or the Dominican Republic. But Cuba has made its presence felt in other ways. The Cuban Revolution, with the social progress

Certain crops in Caribbean countries generate a disproportionate amount of the nations' foreign incomes—so much so that their entire economies are vulnerable to changes in world demand. This harvest of bananas in Dominica is ready for shipment to a fickle world market.

that it entailed for many of its people and the strong sense of nationalism that it stimulated, impressed many West Indians. For new nation-states still in search of an identity, Cuba offered some clues as to how to proceed. For a time, Jamaica experimented with Cuban models of mass mobilization and programs designed to bring social services to the majority of the population. Between 1979 and 1983, Grenada saw merit in the Cuban approach to problems. The message that Cuba seemed to represent was that a small Caribbean state could shape its own destiny and make life better for its people.

The Cuba of Fidel Castro, while revolutionary, is also traditional. Hispanic culture is largely intact. The politics are authoritarian and personality-driven, and Castro himself easily fits into the mold of the Latin American leader, or *caudillo,* whose charisma and benevolent paternalism win him the widespread support of his people. Castro's relationship with the Roman Catholic Church is also traditional and corresponds to notions of a dualistic culture that has its roots in the Middle Ages. In Castro's words: "The same respect that the Revolution ought to have for religious beliefs, ought also to be had by those who talk in the name of religion for the political beliefs of others. And, above all, to have present that

which Christ said: 'My kingdom is not of this world.' What are those who are said to be the interpreters of Christian thought doing meddling in the problems of this world?" Castro's comments should not be interpreted as a Communist assault on religion. Rather, they express a time-honored Hispanic belief that religious life and everyday life exist in two separate spheres.

The social reforms that have been implemented in Cuba are well within the powers of all Latin American governments to enact. Those governments, in theory, are duty-bound to provide for the welfare of their peoples. Constitutionally, the state is infallible and all-powerful. Castro has chosen to identify with the needs of the majority of Cubans, to be a "father" to his people. Again, his actions are not so much Communistic as Hispanic.

Where Castro has run against the grain is in his assault on Cuba's middle class. In a sense, he has reversed a trend that is evident in much of the rest of Latin America—the slow, steady progress of a middle class that is intent on acquiring a share of the power and prestige traditionally accorded to elites. Cuba's middle class was effectively shattered—people were deprived of much of their property; their livelihood;

and, for those who fled into exile, their citizenship. Expatriate Cubans remain bitter toward what they perceive as Castro's betrayal of the Revolution and the middle class.

EMIGRATION AND MIGRATION

Throughout the Caribbean, emigration and migration are a fact of life for hundreds of thousands of people. These are not new phenomena; their roots extend to the earliest days of European settlement. The flow of people looking for work is deeply rooted in history, in contemporary political economy, and even in Caribbean island culture. The Garifuna (black–Indian mixture) who settled in Belize and coastal parts of Mexico, Guatemala, Honduras, and Nicaragua originally came from St. Vincent. There, as escaped slaves, they intermixed with remnants of Indian tribes who had once peopled the islands, and they adopted many of their cultural traits. Most of the Garifuna (or Black Caribs, as they are also known) were deported from St. Vincent to the Caribbean coast of Central America at the end of the eighteenth century.

From the 1880s onward, patois-speaking (French dialect) Dominicans and St. Lucians migrated to Cayenne (French Guiana) to work in the gold fields. The strong identification with Europe has drawn thousands more to what many consider their cultural homes.

High birth rates and lack of economic opportunity have forced others to seek their fortunes elsewhere. Many citizens of the Dominican Republic have moved to New York, and Haitian refugees have thrown themselves on the coast of Florida by the thousands. Other Haitians seek seasonal employment in the Dominican Republic or the Bahamas. There are sizable Jamaican communities in the Dominican Republic, Haiti, the Bahamas, and Belize.

On the smaller islands, stable populations are the exception rather than the rule. The people are constantly migrating to larger places in search of higher pay and a better life. Such emigrants moved to Panama when the canal was being cut in the early days of this century or sought work on the Dutch islands of Curaçao and Aruba when oil refineries were built there in the 1920s. They provided much of the labor for the banana plantations in Central America.

The greatest number of people by far have left the Caribbean region altogether and emigrated to the United States, Canada, and Europe. Added to those who have left because of economic or population pressures are political refugees. The majority of these are Cubans, most of whom have resettled in Florida.

Some have argued that the prime mover of migration from the Caribbean lies in the ideology of migration—that is, the expectation that all non-elite males will migrate abroad. Sugarcane slave plantations left a legacy that included little possibility of island subsistence; and so there grew the need to migrate to survive, a fact that was absorbed into the culture of lower-class blacks. But, for these blacks, there has also existed the expectation to return. (In contrast, middle- and upper-class migrants have historically departed permanently.) Historian Bonham Richardson writes: "By traveling away and returning the people have been able to cope more successfully with the vagaries of man and nature than they would have by staying at home. The small islands of the region are the most vulnerable to environmental and eco-

(United Nations photo/J. Viesti)

Economic hardship in the Caribbean region is exemplified by this settlement in Port-au-Prince, Haiti. Such grinding poverty causes large numbers of people to migrate in search of a better life.

nomic uncertainty. Time and again in the Lesser Antilles, droughts, hurricanes, and economic depressions have diminished wages, desiccated provision grounds, and destroyed livestock, and there has been no local recourse to disease or starvation." Hence men and women of the small West Indian islands have been obliged to migrate. "And like migrants everywhere, they have usually considered their travels temporary, partly because they have never been greeted cordially in host communities."

On the smaller islands, such as St. Kitts and Nevis, family and community ceremonies traditionally reinforce and sustain the importance of immigration and return. Funerals reunite families separated by vast distances; Christmas parties and carnival celebrations are also occasions to welcome returning family and friends.

Monetary remittances from relatives in the United States, or Canada, or the larger islands are a constant reminder of the importance of migration. According to Richardson: "Old men who have earned local prestige by migrating and returning exhort younger men to follow in their footsteps. . . . Learned cultural responses thereby maintain a migration ethos . . . that is not only valuable in coping with contemporary problems, but also provides continuity with the past."

The Haitian diaspora (dispersion) offers some significant differences. While Haitian migration is also a part of the nation's history, a return flow is noticeably absent. One of every six Haitians now lives abroad—primarily in Cuba, the Dominican Republic, Venezuela, Colombia, Mexico, and the Bahamas. In French Guiana, Haitians comprise more than 25 percent of the population. They are also found in large numbers in urban areas of the United States, Canada, and France. The typical Haitian emigrant is poor, has little education, and has few skills or job qualifications.

Scholar Christian A. Girault remarks that, although "ordinary Haitian migrants are clearly less educated than the Cubans, Dominicans, Puerto Ricans and even Jamaicans, they are not Haiti's most miserable; the latter could never hope to buy an air ticket or boat passage, or to pay an agent." Those who establish new roots in host countries tend to remain, even though they experience severe discrimination and are stereotyped as "undesirable" because they are perceived as bringing with them "misery, magic and disease," particularly AIDS.

There is also some seasonal movement of population on the island itself. Agricultural workers by the tens of thousands are found in neighboring Dominican Republic. *Madames sara,* or peddlers, buy and sell consumer goods abroad and provide "an essential provisioning function for the national market."

AN ENVIRONMENT IN DANGER
When one speaks of soil erosion and deforestation in a Caribbean context, Haiti is the example that usually springs to mind. While that image is accurate, it is also too limiting, for much of the Caribbean is threatened with ecological disaster. Part of the problem is historical, for deforestation began with the development of sugarcane cultivation in the seventeenth century. But now, soil erosion and depletion as well as the exploitation of marginal lands by growing populations perpetuate a vicious cycle between inhabitants and the land on which they live. Cultivation of sloping hillsides creates a situation in which erosion is constant.

A 1959 report on soil conditions in Jamaica noted that, in one district of the Blue Mountains, on the eastern end of that island, the topsoil had vanished, a victim of rapid erosion. The problem is not unique to the large islands, however. Bonham Richardson observes that ecological degradation on the smallest islands is acute. Thorn scrub and grasses have replaced native forest. "A regional drought in 1977, leading to starvation in Haiti and producing crop and livestock loss south to Trinidad, was severe only partly because of the lack of rain. Grasses and shrubs afford little protection against the sun and thus cannot help the soil to retain moisture in the face of periodic drought. Neither do they inhibit soil loss."

Migration of the islands' inhabitants has at times exacerbated the situation. In times of peak migration, a depleted labor force on some of the islands has resulted in landowners resorting to the raising of livestock, which is not labor-intensive. But livestock contribute to further ecological destruction. "Emigration itself has thus indirectly fed the ongoing devastation of island environments, and some of the changes seem irreversible. Parts of the smaller islands already resemble moonscapes. They seem simply unable to sustain their local resident populations, not to mention future generations or those working abroad who may someday be forced to return for good."

MUSIC, DANCE, FOLKLORE, AND FOOD
Travel accounts of the Caribbean tend to focus on local music, dances, and foods. Calypso, the limbo, steel bands, reggae, and African–Cuban rhythms are well known. Much of the music derives from Amerindian and African roots.

Calypso music apparently originated in Trinidad and spread to the other islands. Calypso singers improvise on any theme; they are particularly adept at poking fun at politicians and their shortcomings. Indeed, governments are as attentive to the lyrics of a politically inspired calypso tune as they are to the opposition press. On a broader scale, calypso is a mirror of Caribbean society.

Some traditional folkways, such as storytelling and other forms of oral history, are in danger of being replaced by electronic media, particularly radio, tape recorders, and jukeboxes. The new entertainment is both popular and readily available.

Scholar Laura Tanna has gathered much of Kingston, Jamaica's, oral history. Her quest for storyteller Adina Henry took her to one of the city's worst slums, the Dungle, and was reprinted in *Caribbean Review:* "We walked down the tracks to a Jewish cemetery, with gravestones dating back to the 1600s. It, too, was covered in litter, decaying amid the rubble

These peaks in St. Lucia are volcanic in origin.

(Photo Lisa Clyde)

of broken stones. Four of the tombs bear the emblem of the skull and crossbones. Popular belief has it that Spanish gold is buried in the tombs, and several of them have been desecrated by treasure seekers. We passed the East Indian shacks, and completed our tour of Majesty Pen amidst greetings of 'Love' and 'Peace' and with the fragrance of ganja [marijuana] wafting across the way. Everywhere, people were warm and friendly, shaking hands, chatting, drinking beer, or playing dominos. One of the shacks had a small bar and jukebox inside. There, in the midst of pigs grunting at one's feet in the mud and slime, in the dirt and dust, people had their own jukeboxes, tape recorders, and radios, all blaring out reggae, the voice of the ghetto." Tanna found Miss Adina, whose stories revealed the significant African contribution to West Indian folk culture.

In recent years, Caribbean foods have become more accepted, and even celebrated, within the region as well as internationally. Part of the search for an identity involves a new attention to traditional recipes. French, Spanish, and English recipes have been adapted to local foods—iguana, frogs, seafood, fruits, and vegetables. Cassava, guava, and mangos figure prominently in the islanders' diets.

The diversity of the Caribbean is awesome, with its potpourri of peoples and cultures. Its roots lie in Spain, Portugal, England, France, the Netherlands, Africa, India, China, and Japan. There has emerged no distinct West Indian culture, and the Caribbean peoples' identities are determined by the island—no matter how small—on which they live. For the Commonwealth Caribbean, nationalist stirrings are still weak and lacking in focus; while people in Cuba and the Dominican Republic have a much surer grasp on who they are. Nationalism is a strong integrating force in both of these nations. The Caribbean is a fascinating corner of the world that is far more complex than the travel posters imply.

Antigua and Barbuda

GEOGRAPHY
Area in Square Kilometers (Miles): 442
(171) (about 2½ times the size of
Washington, D.C.)
Capital (Population): Saint John's
(21,500)
Climate: tropical

PEOPLE

Population
Total: 65,600
Annual Growth Rate: 0.7%
Rural/Urban Population Ratio: 69/31
Ethnic Makeup: almost entirely black
African origin; some of British,
Portuguese, Lebanese, or Syrian origin
Major Languages: English; Creole

Health
Life Expectancy at Birth: 71 years
(male); 76 years (female)
Infant Mortality Rate (Ratio): 18/1,000
Average Caloric Intake: 90% of FAO
minimum
Physicians Available (Ratio): 1/2,187

Religions
predominantly Anglican; other
Protestant sects; some Roman Catholic

Education
Adult Literacy Rate: 89%

COMMUNICATION
Telephones: 6,700
Newspapers: n/a

TRANSPORTATION
Highways—Kilometers (Miles): 240
(150)
Railroads—Kilometers (Miles): 77 (48)
Usable Airfields: 3

English Harbour

Antigua's English Harbour was the key to British naval power in the
Caribbean—it was the stop-off point where warships were refitted in order
to avoid having to go to England. By the end of the eighteenth century, English
Harbour was at its zenith, and its dockyard could handle almost any need of
the British warships. There were more than 1,000 troops in the shore guard,
and the harbor was a crowded and lively place, with constant parties and
pageants. The importance of English Harbour gave the small, arid island of
Antigua a lasting role in the history of the Caribbean.

GOVERNMENT
Type: parliamentary democracy;
recognizes Queen Elizabeth II as chief
of state
Independence Date: November 1, 1981
Head of State: Prime Minister Lester
Bryant Bird
Political Parties: Antigua Labour Party;
United Progressive Party
Suffrage: universal at 18

MILITARY
Number of Armed Forces: 700 in
defense force
*Military Expenditures (% of Central
Government Expenditures):* 1%
Current Hostilities: none

ECONOMY
Currency ($ U.S. Equivalent): 2.7 East
Caribbean dollars = $1 (fixed rate)
Per Capita Income/GDP: $6,600/$424
million
Inflation Rate: 7%
Total Foreign Debt: $250 million
Natural Resources: seafood
Agriculture: cotton
Industry: tourism; cotton production

FOREIGN TRADE
Exports: $54.7 million
Imports: $260.9 million

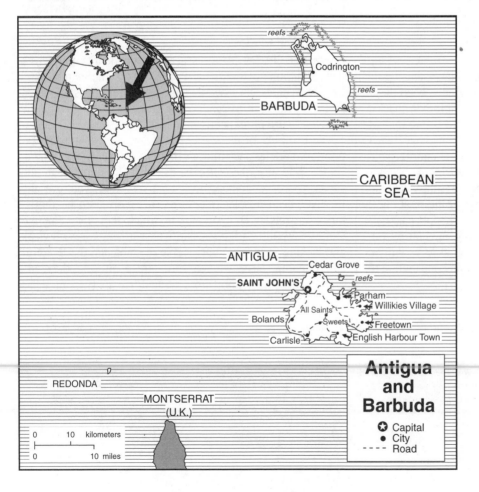

The English settle Antigua **1632**	Antigua abolishes slavery **1834**	Antigua becomes part of the West Indies Federation **1958–1962**	Independence of Great Britain **1981**

1990s

Barbuda talks of secession

The Bird dynasty wins elections to remain in power

Hurricane Luís devastates the islands

ANTIGUA AND BARBUDA: A STRAINED RELATIONSHIP

The nation of Antigua and Barbuda gained its independence of Great Britain on November 1, 1981. Both islands, tenuously linked since 1967, illustrate perfectly the degree of localism characteristic of the West Indies. Barbudans—who number approximately 1,200—culturally and politically believe that they are not Antiguans; indeed, since independence of Britain, they have been intent on secession. Barbudans view Antiguans as little more than colonial masters.

MEMORIES OF SLAVERY

Antigua was a sugar island for most of its history. This image changed radically in the 1960s, when the black-power movement then sweeping the Caribbean convinced Antiguans that work on the sugar plantations was "submissive" and carried the psychological and social stigma of historic slave labor. In response to the clamor, the government gradually phased out sugar production, which ended entirely in 1972. The decline of agriculture resulted in a strong rural-to-urban flow of people. To replace lost revenue from the earnings of sugar, the government promoted tourism.

Tourism produced the unexpected result of greater freedom for women, in that they gained access to previously unavailable employment opportunities. Anthropologist W. Penn Handwerker has shown that a combination of jobs and education for women has resulted in a marked decline in fertility. Between 1965 and the 1980s, real wages doubled, infant mortality fell

dramatically, and the proportion of women ages 20 to 24 who completed secondary school rose from 3 percent to about 50 percent. "Women were freed from dependency on their children" as well as their men and created "conditions for a revolution in gender relations." Men out-migrated as the economy shifted, and women took the new jobs in tourism. Many of the jobs demanded higher skills, which in turn resulted in more education for women, followed by even better jobs. And notes Handwerker: "Women empowered by education and good jobs are less likely to suffer abuse from partners."

CULTURAL PATTERNS

Antiguans and Barbudans are culturally similar. Many islanders still have a strong affinity for England and English culture, while others identify more with what they hold to be their African–Creole roots. On Antigua, for example, Creole, which is spoken by virtually the entire population, is believed to reflect what is genuine and "natural" about the island and its culture. Standard English, even though it is the official language, carries an aura of falseness in the popular mind.

FOREIGN RELATIONS

Despite the small size of the country, Antigua and Barbuda are actively courted by regional powers. The United States maintains a satellite-tracking station on Antigua, and Brazil has provided loans and other assistance. A small oil refinery, jointly supported by Venezuela and Mexico, began operations in 1982.

FAMILY POLITICS

Since 1951, with only one interruption, Antiguan politics has been dominated by the family of Vere Bird and his Antigua Labour Party (ALP). Charges of nepotism, corruption, drug smuggling, and money laundering dogged the Vere Bird administration for years. Still, in 1994, Lester Bird managed to succeed his 84-year-old father, and the ALP won 11 of 17 seats in elections. Lester admitted that his father had been guilty of some "misjudgments" and quickly pledged that the ALP would improve education, better the status of women, and increase the presence of young people in government.

The younger Bird, in his State of the Nation address early in 1995, challenged Antiguans to transform their country on their own terms, rather than those dictated by the International Monetary Fund. His government would take "tough and unpopular" measures to avoid the humiliation of going "cap in hand" to foreign financial institutions. Those tough measures have included increases in contributions for medical benefits, property and personal taxes, and business and motorvehicle licenses. Because Bird and the ALP control patronage and access to government jobs, it is unlikely that the opposition will be able to take advantage of such policies.

DEVELOPMENT

New government policies were announced late in 1994 to enhance revenue collection, curtail public spending, provide tax and duty concessions to attract foreign investment, and reform the public sector. Prime Minister Lester Bird called on international lending agencies to write off 50% of the external debt of Caribbean countries.

FREEDOM

Pervasive government control of the electronic media has resulted in virtually no access for opposition parties or persons representing opinions divergent from or critical of those held by the government. Various governments have used the media in deliberate campaigns of disinformation.

HEALTH/WELFARE

The government has initiated programs to enhance educational opportunities for men and women and to assist in family planning. The new Directorate of Women's Affairs helps women to advance in government and in the professions. It has also sponsored educational programs for women in health, crafts, and business skills.

ACHIEVEMENTS

Antigua has preserved its rich historical heritage, from the dockyard named for Admiral Lord Nelson to the Ebenezer Methodist Church. Built in 1839, the latter was the "mother church" for Methodism in the Caribbean.

The Bahamas (Commonwealth of the Bahamas)

GEOGRAPHY
Area in Square Kilometers (Miles): 13,934 (5,380) (about the size of Connecticut)
Capital (Population): Nassau (172,000)
Climate: tropical

PEOPLE

Population
Total: 259,400
Annual Growth Rate: 1.1%
Rural/Urban Population Ratio: 16/84
Ethnic Makeup: 85% black; 15% white
Major Language: English

Health
Life Expectancy at Birth: 67 years (male); 77 years (female)
Infant Mortality Rate (Ratio): 24/1,000
Average Caloric Intake: 98% of FAO minimum
Physicians Available (Ratio): 1/1,218

Religions
32% Baptist; 22% Protestant; 20% Anglican; 19% Roman Catholic; 7% unaffiliated or unknown

Education
Adult Literacy Rate: 90%

The Bahamas: A Strategic Location

The name "Bahamas" comes from the Spanish *bajamar* ("shallow sea"). This island group, independent since 1973, consists of nearly 700 islands and cays (small islands) as well as almost 2,400 low, barren rock formations. Only about 22 of the islands are occupied on this archipelago.

The Bahamas are strategically located in the Atlantic just off the coast of Florida and southward along the Cuban coast. Because they bridge the entrance to the Caribbean, the Bahamas have had a tumultuous history. Explorers (Christopher Columbus is believed to have landed on one island on October 12, 1492), pirates, and slavers have all had an impact on the islands' cultures.

COMMUNICATION
Telephones: 99,000
Newspapers: 2 dailies

TRANSPORTATION
Highways—Kilometers (Miles): 2,400 (1,480)
Railroads—Kilometers (Miles): none
Usable Airfields: 60

GOVERNMENT
Type: independent state; recognizes Queen Elizabeth II as chief of state
Independence Date: July 10, 1973
Head of Government: Prime Minister Hubert A. Ingraham
Political Parties: Free National Movement; Progressive Liberal Party
Suffrage: universal at 18

MILITARY
Number of Armed Forces: no defense force as such; Royal Bahamas Police Force organized along paramilitary lines; the United Kingdom is responsible for external defense
Military Expenditures (% of Central Government Expenditures): 2.7%
Current Hostilities: none

ECONOMY
Currency ($ U.S. Equivalent): 1 Bahamian dollar = $1 (fixed rate)
Per Capita Income/GDP: $15,900/$4.4 billion
Inflation Rate: 2.7%
Total Foreign Debt: $455 million
Natural Resources: salt; aragonite; timber
Agriculture: vegetables; fish
Industry: tourism; fishing; petroleum; pharmaceuticals; banking; rum

FOREIGN TRADE
Exports: $257 million
Imports: $1.2 billion

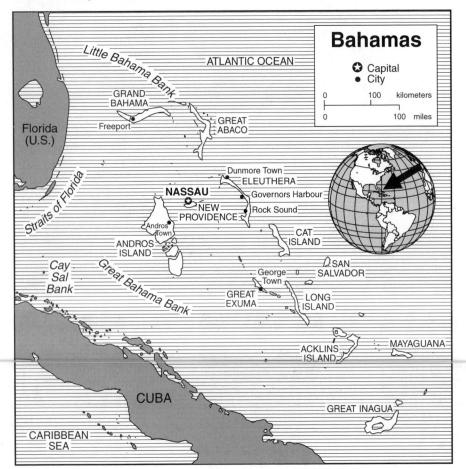

Christopher Columbus first sights the New World at San Salvador Island **1492**	The first English settlement in the Bahamas **1647**	Black-power controversy **1967**	Independence of Great Britain **1973**	Violent crime, drug trafficking, and narcotics addiction become serious social problems **1980s**

1990s

Haitian immigrants become the focus of official hostility	Hubert Ingraham, leader of the Free National Movement, wins a second term as prime minister	New investments create jobs and cut the unemployment rate

BAHAMAS:
A NATION OF ISLANDS

Christopher Columbus made his first landfall in the Bahamas in 1492, when he touched ashore on the island of San Salvador. Permanent settlements on the islands were not established by the British until 1647, when the Eleutheran Adventurers, a group of English and Bermudan religious dissidents, landed. The island was privately governed until 1717, when it became a British Crown colony. During the U.S. Civil War, Confederate blockade runners used the Bahamas as a base. The tradition continued in the years after World War I, when Prohibition rum runners used the islands as a base. Today drug traffickers utilize the isolation of the out-islands for their illicit operations.

Although the Bahamas are made up of almost 700 islands, only 10 have populations of any significant size. Of these, New Providence and Grand Bahama contain more than 75 percent of the Bahamian population. Because most economic and cultural activities take place on the larger islands, other islands—particularly those in the southern region—have suffered depopulation over the years as young men and women have moved to the two major centers of activity.

Migrants from Haiti and Jamaica have also caused problems for the Bahamian government. There are an estimated 50,000 illegal Haitians now resident in the Bahamas—equivalent to more than one fifth of the total Bahamian population of 259,400. The Bahamian response was tolerance until late 1994, when the government established tough new policies that reflected a fear that the country would be "overwhelmed" by Haitian immigrants. In the words of one official, the large numbers of Haitians would "result in a very fundamental economic and social transformation that even the very naïve would understand to be undesirable." Imprisonment, marginalization, no legal right to work, and even the denial of access to schools and hospitals are now endured by the immigrants, who have begun to abandon the Bahamas in large numbers.

Bahamian problems with Jamaicans are rooted differently. The jealous isolation of each of the new nations is reflected in the peoples' fears and suspicions of the activities of their neighbors. As a result, inter-island freedom of movement is subject to strict scrutiny.

The Bahamas were granted their independence of Great Britain in 1973 and established a constitutional parliamentary democracy governed by a freely elected prime minister and Parliament. Upon independence, there was a transfer of political power from a small white elite to the black majority, who comprise 85 percent of the population. Whites continue to play a role in the political process, however, and several hold high-level civil service and political posts.

The country has enjoyed a marked improvement in health conditions over the past few decades. Life expectancy has risen, and infant mortality has declined. Virtually all people living in urban areas have access to good drinking water, although the age and dilapidated condition of the capital's (Nassau) water system could present problems in the near future.

The government has begun a program to restructure education on the islands. The authorities have placed a new emphasis on technical and vocational training so that skilled jobs in the economy now held by foreigners will be performed by Bahamians. While the literacy rate has remained high, there remains a shortage of teachers, equipment, and supplies.

The government of Prime Minister Hubert A. Ingraham and his Free National Movement won a clear mandate in 1997 over the opposition Progressive Liberal Party to continue the policies and programs it initiated in 1992. *The Miami Herald* reported that the election "marked a watershed in Bahamian politics, with many new faces on the ballot and both parties facing leadership succession struggles before the next vote is due in 2002." Ideologically, the two contending political parties were similar; thus voters made their decisions on the basis of who they felt would provide jobs and bring crime under control. Honest government and a history of working effectively with the private sector to improve the national economy have dramatically increased foreign investment in the Bahamas and strengthened Ingraham's position.

Despite new investments, unemployment is still a problem, and many young Bahamians out-migrate. The thousands of illegal Haitian immigrants have added pressure to the job market and worry some Bahamians that their own sense of identity may be threatened. But, in general, there is a new sense of optimism in the islands.

DEVELOPMENT

Because the Bahamian economy is service-oriented, especially in tourism and offshore banking, there are no significant industrial and occupational health hazards. Tourism accounts for nearly half the gross national product.

FREEDOM

Women participate actively in all levels of government and business. The Constitution does, however, make some distinctions between males and females with regard to citizenship and permanent-resident status.

HEALTH/WELFARE

Cases of child abuse and neglect in the Bahamas have risen in the 1990s. The Government and Women's Crisis Centre focused on the need to fight child abuse through a public-awareness program that had as its theme: "It shouldn't hurt to be a child."

ACHIEVEMENTS

The natural beauty of the islands has had a lasting effect on those who have visited them. As a result of his experiences in the waters off Bimini, Ernest Hemingway wrote his classic *The Old Man and the Sea.*

Barbados

GEOGRAPHY
Area in Square Kilometers (Miles): 431 (166) (about 2½ times the size of Washington, D.C.)
Capital (Population): Bridgetown (7,400)
Climate: tropical

PEOPLE

Population
Total: 257,100
Annual Growth Rate: 0.2%
Rural/Urban Population Ratio: 62/38
Ethnic Makeup: 80% black; 16% mixed; 4% white
Major Language: English

Health
Life Expectancy at Birth: 71 years (male); 77 years (female)
Infant Mortality Rate (Ratio): 19/1,000
Average Caloric Intake: 129% of FAO minimum
Physicians Available (Ratio): 1/842

Religions
67% Protestant (Anglican, Pentecostal, Methodist, others); 4% Roman Catholic; 17% none; 12% others or unknown

Education
Adult Literacy Rate: 99%

An Old Democracy

In February 1627, the first permanent settlers arrived aboard the *William and John* to start the British colony of Barbados. So began a democracy that is one of the oldest in the Western Hemisphere; in fact, the framers of the U.S. Constitution borrowed wording from the Charter of Barbados of 1635. Independent of Great Britain since 1966, the government of Barbados contends that its election process is no more chaotic than that of the Republicans and Democrats in the United States.

COMMUNICATION
Telephones: 89,000
Newspapers: 2 dailies

TRANSPORTATION
Highways—Kilometers (Miles): 1,570 (980)
Railroads—Kilometers (Miles): none
Usable Airfield: 1

GOVERNMENT
Type: parliamentary democracy; independent sovereign state within Commonwealth
Independence Date: November 30, 1966
Head of State: Prime Minister Owen Seymour Arthur
Political Parties: Democratic Labour Party; Barbados Labour Party; National Democratic Party
Suffrage: universal at 18

MILITARY
Number of Armed Forces: small Barbados regiment
Military Expenditures (% of Central Government Expenditures): 0.7%
Current Hostilities: none

ECONOMY
Currency ($ U.S. Equivalent): about 2 Bajan dollars = $1 (fixed rate)
Per Capita Income/GDP: $9,200/$2.4 billion
Inflation Rate: 2%
Total Foreign Debt: $652 million
Natural Resources: negligible
Agriculture: sugarcane; subsistence foods
Industry: tourism; sugar milling; light manufacturing; component assembly for export

FOREIGN TRADE
Exports: $161 million
Imports: $703 million

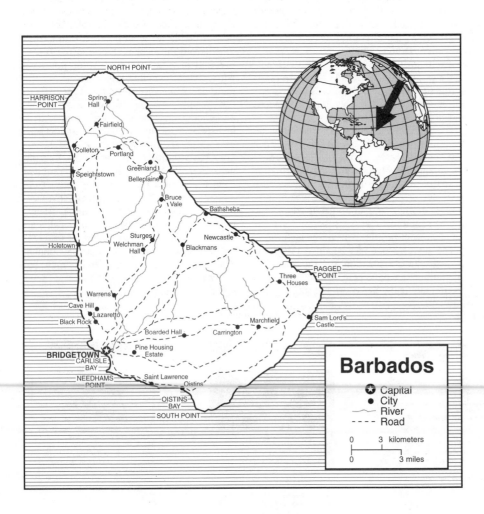

Barbados
- ⊗ Capital
- ● City
- ～ River
- - - - Road

0   3 kilometers

0   3 miles

Barbados is
occupied by the
English
1625

The first sugar
from Barbados is
sent to England
1647

Full citizenship
is granted to
nonwhites
1832

Independence
of Great Britain
1966

1990s

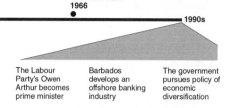

The Labour
Party's Owen
Arthur becomes
prime minister

Barbados
develops an
offshore banking
industry

The government
pursues policy of
economic
diversification

THE LITTLE ENGLAND OF THE CARIBBEAN

A parliamentary democracy that won its independence of Britain in 1966, Barbados boasts a House of Assembly that is the third oldest in the Western Hemisphere, after Bermuda's and Virginia's. A statement of the rights and privileges of Bajans (as Barbadians are called), known as the Charter of Barbados, was proclaimed in 1652 and has been upheld by those governing the island. The press is free, labor is strong and well organized, and human rights are respected.

While the majority of the populations of the English-speaking West Indies still admire the British, this admiration is carried to extremes in Barbados. In 1969, for example, Bajan soccer teams chose English names and colors—Arsenal, Tottenham Hotspurs, Liverpool, and Coventry City. Among the primary religions are Anglican and Methodist Protestantism.

Unlike most of the other islands of the Caribbean, European sailors initially found Barbados uninhabited. It has since been determined that the island's original inhabitants, the Arawak Indians, were destroyed by Carib Indians who overran the region and then abandoned the islands. Settled by the English, Barbados was always under British control until its independence.

A DIVERSIFYING ECONOMY

As compared to other West Indian nations, Barbados, in terms of wealth, is well off. One important factor is that Barbados has been able to diversify its economy; thus, the country is no longer dependent solely on sugar and its by-products, rum and molasses. Manufacturing, financed by foreign investment, now contributes to the country's exports. Tourism is also an important source of revenue.

The Constitution of 1966 authorized the government to promote the general welfare of the citizens of the island through equitable distribution of wealth. While governments have made a sincere effort to wipe out pockets of poverty, a great disparity in wealth still exists.

RACE AND CLASS

Barbados is a class- and race-conscious society. One authority noted that there are three classes (elite, middle class, and masses) and two colors (white/light and black). Land is highly concentrated; 10 percent of the population own 95 percent of the land. Most of the nation's landed estates and businesses are owned by whites, even though they comprise a very small percentage of the population (4 percent).

While discrimination based on color is legally prohibited, color distinctions continue to correlate with class differences and dominate most personal associations. Although whites have been displaced politically, they still comprise more than half of the group considered "influential" in the country.

Even though Barbados's class structure is more rigid than that of other West Indian states, there is upward social mobility for all people, and the middle class has been growing steadily in size. Poor whites, known as "Redlegs," have frequently moved into managerial positions on the estates. The middle class also includes a fairly large percentage of blacks and mulattos. Bajans have long enjoyed access to public and private educational systems, which have been the object of a good deal of national pride. Adequate medical care is available to all residents through local clinics and hospitals under a government health program. All Bajans are covered under government health insurance programs.

SEEKING A LEADERSHIP ROLE

Given the nation's relative wealth and its dynamism, Bajans have been inclined to seek a strong role in the region. In terms of Caribbean politics, economic development, and defense, Bajans feel that they have a right and a duty to lead.

Some of that optimism was tempered in the early 1990s by economic recession. Recovery in 1993 saw a growth of 1 to 2 percent, a result of an International Monetary Fund–induced austerity program.

The Labour Party has continued to push privatization policies. In 1993, an important step was taken toward the greater diversification of the nation's economic base with the creation of offshore financial services. By 1995, the new industry had created many new jobs for Bajans and had significantly reduced the high unemployment rate.

DEVELOPMENT

The government's privatization and economic diversification efforts have already resulted in improvements in the quality of life of Bajan citizens.

FREEDOM

Barbados has maintained an excellent human-rights record. The government officially advocates strengthening the human-rights machinery of the United Nations and the Organization of American States. Women are active participants in the country's economic, political, and social life.

HEALTH/WELFARE

The acting minister of Health and Welfare noted that the treatment of nutrition-related diseases cost taxpayers nearly $50 million in 1996–1997. He felt that the country depended too heavily on imported foods, which Barbadians consider superior to locally grown foods.

ACHIEVEMENTS

Bajan novelist George Lamming has won attention from the world's literary community for his novels, each of which explores a stage in or an aspect of the colonial experience. Through his works, he explains what it is to be simultaneously a citizen of one's island and a West Indian.

Cuba (Republic of Cuba)

GEOGRAPHY

Area in Square Kilometers (Miles): 114,471 (44,200) (about the size of Pennsylvania)
Capital (Population): Havana (2,200,000)
Climate: tropical

PEOPLE

Population

Total: 10,951,400
Annual Growth Rate: 0.7%
Rural/Urban Population Ratio: 26/74
Ethnic Makeup: 51% mulatto; 37% white; 11% black; 1% Chinese
Major Language: Spanish

Health

Life Expectancy at Birth: 75 years (male); 79 years (female)
Infant Mortality Rate (Ratio): 8/1,000
Average Caloric Intake: 121% of FAO minimum
Physicians Available (Ratio): 1/231

Religion

85% Roman Catholic before Castro assumed power

Education

Adult Literacy Rate: 98%

COMMUNICATION

Telephones: 229,000
Newspapers: 1 daily

The Language of Revolution

Señorita ("miss") is no longer viewed as a proper form of address in Havana. Gone from Cuban speech are *señorita*, *señora*, and *señor*. They have been replaced by the revolutionary words *compañera* and *compañero*, meaning "comrade" or "companion." The accepted farewell is *Hasta luego* ("Until later"), taking the place of *Adios*, with its religious connotation of "Go with God."

TRANSPORTATION

Highways—Kilometers (Miles): 26,477 (16,442)
Railroads—Kilometers (Miles): 12,623 (7,877)
Usable Airfields: 181

GOVERNMENT

Type: Communist state
Independence Date: May 20, 1902
Head of State: President Fidel Castro Ruz
Political Parties: Cuban Communist Party
Suffrage: universal at 16

MILITARY

Number of Armed Forces: 180,500
Military Expenditures (% of Central Government Expenditures): 6%
Current Hostilities: none

ECONOMY

Currency ($ U.S. Equivalent): 1.0 peso = $1 (linked to U.S. dollar)
Per Capita Income/GDP: $1,260/$14.0 billion
Inflation Rate: n/a
Total Foreign Debt: $10.8 billion
Natural Resources: metals; primarily nickel
Agriculture: sugar; tobacco; coffee; citrus and tropical fruits; rice; beans; meat; vegetables
Industry: sugar refining; metals; oil refining; food processing; wood products; cement; chemicals; textiles

FOREIGN TRADE

Exports: $1.6 billion
Imports: $1.7 billion

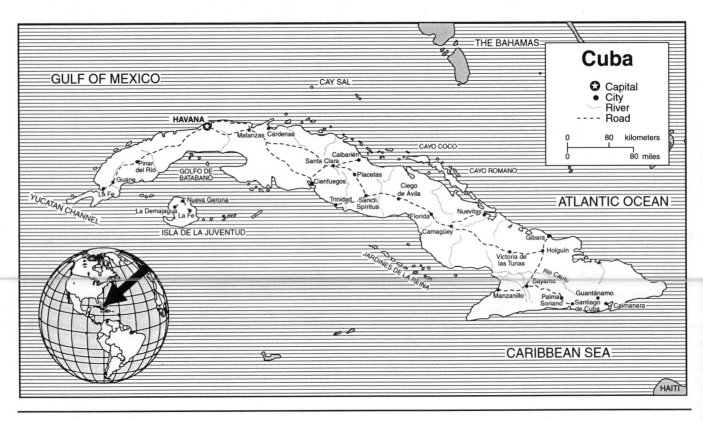

REFLECTIONS ON A REVOLUTION

Cuba, which contains about half the land area of the West Indies, has captured the attention of the world since 1959. In that year, Fidel Castro led his victorious rebels into the capital city of Havana and began a revolution that has profoundly affected Cuban society. The Cuban Revolution had its roots in the struggle for independence of Spain in the late nineteenth century, in the aborted Nationalist Revolution of 1933, and in the Constitution of 1940. It grew from Cuba's history and must be understood as a Cuban phenomenon.

The Revolution in some respects represents the fulfillment of the goals of the Cuban Constitution of 1940, a radically nationalist document that was never fully implemented. It banned *latifundia* (the ownership of vast landed estates) and discouraged foreign ownership of the land. It permitted the confiscation of property in the public or social interest. The state was authorized to provide full employment for its people and to direct the course of the national economy. Finally, the Constitution of 1940 gave the Cuban state control of the sugar industry, which at the time was controlled by U.S. companies.

The current Constitution, written in 1976, incorporates 36 percent of the articles of the 1940 Constitution. In other words, many of Castro's policies and programs are founded in Cuban history and the aspirations of the Cuban people. Revolutionary Cuba has been very successful in solving the nation's most pressing problems of poverty. But those successes must be balanced against the loss of basic freedoms imposed by a strong authoritarian state.

ACHIEVEMENTS OF THE REVOLUTION

Education

One of the Revolution's most impressive successes has been in the area of education. In 1960, the Castro regime decided to place emphasis on raising the minimum level of education for the whole population. To accomplish this, some 200,000 Cubans were mobilized in 1961 under the slogan "Let those who know more teach those who know less." In a single year, the literacy rate rose from 76 to 96 percent. Free education was made available to all Cubans. The literacy campaign involved many Cubans in an attempt to recognize and attack the problems of rural impoverishment. For many women who were students or teachers, it was their first taste of active public life, and because of their involvement, they began to redefine sex roles and attitudes.

While the literacy campaign was a resounding triumph, long-term educational policy was less satisfactory. Officials blamed the high dropout rate in elementary and junior high schools on poor school facilities and inadequate teacher training. Students also apparently lacked enthusiasm, and Castro himself acknowledged that students needed systematic, constant, daily work and discipline.

"Scholarship students and students in general," in Castro's words, "are willing to do anything, except to study hard."

Health Care

The Cuban Revolution also took great strides forward in improving the health of the Cuban population, especially in rural regions. Success in this area is all the more impressive when one considers that between one third and one half of all doctors left the country between 1959 and 1962. Health care declined sharply, and the infant mortality rate rose rapidly. But, with the training of new health-care professionals, the gaps were filled. The infant mortality rate in Cuba is now at a level comparable to that of developed countries.

From the outset, the government decided to concentrate on rural areas, where the need was the greatest. Medical treatment was free, and newly graduated doctors had to serve for at least 2 years in the countryside. The Cuban health service was founded on the principle that good health for all, without discrimination, is a birthright of Cubans. All Cubans were also included under a national health plan.

The first national health standards were developed between 1961 and 1965, and eight priority areas were identified: infant and maternal care, adult health care, care for the elderly, environmental health, nutrition, dentistry, school health programs, and occupational health. A program of spraying and immunization eradicated malaria and poliomyelitis. Cuban life expectancy became one of the highest in the world, and Cuba's leading causes of death became the same as in the United States—heart disease, cancer, and stroke.

Before the Revolution of 1959, there was very little health and safety regulation for workers. Afterward, however, important advances were made in the training of specialized inspectors and occupational physicians. In 1978, a Work Safety and Health Law was enacted, which defined the rights and responsibilities of government agencies, workplace administrators, unions, and workers.

Cuba also exported its health-care expertise; one health authority called Cuba a "health power." It has had medical teams in countries from Nicaragua to Yemen and more doctors overseas than the World Health Organization.

Redistribution of Wealth

The third great area of change presided over by the Revolution was income redistribution. The Revolution changed the lives of rural poor and agricultural workers. They gained the most in comparison to other groups in Cuban society—especially urban groups. From 1962 to 1973, for example, agricultural workers saw their wages rise from less than 60 percent to 93 percent of the national average.

Still, Cuba's minimum wage was inadequate for most families. Many families needed two wage earners to make ends meet. All wages were enhanced by the so-called social wage, which consisted of free medical care and education, subsidized housing, and low food prices. Yet persistent shortages and tight rationing of food undermined a good portion of the social wage. Newly married couples found it necessary to live with relatives, sometimes for years, before they could obtain their own housing, which was in short supply. Food supplies, especially those provided by the informal sector, were adversely affected by a 1986 decision to eliminate independent producers because an informal private sector was deemed antithetical to "socialist morality" and promoted materialism.

Women in Cuba

From the outset of the Revolution, Fidel Castro appealed to women as active participants in the movement and redefined their political roles. Women's interests were protected by the Federation of Cuban Women, an integral part of the ruling party. The Family Code of 1975 equalized pay scales, reversed sexual discrimination against promotions, provided generous maternity leave, and gave employed women preferential access to goods and services. Although women comprised approximately 30 percent of the Cuban workforce, most were still employed in traditional female occupations; the Third Congress of the Cuban Communist Party admitted in 1988 that both racial minorities and women were underrepresented in responsible government and party positions at all levels. This continues to be a problem.

SHORTCOMINGS

Even at its best, the new Cuba had significant shortcomings. Wayne Smith, a former chief of the U.S. Interest Section in Havana who was sympathetic to the Revolution, wrote: "There is little freedom of expression and no freedom of the press at all. It is a command society, which still holds political prisoners, some of them under deplorable conditions. Further, while the Revolution has provided the basic needs of all, it has not fulfilled its promise of a higher standard of living for the society as a whole. Cuba was, after all, an urban middle-class society with a relatively high standard of living even before the Revolution. . . . The majority of Cubans are less well off materially."

Castro, to win support for his programs, did not hesitate to take his revolutionary message to the people. Indeed, the key reason why Castro enjoyed such widespread support in Cuba was because the people had the sense of being involved in a great historical process.

Alienation

Not all Cubans identified with the Revolution, and many felt a deep sense of betrayal and alienation. The elite and most of the middle class strongly resisted the changes that robbed them of influence, prestige, and property. Some were particularly bitter, for, at its outset, the Revolution had been largely a middle-class movement. Castro, for them, was a traitor to his class. Thousands fled Cuba, and some formed the core of an anti-Castro guerrilla movement based in South Florida.

There are many signs that Castro's government, while still popular, has lost the widespread acceptance it enjoyed in the 1960s and 1970s. While Castro still has the support of the older generation and those in rural areas who benefited from the social transformation of the island, limited economic growth has led to dissatisfaction among urban workers and youth, who are less interested in Castro as a revolutionary hero and more interested in economic gains.

More serious disaffection may exist in the army. Journalist Georgie Anne Geyer, writing in *World Monitor,* suggests that the 1989 execution of General Arnaldo Ochoa, ostensibly for drug trafficking, was actually motivated by Castro's fears of an emerging competitor for power. "The 1930s-style show trial effectively revealed the presence of an 'Angola generation' in the Cuban military. . . . That generation, which fought in Angola between 1974 and 1989, is the competitor generation to Castro's own Sierra Maestra generation." The condemned officers argued that their dealings with drug traffickers were not for personal enrichment but were designed to earn desperately needed hard currency for the state. Some analysts are convinced that Castro knew about drug trafficking and condoned it; others claim that it took place without his knowledge. But the bottom line

is that the regime had been shaken at the highest levels, and the purge was the most far-reaching since the 1959 Revolution.

The Economy

The state of the Cuban economy and the future of the Cuban Revolution are inextricably linked. Writing in *World Today,* James J. Guy predicted that, given the economic collapse of the former Soviet Union and its satellites, "Cuba is destined to face serious structural unemployment: its agrarian economy cannot generate the white-collar, technical jobs demanded by a swelling army of graduates. . . . The entire system is deteriorating—the simplest services take months to deliver, water and electricity are constantly interrupted. . . ," and there is widespread corruption and black-marketeering.

Oil is particularly nettlesome. Just as Soviet oil imports fell off and Cuba was forced to make petroleum purchases on the world market, Kuwait was invaded by Iraq. Oil prices skyrocketed. Active development of the tourism industry offers some hope, but Western banks and governments since the mid-1980s have been reluctant to invest in Cuba.

Although Castro prides Cuba on being one of the last bulwarks of untainted Marxism-Leninism, in April 1991 he said: "We are not dogmatic . . . we are realistic. . . . Under the special conditions of this extraordinary period we are also aware that different forms of international cooperation may be useful." He noted that Cuba had contacted foreign capitalists about the possibility of establishing joint

enterprises and remarked that more than 49 percent foreign participation in state businesses was a possibility.

In 1993, Castro called for economic realism. Using the rhetoric of the Revolution, he urged the Legislative Assembly to think seriously about the poor condition of the Cuban economy: "It is painful, but we must be sensible. . . . It is not only with decisiveness, courage and heroism that one saves the Revolution, but also with intelligence. And we have the right to invent ways to survive in these conditions without ever ceasing to be revolutionaries."

A government decree in September 1993 allowed Cubans to establish private businesses. Today, Cubans in some 140 professions can work on their own for a profit. At about the same time, the use of dollars was decriminalized, the Cuban currency became convertible, and, in the agricultural sector, the government began to transform state farms into cooperatives. Farmers are now allowed to sell some of their produce in private markets and, increasingly, market forces set the prices of many consumer goods. Managers in state-owned enterprises have been given unprecedented autonomy; and foreign investment, in contrast with past practice, is now encouraged.

Another indication of Cuba's willingness to experiment with some liberalization of its economy is provided by talks initiated in 1995 with CARICOM states about the possibilities of a free-trade agreement. Total trade between CARICOM and Cuba has increased markedly—from $5 million to $6 million in 1991 to

(United Nations photo)

Fidel Castro has been the prime minister of Cuba since he seized power in 1959. Pictured above is Castro at the United Nations, as he looked in 1960.

Timeline:

The island is discovered by Christopher Columbus
1492

The founding of Havana
1511

The Ten Years' War in Cuba
1868–1878

The Cuban War of Independence
1895–1898

The Republic of Cuba is established
1902

Cuba writes a new, progressive Constitution
1940

Fidel Castro seizes power
1959

An abortive U.S.–sponsored invasion at the Bay of Pigs
1961

The OAS votes to allow member states to normalize relations with Cuba
1975

Mass exodus from Cuba; trial and execution of top military officials for alleged dealing in drugs
1980s

1990s

Castro pursues economic liberalization

Castro announces that 1998 will be his last year in office

Two small planes dropping anti-Castro leaflets are shot down for invading Cuban air space

$56 million in 1996—although it was easier to export from rather than import to Cuba because of a stifling bureaucracy. Indeed, the problems confronted by the free-trade economies of CARICOM with the state-controlled Cuban economy were the subject of joint talks late in 1997.

The new economic liberalism of the Castro regime springs from the need to survive in a world where free-market forces have been embraced by all manner of governments. Castro has always been pragmatic; his adherence to doctrinaire communism may grow increasingly flexible despite rhetorical flourishes to the contrary.

Freedom Issues

Soon after the Revolution, the government assumed total control of the media. No independent news organization is allowed, and all printed publications are censored by the government or the Communist Party. The arts are subject to strict censorship, and even sports must serve the purposes of the Revolution. As Castro noted: "Within the Revolution everything is possible. Outside it, nothing."

In many respects, there is less freedom now in Cuba than there was before the Revolution. Cuba's human-rights record is not good. There are thousands of political prisoners, and rough treatment and torture—physical and psychological—occur. The Constitution of 1976 allows the repression of all freedoms for all those who oppose the Revolution. U.S. political scientist William LeGrande, who was sympathetic to the Revolution, nevertheless noted that "Cuba is a closed society. The

Cuban Communist Party does not allow dissenting views on fundamental policy. It does not allow people to challenge the basic leadership of the regime." But here, too, there are signs of change. In 1995, municipal elections were held under a new system that provides for run-offs if none of the candidates gains a clear majority. In an indication of a new competitiveness in Cuban politics, 326 out of 14,229 positions were subject to the run-off rule.

THE FUTURE

It will be difficult for Castro to maintain the support of the Cuban population. There must be continued positive accomplishments in the economy. Health and education programs are successful and will continue to be so. "Cubans get free health care, free education and free admission to sports and cultural events [and] 80% of all Cubans live in rent-free apartments, and those who do pay rent pay only between 6 and 10% of their salaries," according to James J. Guy.

But there must be a recovery of basic political and human freedoms. Criticism must not be the occasion for jail terms or exile. The Revolution must be more inclusive and less exclusive.

Although Castro has never been effectively challenged, there are signs of unrest on the island. The military, as noted, is a case in point. Castro has also lost a good deal of luster internationally, as most countries have moved away from statism and toward free-market economies and more open forms of government.

Even though a similar trend is apparent on the island, in 1994 and 1995, many Cu-

bans grew increasingly frustrated with their lives and took to the sea in an attempt to reach the United States. Thousands were intercepted by the U.S. Coast Guard and housed in U.S. military facilities at Guantanamo Bay and Fort Howard in the Panama Canal Zone.

The question is increasingly asked, What will happen once Fidel, through death or retirement, is gone from power? Castro's assumption is that the new Constitution, which institutionalizes the Revolution, will provide a mechanism for succession. Over the past few years, he has made some effort to depersonalize the Revolution; his public appearances are fewer and he does less traveling around the countryside.

Change must come to Cuba. More than half of all Cubans alive today were born after the Revolution. They are not particularly attuned to the rhetoric of revolution and seem more interested in the attainment of basic freedoms and consumer goods. Castro is resistant to those demands and appears more and more as a tired revolutionary. Perhaps he realizes that his time has past, for he has announced that he will not run for another term as president when elections are held in 1998.

DEVELOPMENT

The visit by the foreign minister of Belarus in 1997 signaled another step in the reestablishment of ties that existed between the former Soviet Republic and Cuba before 1991. Relations with the Dominican Republic, broken in 1959, were resumed in 1997.

FREEDOM

The Committee to Protect Journalists noted that those who try to work outside the confines of the state media face tremendous obstacles. "The problems of a lack of basic supplies... are dwarfed by Fidel Castro's campaign of harassment and intimidation against the fledgling free press."

HEALTH/WELFARE

In August 1997, the Cuban government reported 1,649 HIV cases, 595 cases of full-blown AIDS, and 429 deaths, a significant increase over figures for 1996. Cuban medical personnel are working on an AIDS vaccine. AIDS has been spread in part because of an economic climate that has driven more women to prostitution.

ACHIEVEMENTS

A unique cultural contribution of Cuba to the world was the Afro-Cuban movement, with its celebration of black song and dance rhythms. The work of contemporary prize-winning Cuban authors such as Alejo Carpentier and Edmundo Desnoes has been translated into many languages.

Dominica (Commonwealth of Dominica)

GEOGRAPHY
Area in Square Kilometers (Miles): 752 (289) (about ¼ the size of Rhode Island)
Capital (Population): Roseau (22,000)
Climate: tropical

PEOPLE

Population
Total: 83,000
Annual Growth Rate: 0.4%
Rural/Urban Population Ratio: 39/61
Ethnic Makeup: mostly black; some Carib Indians
Major Languages: English; French Creole

Health
Life Expectancy at Birth: 74 years (male); 80 years (female)
Infant Mortality Rate (Ratio): 10/1,000
Average Caloric Intake: 90% of FAO minimum
Physicians Available (Ratio): 1/3,130

Religions
77% Roman Catholic; 15% Protestant; 8% others

Education
Adult Literacy Rate: 94%

COMMUNICATION
Telephones: 4,600
Newspapers: n/a

TRANSPORTATION
Highways—Kilometers (Miles): 750 (466)
Railroads—Kilometers (Miles): none
Usable Airfields: 2

The "Switzerland of the Caribbean"

The tiny island of Dominica was discovered by Christopher Columbus on his second voyage to the New World in 1493. The island was sighted on the Christian Sabbath, Sunday (*Domingo* in Spanish), hence the name Dominica. Today, as in 1493, Dominica's very mountainous terrain is densely covered with heavy tropical growth. Described as the most ruggedly beautiful island in the Caribbean, Dominica has been called the "Switzerland of the Caribbean."

GOVERNMENT
Type: parliamentary democracy
Independence Date: November 3, 1978
Head of State/Government: President Crispin Anselm Sorhaindo; Prime Minister Edison James
Political Parties: United Workers Party; Dominica Freedom Party; Dominica Labour Party
Suffrage: universal at 18

MILITARY
Number of Armed Forces: n/a
Military Expenditures (% of Central Government Expenditures): 4.6%
Current Hostilities: territorial dispute with Venezuela

ECONOMY
Currency ($ U.S. Equivalent): 2.7 East Caribbean dollars = $1 (fixed rate)
Per Capita Income/GDP: $2,260/$200 million
Inflation Rate: 1.6%
Total Foreign Debt: $93 million
Natural Resources: timber
Agriculture: bananas; citrus; coconuts; cocoa; essential oils
Industry: agricultural processing; tourism; soap and other coconut-based products; cigars

FOREIGN TRADE
Exports: $48.3 million
Imports: $98.8 million

Dominica is sighted on Christopher Columbus's second voyage
1493

Dominica is deeded to the British by France
1783

Independence of Great Britain
1978

Hurricanes devastate Dominica's economy
1979–1980

Hurricane Hugo devastates the island
1980s

Mary Eugenia Charles becomes the Caribbean's first woman head of government

1990s

Dominica seeks stronger tourism revenues, especially in ecotourism

Hurricanes in 1995 devastate the banana industry

Territorial dispute with Venezuela over Bird Island

A FRAGMENTED NATION

Dominica is a small and poor country that gained its independence of Great Britain in 1978. Culturally, the island reflects a number of patterns. Ninety percent of the population speak French patois (dialect), and most are Roman Catholic, while only a small minority speak English and are Protestant. Yet English is the official language. There are also small groups of Indians who may have descended from the original Carib inhabitants; they are alternately revered and criticized. Many Dominicans perceive the Carib Indians as drunken, lazy, and dishonest. Others see them as symbolically important because they represent an ancient culture and fit into the larger Caribbean search for cultural and national identity. There is also a small number of Rastafarians, who identify with their black African roots.

Christopher Columbus discovered the island of Dominica on his second voyage to the New World in 1493. Because of the presence of Carib Indians, who were known for their ferocity, Spanish efforts to settle the island were rebuffed. It was not until 1635 that France took advantage of Spanish weakness and claimed Dominica as its own. French missionaries became the island's first European settlers. Because of continued Carib resistance, the French and English agreed in 1660 that both Dominica and St. Vincent should be declared neutral and left to the Indians. Definitive English settlement did not occur until the eighteenth century, and the island again became a bone of contention between the French and English. It became British by treaty in 1783.

Today, Dominica's population is broken up into sharply differentiated regions. The early collapse of the plantation economy left pockets of settlements, which are still isolated from one another. A difficult topography and poor communications exaggerate the differences between these small communities. This contrasts with nations such as Jamaica and Trinidad and Tobago, which have a greater sense of national awareness because there are good communications and mass media that reach most citizens and foster the development of a national perception.

EMIGRATION

Although Dominica has a high birth rate and its people's life expectancy has measurably increased over the past few years, the growth rate has been dropping due to significant out-migration. Out-migration is not a new phenomenon. From the 1880s until well into this century, many Dominicans sought economic opportunity in the gold fields of French Guiana. Today, most move to the neighboring French departments of Guadeloupe and Martinique.

THE ECONOMY

Dominica's chief export, bananas, has suffered for some years from natural disasters and falling prices. Hurricanes blew down the banana trees in 1979, 1980, 1989, and 1995, and banana exports fell dramatically between 1993 and 1994. Attempts by the United States in 1995 to force the European Union to end special treatment for former colonies cast a further pall over the banana industry in Dominica. Another drop in banana prices in 1997 prompted

the opposition Dominica Freedom Party to demand that Dominica become part of a single market to take advantage of set prices enjoyed by the producers of Martinique and Guadeloupe. Prime Minister Edison James informed citizens that belt-tightening is necessary to confront the nation's difficult financial situation.

POLITICAL FREEDOM

Despite economic difficulties and several attempted coups, Dominica still enjoys a parliamentary democracy patterned along British lines. The press is free and has not been subject to control—save for a brief state of emergency in 1981, which corresponded to a coup attempt by former prime minister Patrick John and unemployed members of the disbanded Defense Force. Political parties and trade unions are free to organize. Labor unions are small but enjoy the right to strike. Women have full rights under the law and are active in the political system; former prime minister Charles was the Caribbean's first woman head of government.

DEVELOPMENT

Dominica's agrarian economy is heavily dependent on earnings from banana exports to Great Britain. To strengthen the economy, attempts are being made to diversify agricultural production, to develop a tourist industry, and to promote light manufacturing.

FREEDOM

Freedom House, an international human-rights organization, listed Dominica as "free." It also noted that "the rights of the native Caribs may not be fully respected." The example set by former prime minister Mary Eugenia Charles led to greater participation by women in the island's political life.

HEALTH/WELFARE

With the assistance of external donors, Dominica has rebuilt many primary schools destroyed in Hurricane Hugo. A major restructuring of the public health administration has improved the quality of health care, even in the previously neglected rural areas.

ACHIEVEMENTS

Traditional handcrafts—especially intricately woven baskets, mats, and hats—have been preserved in Dominica. School children are taught the techniques to pass on this dimension of Dominican culture.

Dominican Republic

GEOGRAPHY
Area in Square Kilometers (Miles): 48,464 (18,712) (about the size of Vermont and New Hampshire combined)
Capital (Population): Santo Domingo (2,400,000)
Climate: maritime tropical

PEOPLE

Population
Total: 8,089,000
Annual Growth Rate: 1.8%
Rural/Urban Population Ratio: 39/61
Ethnic Makeup: 73% mixed; 16% white; 11% black
Major Language: Spanish

Health
Life Expectancy at Birth: 67 years (male); 71 years (female)
Infant Mortality Rate (Ratio): 50/1,000
Average Caloric Intake: 106% of FAO minimum
Physicians Available (Ratio): 1/2,511

Religions
95% Roman Catholic; 5% others

Education
Adult Literacy Rate: 83%

COMMUNICATION
Telephones: 190,000
Newspapers: 9 dailies

TRANSPORTATION
Highways—Kilometers (Miles): 12,000 (7,488)

Railroads—Kilometers (Miles): 1,655 (1,026)
Usable Airfields: 36

GOVERNMENT
Type: republic
Independence Date: February 27, 1844
Head of State: President Leonel Fernández
Political Parties: Dominican Revolutionary Party; Social Christian Reformist Party; Dominican Liberation Party; Independent Revolutionary Party; others
Suffrage: universal and compulsory at 18 or at any age if married; except members of the armed forces or the police, who cannot vote

MILITARY
Number of Armed Forces: 22,800
Military Expenditures (% of Central Government Expenditures): 0.7%
Current Hostilities: none

ECONOMY
Currency ($ U.S. Equivalent): 13.96 pesos = $1
Per Capita Income/GDP: $3,070/$24.0 billion
Inflation Rate: 14%
Total Foreign Debt: $4.3 billion
Natural Resources: nickel; bauxite; gold; silver
Agriculture: sugarcane; coffee; cocoa; cacao; tobacco; rice; corn; beef
Industry: tourism; sugar refining; textiles; cement; mining

FOREIGN TRADE
Exports: $585 million
Imports: $2.5 billion

The First Cathedral in America

Christopher Columbus discovered the island of Hispaniola (part of which today is the Dominican Republic, the rest Haiti) on his initial voyage to the New World in 1492. After the first northern colony was destroyed by Indians, Columbus established a second colony, only to abandon it when gold was reported in the south. This colony eventually became the city of Santo Domingo, on the Caribbean coast. The Catedrál de Santo Domingo was built soon after the founding of the city. Completed in 1540, it is the oldest cathedral in the Americas. In 1542, the remains of Christopher Columbus and his son Diego were moved from Sevilla, Spain, to this cathedral, allowing the discoverer of the Americas a final resting place in the "New World" that made him famous.

Dominican Republic

- ✪ Capital
- ● City
- ⌇ River
- --- Road

The founding of
Santo Domingo,
the oldest
European city in
the Americas
1496

Independence of
Spain is declared
1821

Haitian control
1822–1844

Independence as
a separate state
1844

The era of
General Rafael
Trujillo
1930–1961

Civil war and U.S.
intervention
1965

The International
Monetary Fund
approves $78
million in a
stand-by loan
1980s

1990s

Leonel
Fernández is
elected president

The minimum
wage is raised
15%

Diplomatic
relations are
restored with
Cuba

DOMINICAN REPUBLIC: RACIAL STRIFE

Occupying the eastern two thirds of the island of Hispaniola (Haiti comprises the western third), the Dominican Republic historically has feared its neighbor to the west. Much of the fear has its origins in race. From 1822 until 1844, the Dominican Republic—currently 73 percent mixed, or mulatto—was ruled by a brutal black Haitian regime. One authority noted that the Dominican Republic's freedom from Haiti has always been precarious: "Fear of reconquest by the smaller but more heavily populated (and, one might add, black) neighbor has affected Dominican psychology more than any other factor."

In the 1930s, for example, President Rafael Trujillo posed as the defender of Catholic values and European culture against the "barbarous" hordes of Haiti. Trujillo ordered the massacre of from 12,000 to 20,000 Haitians who had settled in the Dominican Republic in search of work. For years, the Dominican government had encouraged Haitian sugarcane cutters to cross the border to work on the U.S.–owned sugar plantations. But, with the world economic depression in the 1930s and a fall in sugar prices and production, many Haitians did not return to their part of the island; in fact, additional thousands continued to stream across the border. The response of the Dominican government was wholesale slaughter.

Since 1952, a series of 5-year agreements have been reached between the two governments to regularize the supply of Haitian cane cutters. An estimated 20,000 cross each year into the Dominican Republic legally, and an additional 60,000

enter illegally. Living and working conditions are very poor for these Haitians, and the migrants have no legal status and no rights. Planters prefer the Haitian workers because they are "cheaper and more docile" than Dominican laborers, who expect reasonable food, adequate housing, electric lights, and transportation to the fields. Today, as in the 1930s, economic troubles have gripped the Dominican Republic; the president has promised across-the-board sacrifices.

There is a subtle social discrimination against darker-skinned Dominicans, although this has not proved to be an insurmountable obstacle, as many hold elected political office. Discrimination is in part historical, in part cultural, and must be set against a backdrop of sharp prejudice against Haitians. This prejudice is also directed against the minority in the Dominican population who are of Haitian descent. For example, during the contested presidential election of 1994, President Joaquín Balaguer Ricardo introduced the issue of race when questions were raised about his opponent's rumored Haitian origins.

WOMEN'S RIGHTS

Women in the Dominican Republic have enjoyed political rights since 1941. While in office, President Balaguer, in an unprecedented move, named women governors for eight of the country's 29 provinces. Sexual discrimination is prohibited by law, but women have not shared equal social or economic status or opportunity with men. Divorce, however, is easily obtainable, and women can hold property in their own names. A 1996 profile of the nation's population and health noted that

27 percent of Dominican households were headed by women. In urban areas, the percentage rose to 31 percent.

AN AIR OF CRISIS

Progress toward a political scene free of corruption and racism has been fitful. The 1994 presidential election was marred by what multinational observers called massive fraud. The opposition claimed that Balaguer not only "stole the election" but also employed racist, anti-Haitian rhetoric that "inflamed stereotypes of Haitians in the Dominican Republic." Widespread unrest in the wake of the election, together with pressure from the Roman Catholic Church, the Organization of American States, and the United States, resulted in the "Pact for Democracy," which forced Balaguer to serve a shortened 2-year term as president. New elections in 1996 returned Leonel Fernández to the presidency. Fernández has claimed that Balaguer left the country in a state of "bankruptcy . . . and devastation." Indeed, economic problems have generated an unending series of labor disputes. More than a quarter of the workforce are unemployed. Despite his checkered record, Balaguer, now in his 90s, is expected to run once again for the presidency as the candidate of the Social Christian Reform Party in elections scheduled for the year 2000.

DEVELOPMENT

Balaguer's economic policies initially cut inflation from 100% in 1990 to 3% in 1993, but inflation was again in double digits by 1996. GDP is one of the lowest in the region, and more than 25% of the workforce are unemployed. President Fernández, in an attempt to stimulate trade, resumed diplomatic relations with Cuba.

FREEDOM

Democracy was shaken by massive electoral fraud, political turmoil, and racist rhetoric in 1994 and 1995. New elections in 1996 were more peaceful, but political maneuvering and an economy in crisis have maintained an undercurrent of unrest.

HEALTH/WELFARE

The *Pro-familia* study on population and development identified the main causes of death in children as diarrhea and respiratory sicknesses. Maternal mortality was estimated at 15 to 200 deaths for every 100,000 births. AIDS could be affecting as much as 5% of the population.

ACHIEVEMENTS

The National Theater of the Dominican Republic is a professional showcase of Caribbean arts. It is located on the Plaza de la Cultura along with the Museum of the Dominican Man, the Gallery of Modern Art, and the National Library. The theater has become the cultural heart of the city of Santo Domingo.

Grenada

GEOGRAPHY
Area in Square Kilometers (Miles): 344 (133) (about 2 times the size of Washington, D.C.)
Capital (Population): St. George's (30,000)
Climate: tropical

PEOPLE

Population
Total: 95,000
Annual Growth Rate: 0.5%
Rural/Urban Population Ratio: 70/30
Ethnic Makeup: mainly black
Major Languages: English; French patois

Health
Life Expectancy at Birth: 68 years (male); 73 years (female)
Infant Mortality Rate (Ratio): 12/1,000
Average Caloric Intake: 87% of FAO minimum
Physicians Available (Ratio): 1/4,400

Religions
largely Roman Catholic; Church of England; other Protestant sects

Education
Adult Literacy Rate: 98%

Grenada: Stabilization

Grenada is less than 100 miles off the coast of Venezuela, in a channel through which half of the United States' imported oil enters the Caribbean. In 1983, there was considerable interest in this tiny island when Prime Minister Maurice Bishop and most of his cabinet were killed by the Grenadian military. The United States responded to this seemingly Cuban-inspired coup by sending in U.S. Marines to protect the 700 to 1,000 Americans living on the island. This American "invasion" defused the hostilities in a week. On December 3, 1984, the Grenadians elected a new prime minister, Herbert Blaize, along with his New National Party. Blaize's election was favored by the United States.

COMMUNICATION
Telephones: 5,650
Newspapers: n/a

TRANSPORTATION
Highways—Kilometers (Miles): 1,000 (624)
Railroads—Kilometers (Miles): none
Usable Airfields: 3

GOVERNMENT
Type: independent state; recognizes Queen Elizabeth II as chief of state
Independence Date: February 7, 1974
Head of State: Prime Minister Keith Mitchell
Political Parties: New National Party; Grenada United Labour Party; National Party; National Democratic Congress; Maurice Bishop Patriotic Movement
Suffrage: universal at 18

MILITARY
Number of Armed Forces: 6,500 police; Royal Grenada Police Force
Military Expenditures (% of Central Government Expenditures): n/a
Current Hostilities: none

ECONOMY
Currency ($ U.S. Equivalent): 2.7 East Caribbean dollars = $1 (fixed rate)
Per Capita Income/GDP: $3,000/$250 million
Inflation Rate: 2.6%
Total Foreign Debt: $90 million
Natural Resources: spices
Agriculture: nutmeg; cocoa; bananas; mace
Industry: food processing; garments

FOREIGN TRADE
Exports: $18.6 million
Imports: $133.8 million

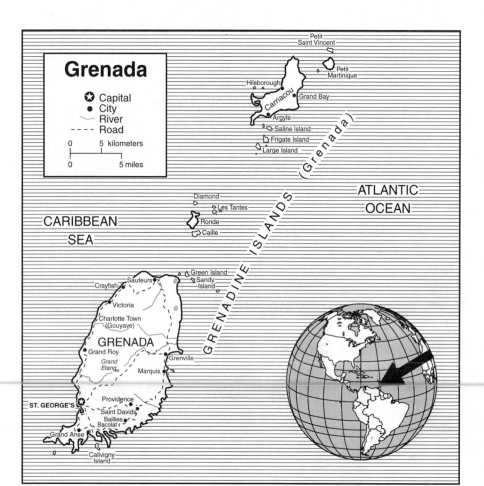

| Grenada is discovered by Christopher Columbus **1498** | England acquires the island from France by treaty **1763** | Slavery is abolished **1834** | Member of the West Indies Federation **1958–1962** | Independence of Great Britain **1974** | A coup brings Maurice Bishop to power **1979** | Prime Minister Maurice Bishop is assassinated; U.S. troops land **1980s** |

1990s

Former mathematics professor Keith Mitchell is elected prime minister in 1995

Prime Minister Mitchell visits Cuba to discuss trade

A proposal to name the new airport after Maurice Bishop proves divisive

GRENADA: A FRESH BEGINNING

On his third voyage to the New World in 1498, Christopher Columbus sighted Grenada, which he named *Concepción*. The origin of the name *Grenada* cannot be clearly established, although it is believed that the Spanish renamed the island for the Spanish city of Granada. Because of a fierce aboriginal population of Carib Indians, the island remained uncolonized for 100 years.

Grenada, like most of the Caribbean, is ethnically mixed. Its culture draws on several traditions. The island's French past is preserved among some people who still speak patois (a French dialect). There are few whites on the island, save for a small group of Portuguese who immigrated earlier in the century. The primary cultural identification is with Great Britain, from which Grenada won its independence in 1974.

Grenada's political history has been tumultuous. The corruption and violent tactics of Grenada's first prime minister, Eric Gairy, resulted in his removal in a bloodless coup in 1979. Even though this action marked the first extra-constitutional change of government in the Commonwealth Caribbean (former British colonies), most Grenadians supported the coup, led by Maurice Bishop and his New Joint Endeavor for Welfare, Education, and Liberation (JEWEL) movement. Prime Minister Bishop, like Jamaica's Michael Manley before him, attempted to break out of European cultural and institutional molds and mobilize Grenadians behind him.

Bishop's social policies laid the foundation for basic health care for all Grenadians. With the departure of Cuban medical doctors in 1983, however, the lack of trained personnel created a significant health-care problem. Moreover, although medical-care facilities exist, these are not always in good repair, and equipment is aging and not reliable. Methods of recording births, deaths, and diseases lack systemization, so it is risky to rely on local statistics to estimate the health needs of the population. There has also been some erosion from Bishop's campaign to accord women equal pay, status, and treatment. Two women were elected to Parliament, but skilled employment for women tends to be concentrated in the lowest-paid sector.

On October 19, 1983, Bishop and several of his senior ministers were killed during the course of a military coup. Six days later, the United States, with the token assistance of soldiers and police from states of the Eastern Caribbean, invaded Grenada, restored the 1974 Constitution, and prepared the way for new elections (held in December 1984).

According to one scholar, the invasion was a "lesson in a peacemaker's role in rebuilding a nation. Although Grenada has a history of parliamentary democracy, an atmosphere of civility, fertile soil, clean drinking water, and no slums, continued aid has not appreciably raised the standard of living and the young are resentful and restless."

Grenada's international airport, the focus of much controversy, has pumped new blood into the tourist industry. Moves have also been made by the Grenadian government to promote private-sector business and to diminish the role of the government in the economy. Large amounts of foreign aid, especially from the United States, have helped to repair the infrastructure.

In recent years, foreign governments such as Kuwait, attracted by the power of Grenada's vote in the United Nations, have committed millions of dollars to Grenada's infrastructure. Some of these partnerships, particularly that involving Japan's access to Caribbean fish stocks, may have severe consequences for Grenadians in the future.

Significant problems remain, however. Unemployment has not decreased; it remains at 25 percent of the workforce. Not surprisingly, the island is experiencing a rising crime rate.

Prime Minister Keith Mitchell of the New National Party has promised to create more jobs in the private sector and to cut taxes to stimulate investment in small, high-technology businesses. He also stated that government would become smaller and leaner. To ease his task, the Grenadian economy has experienced a modest recovery, which had begun in 1993. Privatization has continued, attracting foreign capital. In 1997, the events of 1983 were relived by Grenadians when the proposal to name the airport at Point Saline for the slain Maurice Bishop generated much controversy.

DEVELOPMENT

Mitchell moved to end what Grenadians call "barter trade" and the government calls "smuggling." For years, Grenadian fishermen have exchanged their fish in Martinique for beer, cigarettes, and appliances. The cash-strapped treasury desperately needs the tariff revenues and has used drug interdiction as a means to end the contraband trade.

FREEDOM

Grenadians are guaranteed full freedom of the press and speech. Newspapers, most of which are published by political parties, freely criticize the government without penalty.

HEALTH/WELFARE

Grenada still lacks effective legislation for regulation of working conditions, wages, and occupational-safety and health standards. Discrimination is prohibited by law, but women are often paid less than men for the same work.

ACHIEVEMENTS

A series of public consultations have been held with respect to the reestablishment of local government in the villages. Some 52 village councils work with the government in an effort to set policies that are both responsive and equitable.

Haiti (Republic of Haiti)

GEOGRAPHY

Area in Square Kilometers (Miles): 27,750 (10,714) (about the size of Maryland)
Capital (Population): Port-au-Prince (752,000)
Climate: warm; semiarid

PEOPLE

Population

Total: 6,731,600
Annual Growth Rate: 1.5%
Rural/Urban Population Ratio: 68/32
Ethnic Makeup: 95% black; 5% mulatto and European
Major Languages: French; Creole

Health

Life Expectancy at Birth: 43 years (male); 47 years (female)
Infant Mortality Rate (Ratio): 108/1,000
Average Caloric Intake: 96% of FAO minimum
Physicians Available (Ratio): 1/10,060

Religions

80% Roman Catholic (of which the overwhelming majority also practice Vodun); 16% Protestant; 4% others

---

Land of Gingerbread Houses

The origins of the architecture of Haiti's gingerbread houses are a mystery. Did they spring from the Paris Exposition of 1900, or did they evolve from the styles popular in the United States in the late 1800s? Whatever the reason, Haiti abounds with these elegant, intricate, and multicolored homes. No two are identical. Today, these houses need constant and expensive maintenance; as a result, the Haitian gingerbread house is an endangered species. It is hoped that public awareness will keep them from becoming extinct.

Education

Adult Literacy Rate: 35%

COMMUNICATION

Telephones: 36,000
Newspapers: 6 dailies

TRANSPORTATION

Highways—Kilometers (Miles): 4,000 (2,480)
Railroads—Kilometers (Miles): 40 (25)
Usable Airfields: 14

GOVERNMENT

Type: provisional; still in a state of turmoil
Independence Date: January 1, 1804
Head of State: President René Préval
Political Parties: National Front for Change and Democracy; National Congress of Democratic Movements; Movement for the Installation of Democracy in Haiti; National Progressive Revolutionary Party; Haitian Christian Democratic Party; others
Suffrage: universal over 18

MILITARY

Number of Armed Forces: 7,600
Military Expenditures (% of Central Government Expenditures): 11.0%
Current Hostilities: none

ECONOMY

Currency ($ U.S. Equivalent): 16.18 gourdes = $1 (fixed rate)
Per Capita Income/GDP: $870/$5.6 billion
Inflation Rate: 52%
Total Foreign Debt: $871 million
Natural Resources: bauxite
Agriculture: coffee; sugarcane; rice; corn; sorghum
Industry: sugar refining; textiles; flour milling; cement; tourism; light-assembly industries

FOREIGN TRADE

Exports: $173.3 million
Imports: $476.8 million

ATLANTIC OCEAN

Haiti

⊗ Capital
● City
〜 River
--- Road

0   30 kilometers
0   30 miles

TORTUGA
Port-de-Paix
Le Borgne
Môle Saint-Nicolas
Baie-de-Henne
Cap-Haïtien
Limbé
Fort-Liberté
Grande-Rivière-du-Nord
Ennery
Saint-Raphaël
Les Trois Rivières
Golfe de La Gonâve
Gonaïves
Lafond
Verrettes
Hinche
ÎLE DE LA GONÂVE
Canal de Saint-Marc
Saint-Marc
Montrouis
Rivière Artibonite
Rivière du Libon
Rivière Guayamouc
Lac de Péligre
Mirebalais
Anse à Galets
GRANDE CAYEMITE
Canal du Sud
Jérémie
Baie de Port-au-Prince
Croix-des-Bouquets
Manneville
Dame-Marie
Petit-Trou-de-Nippes
PORT-AU-PRINCE
Léogâne
Pétionville
Anse-d'Hainault
Pestel
Miragoâne
Petit-Goâve
Kenscoff
Les Anglais
Aquin
Marigot
Belle-Anse
Les Cayes
Jacmel
Bainet
Port-Salut
Côtes-de-Fer
ÎLE À VACHE
CARIBBEAN SEA
DOMINICAN REPUBLIC

The island is discovered by Christopher Columbus; named Hispaniola **1492**

The western portion of Hispaniola is ceded to France **1697**

Independence of France **1804**

The era of President François Duvalier **1957–1971**

Jean-Claude Duvalier is named president-for-life **1971**

Jean-Claude Duvalier flees into exile **1986**

1990s

A military coup ousts President Jean-Bertrand Aristide; Aristide returns to power in 1994

In December 1995, René Préval is elected to succeed Aristide

Haiti is admitted as the 15th member of CARICOM

HAITI

Haiti, which occupies the western third of the island of Hispaniola (the Dominican Republic comprises the other two thirds), was the first nation in Latin America to win independence of its mother country—in this instance, France. It is the poorest country in the Western Hemisphere and one of the least developed in the world. Agriculture, which employs about 70 percent of the population, is pressed beyond the limits of the available land; the result has been catastrophic deforestation and erosion. While only roughly 30 percent of the land is suitable for planting, 50 percent is actually under cultivation. Haitians are woefully poor, suffer from poor health and lack of education, and seldom find work. Haiti's urban unemployment is estimated at 40 to 50 percent. Even when employment is found, wages are miserable, and there is no significant labor movement to intercede on behalf of the workers.

A persistent theme in Haiti's history has been a bitter rivalry between a small mulatto elite, consisting of 3 to 4 percent of the population, and the black majority. When François Duvalier, a black country doctor, was president (1957–1971), his avowed aim was to create a "new equilibrium" in the country—by which he meant a major shift in power from the established, predominantly mulatto, elite to a new, black middle class. Much of Haitian culture explicitly rejects Western civilization, which is identified with the mulattos. The Creole language of the masses and their practice of Vodun (voodoo), a combination of African spiritualism and Christianity, has not only insulated the population from the "culturally alien" regimes in power but has also given Haitians a common point of identity.

Haitian intellectuals have raised sharp questions about the nation's culture. Modernizers would like to see the triumph of the French language over Creole and Roman Catholicism over Vodun. Others argue that significant change in Haiti can come only from within, from what is authentically Haitian. The refusal of Haitian governments to recognize Creole as the official language has only added to the determination of the mulatto elite and the black middle class to exclude the rest of the population from effective participation in political life.

For most of its history, Haiti has been run by a series of harsh authoritarian regimes. The ouster in 1986 of President-for-Life Jean-Claude Duvalier promised a more democratic opening as the new ruling National Governing Council announced as its primary goal the transition to a freely elected government. Political prisoners were freed; the dreaded secret police, the Tontons Macoute, were disbanded; and the press was unmuzzled.

The vacuum left by Duvalier's departure was filled by a succession of governments that were either controlled or heavily influenced by the military. Significant change was heralded in 1990 with the election to power of an outspoken Roman Catholic priest, Jean-Bertrand Aristide. By the end of 1991, he had moved against the military and had formulated a foreign policy that sought to move Haiti closer to the nations of Latin America and the Caribbean. Aristide's promotion of the "church of the poor," which combined local beliefs with standard Catholic instruction, earned him the enmity of both conservative Church leaders and Vodun priests. The radical language of his Lavalas (Floodtide) movement, which promised sweeping economic and social changes, made business leaders and rural landowners uneasy.

Perhaps not surprisingly in this coup-ridden nation, the army ousted President Aristide in 1991. It took tough economic sanctions and the threat of an imminent U.S. invasion to force the junta to relinquish power. Aristide, with the support of U.S. troops, was returned to power in 1994. Once an uneasy stability was restored to the country, U.S. troops left the peacekeeping to UN soldiers. The last U.S. forces left in the spring of 1996.

Although there was a period of public euphoria over Aristide's return, the assessment of the *Guardian,* a British newspaper, was somber: Crime rates rose precipitously, political violence continued, and Aristide's enemies were still in Haiti—and armed. Haitians, "sensing a vacuum," took the law "into their own hands."

René Préval, who had served briefly as Aristide's prime minister, was himself elected to the presidency in 1996. According to *Caribbean Week,* Préval has been caught between "a fiercely independent Parliament, an externally-imposed structural adjustment programme, and rumblings from Aristide about 'imperialism' and 'US occupation.'" The division of the Lavalas coalition into strongly opposed factions, together with the withdrawal of a UN presence, has raised tensions further. There has been little progress, and the suffering of millions continues.

DEVELOPMENT

The task of rebuilding Haiti following a devastating trade embargo and the ouster of the military is daunting. Three quarters of the Haitian population are unemployed, and a third depend on aid programs for food and health care.

FREEDOM

The Economist noted that, unless "a rule of law can be made to hold, and a civilian government made to function reliably, all other plans for Haiti will be just so much wasted paper."

HEALTH/WELFARE

Haiti, up until 30 years ago was self-sufficient in food production, must now import about a third of its food needs. Nevertheless, Haiti has a rapidly expanding population, with a doubling time of 35 years overall, far above the Caribbean average of 52 years.

ACHIEVEMENTS

In the late 1940s, Haitian "primitive" art created a sensation in Paris and other art centers. Although the force of the movement has now been spent, it still represents a unique, colorful, and imaginative art form.

Jamaica

GEOGRAPHY
Area in Square Kilometers (Miles): 10,991 (4,244) (slightly smaller than Connecticut)
Capital (Population): Kingston (587,000)
Climate: tropical

PEOPLE

Population
Total: 2,595,300
Annual Growth Rate: 0.8%
Rural/Urban Population Ratio: 47/53
Ethnic Makeup: 76% black; 15% Afro-European; 3% East Indian and Afro-East Indian; 3% white; 1% Chinese and Afro-Chinese; 2% others
Major Languages: English; Jamaican Creole

Health
Life Expectancy at Birth: 72 years (male); 77 years (female)
Infant Mortality Rate (Ratio): 16/1,000
Average Caloric Intake: 119% of FAO minimum
Physicians Available (Ratio): 1/6,335

Religions
56% Protestant; 5% Roman Catholic; 39% others, including some spiritualistic groups

Education
Adult Literacy Rate: 82%

Reggae
Reggae is the only Caribbean music and beat to have had a significant impact outside the region in recent years. The music derives from the traditional rhythms of the Rastafarian cult. Originally called "ska," reggae was introduced to the United States at the New York World's Fair in 1964. Reggae's combination of folk, rock, soul, blues, and revival has become popular in the United States and Europe. The lyrics usually follow a protest theme and are sharply critical of the injustices of society.

COMMUNICATION
Telephones: 127,000
Newspapers: n/a

TRANSPORTATION
Highways—Kilometers (Miles): 18,200 (11,310)
Railroads—Kilometers (Miles): 370 (231)
Usable Airfields: 41

GOVERNMENT
Type: parliamentary democracy; recognizes Queen Elizabeth II as chief of state
Independence Date: August 6, 1962
Head of Government: Prime Minister Percival J. Patterson
Political Parties: People's National Party; Jamaica Labour Party
Suffrage: universal at 18

MILITARY
Number of Armed Forces: 3,500
Military Expenditures (% of Central Government Expenditures): 1.1%
Current Hostilities: none

ECONOMY
Currency ($ U.S. Equivalent): 34.0 Jamaican dollars = $1
Per Capita Income/GDP: $3,050/$7.8 billion
Inflation Rate: 26.7%
Total Foreign Debt: $3.6 billion
Natural Resources: bauxite; gypsum; limestone
Agriculture: sugar; bananas; citrus fruits; coffee; allspice; coconuts
Industry: tourism; bauxite; textiles; processed foods; sugar; rum; molasses; cement; metal; chemical products

FOREIGN TRADE
Exports: $1.2 billion
Imports: $2.2 billion

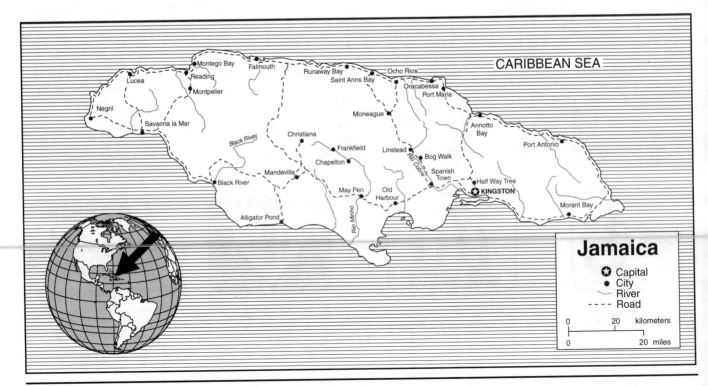

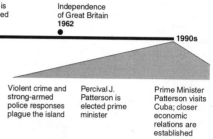

| The first Spanish settlement **1509** | Jamaica is seized by the English **1655** | An earthquake destroys Port Royal **1692** | Universal suffrage is proclaimed **1944** | Independence of Great Britain **1962** | **1990s** |

| Violent crime and strong-armed police responses plague the island | Percival J. Patterson is elected prime minister | Prime Minister Patterson visits Cuba; closer economic relations are established |

JAMAICA:
"OUT OF MANY, ONE PEOPLE"

In 1962, Jamaica and Trinidad and Tobago were the first of the English-speaking Caribbean islands to gain their independence. A central problem since that time has been the limited ability of Jamaicans to forge a sense of nation. "Out of many, one people" is a popular slogan in Jamaica, but it belies an essential division of the population along lines of both race and class. The elite, consisting of a small white population and Creoles (Afro-Europeans), still think of themselves as "English." Local loyalties notwithstanding, Englishness permeates much of Jamaican life, from language to sports. According to former prime minister Michael Manley: "The problem in Jamaica is how do you get the Jamaican to divorce his mind from the paralysis of his history, which was all bitter colonial frustration, so that he sees his society in terms of this is what crippled me?"

Manley's first government (1975–1980) was one of the few in the Caribbean to incorporate the masses of the people into a political process. He was aware that, in a country such as Jamaica—where the majority of the population were poor, ill educated, and lacked essential services—the promise to provide basic needs would win him widespread support. Programs to provide Jamaicans with basic health care and education were expanded, as were services. Many products were subjected to price controls or were subsidized to make them available to the majority of the people. Cuban medical teams and teachers were brought to Jamaica to fill the manpower gaps until local people could be trained.

However, Jamaica's fragile economy could not support Manley's policies, and he was eventually opposed by the entrenched elite and voted out of office. In 1989, however, Manley was returned to office, with a new image as a moderate, willing to compromise and aware of the need for foreign-capital investment. Manley retired in 1992 and was replaced as prime minister by Percival J. Patterson, who promised to accelerate Jamaica's transition to a free-market economy. The government instituted a policy of divestment of state-owned enterprises.

The challenges remain. Crime and violence continue to be major social problems in Jamaica. The high crime rate threatens not only the lucrative tourist industry but the very foundations of Jamaican society. Prime Minister Patterson has called for a moral reawakening: "all our programs and strategies for economic progress are doomed to failure unless there is a drastic change in social attitudes. . . ." A stagnant economy, persistent inflation, and unemployment and underemployment combine to lessen respect for authority and contribute to the crime problem. The Suppression of Crime Act of 1974 was repealed in 1994, however, in part because lawyers objected to extraordinary police powers of search and detention. The nation continues to walk the narrow line between liberty and license.

As is the case in many developing-world countries where unemployment and disaffection are common, drug use is high in Jamaica. The government is reluctant to enforce drug control, however, for approximately 8,000 rural families depend on the cultivation of ganja (marijuana) to supplement their already marginal incomes.

Some of Jamaica's violence is politically motivated and tends to be associated with election campaigns. Both major parties have supporters who employ violence for political purposes. The legal system has been unable to contain the violence or bring the guilty to justice, because of a pervasive code of silence enforced at the local level.

The Patterson government has moved deliberately in the direction of electoral reform in an attempt to reduce both violence and fraud. Until those reforms are in place, however, the opposition Jamaica Labour Party has decided to boycott by-elections.

On the positive side, human rights are generally respected, and Jamaica's press is basically free. Press freedom is observed in practice within the broad limits of libel laws and the State Secrets Act. Opposition parties publish newspapers and magazines that are highly critical of government policies, and foreign publications are widely available.

Jamaica's labor-union movement is strong and well organized, and it has contributed many leaders to the political process. Unions are among the strongest and best organizations in the country and are closely tied to political parties.

DEVELOPMENT

In 1997, Prime Minister Patterson visited Cuba, where agreements were signed for closer cooperation in the medical sphere and with a focus on biotechnology. Agreement was also reached on tourism issues and stressed cooperation rather than competition.

FREEDOM

Despite the repeal of the controversial Suppression of Crime Act of 1974, the Parliament, in the face of persistent high levels of crime, provided for emergency police powers. Some critics charge that the Parliament in essence re-created the repealed legislation in a different guise.

HEALTH/WELFARE

Jamaica's "Operation Pride" was designed to combine a dynamic program of land divestment by the state with provisions to meet demands for housing. Squatter colonies would be replaced by "proud home owners."

ACHIEVEMENTS

Marcus Garvey was posthumously declared Jamaica's first National Hero in 1964 because of his leading role in the international movement against racism. He called passionately for the recognition of the equal dignity of human beings regardless of race, religion, or national origin. Garvey died in London in 1940.

St. Kitts–Nevis (Federation of St. Kitts and Nevis)

GEOGRAPHY

Area in Square Kilometers (Miles): 261 (101) (about 2 times the size of Washington, D.C.)
Capital (Population): Basseterre (15,000)
Climate: subtropical

PEOPLE

Population

Total: 41,400
Annual Growth Rate: 0.8%
Rural/Urban Population Ratio: 58/42
Ethnic Makeup: mainly of black African descent
Major Language: English

Health

Life Expectancy at Birth: 63 years (male); 70 years (female)
Infant Mortality Rate (Ratio): 19/1,000
Average Caloric Intake: n/a
Physicians Available (Ratio): 1/3,125

Religions

Anglican; other Protestant sects; Roman Catholic

Education

Adult Literacy Rate: 97%

COMMUNICATION

Telephones: 2,400
Newspapers: n/a

TRANSPORTATION

Highways—Kilometers (Miles): 300 (187)
Railroads—Kilometers (Miles): 58 (36)
Usable Airfields: 2

GOVERNMENT

Type: constitutional monarchy within Commonwealth; recognizes Queen Elizabeth II as chief of state
Independence Date: September 19, 1983
Head of Government: Prime Minister Denzil Douglas
Political Parties: St. Kitts and Nevis Labour Party; People's Action Movement; Nevis Reformation Party
Suffrage: universal at 18

MILITARY

Number of Armed Forces: n/a
Military Expenditures (% of Central Government Expenditures): n/a
Current Hostilities: none

ECONOMY

Currency ($ U.S. Equivalent): 2.7 East Caribbean dollars = $1 (fixed rate)
Per Capita Income/GDP: $5,300/$210 million
Inflation Rate: 1.6%
Total Foreign Debt: $43.3 million
Natural Resources: n/a
Agriculture: sugarcane on St. Kitts; cotton on Nevis
Industry: sugar processing; tourism; cotton; salt; copra

FOREIGN TRADE

Exports: $32.4 million
Imports: $100 million

Fifty-Fifty Government?

St. Kitts–Nevis declared its independence of Great Britain on September 19, 1983, making it the third two-island country in the Caribbean (the others are Trinidad–Tobago and Antigua–Barbuda). The desire on the part of the citizens of the smaller island of Nevis for an equal say in the government is a source of considerable friction. Allowing people on Nevis—who comprise less than 20 percent of the nation's total population—to have a 50 percent vote in governmental decisions is bitterly opposed by the residents of St. Kitts. This conflict may prove to be a more serious problem now that independence has been gained.

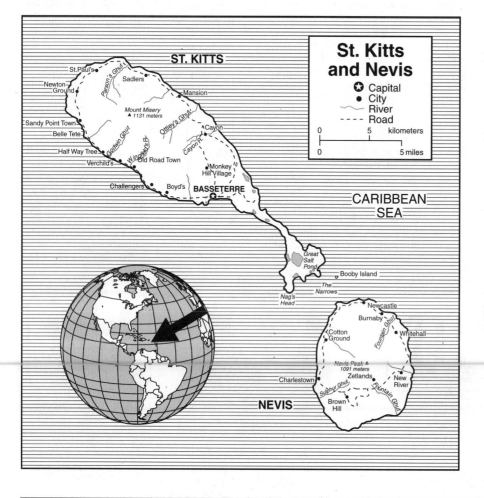

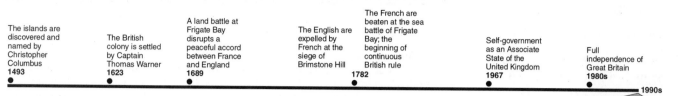

The islands are discovered and named by Christopher Columbus **1493**

The British colony is settled by Captain Thomas Warner **1623**

A land battle at Frigate Bay disrupts a peaceful accord between France and England **1689**

The English are expelled by French at the siege of Brimstone Hill **1782**

The French are beaten at the sea battle of Frigate Bay; the beginning of continuous British rule

Self-government as an Associate State of the United Kingdom **1967**

Full independence of Great Britain **1980s**

1990s

Elections in 1995 bring Denzil Douglas and the St. Kitts and Nevis Labour Party to power

Economic growth slows but tourism expands

ST. KITTS–NEVIS: ESTRANGED NEIGHBORS

As of September 19, 1983, the twin-island state of St. Kitts–Nevis became an independent nation. The country had been a British colony since 1623, when Captain Thomas Warner landed with his wife and eldest son, along with 13 other settlers. The colony fared well, and soon other Caribbean islands were being settled by colonists sent out from St. Kitts (also commonly known as St. Christopher).

The history of this small island nation is the story of the classic duel between the big sea powers of the period—Great Britain, France, and Spain—and the indigenous people—in this case, the Carib Indians. (Although much of the nation's history has centered around St. Kitts, the larger of the two islands, Nevis, only 2 miles away, has always been considered a part of St. Kitts, and its history is tied into that of the larger island.) The British were the first settlers on the island of St. Kitts, but were followed that same year by the French. In a unique compromise, considering the era, the British and French divided the territory in 1627 and lived in peace for a number of decades. A significant reason for this British–French cooperation was the constant pressure from their common enemies: the aggressive Spanish and the fierce Carib Indians.

With the gradual elimination of the mutual threat, Anglo–French tensions again mounted, resulting in a sharp land battle at Frigate Bay on St. Kitts. The new round of hostilities, which reflected events in Europe, would disrupt the Caribbean for much of the next century. Events came to a climactic head in 1782, when the British

garrison at Brimstone Hill, commonly known as the "Gibraltar of the West Indies," was overwhelmed by a superior French force. In honor of the bravery of the defenders, the French commander allowed the British to march from the fortress in full formation. (The expression "peace with honor" has its roots in this historic encounter.) Later in the year, however, the British again seized the upper hand. A naval battle at Frigate Bay was won by British Admiral Hood following a series of brilliant maneuvers. The defeated French admiral, the Count de Grasse, was in turn granted "peace with honor." Thereafter, the islands remained under British rule until their independence in 1983.

AGRICULTURE

Before the British colonized the island, St. Kitts was called *Liamiuga* ("Fertile Isle") by the Carib Indians. The name was, and is, apt, because agriculture plays a big role in the economy of the islands. Almost 90 percent of the nation's economy is based on the export of sugar; the rest derives from the tourist trade.

Because the sugar market is so unstable, the economy of St. Kitts–Nevis fluctuates considerably. Nearly one third of St. Kitts's land (some 16,000 acres) is under cultivation. In a good year, sugar production can exceed 50,000 tons. Although over the years growers have experimented with a number of other crops, they always have come back to sugarcane.

ECONOMIC CHANGE

Unlike such islands as Barbados and Antigua, St. Kitts–Nevis for years chose not to use tourism as a buffer to offset any disastrous fluctuations in sugar prices. On

St. Kitts, there was an antitourism attitude that can be traced back to the repressive administration of Prime Minister Robert Bradshaw, a black nationalist who worked to discourage tourism and threatened to nationalize all land holdings.

That changed under the moderate leadership of Kennedy Simmonds and his People's Action Movement, who remained in power from 1980 until ousted in elections in July 1995. The new administration of Denzil Douglas promised to address serious problems that have developed, including drug trafficking, money laundering, and a lack of respect for law and order. In 1997, a 50-man "army" was created to wage war against heavily armed drug traffickers operating in the region. Agriculture Minister Timothy Harris noted that the permanent defense force "was critical to the survival of the sovereignty of the nation." Douglas also pledged to promote tourism and cut taxes to stimulate small businesses.

The future of St. Kitts–Nevis will depend on its ability to broaden its economic base. A potential problem of some magnitude looms, however: The island of Nevis, long in the shadow of the more populous and prosperous St. Kitts, has raised the possibility of secession. Under the Constitution, the Nevis Assembly can initiate secession proceedings by a two-thirds vote.

DEVELOPMENT

In an attempt to improve an economy that is essentially stagnant, the government of St. Kitts–Nevis, under the auspices of CARICOM, supports the idea of a Caribbean free-trade area. Of particular interest is the inclusion of Cuba in the agreement.

FREEDOM

The election in 1984 of Constance Mitcham to Parliament signaled a new role for women. She was subsequently appointed minister of women's affairs. However, despite her conspicuous success, women still occupy a very small percentage of senior civil-service positions.

HEALTH/WELFARE

Since the economy is so dependent on the sugarcane crop, the overall welfare of the country is at the mercy of the world sugar market. Although a minimum wage exists by law, the amount is less than what a person can reasonably be expected to live on.

ACHIEVEMENTS

St. Kitts–Nevis was the first successful British settlement in the Caribbean. St. Kitts–Nevis was the birthplace of Alexander Hamilton, the first U.S. secretary of the Treasury Department and an American statesman.

St. Lucia

GEOGRAPHY

Area in Square Kilometers (Miles): 619 (238) (about ⅕ the size of Rhode Island)
Capital (Population): Castries (45,000)
Climate: maritime tropical

PEOPLE

Population

Total: 157,900
Annual Growth Rate: 1.2%
Rural/Urban Population Ratio: 52/48
Ethnic Makeup: 90% black; 6% mixed; 3% East Indian; 1% white
Major Languages: English; French patois

Health

Life Expectancy at Birth: 66 years (male); 74 years (female)
Infant Mortality Rate (Ratio): 20/1,000
Average Caloric Intake: 99% of FAO minimum
Physicians Available (Ratio): 1/2,235

Religions

90% Roman Catholic; 3% Church of England; 7% other Protestant sects

Education

Adult Literacy Rate: 67%

COMMUNICATION

Telephones: 9,500
Newspapers: none

TRANSPORTATION

Highways—Kilometers (Miles): 760 (474)
Railroads—Kilometers (Miles): none
Usable Airfields: 3

Drive-In Volcano

St. Lucia is a small, lush, and mountainous island. Amid the deep valleys and beautiful tropical flowers lies the smoldering volcano Soufrière. It is possible to drive a car right to the lip of the fuming crater and boil an egg in one of the many surrounding streams. The area around the crater has a number of hot springs, some of which have been in use as sulphur baths since 1785, when King Louis XVI had the water channeled for the benefit of his troops.

GOVERNMENT

Type: parliamentary democracy within Commonwealth; recognizes Queen Elizabeth II as chief of state
Independence Date: February 22, 1979
Head of Government: Prime Minister Kenny D. Anthony
Political Parties: United Workers Party; St. Lucia Labour Party; Progressive Labour Party
Suffrage: universal at 18

MILITARY

Number of Armed Forces: no army; special unit for defense within police force
Military Expenditures (% of Central Government Expenditures): n/a
Current Hostilities: none

ECONOMY

Currency ($ U.S. Equivalent): 2.7 East Caribbean dollars = $1 (fixed rate)
Per Capita Income/GDP: $4,200/$610 million
Inflation Rate: 0.8%
Total Foreign Debt: $96.4 million
Natural Resources: forests; minerals (pumice); mineral springs
Agriculture: bananas; coconuts; cocoa; citrus fruits; spices; livestock
Industry: garments; electronic components; beverages; corrugated boxes; tourism

FOREIGN TRADE

Exports: $123 million
Imports: $276 million

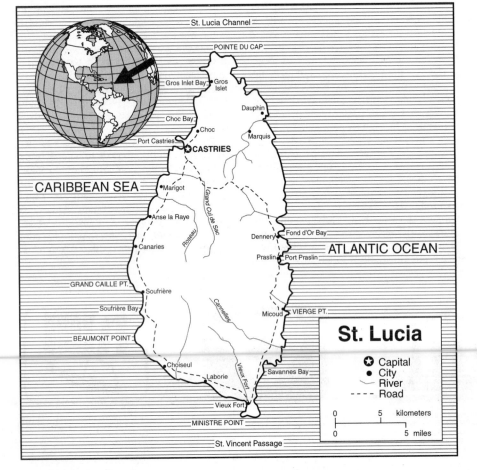

| The English take possession of St. Lucia **1638** | The English regain possession of St. Lucia from France **1794** | Riots **1908** | Universal adult suffrage **1951** | Independence of Great Britain **1979** | 1990s |

Poet Derek Walcott wins the Nobel Prize for Literature

Kenny Anthony of the St. Lucia Labour Party wins the 1997 election

Banana production suffers a serious decline

ST. LUCIA: ENGLISH POLITICS, FRENCH CULTURE

The history of St. Lucia gives striking testimony to the fact that the sugar economy, together with the contrasting cultures of various colonial masters, was crucial in shaping the land, social structures, and lifestyles of its people. The island changed hands between the French and the English at least 7 times, and the influences of both cultures are still evident today. Ninety percent of the population speaks French patois (dialect), while the educated and the elite prefer English. Indeed, the educated perceive patois as suitable only for proverbs and curses. On St. Lucia and the other patois-speaking islands (Dominica, Grenada), some view the common language as the true reflection of their uniqueness. English, however, is the language of status and opportunity. In terms of religion, most St. Lucians are Roman Catholic.

The original inhabitants of St. Lucia were Arawak Indians who had been forced off the South American mainland by the cannibalistic Carib Indians. Gradually, the Carib also moved onto the Caribbean islands and destroyed most of the Arawak culture. Evidence of that early civilization has been found in rich archaeological sites on St. Lucia.

The date of the European discovery of the island is uncertain; it may have occurred in 1499 or 1504 by the navigator and mapmaker Juan de la Cosa, who explored the Windward Islands during the early years of the sixteenth century. The Dutch, French, and English all established small settlements or trading posts on the island in the seventeenth century but were resisted by the Caribs. The first successful settlement dates from 1651, when the French were able to maintain a foothold.

The island's political culture is English. Upon independence of Great Britain in 1979, St. Lucians adopted the British parliamentary system, which includes specific safeguards for the preservation of human rights. Despite several years of political disruption, caused by the jockeying for power of several political parties and affiliated interests, St. Lucian politics is essentially stable.

THE ECONOMY

St. Lucia has an economy that is as diverse as any in the Caribbean. Essentially agricultural, the country has also developed a tourism industry, manufacturing, and related construction activity. A recent "mineral inventory" has located possible gold deposits, but exploitation must await the creation of appropriate mining legislation.

U.S. promises to the region made in the 1980s failed to live up to expectations. Although textiles, clothing, and nontraditional goods exported to the United States increased as a result of the Caribbean Basin Initiative, St. Lucia remained dependent on its exports of bananas. About a third of the island's workforce are involved in banana production, which accounts for 90 percent of St. Lucia's exports. U.S. aid to the region, which topped $226 million in 1985, fell to below $30 million in 1997, leading former St. Lucian prime minister Vaughan Lewis to complain, "We have dropped off the geopolitical map." The North American Free Trade Agreement (NAFTA) was clearly of more importance to the United States.

St. Lucia's crucial banana industry suffered significant production losses in 1997, in large part because of drought. Exports were half of the normal volume, and St. Lucia fell short of filling its quota for the European Union. In addition, the United States won a preliminary judgment from the World Trade Organization that acknowledged that St. Lucia and other Caribbean producers received preferential treatment from Europe under the quota system. Reduced quotas would be disastrous to small local producers.

EDUCATION AND EMIGRATION

Education in St. Lucia has traditionally been brief and perfunctory. Few students attend secondary school, and very few (3 percent) ever attend a university. Although the government reports that 95 percent of those eligible attend elementary school, farm and related chores severely reduce attendance figures. In recent years, St. Lucia has channeled more than 20 percent of its expenditures into education and health care. Patient care in the general hospital was made free of charge in 1980.

Population growth is relatively low, but emigration off the island is a significant factor. For years, St. Lucians, together with Dominicans, traveled to French Guiana to work in the gold fields. More recently, however, they have crossed to neighboring Martinique, a French department, in search of work. St. Lucians can also be found working on many other Caribbean islands.

DEVELOPMENT

A pilot project was developed on St. Lucia to help local farmers diversify their crops so they could provide hotels with a consistent and reasonably priced supply of fresh fruits and vegetables.

FREEDOM

The St. Lucian political system is healthy, with opposition parties playing an active role in and out of Parliament. Women participate fully in government and hold prominent positions in the civil service.

HEALTH/WELFARE

The minister of agriculture has linked marginal nutrition and malnutrition in St. Lucia with economic adjustment programs in the Caribbean. He noted that the success achieved earlier in raising standards of living was being eroded by "onerous debt burdens."

ACHIEVEMENTS

St. Lucians have won an impressive two Nobel prizes. Sir W. Arthur Lewis won the prize in 1979 for economics, and in 1993, Derek Walcott won the prize for literature. When asked how the island had produced two Nobel laureates, Wolcott replied: "It's the food."

St. Vincent and the Grenadines

GEOGRAPHY
Area in Square Kilometers (Miles): 340 (131) (about 2 times the size of Washington, D.C.)
Capital (Population): Kingstown (18,400)
Climate: tropical

PEOPLE

Population
Total: 118,400
Annual Growth Rate: 0.7%
Rural/Urban Population Ratio: 75/25
Ethnic Makeup: mainly black African descent; remainder mixed, with some white and East Indian and Carib Indian
Major Language: English

Health
Life Expectancy at Birth: 71 years (male); 74 years (female)
Infant Mortality Rate (Ratio): 17/1,000
Average Caloric Intake: 91% of FAO minimum
Physicians Available (Ratio): 1/4,737

Religions
Anglican; Methodist; Roman Catholic; Seventh-Day Adventist

Education
Adult Literacy Rate: 96%

COMMUNICATION
Telephones: 6,500
Newspapers: n/a

TRANSPORTATION
Highways—Kilometers (Miles): 1,000 (624)

Railroads—Kilometers (Miles): none
Usable Airfields: 6

GOVERNMENT
Type: constitutional monarchy within Commonwealth; recognizes Queen Elizabeth II as chief of state
Independence Date: October 27, 1979
Head of Government: Prime Minister James F. Mitchell
Political Parties: Unity Labour Party; New Democratic Party; United People's Movement; National Reform Party
Suffrage: universal at 18

MILITARY
Number of Armed Forces: none
Military Expenditures (% of Central Government Expenditures): n/a
Current Hostilities: none

ECONOMY
Currency ($ U.S. Equivalent): 2.7 East Caribbean dollars = $1 (fixed rate)
Per Capita Income/GDP: $2,000/$235 million
Inflation Rate: 4%
Total Foreign Debt: $74.9 million
Natural Resources: n/a
Agriculture: bananas; arrowroot
Industry: food processing

FOREIGN TRADE
Exports: $57.1 million
Imports: $134.6 million

Green Gold

Historically, St. Vincent exported huge amounts of arrowroot (a tuberous plant used to make certain kinds of starch). In fact, its economy was quite dependent on this single crop. Then, in 1954, the price of bananas skyrocketed and U.S. manufacturers replaced arrowroot with cornstarch. Thus, St. Vincent turned to bananas to replace arrowroot as its major crop and major export.

St. Vincent's soil is so fertile that just about any plant will grow and flourish. This, coupled with the rise of the banana market, made St. Vincent a land of "green gold."

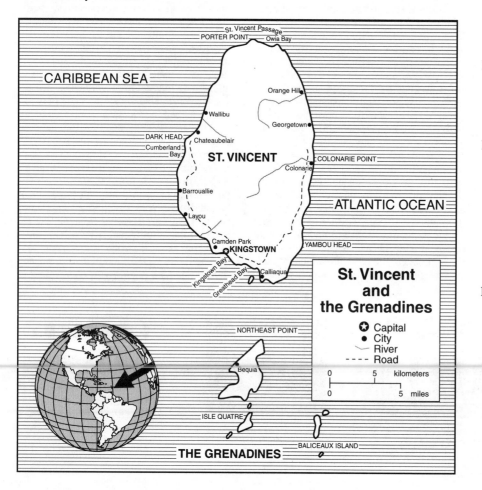

Christopher
Columbus
discovers and
names St. Vincent
1498

Ceded to the
British by France
1763

The Carib War
1795

St. Vincent's La
Soufrière erupts
and kills 2,000
people
1902

Independence of
Great Britain
1979

1990s

A new
minimum-wage
law takes effect

James Mitchell
wins his third
5-year term

The country's
financial
problems deepen

ST. VINCENT AND THE GRENADINES: POOR BUT FREE

Vincentians, like many other West Indians, either identify with or, as viewed from a different perspective, suffer from a deep-seated European orientation. Critics argue that it is an identification that is historical in origin, and that it is negative. For many, the European connection is nothing more than the continuing memory of a master–slave relationship.

St. Vincent is unique in that it was one of the few Caribbean islands where runaway black slaves intermarried with Carib Indians and produced a distinct racial type known as the Garifuna, or black Caribs. Toward the end of the eighteenth century, the Garifuna and other native peoples mounted an assault on the island's white British planters. They were assisted by the French from Martinique but were defeated in 1796. As punishment, the Garifuna were deported to what is today Belize, where they formed one of the bases of that nation's population.

In 1834, the black slaves were emancipated, which disrupted the island's economy by decreasing the labor supply. In order to fill this vacuum, Portuguese and East Indian laborers were imported to maintain the agrarian economy. This, however, was not done until later in the nineteenth century—not quickly enough to prevent a lasting blow to the island's economic base.

St. Vincent, along with Dominica, is one of the poorest islands in the West Indies. The current unemployment rate is estimated at between 20 and 40 percent. With more than half the population under age 15, unemployment will continue to be a major problem in the foreseeable future.

Formerly one of the West Indian sugar islands, St. Vincent's main crops are now bananas and arrowroot. The sugar industry was a casualty of low world-market prices and a black-power movement in the 1960s that associated sugar production with memories of slavery. Limited sugar production has been renewed to meet local needs.

THE POLITICS OF POVERTY

Poverty affects everyone in St. Vincent and the Grenadines, except a very few who live in comfort. In the words of one Vincentian, for most people, "life is a study in poverty." In 1969, a report identified malnutrition and gastroenteritis as being responsible for 57 percent of the deaths of children under age 5. Those problems persist.

Deep-seated poverty also has an impact on the island's political life. Living on the verge of starvation, Vincentians cannot appreciate an intellectual approach to politics. They find it difficult to wait for the effects of long-term trends or coordinated development. Bread-and-butter issues are what concern them. Accordingly, parties speak little of basic economic and social change, structural shifts in the economy, or the latest economic theories. Politics is reduced to personality contests and rabble-rousing.

Despite its severe economic problems, St. Vincent is a free society. Newspapers are uncensored. Some reports, however, have noted that the government has on occasion granted or withheld advertising on the basis of a paper's editorial position.

Unions enjoy the right of collective bargaining. They represent about 11 percent of the labor force. St. Vincent, which won its independence of Great Britain in 1979, is a parliamentary, constitutional democracy. Political parties have the right to organize.

A NEW POLITICAL SPIRIT

While the country's political life has been calm, relative to some of the other Caribbean islands, there are signs of voter unrest. Prime Minister James Mitchell was reelected in 1994 for an unprecedented third 5-year term, but his New Democratic Party lost some ground in the Legislature. In addition, two opposition parties, the St. Vincent Labour Party and the Movement for National Unity, merged to create the new Unity Labour Party. In an effort to recover the initiative, Mitchell has promised major new investments in the crucial banana industry as well as improvements in St. Vincent's infrastructure and social services. Bananas account for 65 percent of St. Vincent's export earnings; they are shipped to European Union countries as a result of a 1992 agreement that set quotas for Caribbean producers. Because the United States won a preliminary judgment with regard to the EU quotas from the World Trade Organization, there is growing concern about the future of the industry.

DEVELOPMENT

In an effort to diversify the economy, a feasibility study was planned for a new international airport and enhanced port facilities to service the tourist trade. Expanded land reform is also under consideration by the government. Prime Minister Mitchell visited Cuba in July 1997 in an effort to expand St. Vincent's trade.

FREEDOM

In 1989, the government took a great step forward in terms of wage scales for women by adopting a new minimum-wage law, which provided for equal pay for equal work done by men and women. The law took effect in 1990. Violence against women remains a significant problem.

HEALTH/WELFARE

Minimum wages range from $3.85 *per day* in agriculture to $7.40 in industry. Clearly, the minimum is inadequate, although most workers earn significantly more than the minimum.

ACHIEVEMENTS

A regional cultural organization was launched in 1982 in St. Vincent. Called the East Caribbean Popular Theatre Organisation, its membership extends to Dominica, Grenada, and St. Lucia.

Trinidad and Tobago

GEOGRAPHY
Area in Square Kilometers (Miles):
5,128 (1,980) (about the size of
Delaware)
Capital (Population): Port-of-Spain
(300,000)
Climate: tropical

PEOPLE

Population
Total: 1,272,400
Annual Growth Rate: 0.1%
Rural/Urban Population Ratio: 35/65
Ethnic Makeup: 43% black; 40% East
Indian; 14% mixed; 1% white; 1%
Chinese; 1% others
Major Language: English

Health
Life Expectancy at Birth: 68 years
(male); 73 years (female)
Infant Mortality Rate (Ratio): 19/1,000
Average Caloric Intake: 121% of FAO
minimum
Physicians Available (Ratio): 1/1,191

The Steel Band

Trinidadians, with an inventive skill that has astounded musicologists,
created a whole range of instruments, from oil drums, gas tanks, pots, and
pans, to empty metal containers of all descriptions. Collectively, these are
known as the steel band. The music from these homemade instruments
became popular after World War II and quickly spread to other islands. The
rhythms have their origin in the islands' black culture, which reaches back
to Africa. The sound is unique and compelling.

Religions
32% Roman Catholic; 24% Hindu;
14% Anglican; 14% other Protestant;
6% Muslim; 10% others

Education
Adult Literacy Rate: 97%

COMMUNICATION
Telephones: 109,000
Newspapers: 4 dailies

TRANSPORTATION
Highways—Kilometers (Miles): 8,000
(4,960)
Railroads—Kilometers (Miles): none
Usable Airfields: 6

GOVERNMENT
Type: parliamentary democracy
Independence Date: August 31, 1962
Head of State: Prime Minister Basdeo
Panday
Political Parties: People's National
Movement; National Alliance for
Reconstruction; United National
Congress; Movement for Social
Transformation; National Joint Action
Committee; others
Suffrage: universal at 18

MILITARY
Number of Armed Forces: about 2,650
*Military Expenditures (% of Central
Government Expenditures):* 4.6%
Current Hostilities: none

ECONOMY
Currency ($ U.S. Equivalent): 5.87
Trinidad & Tobago dollars = $1
Per Capita Income/GDP: $11,280/$15
billion
Inflation Rate: 10.1%
Total Foreign Debt: $2 billion
Natural Resources: oil and gas;
petroleum
Agriculture: sugarcane; cocoa; coffee;
rice; citrus; bananas
Industry: food processing; fertilizers;
cement; petroleum; tourism; automobile
assembly

FOREIGN TRADE
Exports: $1.9 billion
Imports: $996 million

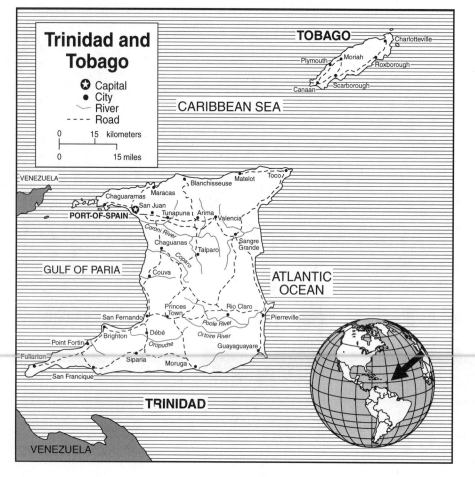

The island now
called Trinidad is
discovered by
Columbus and
later colonized by
Spain
1498

Trinidad is
captured by the
British
1797

Tobago is added
to Trinidad as a
colonial unit
1889

Independence of
Great Britain
1962

Oil-export
earnings slump
1980s

1990s

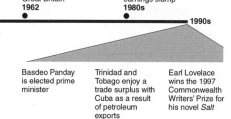

Basdeo Panday
is elected prime
minister

Trinidad and
Tobago enjoy a
trade surplus with
Cuba as a result
of petroleum
exports

Earl Lovelace
wins the 1997
Commonwealth
Writers' Prize for
his novel *Salt*

TRINIDAD AND TOBAGO: A MIDDLE-CLASS SOCIETY

The nation of Trinidad and Tobago, which became independent of Great Britain in 1962, differs sharply from other Caribbean countries, in terms of both its wealth and its societal structure. More than one third of its revenues derive from the production of crude oil. Much of the oil wealth has been redistributed and has created a society that is essentially middle class. Health conditions are generally good, education is widely available, and the literacy rate is a very high 97 percent.

The country also enjoys an excellent human-rights record, although there is a good deal of tension between the ruling urban black majority and East Indians, who are rural. The divisions run deep and parallel the situation in Guyana. East Indians feel that they are forced to submerge their culture and conform to the majority. In the words of one East Indian, "Where do Indians fit in when the culture of 40 percent of our people is denied its rightful place and recognition; when most of our people exist on the fringes of society and are considered as possessing nothing more than nuisance value?"

The lyrics of a black calypso artist that state the following are resented by East Indians:

> If you are an East Indian
> And you want to be an African
> Just shave your head just like me
> And nobody would guess your
>   nationality.

The prosperity of the nation, however, tends to mute these tensions.

Freedom of expression and freedom of the press are constitutionally guaranteed as well as respected in practice. Opposition viewpoints are freely expressed in the nation's Parliament, which is modeled along British lines. There is no political censorship. Opposition parties are usually supported by rural Hindu East Indians; while they have freely participated in elections, some East Indians feel that the government has gerrymandered electoral districts to favor the ruling party.

Violent crime and political unrest, including an attempted coup by black fundamentalist Muslim army officers in 1990, have become a way of life in the nation in recent years. Prime Minister Basdeo Panday, elected in 1996, noted that there were still agendas, "political and otherwise," that divided Trinidadian society. "How much better it will be," he stated, "if all in our society, and particularly those in a position to shape mass consciousness, will seize every opportunity to promote and mobilise the greater strength that comes out of our diversity. . . ."

Trade-union organization is the most extensive among Caribbean nations with ties to Britain, and includes about 30 percent of the workforce. In contrast to other West Indian states, unions in Trinidad and Tobago are not government controlled, nor are they generally affiliated with a political party.

Women are well represented in Parliament, serve as ministers, and hold other high-level civil-service positions. Several groups are vocal advocates for women's rights.

In an attempt to redress imbalances in the nation's agricultural structure, which is characterized by small landholdings—half of which are less than five acres each—the government has initiated a land-redistribution program using state-owned properties and estates sold to the government. The program is designed to establish more efficient medium-size family farms, of five to 20 acres, devoted to cash crops.

TOBAGO

Residents of Tobago have come to believe that their small island is perceived as nothing more than a dependency of Trinidad. It has been variously described as a "weekend resort," a "desert island," and a "tree house"—in contrast to "thriving," "vibrant" Trinidad. Tobagans feel that they receive less than their share of the benefits generated by economic prosperity.

In 1989, the Constitution was reviewed with an eye to introducing language that would grant Tobago the right to secede. The chair of the Tobago House of Assembly argued that, "in any union, both partners should have the right to opt out if they so desire." Others warn that such a provision would ultimately snap the ties that bind two peoples into one. Trinidadian opposition leaders have observed that the areas that have historically supported the ruling party have more and better roads, telephones, and schools than those backing opposition parties.

DEVELOPMENT

Bilateral treaties were signed with the United States to address issues of investment and intellectual property. The government also planned to initiate discussions with Venezuela about a free-trade agreement.

FREEDOM

Freedom of expression on the islands is guaranteed by the Constitution. The independent judiciary, pluralistic political system, and independent and privately owned print media assure that free expression exists in practice as well as in theory.

HEALTH/WELFARE

Legislation passed in 1991 greatly expanded the categories of workers covered by the minimum wage. The same legislation provided for 3 months' maternity leave for household and shop assistants as well as other benefits.

ACHIEVEMENTS

Eric Williams, historian, pamphleteer, and politician, left his mark on Caribbean culture with his scholarly books and his bitterly satirical *Massa Day Done*. V. S. Naipaul is an influential author born in Trinidad. Earl Lovelace is another well-known Trinidadian author.

Articles from the World Press

Regional Articles

Mexico

Central America

South America

Caribbean

Topic Guide to Articles

TOPIC AREA	TREATED IN	TOPIC AREA	TREATED IN
Indians		**Politics**	
Mexico	6. Tlatelolco, Shop Window of the Aztec Empire	*Regional Overview*	1. Latin America Revisited
Central America	8. Mighty Maya Nation	*Mexico*	1. Latin America Revisited
	9. Deforestation from Bad to Worse?		3. Can Democracy Finally Take Root?
South America	15. Brazil: The Meek Want the Earth Now		4. Step into Unknown Political Territory
	16. Conquering Peru		5. PRI's Last Hurrah?
		Central America	11. Democracy Advances in Nicaragua
Industrial Development			12. Panama: Tailoring a New Image
Regional Overview	1. Latin America Revisited	*South America*	13. Remapping South America: Mercosur
	2. Indigenous Cultural and Biological Diversity		14. Bolivia: An Example in the Andes
Mexico	1. Latin America Revisited	*The Caribbean*	17. Cuba Today: Instant Antiquity
South America	13. Remapping South America: Mercosur		18. Island of Disenchantment
		Pollution	
Migration		*South America*	16. Conquering Peru
South America	15. Brazil: The Meek Want the Earth Now		
		Privatization	
Military		*Regional Overview*	2. Indigenous Cultural and Biological Diversity
The Caribbean	18. Island of Disenchantment		
		Roots	
Natives		*Mexico*	7. Laughter and Tears
Regional Overview	2. Indigenous Cultural and Biological Diversity	*Central America*	8. Mighty Maya Nation
Mexico	6. Tlatelolco, Shop Window of the Aztec Empire	**Social Reform**	
	7. Laughter and Tears	*Regional Overview*	2. Indigenous Cultural and Biological Diversity
Central America	8. Mighty Maya Nation	*Central America*	10. After a Long and Brutal Civil War, Academics in Guatemala Remain Cautious
	9. Deforestation from Bad to Worse?		11. Democracy Advances in Nicaragua
South America	15. Brazil: The Meek Want the Earth Now	*South America*	14. Bolivia: An Example in the Andes
	16. Conquering Peru		15. Brazil: The Meek Want the Earth Now
The Carribbean	17. Cuba Today: Instant Antiquity	*The Caribbean*	17. Cuba Today: Instant Antiquity
	19. Soaring Scales of the Silver Basin		18. Island of Disenchantment
		Turmoil	
Natural Resources		*Central America*	10. After a Long and Brutal Civil War, Academics in Guatemala Remain Cautious
South America	15. Brazil: The Meek Want the Earth Now		11. Democracy Advances in Nicaragua
	16. Conquering Peru	*South America*	15. Brazil: The Meek Want the Earth Now
			16. Conquering Peru
Peasantry		*The Caribbean*	18. Island of Disenchantment
Mexico	7. Laughter and Tears		
Central America	11. Democracy Advances in Nicaragua		
South America	15. Brazil: The Meek Want the Earth Now		
	16. Conquering Peru		
The Caribbean	18. Island of Disenchantment		

Article 1   *New Perspectives Quarterly, Volume 14 #2, Spring 1997*

Latin America Revisited

LORENZO MEYER, ABRAHAM LOWENTHAL, ALVARO VARGAS LLOSA

HAS LATIN AMERICA CHANGED, OR DO THINGS REMAIN THE SAME OLD WAY SOUTH OF THE BORDER? DESPITE FREE-TRADE ZONES AND DEMOCRATIC ELECTIONS, DRUG LORDS, CORRUPTION AND GUERRILLAS STILL CAPTURE THE HEADLINES. ESPECIALLY IN MEXICO—ONCE THE MODEL OF GOVERNABILITY IN THE THIRD WORLD—THINGS ARE FALLING APART FAST. MUCH IS DIFFERENT IN LATIN AMERICA TODAY, BUT THE TWO KEY TRANSFORMATIONS THAT WOULD MARK A DEPARTURE FROM THE PAST HAVE NOT TAKEN PLACE—THE RULE OF LAW AND THE REDUCTION OF SOCIAL INEQUALITY. IN THIS COLLAGE OF COMMENT, THREE OF LATIN AMERICA'S MORE SOBER VOICES TAKE STOCK.

Mexico: Turning the Corner or Falling Apart?

LORENZO MEYER is a professor at the Center of International Studies of El Colegio de Mexico in Mexico City and an independent political commentator with a regular column in Excelsior.

MEXICO CITY—On June 28, 1996, while a political meeting was taking place in the small town of Aguas Blancas to mark the first anniversary of the massacre of 17 peasants by local policemen, 50 uniformed and masked men claiming to be members of a newly created Popular Revolutionary Army (EPR) entered the town and also the already complex Mexican political arena.

The initial reaction of the government to the emergence of a second insurgent organization—after the Chiapas rebels—was to call it a farce and minimize its significance. After a few days and a couple of clandestine press conferences given by EPR leaders, governmental officials were willing to admit that the group was in fact a small guerrilla organization operating in Guerrero. Unfortunately, this second version of the EPR was soon substituted by a third one after several bloody attacks on police and military barracks in five states of southern Mexico. Today no one dismisses the EPR as irrelevant and President Ernesto Zedillo has vowed to use

> *As the century comes to a close, Mexico, for so long one of the best examples of governable political systems in the world, is losing this characteristic.*

"the full power of the state" against it. The newest rebel government joins the Zapatista Army on National Liberation (EZLN), in the field since 1994. The total number of well-known armed groups now operating outside the law in Mexico—drug traffickers, bandits, kidnappers, vigilantes, plus bona fide guerrillas—is 85 in 19 states. The police has been unable to cope with this challenge. The Federal Police is in particularly bad shape as a result of years of neglect by the political elite. On August 19, the Attorney General had to ask the support of the army to disarm and dismiss 737 of his 4,200 agents—17 percent of the force—because they were part of the problem and not of the solution. In fact, they were not at the service of the federal government, but of drug dealers or other crime organizations.

The Mexican army, for so long an irrelevant political and social actor, now is active in the field in Chiapas, Tabasco, Guerrero, Veracruz, Oaxaca, Hidalgo, Michoacan, Queretaro and Mexico City. The capital's police department has been handed to generals and colonels as the only way to attempt to regain control of an institution that more often than not is working against society. The Mexican army itself is rapidly becoming an active and indispensable element of support of the governing coalition, a clear indication of the deterioration of civilian institutions. Since last year, the Ministry of Defense has been very active in building a new and direct relationship with its counterpart in the United States, breaking a lone tradition in this area.

As the century comes to a close, Mexico, for so long one of the best examples of governable political systems in the word, is losing this characteristic. And the basis for this assessment is not only insurgency. Two years and several special prosecutors after the assassination of Luis Donaldo Colosio, presidential candidate of Mexico's state party (PRI) and virtually the next president, the crime still remains a mystery. In the meantime, 10 persons involved in one way or another in this dramatic event have died violently, giving substance to the theory of a big conspiracy within the power structure to kill Colosio and cover up the evidence.

THE GOOD OLD DAYS Mexico's governability began to emerge after the builders of the present political system eliminated their enemies in the battlefield during and immediately after the Mexican Revolution (1910–20). But effective suppression of political alternatives was not the only explanation behind the country's governability. It was also the product of a strong presidency and a state party able to introduce strict discipline among the members of the political elite. Last but not least, governability was, above all, the result of a strong political coalition able to provide a mass basis of support of the official party and its natural leader: the president of the republic.

After 1940, and under the undisputed leadership of the president, all strategic political actors—organized labor and peasant unions, the army, state bureaucrats, professional organizations, bankers, industrialists and trade and service organizations—worked out an arrangement mutually acceptable to each and every one of them. The post–revolutionary Mexican political regime provided the necessary positive and negative incentives to strategic actors to discourage behavior dysfunctional to the existing order. This characteristic of post–Second World War Mexico corresponds exactly to a definition of governability.

In its "classical period" (1946–68) and even some time after it, Mexican authoritarianism was very inclusive and had an institutional network very effective as a machine to funnel demands, contradictions and conflicts and give them acceptable solutions. This system of mutual satisfactory compromises began to reach its limits in 1968

when university students—reflecting urbanization and increasing pluralism—demanded effective democratic competition but had brutal repression as an answer. It was around this time that the first guerrilla movements started in modern Mexico with a "dirty war" as the sequel. Armed struggle failed then but some members of those movements waited for better times.

The original political dysfunctions of the '60s and '70s were aggravated by a dramatic economic crisis that started in 1982. The import substitution model inaugurated 40 years earlier became unviable and its dismantling brought a profound economic depression that is still affecting Mexico. The impact of economic restructuring—the opening up of the economy, privatization and budget discipline—was dual. On the one hand, the new market economy increased social marginalization, lowered living standards of the majority of Mexicans, from lower to middle classes, and concentrated income as never before. On the other hand, it diminished dramatically the resources at the disposal of the president, making it very difficult to continue the traditional policies of giving satisfaction to the contradictory demands of the old governmental coalition.

Between 1980 and 1994, common crime in Mexico increased 200 percent. Insecurity in cities and rural areas is the number one problem on the minds of Mexicans, according to surveys.

The combination of economic and political failure coincided with the end of the Cold War and the strengthening of the so-called "third wave of democracy." This combination of internal and external factors helped to produce the first serious electoral challenge to the PRI since 1952. At the right of PRI, the challenger was the half-century old Partido Accion Nacional (PAN); at its left, a coalition of former members of the PRI and militants of the old left (Socialists and Communists) under the leadership of Cuauhtemoc Cardenas (1934–40). The answer of the political establishment to this unexpected turn of events was not very imaginative: a monumental electoral fraud in 1988. But immediately after, the new president, Carlos Salinas, began a reshaping of the traditional coalition. He strengthened the relationship between Mexico and the US, opened the economy to external competition and gave a warm welcome to all kinds of foreign investment. He also reached an informal but very effective understanding with PAN. The basis for this peculiar relationship between an authoritarian president and the democratic right was their mutual interest in dismantling state enterprises, ending public subsidies and introducing Mexico as fast as possible to the process of globalization and, finally, after a century and a half of Jacobean policies, giving legal recognition to the Catholic Church as a cultural, social and political actor. The other side of the coin was a systematic attack of the newly created Partido de la Revolution Democratica (PRD) under the leadership of Cuauhtemoc Cardenas. The actions of the government against PRD included electoral fraud, systematic attack in the mass media as well as open violence. The message of these policies and actions to the radical left was clear: the ballot is useless as a political tool to confront Mexico's authoritarianism as well as the economic and social crisis.

THE UNGOVERNABLE Atul Kholi, looking at India, suggests three basic indicators to measure the degree of governability in any underdeveloped country: A) the nature of the governing coalition, B) governmental effectiveness and C) the capacity of the political system to deal with conflict without resorting to violence.

Let's look at each one in Mexico's case:

In the wake of the Mexican revolution during the 1930s and 1940s, the new political elite was able to build a complex corporate structure that represented almost all strategic political actors. The state/party gave shelter to workers, peasants, bureaucratic and middle-class organizations. Outside the party but equally dominated by the president and the political elite were industrial, trade and financial organizations. Only the Catholic Church was kept outside this coalition, but the government worked out satisfactory *modus vivendi* with the bishops.

The post–revolution political coalition experienced a real crisis when Cuauhtemoc Cardenas, rejecting the new economic policies, left the PRI in 1987. The new coalition based on market economics and the North America Free Trade Agreement (NAFTA) was, by its very nature, much more exclusionary and less stable than the previous one.

In regard to Kholi's second indicator—governmental effectiveness—the situation is even more problematic. According to PRI's platform, the two paramount and traditional goals of the regime are economic growth and social justice. Unfortunately, the so-called "Mexican economic miracle" ended with the short-lived oil boom in 1982. Since that date and up to last year, the average annual growth of the GNP was 2.9 percent—just enough to keep up with Mexican demography. In per capita income growth, Mexico has remained stagnant for 14 years. As far as social justice is concerned, one indicator

> *Mexico requires a strong and legitimate government and political regime. The first step toward that kind of government is to delay no longer the dismantling of authoritarianism and the building of new democratic institutions.*

is telling enough: according to the 1994 household income survey, the poorest half of Mexican families received only 16.2 percent of the available income while the top 10 percent received 41.2 percent.

Non-economic indicators of governmental performance are equally depressing. According to the Ministry of Interior, between 1980 and 1994, common crime increased 200 percent, but federal offenses 400 percent. Insecurity in cities and rural areas is the number one problem on the minds of Mexicans, according to surveys.

The third indicator of governability has to do with the political system's capacity to deal with political conflict in a non-violent way. Colosio's assassination, as well as the killing a few months later of PRI's general secretary, Mario Ruiz Massieu, and the indictment of President Salinas' brother Raul for this crime are just dramatic examples of the same problem: the internal struggle of Mexico's political class has reached a level of violence without precedent since the killing of president-elect Alvaro Obregon in 1928. The violent death of about 400 members of PRD since 1989 also points in the same direction: political violence in Mexico is on the rise.

A PROPOSITION Mexico's protracted transition to democracy and the increasing difficulties in the area of governability are linked. The old authoritarian system is losing legitimacy and effectiveness very rapidly. The PRI no longer reflects the increased diversity of Mexican society, but it refuses to give way to a real plural and democratic system as the best way to process the conflicting demands of all significant political actors.

To fight corruption, deterioration of the environment, rural and urban crime, drug cartels, militarization and similar problems, to neutralize insurgency, to respond effectively to social demands and to continue with economic modernization, Mexico requires a strong and legitimate government and political regime. The first step toward that kind of government is to delay no longer the dismantling of authoritarianism and the building of new democratic institutions. The obstacles Mexico has to surmount to achieve the modernization of its political structures are many and important: inertia, a non-democratic history and civic culture, strong anti-democratic vested interests, a state party that still commands important resources and, finally, a weak president. But the need for this thorough modernization is evident.

© *The Pacific Council on International Policy*

Is Latin America a Good Bet?

ABRAHAM F. LOWENTHAL, director of the Center for International Studies at the University of Southern California, was the founding director of the Inter-American Dialogue, the premier think tank on Western Hemisphere issues. He is now spearheading the new Pacific Council on International Policy headquartered in Los Angeles, of which he is the president.

LOS ANGELES—The prevailing public image of Latin America changes very rapidly in the United States, and indeed elsewhere around the world.

Seven or eight years ago, Latin America was still widely discussed as a series of "basket cases," of hopeless failures supposedly trapped in culture-bound backwardness. Unflattering comparisons were frequently made between Latin America and Anglo America, and especially between Latin America and East Asia. Latin America seemed destined always to lag. The *mañana* attitude was thought to be dominant.

Just four or five years ago, by contrast, Latin America was enthusiastically hailed for its new boom. Substantial foreign capital entered the region, over $50 billion per year, on average, during each year of the early 1990s. The mood about Latin America's economies, particularly among international investors, was little short of euphoric.

Similar extremes have characterized discussion of Latin America's political climate—sharply negative during the authoritarian period of the late 1970s and early 1980s and then increasingly positive in the late 1980s and early 1990s, as the region moved toward democratic governance. Only a few years ago, it used to be asserted that Latin Americans were culturally disposed toward authoritarian rule, and that corruption and lack of accountability were deeply ingrained. But with Latin America's democratic transitions of the late 1980s, US officials claimed under President Bush that the region was fast becoming the "first completely democratic hemisphere in human history." Similar claims were made by Clinton Administration spokesmen in connection with the Miami Summit of the Americas in December 1994.

During the past three years, however, new concerns have emerged about Latin America. The Chiapas uprising in Mexico on January 1, 1994, was a shocking re-

minder that NAFTA has not solved all of Mexico's problems. The assassination just a few weeks later of the presidential candidate of Mexico's ruling party, the PRI, and then several months later, of PRI's secretary general caused serious additional worries, reflected in the precipitous decline of the country's reserves. Other doubts were raised, for various reasons, in Argentina, Brazil, Colombia, Peru, Venezuela and elsewhere.

All these concerns were heightened and underlined by the Mexican devaluation in December 1994, the collapse of the peso and of the Mexican stock market that followed, and by the nose-dives which occurred as a result of the "Tequila effect" in several other Latin American markets. The allegations, denunciations and innuendoes which have rocked and roiled Mexico in the past couple of years have further damaged the whole region's image.

The flight of Ecuador's vice president into exile to escape corruption charges, the resurgence of guerrilla violence in Peru, the daring jail break by imprisoned leftists in Chile; these and other incidents grab media attention. Once again, Latin America has begun to be painted by some in somber tones.

As someone who has followed Latin America closely for many years, through various cycles and fads, I would question both the uncritical optimism about Latin America which was fashionable in the early 1990s and also broad-brush pessimism now being heard in some quarters. Latin America's political and economic advances during the past decade have been real but fragile, widespread but uneven, significant but still quite limited, promising but by no means assured.

THREE FUNDAMENTAL SHIFTS Three shifts have unquestionably been taking place in Latin America during the past few years: an emerging consensus among economic policy-makers on the main tenets of sound policy; the even more universal embrace of constitutional democracy as an ideal; and a growing disposition toward pragmatic cooperation with the industrial countries and particularly with the US.

By the late 1980s, most Latin American economic policy-makers had come to share a diagnosis of the region's fundamental maladies and a set of prescriptions for restoring its health. Throughout Latin America and the

> *Latin America's political and economic advances during the past decade have been real but fragile, widespread but uneven, significant but still quite limited, promising but by no means assured.*

Caribbean, it came to be understood that it is essential to bring inflation under control, even though that means drastically reducing public expenditures. It became accepted, as well, that the import substitution approach to economic growth—however successful it was in some countries during the 1950s and 60s—has been exhausted everywhere, and that the region's recovery depends primarily on boosting exports, which in turn necessitates market openings, competitive exchange rates, and an end to various subsidies and other forms of protection.

It was also agreed that Latin America must sharply prune the state's industrial and regulatory activities, privatize most public enterprise, facilitate competitive markets, stimulate the private sector and attract foreign investment. The emergence of this region-wide consensus among economists and economic policy-makers is a paradigm shift of historic dimensions.

Equally striking has been the broad accord on the desirability of constitutional democratic politics. Just 30 years ago, in the late 1960s, self-proclaimed "vanguards" on the left and "guardians" on the right openly expressed disdain for democratic procedures, and both of them claimed significant followings. In recent years, however, a wide spectrum of Latin American opinion has come to recognize the value of democratic governance. Most Latin American elites, as well as the public at large, now agree that, to be legitimate, government authority must derive from the uncoerced consent of the majority, tested regularly through fair, competitive and broadly participatory elections.

The regional turn toward harmonious relations with the US has also been unmistakable. For years, many Latin Americans defined their foreign polices primarily by expressing independence, even outright opposition, to Washington. All this has changed. Most Latin American governments and many opposition movements in Latin America today seek stronger links with the US. Mexico made the most dramatic move toward US-Latin American cooperation when President Carlos Salinas de Gortari and his team began in 1990 to pursue a North American Free Trade Agreement (NAFTA) with the US and Canada. Most other Latin American countries actively work to improve their ties with the US, sometimes even at the expense of their relations with other Latin American nations. Only Fidel Castro's Cuba holds on to

Most Latin American elites, as well as the public at large, now agree that, to be legitimate, government authority must derive from the uncoerced consent of the majority, tested regularly through fair, competitive and broadly participatory elections.

its anti-Americanism, and even Cuba would probably be open to rapprochement, if Washington were only willing.

These turns toward free market economics, democratic politics and inter-American cooperation are not accidental or unconnected. They are not insignificant, nor are they merely cyclical. They respond to profound regional experiences during the last generation and to a radically transformed global context.

REFORMS AT RISK Yet these important shifts are still at grave risk, and they will surely not last through the 1990s in every country, at least in their current form. There will be bumps in the road, detours and frank reversals.

The region-wide promulgation of market-oriented economic reforms was deceptively easy. It was indeed stunning that such similar measures could be announced in short order in extremely different countries, often by presidents who had actually campaigned against such reforms. But this convergence owed much more, in most cases, to the lack of credible alternatives and to weak and disoriented oppositions than to broad-based national consensus or to unshakable conviction by political leaders. Except in Chile and perhaps in Argentina, the political base for the economic reforms is still quite tentative, firmly supported only by leading technocrats and some segments of the private sector.

Unless Latin America's economic reforms soon generate demonstrable and broadly felt results, they may not become solidly entrenched. Changes in policy or at least in emphasis and pace may occur in several countries if it becomes generally perceived that income concentration is worsening, and that social, economic and in some cases ethnic divisions are widening. It is difficult, if not impossible, for governments to sustain popular backing for reforms that at first enrich a privileged few without providing a credible promise of mass prosperity. Strong social safety nets and improved public services would help make the reforms palatable, but they are hard to achieve when the economic reforms, and years of low growth and fiscal crisis, have cut back the state.

The dwindling of public support for the economic programs has become increasingly evident throughout much of Latin America recently, especially in the violent outbursts experienced in provincial Argentina, rural Colombia and southern Mexico; the mounting social and labor protests in several other countries; and the gains registered by opposition parties in many countries. These opposition forces are not uniform, of course, and the reasons for their advances vary from case to case, but there is little denying that incumbents who initiated the reforms have been losing ground in many countries.

ECONOMIC VULNERABILITY Latin America as a whole can probably not achieve and sustain economic dynamism throughout the 1990s, let alone grow at rates comparable to the East Asian "tigers." Chile has managed more than a dozen consecutive years of impressive growth, to be sure, after long years of painful structural reform. But growth has not yet proved sustainable at even moderate levels in most other countries. In fact, Latin America's overall rate of growth during the 1990s has been quite modest, not to say mediocre. Other than Chile, only Argentina, Colombia, Costa Rica and Panama have thus far sustained moderate to high rates of growth (averaging over 4 percent per year) in the '90s. Of all the countries in Latin America and the Caribbean, only eight (Colombia, Argentina, Chile, Uruguay, Belize, Jamaica, Panama and Costa Rica) had higher per capita incomes in 1993 than in 1980; in some cases, there has been no gain in real per capita income since the early 1970s.

Much of the capital entering Latin America has been portfolio rather than direct investment.

The flow of voluntary capital into several Latin American countries since 1990 has been encouraging by contrast with the lean years from 1982 through 1989. But much of the capital entering Latin America has been portfolio rather than direct investment. Most of it is selectively concentrated in a few large low-risk firms, and it can be and has been withdrawn quickly by mutual funds and institutional investors with worldwide alternatives. A good deal of it, moreover, is flight capital—originally taken out of Latin America by elites and prone to leave again whenever there is trouble. Much of the foreign investment in Latin America in the early 1990s was drawn to the region in part by high interest rates and by quick stock market spurts as well as by relatively low interest rates prevalent in industrial countries; even minor upward adjustments in industrial-country interest rates produced some outflow of capital from Latin American markets in 1994–95. Equally or perhaps more troubling, Latin America's dependence on foreign capital remains very high because rates of saving and investment in the region remain so low.

Latin America's economies, in short, have made strides, but they are not yet out of the woods. If Latin America's external environment were more supportive—that is, if growth rates in the industrial countries could rebound, if international protectionism could be avoided, if interest rates stayed low and/or further debt relief

were achieved—there might be good reason to hope that most Latin American economies could advance in a mainly uninterrupted fashion through the rest of the 1990s. But these propitious international circumstances are far from present.

SHORT ON DEMOCRACY The regional turn toward democracy is also highly vulnerable. Indeed, effective democratic governance in Latin America now exists only in those very few countries—Chile, Costa Rica, Uruguay and the Commonwealth Caribbean—where democratic traditions were already well implanted 35 or 40 years ago, and even in some of these countries it is still challenged.

Peru's turn to renewed and thinly veiled authoritarian rule through President Alberto Fujimori's autogolpe of 1992 may be unique because of the national consensus against the extremist Shining Path movement and the broad distrust there of most institutions. But the threat to democratic governance is by no means confined to Peru. What was most striking about the nearly successful military coup in Venezuela in February 1992 and the even bloodier attempt in November of that year, for example, was that they appeared to have considerable support within the military and to be accepted with equanimity, if not outright enthusiasm, by quite a few Venezuelans. This widespread repudiation of the established Venezuelan parties laid some of the basis for the eventual ousting of President Carlos Andres Perez and then the return to the presidency of former President Rafael Caldera, winning the presidency as an independent running against the two established parties, with the support of only 17 percent of the electorate.

Brazil has also faced grave difficulties, with several failed presidents, extraordinarily weak parties, massive corruption, rampant street crime, rural violence and police repression. That elected president Fernando Collor could be peacefully removed from office in 1993 for larceny—and that 18 members of Congress could also be recommended for expulsion for taking bribes and kickbacks—showed Brazil's resilience and public respect for constitutional procedures and norms, as well as the strength of the press and other civic groups. But this false start for Brazilian democracy took its toll, making it very difficult for the largest country in Latin America to adopt and implement coherent policies. With a highly qualified elected president, former Senator and Finance Minister Fernando Henrique Cardoso, and with a growing national consensus for significant economic and political reforms, Brazil today is at its most promising and hopeful moment in many years, but the country still has a lot of catching up to do.

The pervasive corruption and violence associated with narcotics has been undermining state authority in Bolivia, Colombia, Ecuador, Panama, Peru, Suriname, as well as Mexico. Guerrilla violence still erodes or hampers democratic governance not only in Peru but in Colombia, Guatemala and southern Mexico. Throughout most of Latin America, civil-military relations remain an unresolved problem, exacerbated by the drastic effects of budget austerity on military salaries and perquisites, and by uncertainty about the role of the armed forces in a changed world environment.

And more than 80 years after its revolution, Mexico is still far from truly "effective suffrage" or providing equal justice under law throughout the country. Polls before the 1994 presidential elections showed that nearly half of the Mexican population doubted that their votes would be respected. More than 70 percent distrust government explanations of the Colosio assassination. Confidence in the rule of law can hardly have been enhanced by the dizzying series of allegations, revelations and rumors. Legitimacy cannot easily be built or maintained in such circumstances. It is hard to be sure whether Mexico's traumas will ultimately enhance the prospects for political reform and democratic opening, or whether they will eventually produce an authoritarian backlash.

In country after country, polls show that most people still favor "democracy" as a form of government but are increasingly skeptical of all democratic political institutions. The hard truth is that representative democracy is not being successfully "consolidated" in most of Latin America, in many cases because it has yet to be truly constructed. Sustained political stability based on legitimate and valued institutions has not yet been achieved in most of Latin America.

THE SOCIAL QUESTION Latin America's chances for sustaining economic and political advances depend in part on overcoming widespread poverty and vast inequalities, but these problems have on the whole been getting worse. According to UN statistics, some 46 percent of Latin Americans lived at poverty levels in 1990, 4 percent more than a decade before. More than 200 million people survive without basic necessities, according to UN definitions; many of these subsist in extreme poverty, unable to maintain the minimum caloric intake required for human health.

After more than a decade of depression, austerity programs and structural adjustments, millions of Latin Americans who earlier thought they had made it to the middle class have been newly impoverished. The economic reforms have provided benefits to a few, but in the short run they have reduced real wages and increased uncertainty for many. Although it has become unfashionable worldwide to talk about class struggle, the divisions in Latin America have become notably sharper. The gap between those who live in the 21st century, with their cellular phones and Internet connections, and those living in the 19th century or even earlier, grows ever larger and more unbridgeable. Income distribution, long more inequitable in Latin America than elsewhere in the world, has become even more unequal in most countries. Reduced investments in health, education and other such services in the 1980s will have their worst effects in the late 1990s. For Latin America's poor, the 1990s are literally the time of cholera—and of tuberculosis, malaria and other infectious diseases.

In many Latin American countries, the "social question" is reaching critical dimension. Pervasive social breakdown is reflected in such horrible practices as kidnapping for ransom and the sale or killing of children. These grim realities reflect—and feed, in turn—a high degree of frustration and alienation. Emigration has been burgeoning, even from countries (like Brazil) where this has not previously occurred. Insurgencies remain a threat in several nations. Evangelical religious sects and messianic movements are exploding. All these conditions make for volatility, not for sure and steady progress.

Latin America's chances of successfully confronting its social agenda may depend significantly on political forces long opposed by the US in the Cold War context. A political space now exists in many Latin American nations for a modern social democratic movement, one which accepts the democratic political rules and the main tenets of modern economic doctrine but confronts the issues of equity that have been largely neglected thus far by most reigning technocrats. Latin America's new generation of leaders emerging from the left—Cardoso and Lula in Brazil, Jose Octavio Bordon and Chacho Alverez in Argentina, Ricardo Lagos and Sergio Bitar in Chile, Ruben Zamora in El Salvador, Andres Velásquez in Venezuela and others—stand to gain from a region-wide dissatisfaction with politics—as usual and widespread frustration at the failure of the economic reforms thus far to alleviate mass poverty or the pauperization of the middle class. Whether these leaders are yet ready to de-

> *The gap between those who live in the 21st century, with their cellular phones and Internet connections, and those living in the 19th century or even earlier, grows ever larger.*

velop sound action programs and can build a sustainable consensus to implement them remains to be seen, however. The Cardoso presidency in Brazil is an important test.

MEDIUM-TERM PROSPECTS Those who want to be optimistic about Latin America often point to Chile—growing well, with improved equity, and with democratic politics as a blueprint for the future. But it is wrong to project Chile's success in achieving both sustained economic growth and democratic political stability as a sure predictor of how the whole region will evolve; Chile has had several historic advantages, not the least of which is the legacy derived from several generations of democratic politics.

The countries of Latin America and the Caribbean are not simply strung along on a spectrum, ineluctably going in a set order through the same stages of development. Their paths are diverging, and will probably diverge still further in the future.

Even before NAFTA, for instance, more than 70 percent of Mexico's trade was with the US and more than 6 percent of Mexico's work-force was employed in this country, remitting at least $3.5 billion a year back to Mexico. A similar trend toward functional North American integration is evident with the Caribbean islands. US airlines and telephone companies treat the Caribbean islands as if they were domestic, not foreign; it is hard to define the border between the mainland and the Caribbean in economic, social demographic or political terms—but it is certainly north of Miami!

But while Mexico, many Caribbean islands and part of Central America have been integrating with the US, Peru and to some extent Colombia have disintegrated internally; Argentina and Brazil have been trying to nurture a subregional common market, Mercosur; and Chile has been steadily diversifying its ties throughout the Americas, Asia and Europe. For many purposes, therefore, it is less sensible than ever to generalize about Latin America and the Caribbean.

Most Latin American and Caribbean countries today do share two difficult internal tensions, however. One is between the imperatives of political and economic liberalization, between the opening of democratic politics and of market economies. For reasons of national experience and ideology, people in the US like to think of these processes as not only compatible but as necessarily related—as two sides of the same coin, united by the element of free choice. But in Latin America's circumstances—as in those of Eastern and Central Europe, of Russia and of East Asia—the claims from an impatient populace and the demands of economic elites are not easily reconciled, at least in the short and medium term. It will take superb political craftsmanship to build the coalitions necessary to manage these tensions successfully, and this skill remains everywhere in short supply.

A second important tension is between streamlining states and ridding them of excess functions and personnel, on the one hand, and strengthening their capacity to provide crucial public services and exert legitimate authority, on the other. Over the last decade, reforms to reverse failed statist policies, combined with fiscal crisis, have further weakened Latin American governments, which were never strong in administrative and management capacity. In many Latin American countries, therefore, building effective and efficient state capacity—rather than further cutting back the state—is a central task for the 1990s.

It is by no means clear, in sum, whether and when all Latin American and Caribbean countries can turn the many corners that must be successfully negotiated to assure sustainable economic development plus effective and enduring democratic governance. Euphoria about Latin America—propagated in recent years by the emerging market funds, investment promotion boards and the *Wall Street Journal's* editorial page—was as unjustified as indiscriminate bearishness was seven or eight years ago. But so is the new gloom beginning to percolate in some quarters. Mexico's political and economic troubles, although they have been severe, should not touch off a new cycle of decline there or elsewhere in Latin America. If they do, it will be mainly because exaggerated and undifferentiated international concerns—in the US, Canada, Europe and in Japan—themselves help produce self-fulfilling prophecies.

The next few years could still see significant setbacks in Latin America: economic stagnation in some countries, renewed inflation in others, political or policy instability, and perhaps reversion toward authoritarian rule in some cases. It is dangerous to sweep these real possibilities under the rug.

But it is equally wrong to ignore the social, economic, political and policy gains made in many Latin American countries in recent years. Latin America's future is far from assured, but it is on the whole promising, at least in the medium and longer term. In a world of considerable uncertainty and widespread disillusion, Latin America still has clear potential for positive advance, even against severe obstacles. Latin America is not a sure thing, but it is a reasonable bet.

> *Building effective and efficient state capacity—rather than further cutting back the state—is a central task for the 1990s.*

Bad Reforms Imperil Latin America's Free Market

ALVARO VARGAS LLOSA, a Peruvian journalist, is co-author with Cuban novelist Carlos Alberto Montaner and Colombian journalist Plinio Apuleyo Mendoza of the best-selling book, Manual of the Perfect Latin American Idiot (Plaza & Janes, Madrid, 1997).

LONDON—There is a perilous new myth which claims that Latin America is at present experiencing a free-market revolution. A grave danger resides in the fact that the courageous but limited experiments in reform are giving rise to a powerful populist opposition and weakening the case for the free market precisely because they are so incomplete.

If the limited reforms that have brought about fewer state-owned enterprises, reduced inflation and increased foreign investment were enough to bring about stability and prosperity—indeed a capitalist revolution—then Latin America would have been prosperous a long time ago. After all, there have been periods in the past when monetary policy was not wildly out of control and the wave of state ownership had not yet begun. During that time foreign investment was omnipresent; so much so, that all of our Socialist revolutions—from Mexico in 1910 to Bolivia in 1952 to Cuba in 1959 to Peru in 1968—arose in the name of "sovereignty." And yet the misery persisted.

If competent macroeconomics are sufficient for a free and prosperous society, why is Latin America still backward even though, since 1940, we have grown an average 5 percent a year; more than Europe has grown in that same period?

The answer lies in a simple but often misunderstood irony: Partial reforms and the single-minded focus on macroeconomic management—without commitment to private property, competitive markets and strong judicial and democratic political institutions—result in mercantilistic systems where the vast majority are denied the opportunities and benefits of economic growth.

There are two great weaknesses in the current reform process in Latin America. The first is that reformers are confusing private enterprise with free-market capitalism.

> *Ill-conceived privatizations have replaced public monopolies with private monopolies, transferring the ownership of certain sectors of the economy while still protecting markets and scandalously fueling corruption.*

Second, reformers are focusing on macroeconomic management without considering institutional frameworks.

Private ownership is not a panacea for an economy. Ill-conceived privatizations have replaced public monopolies with private monopolies, transferring the ownership of certain sectors of the economy while still protecting markets and scandalously fueling corruption. Telephone systems demonstrate the problem. Throughout Latin America, users are suffering high rates and poor service because telephone companies have been sold as private monopolies. This is true in Peru, Mexico, Argentina. Users then wrongly deduce that capitalism is the cause of this abuse. They fail to understand that this is what happens when you transfer a closed market from public to private control.

The same situation happens in a variety of other service industries. Public transport in Buenos Aires is privately owned, but each route is monopolized by one company, thereby turning Argentines against the whole idea of privatization.

The inadequacies of these privatizations are being used by enemies of reform in Latin America such as the powerful Colombian telephone union, which controls most of the 14,000 workers of Colombian Telecom, the state-owned telephone company. To defend state ownership and block privatization, the union points out the flaws of Peru's privatized telephone monopoly.

Protecting these private monopolies has also led to the equally dangerous perception that liberalization means giving privileges to the rich. Of the 15 Mexicans featured in *Fortune's* latest list of the richest people in the world, there is not one who has not benefited (however legally) from state-granted privileges. Mexicans see little reason to bless a reform process that has left them impoverished and disenfranchised.

Around the continent there are also so-called "strategic" areas of the economy where privatization is not even contemplated. Take the oil industry, for example. Consider Venezuela. Despite a phenomenal $250 billion generated in the past 20 years by the state-owned oil company, an estimated 80 percent of Venezuelans live below the poverty line today. And yet even the suggestion of privatizing Venezuelan oil is met with hysteria. This is also the case with oil in Mexico and copper in Chile.

On the macroeconomic front, some Latin American countries have made bold changes, but at the same time they have blatantly ignored the importance of institutions—justice, private property, solid money and democracy. The result is a reform process with weak links that invites disaster.

Lack of institutional reform is widespread. Private-property rights are often either ignored or eschewed by government. During the 1980s, in a silent process, Peruvian peasants *de facto* privatized 60 percent of the land that had been collectivized by the Socialist agrarian reform of the 1970s. Yet formal property titles are still not available for the Peruvian Andes' 4 million *patceleros.*

In Mexico, property rights, a crucial institution in any free society, can hardly be present under Article 27 of the constitution, which states that "the nation" is the owner of all the land. The heralded reform of the collectively owned *ejido* has not translated into property rights for peasants.

In Peru, there can be little trust in the country's institutions when the judiciary was disbanded in a *coup d'état* by the president himself in 1992, later replaced by a new, politically dependent court. This institution made no attempt to prevent Peru from becoming, according to a 1998 Amnesty International report, the country with the most political prisoners in Latin America after Cuba (approximately 1,100).

The authoritarian structure of Peru's current system has been exposed during the hostage crisis at the Japanese embassy in Lima. That crisis, for which the blame must be put on the cruel Tupac Amaru terrorists, has revealed that Mr. Vladimiro Montesinos, Peru's corrupt strongman behind Alberto Fujimori, is not as efficient as we were led to believe—the entire intelligence service hierarchy is among the hostages! It has also shown that the Peruvian military's obsession with Ecuador is a national security risk. While they were busy buying a squad of MIG fighters from the former Soviet republics and placing key military personnel at the northern border, the internal enemy was preparing its most spectacular blow.

Finally, the hostage crisis has also revealed that political prisoners (many of whom are not terrorists) are held in jails that resemble medieval dungeons.

Leaving aside the extreme case of Peru, which country has undertaken a new reform of its justice system? None. Latin America divorces economic liberty from its essential political and institutional base.

Latin America has never tried liberal reform. What I've called "The Latin American Idiot" (the conventional wisdom of the leftist Latin American intellectuals) instead has always attributed our failures to conspiracies—the Monroe Doctrine, the United Fruit Company, the IMF, the World Bank. The latest enemy is neoliberalism—that is, free-market reform. Once again, the blame is in the wrong place.

Article 2

Cultural Survival Quarterly, Winter 1995

Indigenous Cultural and Biological Diversity:

Overlapping Values of Latin American Ecoregions

Bruce A. Wilcox and Kristin N. Duin

Bruce Wilcox is Director of the Institute for Sustainable Development based in Menlo Park, California. Kristin Duin is a biologist from Stanford University and an intern at the Institute.

It is well known that the number of culturally distinct indigenous populations tends to be high in tropical rain forests, the most biologically rich and ecologically significant ecosystems in the world. Yet the overall correspondence of cultural diversity with globally significant biological values within and between ecosystems generally is less well known. We had the opportunity to measure this correspondence on the basis of two recently completed map-based data sets. A pioneering project backed by The World Bank and implemented by David Olson and Eric Dinerstein at World Wildlife Fund—US (the results of which are to be published early in '95) has produced a preliminary set of 218 ecoregions in Latin America. Meanwhile, a decade-long project to map indigenous groups in South America has been recently completed by Manual Lizarralde of the Department of Anthropology at U.C. Berkeley, complementing Mac Chapin's Central American map (*CSQ*, Fall, 1992).

In parallel with the above developments, our group has been working on an operational framework for applying valuation concepts based on ecological economics to the measurement of sustainability, in collaboration with The 2050 Project at the World Resources Institute in Washington, D.C. This work involves employing the notion of "biological utility," or the beneficial role of ecosystem function and biodiversity

in the sense of the "goods and services" provided by different kinds of natural ecosystems; forest and woodland, savanna/grassland, wetland, shrubland, scrubland and desert, and the many subtypes of these and other terrestrial ecosystems. Different ecosystems in general, and in different locations in particular, vary greatly in their biodiversity and ecological properties of utility to humans. For example, forest and woodland tend to support large numbers of species, especially trees, of enormous value as harvestable resources, along with genetic resources for the improvement of domesticated species. Wetlands, on the other hand, which generally have much lower levels of species and genetic diversity, are of higher value for the storage and cleansing of water resources and regulation of water flows. Yet both are the most important terrestrial ecosystems for the storage or accumulation of carbon, thus for the amelioration of global climate change.

Because an ecoregion is effectively an area delineated on the basis of biotic features including the dominant ecosystem type, various measures of utility value can be attributed to a single ecoregion unit or a collective set constituting a larger biogeographic or geopolitical area, or major ecosystem category (e.g., all of the tropical moist forest in Latin America). So, along with the measurement of indigenous cultural significance, utility value in terms of the contribution to globally significant functions, like maintenance of genetic resources or amelioration of global climate change, is mappable. The result can be an "accounting," which theoretically can be made at different aggregate geographic scales, of the value of different regions in terms of their contribution to at least these aspects of global sustainability.

Biological Utility and Cultural Diversity

The linkage between indigenous cultural diversity and biological diversity has been shown to be as complex as it is inextricable by Madhav Gadgil of the Indian Institute of Science in Bangalore and his collaborators. They have found, for example, that traditional endogamous groups in India, including tribal peoples, partition the biological resource base, exploiting different niches in a manner of speaking. Some groups specialize as honey gatherers, others as shifting cultivators (traditional cultivators who clear forest plots, cultivate them for several years, then leave them fallow to be reclaimed by the forest while moving on to clear and cultivate a new plot), and so on. This obviously results in a greater efficiency of biological resource use than is possible when the economic production system is "industrialized," which basically involves "homogenizing" the resource base, reducing both cultural and biological diversity. Industrial development generally results in the transformation of environmentally heterogeneous landscapes into ones dominated by large blocks of state or privately controlled lands used for intensive agriculture, plantation forestry, parks, industrial activity, and urban settlements.

There presumably is much to be learned by societies engaged in industrial modes of production from cultures whose production systems are compatible with or may even enhance intrinsic levels of biodiversity. By "intrinsic levels" we mean amounts of habitat, species, and genetic diversity comparable to that which would exist in the absence of human activity. It has become a more or less accepted principle among ecologists

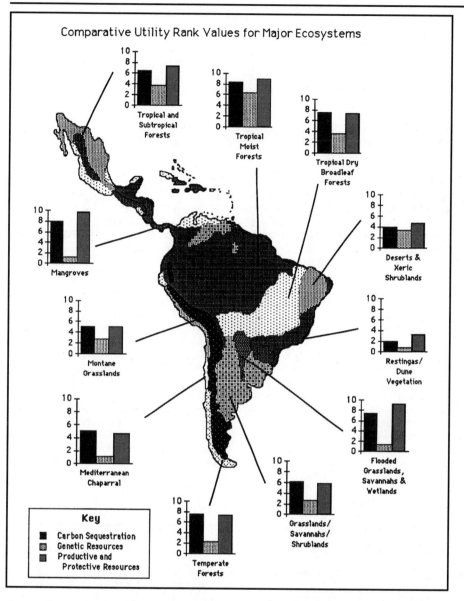

Comparative Utility Rank Values for Major Ecosystems

Tropical and Subtropical Forests

Tropical Moist Forests

Tropical Dry Broadleaf Forests

Deserts & Xeric Shrublands

Mangroves

Restingas/ Dune Vegetation

Montane Grasslands

Flooded Grasslands, Savannahs & Wetlands

Mediterranean Chaparral

Grasslands/ Savannahs/ Shrublands

Temperate Forests

Key
- ■ Carbon Sequestration
- ▦ Genetic Resources
- ▩ Productive and Protective Resources

that moderate levels of physical disturbance, such as often imposed by traditional forms of resource exploitation, enhances ecological complexity, landscape heterogeneity, and species diversity, thus promoting overall biodiversity. Also, empirical evidence exists showing indigenous cultivators' plantings of perennial species, for example, increases overall species diversity at a site. This has been shown by Dominique Irvine in her research on the Runa people of the Ecuadorian Amazon. Based on these two lines of evidence and population biology and ecological theory in general, a strong argument can be made that traditional use of biological resources, even with a cautious mix of conventional land and resource use, could maintain and even enhance biodiversity. Yet despite this possibility, excessive rates of population growth in the South and consumption in the North are overwhelming the land and biological resource base globally. Gadgil provides an interesting slant on the distinction between indigenous and industrial cultural perspectives of biodiversity which has important consequences to global sustainability. He points out that a convenient, although not always exclusive, dichotomy can be drawn between "ecosystem people" and "biosphere people." Ecosystem people derive their sustenance from biological resources in their vicinity, while biosphere people (most of us reading this article), base their sustenance on biological and non-renewable resources from distant sources, often including the ecosystems in which indigenous people live. The distinction is not simply academic. People physically dis-

tant from the biological resources they consume tend to undervalue them, indirectly facilitating their over-exploitation and the degradation of the ecosystems producing them. By contrast, those with a direct stake in the biotic integrity of an ecosystem supplying their needs, tend to be conscious of their dependency. This is precisely the consciousness required by society at large for global sustainability.

The concept of biological utility may be one way to help build this consciousness. "Utility" is simply the notion that humans value things that provide them with some use or instrumental benefit. This contrasts with intrinsic value which we attach to things we believe have value in their own right. It is often argued as dangerously anthropocentric to ascribe utility or economic value to things like biological or cultural diversity which clearly are inherently valuable regardless of any monetary or other quantitative measures. However, the measurement of utility value provides a more objective means of identifying which components of nature or culture are considered more important than others. The alternative, which is to insist everything be valued equally, results in little value being ascribed to anything. In fact, as Brent Berlin of U.C. Berkeley (now at the University of Georgia) and others have shown, indigenous people classify biological diversity based on utility value. This contrasts the system of biological classification used in Western science.

In indigenous cultures, rational stewardship (conservation) of biological resources is effectively based on a knowledge of functional utility and institutionalized in the form of taboos. For example, in many tropical forest ecosystems figs (Ficus spp.) act as keystone species, and this recognition by tribal cultures in India is the basis of the reverence held for *Ficus religiosa* and the taboos against the cutting of such trees. Unfortunately, such rational connections based on biological utility are less well developed among non-traditional and non-indigenous societies. Recognizing attributes of biodiversity that represent utility benefits is an obvious first step toward the institutionalization (formal or informal) of modes or methods of sustainable resource use.

Biological Utility of Latin American Ecoregions

A thorough accounting of functional connections between human welfare, in terms of global sustainability and ecosystems, is both impossible and impractical. Not only is the number of scientifically demonstrated connections a small fraction of the total that may possibly exist, but the perception of utility is "user-dependent." The "direct output benefits" of ecosystems—tangible commodities represented by plants and animals consumed directly or marketed as food, fiber, forage, or chemically active compounds—generally overlap very little among traditional users of biological resources and industrial society. The other major class of utility values, represented by the so-called "indirect functional benefits" of ecosystems, tend to overlap more, and particularly so if "function" is considered on a larger scale—spatially and temporally. For example, the role of forests in the maintenance of global and regional climate benefits indigenous, and non-indigenous "biosphere" people alike.

Unfortunately, despite such overlapping dependencies, the response to ecological degradation in many biodiversity rich areas tends toward the designation of natural areas as parks and protected enclaves from which indigenous control of resources is minimized or excluded. More than this, however, the focus on biodiversity by non-indigenous and non-ecosystem people has been on popular, charismatic and mythological elements, such as "endangered species" and "rain forests." Important utility benefits of ecosystems, essential to all people as well as the survival of charismatic elements of biodiversity, are often over-looked. These indirect functional benefits derive from *ecological* functions or processes, or other attributes related to physical structure in ecosystems, that do not necessarily correspond to high levels of globally unique biodiversity.

Some kinds of ecosystems like rain forests apparently do have higher biological utility value, as well as high element diversity, measured in terms of the benefits for society at large, including indigenous people. However, it is important to know how these broader utility values vary among different types of ecosystems as a means of assessing the social and economic impacts of deforestation and other pressures on ecosystems. Part of our research was conducted within USAID's Biodiversity Support Program (BSP), and was directed toward contributing a valuation framework for setting conservation investment priorities on a country basis. This effort, particularly the development of ecoregion maps by Olson and Dinerstein afforded an opportunity to attach utility value to specific terrestrial ecosystems in Latin America and the Caribbean.

The mapping of ecoregions and indigenous populations provided a unique opportunity to determine the extent to which measures of biological utility value, as perceived by society at large, and cultural diversity correspond. A high correspondence would demonstrate, for example, that the ecosystems most important to maintaining indigenous cultural diversity are also the most important to maintaining global ecosystem functions such as the amelioration of global climate change, the maintenance of genetic resources, and protective and productive functions of ecosystems. This would have implications beyond development agency investment priorities, by suggesting a reexamination of the perception of values and benefits held by those of us in industrial society vis à vis those of indigenous people.

In our preliminary analysis reported here, 57 aggregated ecoregion units comprising the eleven Major Habitat Types in Latin America were scored and ranked according to the number of distinct linguistic/ethnic indigenous populations that occurred within their boundaries as well as their utility value. (In all, 218 base ecoregions currently are identified in the Olson and Dinerstein ecoregion scheme.) As indicators of utility value we used measures of carbon

Figure 1

Habitat Type	Biomass Carbon Content[1]	Forest Tree Genetic Resources[2]	Centers of Plant Diversity[3]	Origins of Important Crop Species[3]	Domesticated Animal Origins[3]	Net Primary Productivity[4]	Indigenous Populations	Base Ecoregions
Tropical Moist Forests	16	95	40	18	14	1800	334	54
Tropical Dry Broadleaf Forests	7	70	12	12	11	800	89	32
Tropical and Subtropical Forests	7	48	9	1	0	1300	56	15
Temperate Forests	17	1	2	0	1	1300	2	4
Grasslands/Savannahs/Shrublands	3.3	17	3	4	5	850	46	16
Flooded Grasslands, Savannahs and Wetlands	3	5	0	2	3	2000	21	13
Montane Grasslands	1	7	9	1	6	600	13	13
Mediterranean Chaparral	1	3	0	0	0	250	2	2
Deserts and Xeric Shrublands	0.5	39	9	9	7	250	31	27
Restingas/Dune Vegetation	0	1	0	0	0	0	0	3
Mangroves	7	2	2	0	2	2000	10	39

Indicators of Biological Utility, Cultural Diversity and Biodiversity in Latin America

[1] Units are in kg/m². Data source is J. S. Olson, J. A. Watts, L. J. Allison, "Carbon in Live Vegetation of Major World Ecosystems," Oak Ridge National Laboratory, 1983.

[2] Food and Agriculture Organization of the United Nations, "Appendix 7: Forest Genetic Resources Priorities, in the Report on the 8th Session of FAO Panel of Experts on Forest Gene Resources," Rome, 1994.

[3] Updated from original data in WCMC, "Global Biodiversity; Status of the Earth's Living Resources," Chapman and Hall, 1992.

[4] Units are in g/m²/yr. Data Source is H. Likens and R. Whittaker, "Primary Productivity of the Biosphere," Springer-Verlag, 1975.

sequestration, genetic resources, and protective and productive benefits collectively associated with the ecoregions that constituted a Major Habitat Type. The scores were based on measured values drawn from the scientific literature, such as rates of biomass storage or accumulation. Where quantitative measures were unavailable, but clear qualitative differences exist, ecoregions were simply given scores based on their relative rank for a particular function. The first two utility values are global in the sense of the scale on which they benefit humans: The amelioration of global climate change through the sequestering of carbon in plant matter and the accumulation of carbon in the form of soil organic matter; and the maintenance and continued evolution of gene pools necessary for the improvement of the World's economically most valuable crops and livestock. The third category captures an ecosystem's utility or functional value in two senses, its protective and productive capacity. The former refers to an ecosystem's buffering capacity against regional or local environmental change: drought, storms, floods, etc. Productive capacity refers to the rate of biomass production, which ecologists measure as "net primary production," and the "export" of nutrients or provision of fishery habitat upon which other

(particularly aquatic and marine) ecosystems depend. The Vareza flood forests of the lower Amazon for example, and the mangroves that occur throughout coastal zones in the tropics are the ecological foundation for traditional and commercial fisheries. In a parallel sense, the Amazon Basin "exports" precipitation to surrounding regions, making possible rainfed crop and livestock production, as well as providing water resources for domestic and industrial use.

Geographically Coinciding Values and Benefits

The biological utility, biodiversity, and cultural diversity indicator measures for Major Habitat Types are shown in the Table. The relative rankings of each Major Habitat Type for each of the three utility value categories are shown in Figure l. A more detailed study presenting analysis at a higher level of resolution (i.e., the aggregate ecoregion and base ecoregion levels) is planned. Although not shown here, measures of biological utility value are generally correlated with those of element biodiversity, including estimates of species richness and endemism, which were made preliminarily by expert groups at the BSP biodiversity priority setting workshop in Miami in October. The data in the table

allow further comparison of variables representing the three utility value categories, indigenous cultural diversity (number of distinct indigenous populations), and biodiversity in terms of habitat diversity within Major Habitat Types (Number of Base Ecoregions). The comparisons of most interest to us here, the relationships between the types of diversity—biological and cultural—and between cultural diversity and biological utility, show strong positive correlation (Figure 2). Mangroves are the only habitat type diverging markedly from this pattern by having far fewer indigenous populations than expected. This perhaps should not be surprising since the coastal location and inhabitability of mangroves makes their mapped distributions least likely to overlap with those of indigenous populations.

Behind these data, there are a number of interesting patterns for various smaller scale ecoregion units. For example, it is apparent that among ecoregions consisting of tropical moist forest, those of the Amazon Basin, in addition to being the most species rich, score highest in biological utility value while supporting the largest number of indigenous populations (with 334, or over two-thirds of the total diversity recorded for all of Latin America). Yet Tropical Dry Forests, which often are overlooked for

Figure 2

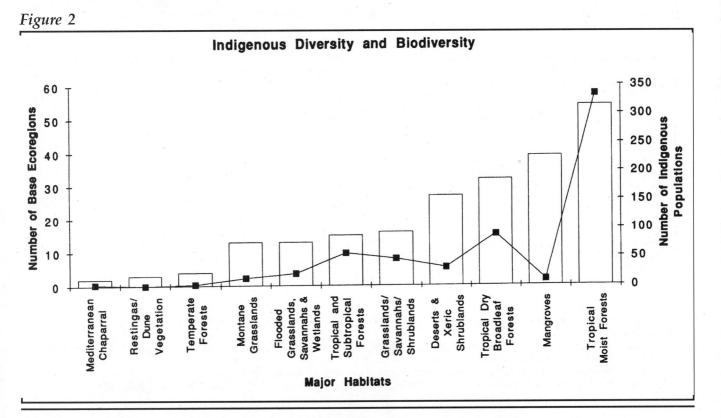

their conservation value, are hardly lacking in cultural and biological diversity overall, or in interesting ecoregional patterns. In total, 89 indigenous groups were recorded for tropical dry forests in Latin America. While not having nearly as high value on the basis of indicators affected primarily by rainfall, such as carbon storage and net primary production, dry forests are nonetheless relatively rich in genetic resources. The aggregate ecoregion unit encompassed by Mexican dry forests is particularly noteworthy in this regard. This "ecosystem" not only supports a relatively high indigenous cultural diversity (about 30 distinct groups), albeit much of it assimilated or displaced, it also represents one of the world's most important repositories of genetic resources. Its forest tree genetic resources rival that of any tropical moist forest region. Even more significantly, its crop plant genetic resources, which include wild relatives of maize (*Zea maize*), cotton (*Gossypium* spp.), peppers (*Capsicum* spp.), and squash (*Cucurbita* spp.), are the basis of some of the world's most valuable commercial crops. Thus our results show that even within a major habitat type such as dry forests, biological diversity, both of utility and non-utility, and indigenous cultural diversity seem to be highly correlated. In this instance, protecting the integrity of ecosystems containing the biological diversity most important to the food security of present and future generations, could simultaneously maximize the protection of indigenous cultural diversity.

We were frankly surprised to find such a strong correlation between biological diversity utility value and cultural diversity, especially since our utility indicators are based on value from a global or regional, but not local use perspective. We will be continuing our research to see how these patterns hold up at a higher level of ecogeographic resolution. Certainly the occurrence of a large number of indigenous groups, whose use of biological diversity is probably as proportionately diverse, is an automatic expression of high utility value for an ecosystem. However, why should such ecosystems also rank high in utility measures based on an industrial society perspective?

Considering some basic ecological and co-evolutionary principles, the correspondence may not be so surprising. For cultures dependent entirely on biological resources the possibilities for diversification and coexistence should, in theory, be greatest where the resource base is richest. Biotic richness in this regard has two major components, productivity, such as that measured by net primary production (essentially the rate of accumulation of plant biomass), and diversity, primarily in the form of the variety of biological resources to exploit. Thus as ecologists have found in studying the distribution and abundance of plants and animals, species diversity tends to increase with habitat diversity and increasing productivity or energy flow through an ecosystem. The theoretical explanation is that there are lower limits to population size and upper limits to niche overlap for species persistence. Therefore the higher the productivity and diversity of a habitat, the greater the opportunity for biological diversification; and the same may hold for indigenous cultures.

However, there is an additional explanation for these patterns. Stanford anthropologist William Durham, an expert on historical land use conflicts involving indigenous people, leans toward a cultural competitive exclusion explanation: Colonizing European populations are likely to have displaced indigenous populations disproportionately from preferred "European-like" habitats (such as scrubland and savannah-woodland)—leaving rainforests to the last!

Whatever the causative agent, the results of our analysis show that contemporary industrial society and indigenous societies may be more interdependent than is often appreciated. If the results of this analysis hold up after further study, they will help confirm scientifically what perhaps most know intuitively: all societies are mutually interdependent with each other and on natural ecosystems, and this interdependency crosses all spatial and temporal scales.

Article 3

World Press Review, September 1997

Can democracy finally take root?

Dawn in Mexico

For a change, the news from Mexico is good. Plagued in recent years by poverty, scandal, and crisis, Mexico has held the cleanest elections in its history, and the result has been a shock to the old order. With gains by opposition parties throughout the country, this may be the start of a new political pluralism.

LaJornada

Since July 6, Mexico has been experiencing a mood of exultation the likes of which it had not felt since that happy day in 1911 when Francisco Madero marched into the capital following the fall of the 30-year dictatorship of Porfirio Díaz. The reign of the Institutional Revolutionary Party (PRI) has been even longer.

Formed in 1929, the PRI has outlived such venerable political mummies as the Communist Party of the Soviet Union and Spain's Franco dictatorship. Created to put an end to the uprisings, coups, and assassinations that followed the 1910 revolution's victory on the battlefield, the official party fell victim to the same ills it had overcome 60 years before: political crimes, corruption, a Sicilian-style conspiracy of silence—the whole Macbeth-like witches' brew, liberally seasoned with skeletons in the closet, graveyard excavations reminiscent of Dracula, soap-opera infatuations, and disappearances worthy of a Hitchcock thriller.

Now the PRI has lost control of the office of mayor of Mexico City (the largest urban area in the world) and its absolute majority in the Chamber of Deputies, as well as two more state governorships in addition to the four already held by the National Action Party (PAN). More than half the country is now governed by the opposition. For us Mexicans, the paradox is that the abnormal state of affairs we have inherited from the PRI had come to seem normal, and normal democracy now seems abnormal. We will have to get used to normalcy.

The PRI and some of its allies in the private sector tried to exploit this paradox during the campaign. If the PRI's "normalcy" were disrupted, they warned, the result would be ungovernability, chaos, or even intervention by the U.S.

Well, after July 6, Mexico's old regime, like the Wicked Witch in *The Wizard of Oz,* has vanished into thin air. And Mexico, instead of plunging into chaos, has not only experienced a rebirth of hope but an objective situation that is much more stable. The stock market, foreign investment, the strength of the peso against the dollar, the confidence shown by major Mexican corporations—all of these indicators, far from plummeting, have shown spectacular improvement. Democracy generates confidence.

> *"The old regime, like the Wicked Witch, has vanished."*

Let's be wary of over-optimism, some warn. The old PRI is a wounded dinosaur still capable of lashing out. But the PRI cannot distort the confidence generated by the electoral process and channel it into a renewal of fear. Rather than weep over its setback, the PRI should give some serious thought to its future. Does it have one? Given its territorial spread and organization, the answer should be yes. But that does not relieve the PRI of the need to take a hard look at itself.

Its lack of political principles, its ideological vagueness, its chameleon-like opportunism have enabled the PRI to pose successively as revolutionary, nationalist, socialist, statist, populist, and pro-free market. What will be the PRI's true face now? Perhaps, after wearing so many masks, the PRI has become faceless. What it does have are many intelligent, concerned, and honest members. It is up to them to reform their party so that they may take their place as one party among others, not *the* party.

Another scare tactic used during the campaign was to warn that democracy would draw a negative reaction from the U.S. This argument also was demolished on July 6. Washington's traditional support for authoritarian regimes in Mexico in the name of security was never a comfortable position. The results of the election make things much easier for the Clinton administration's Mexico policy. Dealing with a democratic system is more complex but easier. The foreign policy initiatives of President Ernesto Zedillo will be closely watched by the new

Congress, just as those of President Bill Clinton are watched by his. In other words, Mexico's relations with the U.S. will be more like American relations with Mexico—more scrutinized, more critcized, and more negotiated. But, when all is said and done, that is normal in a democracy.

—Carlos Fuentes, "La Jornada" (leftist), Mexico City, July 10, 1997. Carlos Fuentes, the author of more than two dozen novels, writes often on Mexican-U.S. relations.

Article 4

World Press Review, September 1997

A Step into Unknown Political Territory

Can Congress Curb the President?

EL MERCURIO

Following a resounding victory for the opposition in July's elections, Mexico awoke with a new political map that represents a situation unprecedented in the nearly 70 years that the Institutional Revolutionary Party (PRI) has monopolized government.

"These are the most important elections of the 20th century in this country," says analyst Adolfo Aguilar Zinser, who won a seat in the Senate as a candidate of the Mexican Green Environmentalist Party (PVEM). Nobel laureate Octavio Paz said in the daily *Reforma* that the election "perhaps heralds a new era in the history of Mexico." Others saw the vote as signaling the passing of the ruling party. "The PRI is dead. The funeral may be long and wearisome, but the PRI is a drowning man thrashing in the water," says political scientist Carlos Monsiváis.

For the first time since it came to power in 1929, the ruling party lost its absolute majority in the Chamber of Deputies. The PRI won 229 of the lower house's 500 seats, a substantial drop from the 298 it won in 1994. Still, the party remains "the majority party and leading political force in the country," says PRI Chairman Humberto Roque Villanueva. As a consolation prize to offset its losses, the PRI won the governorships of the states of San Luis Potosí, Campeche, Colima, and Sonora.

Despite its failure to win a single governorship, the big winner was the Party of the Democratic Revolution (PRD). In the Chamber of Deputies, it nearly doubled its representation, climbing from 65 to 129 seats and cap-

turing 25.9 percent of the vote. It also confirmed its position as the leading political force in the capital district, where its victorious mayoral candidate, Cuauhtémoc Cárdenas, pulled in almost 48 percent of the votes. The PRD also won control of Mexico City's Legislative Assembly and won a majority in 28 of the city's 30 lower-house electoral districts.

Gains were scored by the conservative National Action Party (PAN), although on a more modest scale than its leaders had hoped. In the Chamber of Deputies, PAN climbed from 119 to 126 seats, drawing 27.7 percent of the vote. It won the governorships of Nuevo León and—the big surprise of the election—Querétaro, states that were also electing local authorities. But its candidate for mayor of Mexico City, Carlos Castillo Peraza, came in a disappointing third.

In the Senate, where 32 of the 128 seats were up for grabs, the PRI lost 20 seats but retained a majority. PAN held on to second place, and PRD remained third. The news here was the victory of Aguilar Zinser of the PVEM.

The outcome of these elections implies a sharp change of course in Mexican politics. As President Ernesto Zedillo acknowledged in a televised address to the nation, the country "has taken an irreversible, definitive, and historic step toward normalcy." Zedillo said that "a great celebration of democracy has taken place. The will of the Mexican people has been respected and strengthened." He congratulated the political parties that took part in the election and said the results were due to electoral reform sponsored by his administration last year.

That reform deprived the government of the upper hand in the election process and on the board of the Federal Election Institute.

According to Gabriel Sánchez Díaz, chairman of a citizens' advisory group, "these were the cleanest of elections. They turned out better than those of 1994 and 1991. They are dramatically different from those of 1988," when a controversial "breakdown" of the computerized vote-tally system apparently deprived presidential hopeful Cuauhtémoc Cárdenas of his victory over Carlos Salinas de Gortari.

The outcome of these elections, say analysts, will be a pluralistic Mexico. Everyone agrees that it will now be necessary to negotiate in order to move bills through Congress. Mexico is venturing into unknown territory. Although everyone seems disposed to dialogue, "no one knows what will happen, because we are entering a period of uncertainty in which no one has a definite strategy, simply because we have never been in a situation such as this," says Aguilar Zinser. In *Reforma*, Paz wrote that "the future is unpredictable and many problems await us. . . . Let us remember that democracy is not just a theory but a practice."

The big unanswered question is what kind of relationship will emerge between a PRI administration and a Chamber of Deputies dominated by the two main opposition parties. "We do not know what will happen when Congress calls the president to account. [He] has never been held accountable to the legislature because it seems to cast discredit on him and tarnish his image of power," says Aguilar Zinser.

Another important transition is the one that will take place in Mexico City. Cárdenas, who will take office on December 5, says that he will turn his attention to organizing his staff and choosing his "cabinet." He hopes to have "very respectful dealings" with President Zedillo. Cárdenas adds that his new administration will focus on keeping his campaign promises. "We will fight corruption and organized crime, we will clean up the administration, and we will have an efficient government very close to the people, one that strives to meet the needs of the people of Mexico City."

Despite declarations of goodwill, two clouds hang over the Cárdenas administration's future. Will he govern with an eye to the presidential race in the year 2000? And will the federal government use the opportunity to create problems for him that could undermine that goal?

During his victory rally at the Plaza del Zócalo in Mexico City, Cárdenas said, "We're getting ready to win in 2000." Analysts said it is very likely that the leader of the PRD—who ran for president in 1988 and 1994—will use his new position as a springboard to the presidency.

In light of that, it is quite probable that the government will decide to create stumbling blocks for Cárdenas, who does not have authority over the whole budget for the capital city and does not control the police force, which is accountable to the federal government. The aim would be to damage Cárdenas's image in order to undermine him in the public eye.

—*Juan Ignacio Brito, "El Mercurio" (conservative), Santiago, July 8, 1997.*

Article 5   *The World & I*, August 1997

The PRI's Last Hurrah?

President Ernesto Zedillo has been walking a tightrope in modernizing and improving Mexico's Byzantine politics.

GEORGE W. GRAYSON

President Ernesto Zedillo's upbeat predictions, even before the current economic recovery began, prompted labor chiefs and other mossbacks within his own Institutional Revolutionary Party (PRI) [see boxes on Mexico's three main political parties] to observe wryly that the 45-year-old chief executive would change the national symbol from the eagle to the seal, the only marine creature that applauds—just before his head goes underwater!

In fact, Zedillo may have the last laugh, for the Yale-trained economist approaches the mid-point in his six-year term with far higher public-approval ratings than the PRI. Indeed, the prospect of the party's losing the mayorship of Mexico City on July 6 led a local doomsayer to warn darkly of the "demise of the PRI." The party stands as the world's longest-ruling party since the collapse of communism.

Yet, despite pummelings at the polls and the recent defection of militants, the PRI still shows signs of life. As a matter of fact, Emilio Chuayffet Chemor, 45, a wily former governor of Mexico state and Zedillo's de facto prime minister, hopes to parlay his party's disappointing midyear performance in the capital into a strong presidential bid in 2000.

How has Zedillo responded to the December 1994 peso devaluation, which sparked a 6.9 percent drop in GDP? What impact has the economic crisis—cum Salinas family melodrama—had on the ruling party? Has the president honored his preelection pledge to remain at arm's length from the PRI? Why might

a setback in Mexico City revitalize his party's chances of retaining the presidency when Zedillo steps down in 2000?

Zedillo and the peso crisis

On December 1, 1994, hundreds of foreign dignitaries and business leaders hobnobbed with local notables at the swearing-in of Mexico's 80th chief executive. After donning the red, white, and green presidential sash, the austere, bespectacled Zedillo pledged to continue and even to broaden the efforts of his predecessor Carlos Salinas de Gortari, to liberalize the country's once-state-hobbled economy.

Zedillo's most dramatic pronouncements, however, focused on the country's authoritarian political system, dominated by the PRI since 1929. Mexican politics had long manifested presidential supremacy over other branches of government, hostility toward political adversaries, corruption, and electoral fraud. Indeed, critics have often gibed that "democracy exists 364 days a year in Mexico—it's only missing on election day."

To overcome this onerous legacy, the new president vowed to open access to the political process, shift power from the executive to the legislative and judiciary branches, empower states and municipalities, and welcome a dialogue with the major opposition parties: the center-right National Action Party (PAN) and the nationalist-leftist Democratic Revolutionary Party (PRD).

As for taking on the corruption known to suffuse Mexico's Byzantine regime, Zedillo concluded: "Government

is not the place to amass wealth. . . . Those who aspire to do so should leave my government and pay strict attention to the law."

In addition, Zedillo called for "definitive electoral reform," to include fair media access and public campaign financing for all parties; limits on and scrutiny of those expenditures; and full autonomy for the Federal Electoral Institute, which is charged with organizing, monitoring, and validating Mexican elections.

Such promises meshed with Zedillo's preelection commitment to maintain a "healthy distance" between the government and the party, to the extent that he would limit his role to that of a "passive militant" who would remain aloof from intra-PRI decision making.

For the party's peasant and trade-union hard-liners—derisively known as "dinosaurs"—these words represented the political equivalent of gargling razor blades. Nonetheless, the old guard buttoned its lips lest Zedillo follow Salinas' example—namely, filling the air with modernizing rhetoric while unilaterally silencing political malcontents.

The celebrations surrounding Zedillo's inauguration provided a calm before the storm. Three weeks after taking office, the new chief executive confronted a challenge much graver than that posed by his choleric PRI warhorses.

A hemorrhage of capital out of the Mexican economy made it impossible for Finance Secretary Jaime Serra Puche to cover a current-account deficit that soared to $28 billion in 1994. On December 20 of that year, after publicly vacil-

The Principal Players

- Ernesto Zedillo, the current president, saw his popularity plummet during the recent peso crisis.

- Emilio Chuayffet Chemor, Zedillo's de facto prime minister, hopes to succeed to the presidency in the 2000 election.

- Zedillo's predecessor, Carlos Salinas de Gortari, and Carlos' brother, Raul Salinas, have received the blame for most of the financial problems.

- Zedillo's main competition comes from Cuauhtémoc Cárdenas, cofounder of the left-of-center PRD.

lating over devaluation for several days, he announced that the central bank would no longer use its meager hard-currency reserves to prop up the peso.

The rest is history: The peso went into a tailspin; Zedillo replaced Serra Puche with another U.S.-educated Ph.D., Guillermo Ortiz Martínez; a "tequila effect" bedeviled other Latin American economies; U.S. President Bill Clinton crafted an ambitious and controversial bailout package for Mexico; and a prolonged time of troubles beset a nation that Salinas had vowed to catapult from the Third to the First World.

Mexicans lampooned their leader: A popular joke commended Zedillo as the only winner of three Nobel Prizes: in physics, because he made the peso float; in chemistry, because he transmuted the economy into dung; and in literature, because he realized *Les Misérables* in 19 days, a feat that took Victor Hugo 19 years.

In a late February 1995 fight for political survival, Zedillo broke a taboo against incumbents attacking predecessors and their families. In what became a political tragicomedy, the beleaguered president ordered the arrest of Raúl Salinas, who had not only held a key post in his brother's administration but also managed a family fortune that had ballooned during the government sell-off of state assets to Salinas' friends. Authorities charged Raúl with masterminding the murder of PRI Secretary-General José Francisco Ruiz Massieu, once married to his and Carlos' sister.

The gradual unfolding of the drama—replete with the outgoing president's flight into self-imposed exile, revelations of bulging Swiss bank accounts, charges of homosexual liaisons, and accusations of ties to narcotraffickers—diverted the spotlight from Zedillo. The festering scandal allowed an increasingly self-assured, strong-willed president to pursue a tough austerity program that paid

dividends the following year when $7.6 billion in direct investment flowed into Mexico. The IMF predicts a 4.5 percent growth in GDP amid a 17.5 percent price rise in 1997.

Impact on the PRI

Irate over both the economic sacrifices imposed on them and the hangover from Salinas' departure from office, voters vented their spleens on the PRI in successive state elections. In 1995, PAN candidates won convincingly the governorships of Jalisco, Guanajuato, and Baja California. In Guanajuato, for example, Vicente Fox Quesada—a flamboyant blue-jeans-wearing Coca-Cola executive-turned-politician—scored a 2–1 landslide, marking the PRI's worst recorded defeat at the state level.

In 1996 the political thrashing continued, as opposition candidates achieved unprecedented gains in municipal elections in Coahuila, Hidalgo, and Mexico state. The PRI suffered its most embarrassing loss in Mexico state, which wraps around three-quarters of the capital and stands as a microcosm of the country, embracing urban, suburban, small-town, and rural areas. The PRI entered the election in control of municipal governments encompassing 97 percent of Mexico state's 12.5 million residents. After the contests, the party's mayors governed only half the population.

For several reasons, the electoral rebuff proved an especially bitter pill for the PRI to swallow: First, the revolutionary party boasts a remarkably effective organization in Mexico state, the country's most populous. Second, even though a product of the state's vaunted political machine, Government Secretary Chuayffet could not deliver victory in his own backyard.

Finally, *priístas* (PRI militants) feared that the outcome could foreshadow the mid-1997 vote for mayor in Mexico City:

The state melds into the capital; its residents fall into the same media market as the *capitalinos*; and concerns about jobs, salaries, street crime, and pollution pervade the entire metropolitan population.

Just as troubling, these defeats sparked defections from the PRI: Sen. Layda Sansores jumped ship when the party failed to nominate her for governor of Campeche, a post she then chose to pursue as the PRD nominee. Ex-Tabasco governor and party heavyweight Enrique González Pedrero also bolted to the PRD, which guaranteed him a Senate seat. Others followed suit.

Admittedly, Zedillo feared a victory by the PRD's Cuauhtémoc Cárdenas over PRI standard-bearer Alfredo del Mazo González in the Federal District. However, he worried even more about his party losing its majority in the Chamber of Deputies, whose 500 seats would also be up for grabs on July 6. The loss of parliamentary control would imperil legislation designed to privatize more economic sectors, intensify Mexico's participation in the global economy, and shift more power away from the president and toward other branches of the federal government and to the states.

Zedillo quickly abandoned any pretense of keeping a healthy distance from the PRI. In combination, these developments drove home to Zedillo the midterm election's significance for the remainder of his term. Since early 1996, the chief executive has increasingly identified with and become involved in his party.

After all, unlike the Machiavellian Salinas, he boasts neither an independent power base nor a robust political team. Besides Finance Secretary Ortiz Martínez, Zedillo's only politically active confidants are Sen.-elect Esteban Moctezuma, outgoing Mexico City Mayor Oscar Espinosa Villarreal, and PRI President Humberto Roque. Along with the PRI hierarchy and the government ministry, he obligingly continued his party's tradition of the top-down selection of candidates for the July contests.

On April 12, Zedillo gave a pep talk to all his party's legislative aspirants. Two days later, he attacked the opposition as champions of "destructive change, hypocrisy, intolerance, and vindictive aggression." Finally, he enthusiastically endorsed the mayoral bid of del Mazo, though many PRI insiders had proffered that Senate President Fernando Ortiz Arana forgo the governorship of Querétaro in favor of running for the Federal District's top job.

MEXICO'S THREE MAJOR PARTIES

Institutional Revolutionary Party (Partido Revolucionario Institucional, or PRI)

President Plutarco Elías Calles established the forerunner of the PRI in 1929 to promote unity among regional military, political, and economic leaders in the aftermath of President-elect Alvaro Obregón's assassination. In 1938, President Lázaro Cárdenas reorganized the party along functional or "corporatist" lines, with four sectors: (1) agrarian/peasant, (2) labor, (3) popular/white-collar, and (4) military.

Although the military sector was abolished in 1940, the party—despite various reforms—retains important elements of its corporatist past. However, old-line peasant and labor leaders—derided as "dinosaurs"—have increasingly lost power to change-oriented politicians and foreign-educated technocrats like Salinas and Zedillo. Yet these leaders hold on to their control of the legislature and block needed reforms.

Nonetheless, the PRI continues to embrace "revolutionary nationalism"—a farrago of beliefs revolving around support for the revolution, the president, and social reform. Zedillo's strong commitment to a democratic opening aside, the party is associated in the public's eye with electoral fraud and the recent recession, causing it to lose votes to the PAN and PRD. Defections have beset the party apace with its decline in popular support.

The PRI won 48.7 percent of the presidential vote in 1994; it holds 300 seats in the 500-member Chamber of Deputies, 119 seats in the 152-member Senate, and 27 governorships.

National Action Party (Partido Acción Nacional, or PAN)

Catholic laymen founded the party in 1939 in reaction to the nationalization, agrarian-reform, and "socialist" educational policies of President Cárdenas, the father of Cuauhtémoc. Its greatest influence lies in the north, where it holds the governorships of Baja California and Chihuahua, as well as in the central Bajío region, Yucatán, and in cities.

Although Salinas prempted much of its pro-business, market-focused program, the PAN leadership frequently worked hand-in-glove with the PRI-dominated government on such major issues as reprivatizing the banks, approving NAFTA, attenuating the constitution's anticlerical provisions, altering the status of *ejido* communal farms, and revamping electoral statutes. Hard-charging, U.S.-oriented businessmen (known as the "Barbarians of the North") who joined the PAN in recent years coexist, sometimes uneasily, with traditional *panistas* known for their devotion to social-Christian principles and the needs of small business.

The PAN, which won 25.9 percent of the 1994 presidential vote, boasts 119 seats in the Chamber of Deputies and 25 seats in the Senate. In addition, *panistas* occupy the governorships of Baja California, Chihuahua, Guanajuato, and Jalisco, as well as scores of important mayoral offices.

Democratic Revolutionary Party (Partido Revolucionario Democrático, or PRD)

Former PRI leaders Cuauhtémoc Cárdenas and Porfirio Muñoz Ledo spearheaded the party's creation of Mexico's most eclectic party. They sought to institutionalize the substantial support garnered by the National Democratic Front, under whose banner Cárdenas sought the presidency in the fraud-marred 1988 presidential election, won by Carlos Salinas de Gortari.

The Democratic Current (a PRI breakaway group), the Mexican Socialist Party, and an amalgam of communist, socialist, and ex-guerrilla organizations constituted the PRD in 1989. During his recent race for mayor of Mexico City, Cárdenas toned down the party's leftist-nationalist rhetoric to present himself as a mainstream candidate devoted to revising—not discontinuing—NAFTA, market-oriented domestic policies, and other reforms advanced by Salinas and Zedillo.

The PRD captured 16.6 percent of the vote in 1994 presidential contest; it holds 71 seats in the Chamber of Deputies and 8 seats in the Senate.

—G.W.G.

Chuayffet and the PRI's future

The main threat to the ruling party's future lies in accelerating fragmentation rather than a sudden demise. Several dynamics contribute to the erosion of the PRI's once-unassailable strength. First, the pursuit of internal democracy challenges the power of the PRI's *campesino* and labor sectors, long a reliable source of votes, whether by hook or by crook.

In addition, there is the possibility of a knock-down, drag-out leadership fight when Fidel Velázquez—the acting 97-year-old patriarch of the PRI-linked union confederation—passes from the scene. The growth of the PAN and PRD and the mushrooming of human-rights organizations, neighborhood associations, and other less formal elements of civil society are evidence of an increase in competitors and critics. Finally, there is Zedillo's move to unilaterally disarm the presidency, an institution traditionally endowed with enormous authority to forge coherence within the PRI and whip opponents into line.

Ironically, a victory by Cárdenas in Mexico City could heighten the PRI's chances of holding on to Los Pinos presidential palace in the next presidential election, just three years away. Chuayffet has the most to gain from an opposition triumph. The outcome would bear out his professions of faith in democratic elections; boot del Mazo from the political stage; discredit Roque as the PRI president who "lost" Mexico City; and chill the ambitions of Ortiz Martínez and Moctezuma, whose neoliberal policies have alienated the capital's voters.

Even though economic conditions should improve, an opposition mayor will likely face marches, demonstrations, and strikes launched not only by aggrieved citizens but also by organized labor, which harbors no love for the PRD or the PAN. After a couple years of social discord highlighted by continual protests, staged traffic jams, and other signs of discontent, Chuayffet could present himself as a seasoned, fair, no-nonsense leader capable of ensuring stability.

No one expects Chuayffet to just waltz into the presidency: If elected Distrito Federal mayor (as polls in mid-June forecast), Cárdenas will use city hall as a bully pulpit for his third presidential race in a dozen years. Fox, Guanajuato's hard-charging populist governor, would make a formidable candidate for the PAN, although Mexico's center-right party—like the PRD and PRI—currently suffers from internal tensions, sharpened by its disappointing performance in Mexico City.

As for the PRI, Zedillo—whose stock should climb higher when macroeconomic gains trickle down to average citizens—clearly favors his alter ego, the young, movie-star-handsome Moctezuma. And the intrepid Ortiz Arana—after a 30-year career in which he presided over three legislative bodies, the PRI, and a major state—has a Rolodex of supporters that is without peer in Mexico.

Still, should Chuayffet reach the presidential palace, he would keep the eagle at the center of the Mexican flag, relegate the clapping seal to the circus or the aquarium, and reestablish the PRI as a viable entity within an ever-more plural and competitive political system.

George W. Grayson, the Class of 1938 Professor of Government at the College of William and Mary, has just written his eighth book on Mexico, Mexico: From Corporatism to Pluralism, *published by Harcourt-Brace later this year.*

Article 6

The UNESCO Courier, November 1996

PRE-COLUMBIAN AMERICA

Tlatelolco, shop window of the Aztec empire

BY MARÍA REBECA YOMA MENDINA AND LUÍS ALBERTO MARTOS LÓPEZ

MARÍA REBECA YOMA MEDINA AND LUÍS ALBERTO MARTOS LÓPEZ are Mexican archaeologists.

In pre-Columbian Mexico a great market was held in the Aztec city of Tlatelolco. Its size and organization amazed the Spanish conquistadors, who had seen nothing like it in sixteenth-century Europe.

Tlatelolco was a part of the Aztec capital, Tenochtitlán which, so legend has it, was founded on an island in Lake Texcoco in 1325. The site was ideal for exploiting the lake's resources, but seed, fruit, vegetables, building materials and many other essential goods had to be brought in from outside. In 1337, an Aztec splinter group founded an independent city, Tlatelolco, on an island north of Tenochtitlán. The two cities soon became rivals. Tlatelolco's strategic position and the extraordinary business acumen of its inhabitants were such that it acquired a formidable commercial reputation.

A market suburb

At first the market of Tlatelolco dealt exclusively in primary products, but economic and social development slowly encouraged the growth of trade in luxury goods. This became so important that an institution specializing in long-distance trade was set up. It was known as the *Pochtecayotl* and set up a trading network that reached as far as the provinces of the Mayan empire.

In 1473, after a war in which no quarter was given, Tlatelolco was defeated in battle by an army from Tenochtitlán. Overnight the proud city became a suburb of Tenochtitlán. In view of the market's reputation and size, however, the victors decided to encourage its expansion by transporting to it a wide variety of rare products from other cities and regions of the Aztec empire.

The conquistadors' amazement

When the Spanish conquered Mexico, the market of Tlatelolco was at the height of its prosperity. Contemporary Spanish chroniclers describe how the market place was located to the east of the city's great ceremonial enclosure on a vast square esplanade with sides 200 metres long, fully paved and level and surrounded by arcades housing shops. At the centre of the square was the *momoztli*, a kind of truncated stepped pyramid which was used for celebrations, ceremonies and other public events.

Hernando Cortés, the Spanish conqueror of Mexico, wrote that "This city has many squares where trade and commerce go on all the time. One square is twice the size of Salamanca and surrounded with arcades that more than 70,000 people pass through every day, buying and selling."

Admirably sited near the quay of La Lagunilla, where boats laden with merchandise tied up, the market was also joined to the mainland by three causeways.

As the shop window of the Aztec world, Tlatelolco market offered its customers an amazing variety of exotic products from the four corners of the empire—fruit, animals, medicines, cloth, hides, pottery, instruments, tools and materials of all sorts. It also provided many services: public baths, cafés, barber shops, porters and slave markets.

Cacao currency

The merchants, known officially as *tlamacaque*, were generally also the producers. Middlemen known as *regatonería*, who bought cheap and sold at a profit, did not appear until the colonial period.

Barter was the normal practice, but some commodities also served as currency. Cacao was grown for this purpose in certain parts of the empire, with the consequence that its production was strictly controlled by the government. The basic unit was the bean for inexpensive items and the sack of 8,000 beans (*xiquipiles*) for expensive items.

Handkerchief-sized squares of cotton known as *quachtli* were also used as currency. They came in three sizes, equalling 65, 80 and 100 cocoa beans respectively. A canoe was worth a *quachtli* of 100 beans. A slave who could sing was worth 30 *quachtlis*, and an excellent singer and dancer could fetch 40 *quachtlis*, or 4,000 cocoa beans.

Gold dust was another form of payment. It was poured into feather quills, whose value was based on their length and diameter. Small change came in the form of small, thin, T-shaped copper coins, nuggets of gold, copper or pewter, chips of jade and even the red shell from a mollusc now known as the spondylus.

These trading activities obeyed well-established laws and rules, for the market, like other institutions in pre-Columbian Mexico, functioned on a "correct and fair" (*in qualli, in yectli*) basis. No business could be transacted outside the market area, where each merchant was allotted a place corresponding to the nature of his wares. Lengths of rope and receptacles of various capacities were standardized and used to measure quantities. The price of each article was fixed in advance, and any merchant caught cheating on measures or price was severely punished.

There was a chamber where twelve judges sat in permanent session to ensure fair dealing and settle differences. Superintendents regularly went on rounds to maintain security and prevent fraud.

When they founded Mexico City, the Europeans created two new markets but neither ever attained the size or the splendour of Tlatelolco. But Tlatelolco did not survive the Spanish conquest.

Laughter and Tears

Mexico's Paradoxical Proverbs

Jeff M. Sellers

Jeff M. Sellers is a free-lance writer based in Madrid who formerly lived in Mexico. His book Folk Wisdom of Mexico, *published in May 1994 by Chronicle Books, can be ordered by calling 1-800-722-6657.*

Like most young children growing up in Mexico City, Alfredo Villafranca learned right from wrong through the country's time-honored proverbs and sayings. If his grandmother was always telling him, "Don't do good that could look bad" (No hagas cosas buenas que parezcan malas), then the paradoxical message of that proverb surely had its source in something or someone even older. Young Alfredo was learning not only right from wrong but the time-worn ironies of his ancestors.

At first glance, perhaps especially to those in the United States, the proverb "Don't do good that could look bad" may indicate a folksy concession to practicality, a shameless regard for what others think at the expense of doing what is right. In Mexico, however, it is an appeal for sincerity, purity, or totality in doing right. If good deeds look harmful from an outsider's perspective, it's probably because they are indeed pernicious or stained by impure motives. The proverb in its older form is followed by the phrase "nor bad things that could look good."

"Everyone tells you this from a very early age," says Villafranca, now a thirty-year-old graduate student in journalism ethics. "Don't do good things that could look bad, nor bad things that could look good, always do good things that look good. That is, be totally sincere."

In this way the proverb sometimes carries a sense that the road to hell is paved with good intentions. Going out with friends who are given to drunkenness or drugs, for example, though well-intentioned and innocent, looks bad and indeed carries with it some danger, says Villafranca. Or, as another Mexican proverb says, "When the river sounds, it's because it carries water" (Cuando el río suena, es que lleva agua).

"Friends who are involved in drugs—you're near them, and although your mother knows you're not involved in drugs, she'll say, 'Don't do good that could look bad,' " says Villafranca. "It's a corrective."

The folk wisdom of Mexico is rich in paradox, which might be expected from a people who daily live the apparent contradictions of the individual and the community, solitude and *fiesta*, impassivity and grief. Experiencing as well the curious juxtapositions of rich and poor, Virgin Mary and Malinche (the Aztec concubine taken by Hernán Cortés, symbolically forming the new race), fatalism and faith, the paradoxical Mexicans produced a folk wisdom that often expressed at least two things at once, usually laughter and tears.

This is the peculiarity of Mexican sayings, though their messages may be universal and their roots European. Nearly every scholar who has chronicled Mexican sayings has done so with trepidation, acknowledging first that their origins often lie in Spain and that, as a result, similar shoots will appear in the sayings of other Latin American countries. But Mexican linguist Dario Rubio, to whom many observers of Mexican culture pay homage, regarded most of the nation's sayings as unique in form and content.

Their piquant messages and blend of Castilian and Aztec-descended diction reveal Mexico's particular and "immense bitterness, her never realized ideals, her always dying hopes . . . which lead to wanting to go on to something less cruel, less bitter, some consolation," Rubio wrote in 1932.

Laughing at Death

Sorrow also sings, when it runs too deep to cry. Such is the poetic translation of the Mexican proverb that literally means, "Pain is also sung, when crying isn't possible" *(También de dolor se canta cuando llorar no se puede).*

Something of the Mexican indifference toward life that writer/philosopher Octavio Paz describes can be seen in this proverb, as the saying refers primarily to singing smiley songs in the face of tragedy. If harsh conditions and heartbreak have been common in Mexico's history, then song has played a masterful role as one of the masks that both protect against and express sorrow. These dual purposes are served by both the most frivolous bar tune and the most heart-wrenching ballad. The sad ballad protects with a culturally acceptable expression of sublimated sorrow, and the festive tune may be a form of weeping for those who have no more tears to shed.

"Sorrow also sings, when it runs too deep to cry" most often refers to death or other profound loss. If the Mexican shows indifference toward life, this also reflects indifference toward death, says Paz.

The proverb is very popular in Mexico, according to Villafranca. "It's very beautiful, and Mexican culture is very, very special in this," he observes. "Suffering and pain are expressed in Mexico with songs, primarily about death, death as a representation of all our problems, shortages, illnesses. It speaks of a small chance of having hope, of seeing things more positively. Under suffering or pain, we always have this opportunity to make fun of it."

Some Mexicans ask that festive *manachi* bands appear at their funerals, notes Mario Martinez, a thirty-year-old law student from Tijuana. "They're just kidding, but you have to remember the Aztecs and their response to death," says Martinez. "The tomb was not so much a disaster but an offering to the gods."

The Mexican celebration on November 1, the Day of the Dead, is a graveside vigil in which food and other goodies are offered to the deceased. The custom hearkens back to the Aztec view of death as a passageway to further journeys, for which cadavers were equipped with gifts for the gods.

"They had a mission. They had to bring something to the gods, food or flowers and personal things, and so they were buried that way," explains Martinez. "Even before the Catholics arrived [rendering November 1 All Saints' Day], food and flowers were being offered, and death was a ritual, a party. Someone was going to communicate for you to the gods, so the emphasis was not so much on death but on another vision, and there was no reason to cry."

Living intimately with death, being more familiar with it than people who try not to think about it, the Mexican more easily stands before it and sings. Perhaps it is this indifference that is behind Mexico's paradoxical answer to the English saying that time heals all wounds: *El tiempo cura y nos mata* ("Time heals, and then it kills").

Concepts of Time

Mexico laughs at death while showing its generous perspective of time in a macabre saying, "In a hundred years, we shall all be bald" (*Dentro de cien años, todos seremos calvos*).

Deftly making light of death's power, while showing respect for it, the saying implies that even if all men were not created equal, they will be so soon enough. A nice round time frame, a century, is introduced, putting human life in its place within the magnitude of time.

Mexican life rhythms leave more time for family and neighbors, talking in the town square, or even getting work done. During evening hours, when much of the world is watching prime-time TV, the Mexican is working steadily, having spent the afternoon with the family enjoying good food. Out of this generous concept of time

emerged a profoundly simple proverb, "There's more time than life" (*Hay más tiempo que vida*).

The proverb simply suggests that one needn't be hasty or anxious. In a tricky conceptual twist, though, the abundance of time is seen as extending beyond our life spans at both ends, before birth and after death. Thus the proverb presents another paradox: An allusion to the brevity of life serves to assert that one should slow down.

"There is more time than life" is the apt response to those who question whether there is enough time to do a job well, visit a loved one, or finish a good meal. It gently splashes the poser of the question with a perspective grander than the myopic one that prompted the question in the first place. There is the sudden realization that time is vast, dwarfing human life in all its haste and bustle. With this humbling reassurance, the proverb suggests we should not only take our time but take it easy.

"In daily life, it is used to calm people down," says Martinez. "I probably heard it most in my life from my mother at mealtime. I might be feeling very pressured by something at school, and my mother would say 'Relax, there's more time than life.' "

In Mexico, sayings favoring the proverbial turtle over the hare abound. "Better a stride that will last than a trot that tires fast" (*Más vale paso que dure y no trote que canse*) is one example. But "there is more time than life" carries a deeper philosophical content than most others. Its typical Mexican whimsy could suggest that if time is abundant and hence cheap and life is short and hence valuable, then one should freely borrow from the one to enrich the other.

The fun to be had with the concept of time is seen in other Mexican sayings. "The lazy work twice as much" (*El flojo trabaja doble*) snaps at those whose shoddy workmanship obliges them to spend as much time in the redo as they did originally. More contemplative but just as ironic is the sideways saying "No pain lasts one hundred years, nor could anyone outlast them" (*No hay mal que dure cien años, ni enfermo que los resista*). This could be the bright side of chronic pain: On the one hand, the reassurance that no pain lasts as long as a century; on the other, the reminder that even if there were such a pain, it would kill us long before that. But this is only the proverb's tongue-in-cheek vigor. The essential message is that, like darkness before the dawn, current difficulties do pass.

If this encouragement is ironic, perhaps its very gloominess has kept it alive over the centuries. An earlier form of the proverb appears in literature from Madrid dating from 1675. In a volume of idiom published after the bitter close of Spain's golden age (Gerónimo Martín Caro y Cejudo's *Refranes y Modes de Hablar*), the saying is "There is no good that lasts one hundred years, nor does evil last a century" (*No hay bien que cien años dure, ni mal que a ellos lleque).* By 1922 this appears in a Madrid dictionary of proverbs and sayings as "There is no evil (or pain) that lasts one hundred years"; the editor of this reference work, José Manía Sharbi, notes that some sources add, " . . . nor could a body outlast them." Thus, whether it was Spanish or Mexican irony that contributed the fatal final phrase remains unknown. What is certain is that the morbid irony of the proverb in its current form resonates within the Mexican soul.

The soul that rests confidently in the doorway of death and the abundance of time also takes heart in the proverb "He who gets drenched at dawn has the rest of the day to dry out" *(El que temprano se moja, tiempo tiene de secarse).* Here again, time is a key ally. He who suffers a bad experience early in life (or early in the day game, or battle) has all the more time to recover, according to this proverb. Its literal translation is "He who gets wet early has time to dry out."

In an earlier form, the proverb was not so poetic or uplifting; it seems to have relied on wetness as a euphemism for drunkenness. Indeed, the earlier form says, "He who gets wet early on has a *place* to dry out" *(El que temprano se moja, lugar tiene de secarse).* Rubio had heard it said that the saying was employed when inviting someone to have some wine first thing in the morning.

Aztec Voices

Rubio, who published the first authoritative collection of Mexican proverbs in 1937, wrote that Mexico would lack nothing in spicy expression even without the original forms of the sayings imported from Spain. Hence, regarding the influence of the Aztec language on Mexican culture, Rubio dared to declare: "If all the voices of Nahuatl origin were to disappear from Mexican Spanish, it would produce a truly horrible chaos."

Mexican proverbs are rife with Nahuatl or Nahuatl-descended words. In "Every man is entitled to make a kite from his pants" *(Cada quien puede hacer de sus calzones un papalote),* the individualistic side of the Mexican personality is reflected with diction distinct from the Spanish original: The word for "kite" is *cometa,* but in the Mexican version it appears as *papalote,* from the Nahuatl word *papalotl,* meaning butterfly.

This jolly proverb tells of the free spirit born of the Mexican's essential solitude, for, as important as the collectives of family and community are, the Mexican is profoundly solitary, according to Paz. The proverb's original language was so harsh and vulgar that only base classes used it to indicate that any fool can do whatever he pleases without having to answer to anyone. The original version from Spain, which spoke of making a kite from one's *culo* (graciously translated "buttocks"), has been softened by replacing it with *calzones,* meaning "pants."

Mexico's famous fatalism is detected in another saying that reflects the Nahuatl voice: "He who is born for tamales, on him the husks will fall from heaven" *(Al que nace p'a tamal, del cielo le caen las hojas).* Lucky people don't have to work at what they want, according to this saying, which makes superb use of the Mexican food staple *tamal,* descended from the Nahuatl *tamalli.* This word meant for the Aztecs what *tamal* means for the Mexican today: ground cornmeal with a filling of peppers or meats, steam cooked in the corn husks in which it is wrapped.

Likewise, it is the Nahuatl-descended word for prickly pear, *nopalli,* that can be heard as *nopal* in the proverb *"Al nopal lo van a ver sólo cuando tiene tunas"* (The prickly pear has company only when it bears fruit).

This is said in jest to those who appear in one's doorway only when they need something. The saying can be employed with varying degrees of sarcasm in the home, workplace, or political realm. According to Rubio, it seems to have had its origins in one of the verses of "Jarabe Tapatío," a traditional Mexican song:

> *Ingratas, crueles fortunas,*
> *He llegado a comprender*
> *Que al árbol lo van a ver*
> *Sólo cuando tiene tunas*
> *Sólo cuamdo tiene tunas*
> *Menos ni se acuerdan dél.*

> Ungrateful, cruel fortunes
> I've come to understand
> The tree is visited
> Only when it bears fruit
> Only when it bears fruit
> Or else it's not even remembered.

Dreams of the Poor

Mexican proverbs came from the ground. They are eminently earthy and reflect an earthly perspective, particularly that of the poor and the rural.

"Mexican proverbs may not be as old as rock, but they are at least as old as the largest trees in the *zócalos* [public squares] of rural towns," says Chicano poet Gary Soto in Chronicle Books' *Folk Wisdom of Mexico.* "It takes only a kitchen table, or two chairs situated under a mulberry tree, to hear a chattering of rural history summed up with an appropriate proverb."

Exposure to enough Mexican proverbs leaves one with the dust of hardship in the mouth. Thirst and cold are expressed in "The sun is the blanket of the poor" *(El sol es la cobija del pobre),* indicating that the poor take their warmth directly from the original source, or not at all. Likewise, hunger and perhaps despair can be heard sighed in the predawn darkness, in "Dreaming is the food of the poor" *(El sueño es alimento de los pobres).* The word for "dream," *sueño*, is idiomatically "sleep," and in either case the message can be taken starkly: It relieves hunger, until awaking.

It could be said that such proverbs paradoxically express at once consolation and anguish. "Bewail your poverty, and not alone," goes one saying (*Llórate pobre, y no te llores solo*). If one must endure such misery, the company of family and friends can remove the fatal edge. Another proverb, which speaks of the supposedly indomitable human spirit, is raw enough: "Man can adapt to anything except not eating" (*A todo se acostumbra el hombre, menos a no comer*).

A few cannot resist taking jabs at the rich, who historically were associated with corruption or oppression: "God gives money to the wealthy because without it, they would starve to death" (*Dios les da el dinero a los ricos, porque si no lo tuvieran, se morirían de hambre*).

If the rich were to be taunted, invariably money itself would come in for the same treatment. "Money buys only what is cheap" (*Sólo lo barato se compra con el dinero*) goes one proverb, asserting the priceless value of life's immaterial gifts. Unlike the English saying that the best things in life are free, the Mexican proverb tells more directly what money can buy.

Technology, imports, television, fashion, and the like have invaded Mexico's urban centers, bringing with them materialistic values that have challenged the traditional contentment with earning only enough to feed and clothe one's family. There are entire towns in Mexico, though, in which "people are still playing very ancient roles," to whom getting ahead and getting more would be strange goals indeed, according to Martinez. To those who are rich in family, friends, and faith, money buys only what is cheap.

It would be naive to imagine that the poor do not long to be rich. For some, these are the only two kinds of people there are, hence the proverb "Better to be a rich man's dog than a poor man's saint" (*Más vale ser perro de rico que santo de pobre*), an appeal for practicality. An elevated position that comes without livelihood is uncomfortable at best; better to have a low position with a means for living. Servile though the position may be, at least it guarantees being fed, and the impractical is best left to the otherworldly. Such a sentiment, as well as the counterpoint that money buys only what is cheap, might be overheard in any Mexican street café.

A Fatal End

The longings of the poor are expressed in many Mexican sayings, but perhaps none so subtly as in the somewhat obscure "There are no gardens like those grown by the poor" (*No hay jardines como los que hacen los pobres*). Flora, whether cultivated or wild, is dear in Mexico, but the saying is mainly figurative in speaking of the poor's designs and daydreams for fruits, flowers, and vegetables on land they don't have. The gardens of the poor are the most beautiful of all, if only because they exist only in yearning.

Sayings and proverbs are not used uniformly. This proverb can be taken to refer to those of humble means, creating in their small plots all the vision and beauty that poverty keeps them from otherwise expressing. It might be said, therefore, of someone who sublimates frustrated ambitions into eccentric hobbies.

Even proverbs with a single meaning can be used in various ways. As observed earlier, "Don't do good that could look bad" is a warning and corrective, but it also offers a tactful way of disagreeing with someone while appearing to agree, says Maria Jesus Urtaran of Mexico City.

"Someone may have done something wrong, but they try to justify it," says Urtaran. "So you pretend with them that they're innocent and leave it at that: 'Fine, but don't do good that could look bad.'"

The common proverb "He who is a parrot is green wherever he is" (*El que es perico, dondequiera es verde*) might be used in various ways, but its basic meaning is that the capable in one situation will be ever capable in another. This is heard from parents, teachers, coaches, and schoolmates from one's earliest years.

"Let's say I'm playing dominoes and I'm well known for that, and then my friends want to play cards, a different game," says Martinez. "I'll say, 'No, I don't know how,' and they'll say, 'He who is a parrot is green wherever he is.' And what they're trying to suggest to me is that, in reality, I'm no good. If I were any good, I'd play cards as well as I play dominoes."

The saying serves to affirm that whatever one is, one will be in any place or circumstance: brave or cowardly, intelligent or idiotic. Here is a trace of the Mexican sense that all is fated, or, as another saying goes, "He who was born to die by hanging will not die by drowning" (*Quien nació para ahorcado no morirá ahogado*).

Likewise, fatalism can be seen in "Today's butcher is tomorrow's beef" (*El carnicero de hoy es la res de mañana*), a warning to the powerful and presumptuous that, ultimately, vicissitudes could leave them in ruin. Urtaran points to various Mexican political bosses who have been jailed in the past few years.

Most common among the proverbs of fatalism is the idea that one's irreversible destiny is set from birth. When the Mexican says, "He who enjoys being an ox will lick even his yoke" (*El que por su gusto es buey hasta la coyunda lame*), or the more tricky "Everyone has the luck he deserves" (*Cada quien tiene la suerte que merece*), what is meant is that from birth one was fated for whatever one enjoys, does, or is. If one enjoys being as servile as an ox, from birth it was ordained; if one enjoys good luck from the merits of hard work, or misfortune thanks to misdeed, either way, it was determined at birth. More succinctly, "Some are born to be saints and others to be coal" (*Unos nacen para santos y otros para ser carbón*).

Ingrained fatalism may play a big part in the Mexican's silent gaze before ill fortune, but its interplay with faith cannot be ignored. Consciousness of God and the after-life traditionally underlie the Mexican worldview. The debilitating resignedness of fatalism may be the opposite of the faith that inspires, but in the paradoxical Mexican view, fatalism is itself a kind of faith. In varying degrees, it may reflect trust that a Judge will do ultimate justice. So the silent gaze may owe its unnerving steadiness to equal parts of fatalism and faith, as expressed in "God speaks for him who holds his peace" (*Dios habla por el que calla*).

Even before the arrival of Spanish Catholicism, the as-cetic Aztec culture took a celestial perspective of suffer-ing that honored silence as the proper response. Suffering in silence thus has pre-Hispanic antecedents. Although the church has done its part to fight injustice (Mexican independence was initiated by priests), the overarching residual of Catholicism in the Mexican con-science is that ultimate justice will be done later; maybe in this life, maybe not. Maybe visibly, maybe not: "No evil comes but to bring some good" (*No hay mal que por bien no venga*).

Romance

There's no fate worse than a life without love," says one proverb (*No hay suerte peor que una vida sin amor*).

The tragedy so common to Mexican experience naturally finds its way into the realm of romance. "The lovesick speak even to the stones" (*El que padece de amor, hasta las piedras habla*), says one; another refers perhaps ironically to the salve of new love for the pain of love lost: "One nail drives out another" (*Un clavo saca al otro*).

To those contemplating giving another chance to a bro-ken relationship, one might say, "Love is like a cake, it should not be served reheated" (*El amor es como los pas-teles, que recalentados no sirven*). That is, if things go badly, the original intensity of feeling cannot be recovered. And, for those intent on rushing things, there is "For love to last, it must be discreet" (*El amor para que dure ha de ser disimulado*).

Perhaps most common of them all and not necessarily limited to amorous matters is "Better alone unattached than unsuitably matched" (*Es mejor estar solo que mal acompañado*). This can also be heard among bickering friends or even erstwhile political mates.

The proverbs of Mexico take their forms from the im-ages of the country's very ash and color, from nails and cakes, coals and parrots. From the ache of injustice and a darkly fired strength of spirit comes wisdom that makes light of the weight of the world: death, time, tears. Flippant little sayings are seared into the conscience and define the world in endurable terms. As they are so often paradoxical, sometimes the most morbid sentiments are said with the biggest grins. In this, the humble Mexican is proud in a way that is in no sense gratuitous.

Article 8

Archaeology, September/October 1996

A MIGHTY MAYA NATION

How Caracol built an empire by cultivating its "middle class"

BY ARLEN F. CHASE AND DIANE Z. CHASE

By the close of the seventh century A.D. the Lowland Maya settlement of Caracol had become one of the most populous cities in the Precolumbian world. The 65-square-mile metropolis was home to more than 120,000 people whose stone and thatch dwellings stood amid lush gardens on terraced hillsides and valleys. At the northern edge of a high plateau, three large plazas sur-rounded by pyramids, palaces, administrative buildings, and ballcourts formed the heart of the city, from which paved roads extended to distant suburbs. Caracol had

grown from a modest town to a bustling city in the span of a century (ca. A.D. 550–650). Its people enjoyed a pros-perity unparalled in the Mesoamerican world. Military victories over rival cities, such as Tikal, Naranjo, and Ucanal, had assured political preeminence over some 4,500 square miles of territory. What led to Caracol's rapid development and unique place in Maya history? More than a decade of excavation by our team from the University of Central Florida has yielded some surpris-ing answers.

Caracol is located in the remote rain forest of the Cayo District of western Belize. Discovered in 1937 by a la-borer in search of timber, it attracted the attention of Linton Satterthwaite of the University of Pennsylvania, who in the 1950s drew and photographed most of the site's carved stelae and altars and produced a site plan depicting 78 structures. A. Hamilton Anderson, the first archaeological commissioner of Belize, excavated three tombs as part of the University of Pennsylvania project and undertook two additional short seasons of excavation in the mid-1950s. In 1980 a terrace system was briefly studied by Paul Healy of Trent University in Ontario.

At the start of our work in 1983 we expected to find a midsized Classic Maya city typical of the Southern Lowlands, where major monuments and buildings would be concentrated in the heart of the city, beyond which would lie only scattered settlement. Three years into the project we realized that Caracol was quite different from other Lowland Maya cities. We knew there were more than 78 structures; what we had not expected was a settlement so large and dense that our mapping teams would have difficulty finding the site's outer limits. Unlike Tikal and Calakmul, Caracol had been laid out on a radial plan much like Paris or Washington, D.C. Luxury goods, such as jadeite pendants, eccentrically shaped obsidian objects, and exotic shells, that are confined to the ceremonial precincts of other sites, were found throughout the city. Vaulted masonry tombs, traditionally believed to have been reserved for royalty, were discovered not only in temples and pyramids, but also in humble residential units. Clearly some sort of social policy had been at work here that was unique in the Maya world.

We know from excavations on the outskirts of Caracol that a few scattered hamlets had been established there by ca. 900 B.C. For nearly a millenium the population remained relatively stable. By the first century A.D. monumental architecture was under construction, indicating that the site's elite had the ability to mobilize labor and resources. The Temple of the Wooden Lintel on the eastern side of one of Caracol's main plazas achieved its final form around A.D. 70. Deposits found in the core of this building contained jadeite, shells from the Pacific, and cinnabar, attesting participation in an extensive trade network. By the second century A.D. Caracol had built its most impressive edifice, which we named Caana, Maya for "Sky House," a massive platform atop which temples, palaces, and other buildings were erected. Adjacent to it stood the plastered pyramids and shrines of the Eastern Acropolis, where a woman who had died ca. A.D. 150 was buried. In her grave were 34 pottery vessels and a mantle made of more than 7,000 shell and jadeite beads and fringed with cowrie shells and tapir teeth, indicating the prosperity enjoyed by some of Caracol's early inhabitants.

During the next four centuries Caracol grew steadily in size and population. Outlying settlements such as Ca-

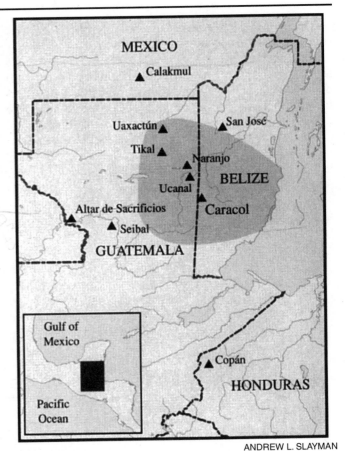

ANDREW L. SLAYMAN

Shaded area of map shows region controlled by Caracol at its height in the mid-seventh century A.D.

hal Pichik and Hatzcap Ceel, five and six miles away, were annexed and eventually incorporated into the expanding city. Construction continued in the central plazas, where even more high-status burials—in front of the Temple of the Wooden Lintel, in the Southern Acropolis, and on the summit of Caana—suggest the site was becoming increasingly prosperous and extending its trade contacts. The placement of yet other tombs in small household shrines suggests that ordinary citizens were beginning to take part in ritual activities normally reserved for the elite, a social development that would accelerate with the passage of time, setting the stage for Caracol's Late Classic success.

According to hieroglyphic inscriptions found on an earlier structure within Caana, on several carved stone monuments, and on a building stairway at Naranjo 25 miles to the northwest, the city embarked on military campaigns throughout the Southern Lowlands in the mid-sixth century. The inscriptions tell us that Caracol defeated Tikal, one of the region's most powerful cities, in A.D. 562, during the reign of Yahaw Te K'inich (Lord Water), and then consolidated its political position by defeating Naranjo and, presumably, a host of minor centers under the king's son K'an II. Naranjo was annexed in

J. BALLAY,
CARACOL ARCHAEOLOGICAL PROJECT
Agricultural terraces and residential units dominate the landscape in artist's reconstruction, above, of outlying settlement at Caracol. At left, a household shrine and dwellings surround a central courtyard, or plazuela, *a residential plan common throughout Caracol.*

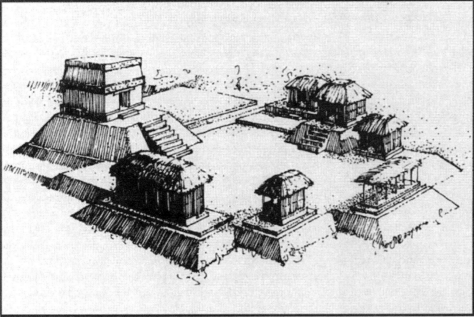

A.D. 631, possibly to have better control over tribute coming from Tikal. Naranjo and Caracol may even have been connected by a long causeway, parts of which have been detected on Landsat photographs. Strategic alliances were also formed with the ruling families of several key cities, most notably Calakmul to the north. By the mid-seventh century Caracol had become the seat of a small empire, collecting tribute from many of its former rivals and their allies.

In the century following the victory over Tikal, Caracol's population swelled from some 19,000 to more than 120,000—nearly double the maximum estimated population for either Tikal or Calakmul. Even four to five miles from the city center, as many as 2,500 people inhabited each square mile, a population density unparalleled in the ancient Maya world. To maximize the land's agricultural potential, thousands of miles of stone terraces were built and hundreds of reservoirs created. The city also embarked on a massive building program that included expansion and refurbishment of many principal monuments, including Caana and the Central, Eastern, and Southern acropolises, as well as the construction of a road system linking the city center to outlying areas. As Caracol grew, it absorbed many settlements, sometimes converting their plazas and temples into administrative centers. In some cases new centers were established in previously unoccupied areas, stimulating the development of new residential zones for the site's burgeoning population. The new settlements were connected to the core of the city by additional roads, facilitating the management and economic integration of the area. The road system also permitted rapid mobilization of Caracol's army, whose victories provided tribute labor to expand the city and strengthen its resource base.

Residential areas at Caracol consisted of *plazuela* units—groups of variously sized dwellings generally built on the north, south, and west sides of a central courtyard or small plaza. These units may have been occupied by members of extended families. Many courtyards had squarish structures on their eastern sides that served as shrines and family mausoleums. These ranged from simple wood-and-thatch structures on small platforms to masonry edifices atop pyramids. Inside both platforms and pyramids were vaulted tombs, many containing the remains of more than one individual, along with polychrome ceramic vessels, shell accessories, and ceramic incense burners used in rites venerating the dead.

Residential units with eastern shrines are found throughout the Southern Lowlands, but not as often as at Caracol, where they make up about 60 percent of all dwelling groups recorded to date. Distances between units vary from 150 to 450 feet, depending on the location of terraced fields and the steepness of the terrain. Conspicuously absent in Caracol's outlying settlement areas are housing units grouped around connecting plazas, a common residential feature at Tikal and Copán. The absence of such units may reflect tight control over town planning.

While differences in material culture and life-styles surely separated the upper and lower levels of Maya society, the gap between them seems to have been substantially bridged at Caracol. The distribution of vaulted masonry tombs and the presence of luxury items in the simplest residential units suggest that the people here were somehow sharing the wealth. Moreover, as the Late Classic period progressed more and more of the site's

inhabitants appear to have enjoyed the "good life." Any gap in quality of life that may have existed between elites and commoners rapidly closed as a sizeable "middle class" developed. Nowhere is this more evident than in Caracol's mortuary practices. We have excavated 213 burials at the site, 86 of which were in vaulted masonry chambers, many in the eastern shines of the *plazuela* units. Most of these chambers have passages allowing reentry to bury additional family members, to remove bone relics of ancestors, or to perform funerary rituals. Some tombs were emptied and reused. The newly dead were sometimes placed on wooden palettes. The bundled bones of ancestors would also be put in the chambers with offerings of shell, jadeite, and pottery. Incense was burned in front of the shrines, where offerings, including specially made ceramic vessels containing human fingers amputated in rituals, would be deposited.

Aspects of Caracol's burial practices are unlike those known from other Maya sites. The placement of more than one person in a single grave is relatively common at Caracol, occurring in 42 percent of its Late Classic burials. At Tikal less than two percent of Late Classic burials contain the remains of more than one person; the practice is even less common at other Southern Lowland sites. The widespread distribution of masonry tombs and their occurrence in *plazuela* units of all sizes attests their importance to the population. Though more are sure to be found as the investigation of the site progresses, the number of vaulted tombs encountered to date, some 120, already far exceeds the number found at Tikal, where only 23 have been discovered, most dating to the Early Classic period.

At Caracol we have found eight Late Classic tombs with texts on red-painted stucco panels and red-painted capstones. These texts, providing either the date of the chamber's consecration or the date of an individual's death, are usually associated with Caracol's royalty. Inscriptions alone, however, do not necessarily suggest elite status since texts are found on a variety of artifacts from nonelite burials.

One of the more telling indicators of Caracol's shared wealth is the frequency of inlaid dentition, a cosmetic modification interpreted elsewhere as signifying high social status. Only a few individuals with teeth inlaid either with jadeite or hematite are found at most Maya sites. At Caracol we have studied the remains of more than 50 people with inlaid teeth, nearly all of which date to the Late Classic period. This is more than twice the number of such individuals found at the Southern Lowland sites of Tikal, Seibal, San José, Uaxactún, and Altar de Sacrificios combined. People with inlaid teeth were buried throughout Caracol in both elaborate tombs and simple graves, suggesting that all levels of society had access to this cosmetic practice.

Ceramic incense burners and specially made ceramic cache vessels, considered elite items at many Maya sites, also seem to have been widely used at Caracol. Incense burners are found throughout the city and in a greater variety of contexts than at other Maya sites. We have found complete incense burners on the stairways of residential groups and in seven tombs, all dating between ca. A.D. 450 and 700. This contrasts with Tikal, where incense burners are largely found in association with the site's central plaza. Ritual offerings traditionally associated with elite ceremonial structures at other Maya sites are found in nearly all of Caracol's *plazuela* units, often buried in the courtyard areas in front of the eastern shrines. Many of these deposits date from ca. A.D. 550 to 700 and form a major part of the ritual paraphernalia associated with Caracol's veneration of the dead. The most common ritual deposits consist of small bowls placed rim-to-rim and found either empty or containing the bones of human fingers, from both adults and children. We believe that fingers were removed from the living as part of funeral rituals and in rites venerating the dead. In most cases only one digit was removed. One such cache, however, contained bones from 22 fingers in a single set of bowls. Virtually every excavated *plazuela* unit contained at least one cache of this type.

In Late Classic *plazuela* groups we have found more than 50 large, lidded urns, most with modeled or painted faces. A dozen such urns contained obsidian carved in exotic shapes; others held pyrite mirrors, *Spondylus* shells, and pieces of malachite. Caches in pottery vessels with faces and those with finger bones were also found in the Central and the Eastern acropolises, indicating that high-status residents of Caracol were sharing in society-wide rituals.

Caracol's rapid development was surely related to its social policies, presumably initiated prior to its known military conquests. To manage people effectively, the city's leaders encouraged a form of social cohesion that stressed the development of a distinctive identity rooted in ritual activity and bolstered by prosperity. This system worked for more than three centuries. Then, after A.D. 800, the people began to abandon the policies that had integrated them. Luxury items are found only in palaces, suggesting that the rich and powerful kept such goods to themselves. Simultaneously, outlying populations discontinued common ritual practices. About A.D. 895 much of the core of Caracol was burned, by whom we do not know. The Late Classic investment in road and field systems, however, continued to benefit residents of the outlying areas. For another 150 years they farmed the fields much as they always had and made occasional offerings in the abandoned central buildings. By A.D. 1100 Caracol's social identity was gone, and all vestiges of the once mighty nation had been engulfed by the rain forest.

ARLEN F. CHASE *and* DIANE Z. CHASE, *professors in the department of sociology and anthropology at the University of Central Florida in Orlando, have been directing excavations at Caracol since 1985. Project funding has been provided by the Dart Foundation, the Government of Belize, the Harry Frank Guggenheim Foundation, the Institute of Maya Studies, the National Science Foundation, the University of Central Florida, the United States Agency for International Development, and donations to the University of Central Florida Foundation, Inc.*

Article 9   *The Tico Times*, July 25, 1997

Deforestation From Bad To Worse?

By Guillermo Escofet

Tico Times Staff

Despite government claims that deforestation in Costa Rica has finally been brought under control, environmentalists charge that more trees were cut during the last logging season than in previous years.

Much of the blame is being put on the very laws recently passed to stop Costa Rica's rapid loss of forest cover. Critics say the laws have created loopholes loggers are pouncing on to destroy the few forests remaining outside the country's National Park system.

The hardest hit areas appear to be the Peninsula of Osa, Talamanca and Tortuguero, where the country's few remaining large tracts of virgin rainforest stand.

"Any talk of deforestation coming to a halt is just a lot of hot air by President José María Figueres and Environment Minister René Castro to promote their "joint implementation" scheme abroad," said biologist Quírico Jiménez, author of a pioneering study on Costa Rica's endangered tree species.

Castro insists that logging in wild forests decreased last season, and that, overall, more trees were planted than felled.

"This year Costa Rica will be able to prove it has become a net reforester," he told The Tico Times.

The problem is that there is no hard evidence to support either argument. Despite the satellite and aerial photography technology available, Costa Rica lacks a systematic, year-by-year method of measuring forest cover, making it impossible to say for certain whether forests shrank or grew over the past year.

What is evident, though, is a strong feeling among concerned citizens and environmental groups that the pace of deforestation has accelerated. The Tico Times has been flooded in recent months by letters and faxes denouncing abuses in many parts of the country, and Castro himself admits that forestry authorities are receiving more complaints than ever—an average of more than three per day.

However, Castro attributes this to improved law enforcement mechanisms that have made it easier for people to report violations, and to confusion caused by the new legislation.

"There's an important change in the game rules, and that creates confusion and uncertainty among all players," he said.

The legislation causing all the fuss is the New Forestry Law introduced in April last year, and the reglamento (a law's enforcement framework) that followed it in December.

Also worrying environmentalists is a change in the Land Title Law that makes it easier for people to claim land in conservation areas; and the decentralization and devolution of powers previously concentrated in the General Forestry Administration.

Hailed as a landmark in the fight against deforestation, the Forestry Law banned all further land-use changes in natural forests, and deregulated forestry plantations.

However, critics say the law's good intentions were corrupted by the influence of the loggers' powerful lobby group, the Forestry Chamber, which ensured that clauses and qualifications were added to crucial articles in the law and its reglamento.

"The Forestry Law was drawn up by the Forestry Chamber under the nose of the Environment Ministry," Jiménez charged.

Although not as unequivocal, the Environmental Law Center's (CEDARENA) forestry expert, Eugenia Wo Ching, said the Chamber did have a consultant present at all stages of the legislative process.

Aspects of the law that have most alarmed environmentalists are:

* Article 3, which allows a change of land use for forests smaller than two hectares. Castro defended this by saying that such stands are not biologically viable.

Eleven forestry experts consulted by The Tico Times disagree, stressing that the thousands of small patches of forest that dot Costa Rica's countryside act as important biological corridors for animal and plant species.

* Article 21, which handed municipalities the power (previously held by government forestry officials) to issue logging permits for farmland and non-forested areas, for a maximum of 20 trees per person.

Critics say municipalities do not have the expertise for this type of work, and can be easily fooled or bribed by loggers. Castro admitted the municipalities need more preparation, but said the majority have so far acted responsibly.

* Article 20, which gives logging authorization powers to private forestry engineers ("regentes forestales") in the same areas covered by the municipalities, and lumber plantations.

Critics say officials are now approving logging management plans from their desks, taking what regentes say at face value. Castro said this has reduced work pressure on officials, allowing them to concentrate their efforts on more important tasks.

* Articles 1 and 18, which some people say leave a loophole for loggers to gain legal access to National Parks and Biological Reserves, where logging until now has been strictly prohibited. Castro flatly denied this, adding that, if anything, the new law imposes tougher controls in conservation areas.

* Article 56, which eliminated the plastic tags used to identify legally-cut logs during their transportation.

Critics charge that this has made it more difficult to detect illegal shipments during road checks. The tags were reintroduced in the reglamento, after the government realized that their abolition had been a mistake.

* Article 8 of the Land Title Law of National Reserves, which introduces five easy ways to obtain land titles in protected areas. Environmentalists say this legislation was pushed through under

pressure from the Forestry Chamber to gain access to protected areas around Corcovado National Park on the Osa Peninsula, where most of the land is unclaimed. By law, a land title is required to obtain a logging permit.

Castro defended this by saying that resources on privately-owned [land] are better looked after.

Vociferous opposition to these laws from environmental pressure groups has prompted legislators into action.

Currently under review in the Legislative Assembly is a reform bill introduced by opposition Social Christian Unity Party deputy Rodolfo Brenes to remove logging authorization powers from municipalities, allegedly following widespread abuses in the northeastern districts of San Carlos, Guápiles and Sarapiquí.

An injunction against the law's reglamento is also being drawn up by ruling National Liberation Party congressman Luis Martínez, to be filed soon with the Constitutional Chamber of the Supreme Court (Sala IV). According to Martínez, the reglamento undid much of the good work incorporated into the law.

Castro blamed the perceived increase in illegal logging on several factors, starting with elimination of the identity tags traditionally nailed to legally-felled timber.

"We committed an error," he admitted. "We thought the (tagging) system was obsolete, and never realized so many ordinary people actually gave them importance as a way of telling whether a shipment of lumber was legal or not."

"The result is that we ended up with many mistaken complaints from people who would see trucks drive past without tags and naturally assume they were carrying illegal lumber."

The Minister also explained that a corps of 100 park rangers was recently invested with police powers and pro-

vided with a back-up force of 700 permanent volunteers. This, he said, has created a more effective law-enforcement force that is pushing through more complaints than before.

In addition, the Environment Ministry set up a hotline (tel. 192) to make it easier for the public to report violations.

Finally, said Castro, as of last year, many tree plantations reached maturity, so a large proportion of the lumber cut last season came from cultivated forests.

However, the Minister's assertion that the country's forests are increasing is dismissed by environmentalists as wishful thinking.

To support his theory, Castro points to satellite images of the Central Mountain Range—containing 10 percent of Costa Rica's forested land—which, he insists, show forest cover growing by a total of 1,000 hectares a year. If this can occur in one of the most heavily populated agricultural areas in Costa Rica, he argues, there's a good chance the same thing is happening elsewhere.

To prove it, Castro will be commissioning similar satellite shots of the rest of the country, to carry out a nationwide study to be presented at the Central American Forestry Congress in September.

"I have the hypothesis that what we've seen in the Central Range is taking place all over the country," he said.

However, Arturo Sánchez, chief researcher at the University of Costa Rica's Sustainable Development Research Center, questions the methodology used to interpret these images.

"International quality standards were not followed," said Sanchez, who carried out Costa Rica's last nationwide forest cover inventory in 1992 using NASA Pathfinder images, and is currently working on an update that should be ready by next January.

Sánchez has studied the same images Castro is referring to, and said the growth in forest cover they supposedly

show consists mostly of either underbrush or tree plantations, neither of which replicate the ecosystems and rich biodiversity in primary forests.

The only hard figures available on a year-by-year basis are those showing the number of logging permits issued by the National System of Conservation Areas (SINAC), the government body that regulates forestry activities in Costa Rica.

However, these are misleading—because the number of permits normally gives a very conservative estimate of the number of trees actually destroyed, and because the rules of how the permits are issued changed under the new law.

On paper, it appears that the total cubic meters of lumber allowed to be extracted from forests last season more than doubled in relation to 1995. Permits were granted for over one million cubic meters, as opposed to 431,566 the previous year, or 309,835 in 1994.

However, as the head of the SINAC, Raúl Solórzano, explained, under the new Forestry Law, logging permits can now span several years, depending on the duration of the applicant's forestry management plan. So while before, applicants had to obtain separate permits every year to cut the trees stipulated in their management plans, authorization is now given in one fell swoop, covering, if need be, up to 10 to 15 years. This would explain the large volume of lumber authorized in the period 1996-97.

Solórzano added that the demand for lumber in the country's sawmills hovers constantly between 1.2 to 1.5 million cubic meters per year, yet the volume officially extracted through authorized loggings in previous years has always been far below this. This implies, he said, that the rest was obtained illegally.

"If there are now more permits, it's because things are legal now," said Solórzano.

Article 10 The Chronicle of Higher Education, July 11, 1997

After a Long and Brutal Civil War, Academics in Guatemala Remain Cautious

Universities have been traumatized by decades of military dictatorship and strife

BY COLIN WOODARD

GUATEMALA CITY

SIX MONTHS after a United Nations–brokered peace agreement brought an end to a long and brutal civil war in Guatemala, educators here have yet to get used to the idea.

"It is very good that the war is over, but I am pessimistic about the peace," says Jorge Solares, director of the Inter-Ethnic Studies Center at the University of San Carlos of Guatemala. "There is intellectual freedom now, but we are very unsure of the permanence of that freedom. It makes us very cautious."

An estimated 140,000 people were killed during the 36-year-long war, among them many outspoken academics and student leaders. The peace agreement ended the fighting, but not the fear. In many neighborhoods here in the capital, private property is protected by razor wire and patrolled by guards with pump-action shotguns.

Scholars and intellectuals say major education reforms are needed if peace is to take root here. But decades of military dictatorship and civil war have traumatized the university system, which is reacting only slowly to the current democratization of Guatemalan society.

Although the civil war began in 1960, its origins go back centuries. Mayan Indians always have made up a majority of the population in what is now Guatemala, but since the Spanish conquest they have been a disenfranchised underclass. Pushed from their lands, deprived of education and basic health care, and subject to virulent racial discrimination, most Maya still serve as an inexpensive labor reserve for a relatively few rich landowners. When a coup sponsored by the U.S. Central Intelligence Agency in 1954 ended Guatemala's brief experi-

ment with land reform, the stage was set for the guerrilla war and counterinsurgency operations that followed.

DEMOCRATIC, MULTICULTURAL SOCIETY

With the end of the Cold War, Western countries pressured the Guatemalan government to negotiate a settlement with the marginalized but undefeated guerrillas. The peace accords that were finally signed in December seek to reshape Guatemala as a democratic, multicultural society. But the underlying causes of the civil war will be enormously difficult to address: The Maya account for 60 per cent of the country's population, but they control only a tiny fraction of its wealth. An official with the United Nations team monitoring the peace process estimates that 70 per cent of the Maya in Guatemala live in poverty, and that more than 80 per cent are illiterate.

Sources from across the political spectrum here agree that expanding educational opportunities for the country's poor is vital to the success of the peace.

"We need to redefine the country to reflect reality. This is a multicultural, multilingual society, and there's room for everyone if there's mutual respect and equal opportunities," says Estuardo Zapeta, who was the country's first Ma-

yan newspaper columnist and is now the Education Ministry official responsible for planning the expansion of the educational system. "As long as we leave the Maya illiterate, we're condemning them to being peasants. And if that happens, their need to acquire farmland will lead us to another civil war."

The peace agreement requires the government to increase annual spending on education by 50 per cent and to insure that, by the end of the decade, all students in Guatemala complete at least three years of universal education.

"The problem is, the private sector is completely opposed to increasing taxes, even though we have the lowest rates in the hemisphere," says Dinora Azpuru de Cuestas, a senior political analyst at the Association for Social Science Research, a state-supported think tank.

Most of the new money for education will go to improve primary and secondary schools, according to Mr. Zapeta. He estimates that one million Guatemalan children have no access to education at any level—an astonishing figure in a country with a total population of 10.6 million. "Many communities have no teacher at all, let alone a school building," he says. "The big imperative for the higher-education system is to train bilingual teachers who can work in these communities."

"Many communities have no teacher at all, let alone a school building. The big imperative for the higher-education system is to train bilingual teachers who can work in these communities."

22 INDIGENOUS MAYAN LANGUAGES

As is many other parts of the world, "mother language" education has been a controversial issue in Guatemala, where perhaps half of the Mayan majority does not speak Spanish. Complicating matters further, most of the 22 indigenous Mayan languages are not mutually comprehensible, so Spanish is used for inter-tribal communications. Because Mayan languages are not recognized by the state, few bilingual teachers have been trained.

A 1995 review by the World Bank of a bilingual education program here that the bank and the U.S. Agency for International Development have supported for the past two decades found that while the up-front cost was higher than that of traditional Spanish-only schooling, it ultimately reduced per-student costs by almost 5 per cent, because it was more efficient and productive. Bilingual schoolchildren in the program were found to "have higher attendance and promotion rates and lower repetition and dropout rates," and to receive higher grades in all subjects, including Spanish, than other students did. The study also found that students in the program went on to high school and higher education at a higher rate than did those in other schools.

But the program reaches only 15 per cent of students in the first to fourth grades. Mr. Zapeta says the Education Ministry would like to expand it significantly but is frustrated by the shortage of bilingual teachers.

"This is where higher education comes in," he says. "One of the country's top priorities is to train 35,000 bilingual schoolteachers. International donors should be creating these human resources. But the donors need results in two to three years, so they don't fund these sort of things."

At Guatemala's universities, change is coming slowly. Of the country's five universities, four are private, and all are in the capital. The state-supported by autonomous University of San Carlos of Guatemala is by far the largest—its 75,000 students represent three-quarters of the national enrollment in higher education. One Western diplomat refers to the university as Guatemala's "great, left-leaning, state behemoth," because of its Marxist reputation and its resistance

to reform. Professors and students at San Carlos often were targeted for assassination during the civil war, because the institution was widely regarded as a training ground for the guerrilla movement.

Sources familiar with the university say it served as a center of political activism and civil protest—a pattern repeated at other Central American universities. "The problem is that the emphasis is still on political activism, to the detriment of real teaching and research," says Dr. Azpuru de Cuestas, the political analyst. Faculty and staff members "have only just begun to recognize the need to adapt to the normalization of the situation," she says.

"University intellectuals and researchers will play a major role in this country's social transformation," says Dr. Solares, of the inter-ethnic–studies center at San Carlos. "We need to present an organized front to improve the education system. If not, we will continue to fail for lack of resources."

Although under Guatemala's constitution, San Carlos receives a healthy 5 per cent of the national budget, Dr. Solares says the government is always late in transferring the funds, complicating efforts to increase enrollment and expand course offerings.

Guatemala's universities enroll a mere 1 per cent of the country's college-age population. At San Carlos, Maya constitute only 5 per cent of all students, says Mr. Zapeta of the Education Ministry. "There is talk of increasing Mayan enrollment" at San Carlos, he says, "but to have any possibility of reflecting the real proportion of the population, there must be wider access to primary and secondary schooling."

TRAINING MAYAN INTELLECTUALS

In the foothills overlooking this city, the Jesuit-run Rafael Landivar Univer-

> *"As long as we leave the Maya illiterate, we're condemning them to being peasants. And if that happens, their need to acquire farmland will lead us to another civil war."*

sity has focused its resources on training Mayan intellectuals and developing textbooks and teaching materials in indigenous languages. "I agree that primary education is essential, but it's also very important that there be a Mayan intelligentsia at this critical time in the shaping of our country," says Guillermina Herrera Peña, vice-rector general of the university.

With support from international organizations and donor nations, since the mid-1980s the university has operated a linguistics institute that promotes the use of indigenous languages. During the height of the civil war in the '80s, the Jesuit university was quietly training Mayan students as indigenous-language specialists.

"We chose linguistics because it was more politically inert than, say, anthropology," Dr. Herrera recalls. "If we had drawn much attention to ourselves, it could have easily meant the closing of the university." The institution's sister Jesuit universities in Nicaragua and El Salvador accused it of being too cautious, she says, "but the environment was even more dangerous here."

Since the end of the civil war, Rafael Landivar University has increased its research projects on the Maya and stepped up its recruitment of Mayan students. Grammar books have been prepared for 10 Mayan languages, along with bilingual teaching manuals, indigenous-language texts, and children's books. According to Dr. Herrera, the number of Mayan students who win scholarships to attend the university is increasing, and all incoming students—the vast majority of whom are not Maya—are now required to take a general course in ethnic identity to help them develop a greater appreciation of the diversity of the country's population.

"We live in times of hope," she says. "If the spirit of goodwill I see here today were present decades ago, perhaps we wouldn't have had a war."

Democracy Advances in Nicaragua

by Tom Carter

In the United States political parties, presidential candidates, and issues are virtually interchangeable. In Nicaragua, by contrast, a genuine political war is going on for the heart, soul, and future of the nation.

It will take years to resolve, but, at least for the moment, those favoring a free-market economy and democracy have the upper hand.

On October 20, 1996, some two million people went to the polls in general elections. By a margin of nearly 51–39 percent, the people of Nicaragua voted for Liberal Alliance candidate Arnoldo Alemán over the Marxist Sandinista, Daniel Ortega.

Alemán, a 50-year-old lawyer and coffee planter who had spent time in a Sandinista prison, was elected president in the first transition from one democratically elected government to another in the history of the country.

"For the first time in more than 100 years of Nicaraguan history, one civilian, democratically elected president will hand over power to another," President Violeta Chamorro told reporters at the inauguration. She left office with her popularity at its highest point ever.

At a January 10 ceremony, promoted as the consolidation of Nicaragua's nascent democracy, Alemán received the presidential sash from Chamorro. Her nearly seven years in office had seen the end of an eight-year civil war during the Sandinista regime and the return of capitalism.

"We will not return to the past. The long, dark night is over," Alemán told thousands of supporters in Nicaragua's national stadium in Managua at his swearing-in.

BUDDING OF HOPE

Alemán also made overtures to the Sandinistas, asking their help in reconciling the long-divided nation.

Adding to the general optimism are signs of economic growth as Nicaragua emerges from the economic collapse of the 1980s. The economy grew by 5.5 percent in 1996, and outgoing government officials have predicted up to 7 percent growth in 1997.

"After five years, I can say with responsibility that we are an emerging country with a future and capacity to grow," outgoing Central Bank President Evenor Taboada told David Koop of Reuters News Service just prior to the inauguration.

Several days after the inauguration, Alemán met with Ortega and other top Sandinista officials in a session both sides described as "positive and productive."

Alemán and Ortega said they agreed in principle to name a high-level commission to study Nicaraguan poverty, property disputes created by Sandinista confiscations, and foreign investment needs.

"It was a normal discussion, correct and satisfactory," Alemán said after the meeting.

"This is a good signal that the country is now on the road of dialogue that has always been the best weapon to move the country forward without bloodshed," he said.

Ortega, who led the Marxist revolution that toppled dictator Anastasio Somoza Debayle and who ruled Nicaragua in the 1980s, called the meeting "beneficial." He said: "The ideal would be for us not to have confrontations or submit to violence. But that depends on the steps they take. It is in their hands to reach stability."

Ortega has threatened that Nicaragua would see a return to violence if the government follows policies that harm the country's poor.

The uneasy truce between the political leaders here is cause for quiet celebration in this notoriously divided Central

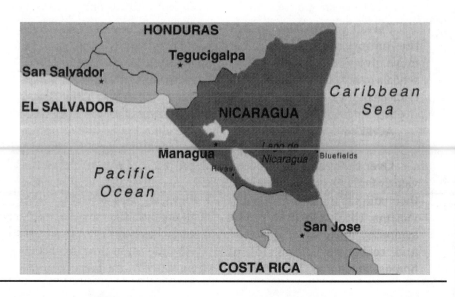

SORTING OUT THE LAND-REFORM MESS

During the Sandinista period from 1979 to 1990, nearly 40 percent of Nicaragua's agricultural sector was confiscated in a land-reform scheme.

More than 200,000 campesinos received plots of land once owned by members of dictator Anastasio Somoza's ruling elite. But the title to the land remained with the Sandinista government.

Also, in the last days of Sandinista rule, members of the government expropriated thousands of homes for themselves in what came to be known as the *piñata*, after the children's game that involves striking a papier-mâché effigy with a stick and grabbing for the prizes that fall out.

Former Sandinista President Daniel Ortega still lives in a mansion seized from Arnoldo Alemán's current campaign manager during that period.

When Violeta Chamorro was elected president in 1990, those who had lost property to the Marxists demanded the return of their homes, or at least fair compensation.

Sen. Jesse Helms (R-North Carolina) has repeatedly held up U.S. aid to Nicaragua on the grounds that U.S. citizens, including Nicaraguans who were naturalized during their exile, have not had their property claims properly reviewed and fairly settled.

Today, the property title question—who owns the land—remains the most contentious issue for the future of Nicaragua and the single biggest roadblock to foreign investment.

"The land title is a difficult issue," said former Secretary of State James Baker III, shortly after observing the Nicaraguan elections. "What is critical and most important [in Nicaragua] is that conditions are appropriate for investment. All this farmland that could be devoted to agribusiness uses, if you ever straightened out the land titles, could bring in a lot of investment."

T.C.

say, the Sandinistas would have won far fewer votes than they did.

But there is some evidence that the hard-core support is waning. The Sandinistas are divided among themselves, and while Ortega is the party leader, his Sandinista critics point out that he cannot seem to win an election. And in postelection demonstrations over the Managua mayorship, the Sandinistas were unable to bring the crowds into the streets as they did in the early days of the Chamorro presidency.

On the other hand, the uncompromising Sandinistas, who have shown a troubling ability to disrupt Nicaraguan life in the past, are displeased with the Nicaraguan Supreme Court, which struck down numerous laws passed since October by the then Sandinista-controlled National Assembly.

Uncharacteristically quiet in the days before Alamán's inauguration, the Sandinistas were enraged by the court's decision in early January to nullify dozens of Sandinista-sponsored laws passed in recent weeks.

They accused the court of bowing to pressure from Alemán's Liberal Alliance coalition in overturning the laws, which were passed by the National Assembly in sessions boycotted by pro-Alemán legislators.

"The decision was a coup d'état, with the collusion of the current and incoming governments," Sandinista legislator Rafael Solis told wire service reporters in January. "It puts the country in a crisis situation, with unpredictable consequences."

"The Supreme Court decision will not help Nicaragua's democratic transition," said Sandinista leader Victor Tinoco.

American nation, but the undercurrents of division and violence are just below any surface calm.

The United Nations ranks Nicaragua as the second-poorest country in Latin America, just slightly better off than Haiti. More than 70 percent of its population lives below the poverty line.

THREAT TO STABILITY

The Sandinistas won just 38 percent of the vote in October. Still, in a country that put up 23 different political candidates for president, the Sandinista cadres remain the best-organized and angriest political machine in the country. Without their tightly knit organization of grassroots activists, many observers

On Track to Stability

- **The rightist Liberal Alliance defeated the Sandinistas to win last fall's presidential elections by a margin of 51–39 percent.**

- **This achieved the country's first transition from one democratically elected government to another.**

- **While the nation remains very poor, its economy grew by 5.5 percent in 1996, and possible 7 percent growth is predicted for 1997.**

- **The Marxist Sandinistas, who have threatened to disrupt the country if the poor are not property tended to, still present a menacing, though much-subdued, profile.**

Nicaragua

Official Name: Republic of Nicaragua

Capital: Managua

Geography: Area: 50,800 square miles (about the size of Louisiana). Location: Central America. Neighbors: Honduras on north; Costa Rica on south.

Climate/Topography: Atlantic and Pacific coasts are each more than 200 miles in length. The volcano-studded Cordillera Mountains run northwest to southeast through the middle of the country. Between this and a volcanic range to the east lie Lakes Managua and Nicaragua.

People: Population: 4.3 million. Ethnic groups: Mestizo, 69 percent; white, 17 percent; black, 9 percent; Indian, 5 percent. Principal language: Spanish (official).

Religion: Roman Catholic, 95 percent.

Education: Literacy: 66 percent.

Economy: Industries: oil refining, food processing, chemicals, textiles. Chief crops: bananas, cotton, fruit, coffee, sugar, corn, rice. Minerals: gold, silver, copper, tungsten. Arable land: 9 percent. Per capita GDP: $1,570.

Government: Republic.

FLASH POINTS

Chamorro, 67, a gray-haired, grandmotherly figure, leaves office with the praise of the international community. She is popular because she ended Nicaragua's civil war and returned the country to democracy and the free market.

But the country remains polarized to a degree unfathomable in the United States.

After the election, Ortega and his party, citing election fraud, refused to accept the results that gave the presidency, the Managua mayorship, and the National Assembly to the Liberal Alliance.

Just hours before Alemán took the presidential sash, Managua police arrested two men carrying dynamite, foiling an apparent attempt to kill Alemán. One was identified as a former Sandinista intelligence officer.

Ortega later admitted that he knows the Sandinista party member who was arrested with dynamite. Some press reports said the man was once a member of Ortega's security detail.

"I have a relationship with him, as I have with thousands of Sandinistas of this country," Ortega said in a statement.

Also, the day before the inaugural ceremony, an unknown group ambushed a Nicaraguan army patrol, killing six soldiers in the province of Matagalpa.

Most suspect that the ambush was the handiwork of former civil war combatants, from the left and right, who have turned to crime.

Alemán, in a final effort to bring peace to the countryside, has called on the men to lay down their arms or face the full brunt of the government's power.

Nicaragua specialists note that the two camps, the right-wing Liberal Alliance and the Marxist Sandinistas, remain bitter enemies and will probably clash continually during the next few years. This, they say, will undermine but not strangle the growth of democracy.

Alemán is a burly anti-Sandinista who made a name for himself as mayor of Managua with a massive public works program that featured downtown cleanup, new streets and fountains, and a rapid-response team to whitewash revolutionary Sandinista graffiti.

Once a leader of the Somocista Youth Movement, named for dictator Somoza,

Alemán is supported by Nicaraguan exiles in the United States, rural peasants, and the urban anti-Sandinista vote.

In addition to political differences, Alemán has a personal dislike for the Sandinistas. In 1989, they expropriated his coffee farm as his wife lay dying of cancer. His running mate, Enrique Bolanos, is also a victim of Sandinista expropriations.

The middle ground—for the last six years occupied by Chamorro and her now shattered UNO coalition—had no real candidate or voice in the October election.

TAMING THE TIGER

Given the extremes, perhaps the most remarkable accomplishment of this election is that Nicaraguans are consolidating their fledgling democracy by resolving their political differences with ballots instead of guns.

Just three years ago, the National Assembly was paralyzed after former Contras unsatisfied with their lot in the peace armed themselves and took over a town. The Sandinistas responded by kidnapping members of the legislature, including Contra leader Alfredo Cesar, whom they released after making him parade about in his underwear.

The Chamorro government inherited a looted national treasury, the highest per capita external debt burden in the world, and an economy in shambles. The Alemán government will have it only somewhat better.

Per capita income is about $400. Unemployment is over 50 percent. And in *under*employment, and as much as 80 percent of Nicaragua's 4.4 million people are affected. Kidnapping and violent crime are rampant, with the number of crimes last year double the 1989 rate. The cost of living rivals Miami's, and there is little help on the horizon.

At the insistence of international credit institutions, an economic plan of government austerity, deregulation, lower taxes, privatization of state enterprises, and bureaucratic downsizing is the order of the day.

Foreign aid accounts for one-third of Nicaragua's $1.8 billion gross domestic product. In renewing their commitment for the next three years, the foreign donors made it clear, last summer, that they expect the country to stay the course.

Inflation, at 14,000 percent when Chamorro came to office, is under control at about a 12 percent annual rate. Due to increased coffee and seafood exports, Nicaragua has experienced several years of 3–5 percent growth.

The Maturing of Daniel Ortega

On October 21, 1996, the day after the Nicaraguan national elections, several senior U.S. statesmen talked with a small group of reporters, including Tom Carter.

Question: How has Sandinista leader Daniel Ortega changed from the man you knew in 1979, until today?

Former President Jimmy Carter: He's matured. When I first met him in 1979, he was like a college kid who had won a revolution and didn't know a darn thing about [governing]. He was a young revolutionary who knew how to fire an AK–47 and overthrow a dictator but didn't know how to run anything.

There is more of a comparison between then and 1990. I was contacted by the Sandinistas when I was in Ghana and asked if I would be willing to come down here and monitor the election. I was being asked to confirm what the Sandinistas thought would be an inevitable victory.

When President Bush was elected, the [Sandinistas] turned to the Carter Center, and out of that was evolved the 1990 elections, which turned out to be quite honest. When the Sandinistas lost, this was when we had to convince them to accept the elections.

They did accept the 1990 election when they had total control of the military and could have disavowed it. I think that shows a certain amount of maturity.

James Baker III (secretary of state under President Bush): I don't think that Ortega would have accepted the results in 1990 had President Carter not been down here to encourage that.

Carter: We could have never come down here if President Bush had not abandoned his commitment to the Contra cause.

Question: Mr. Baker, do you accept that word *abandon*?

Baker: No. I would phrase it differently. I do think we changed the policy. What we did was we decided to see whether we could achieve a compromise with congressional Democrats that would protect the Contras and relocate them and provide funds for humanitarian assistance. I wouldn't say we abandoned the Contras, but we certainly changed the policy.

One of the arrows in [Carter's] quiver [that he used to convince Ortega to accept the 1990 election] is that we did not abandon the Contras. We maintained them as a fighting force with humanitarian and relocation assistance, and if Ortega had thumbed his nose at the election results, that was always in the background. I feel certain that under those circumstances, we could have gone back to Congress and gotten more military aid.

Carter: That is true.

The Sandinista army, once at 38,000, is now down to just 12,000 men and under nominal civilian control.

The day after the election, former Secretary of State James Baker III and former President Jimmy Carter gave their post-mortems on the election and Nicaragua's future in general.

Both men said democracy in Nicaragua is in its infancy, but the elections, in which people stood in broiling sun for hours to cast their ballots, were an inspiration. However, both men cautioned that with Nicaragua's many economic problems and political divisions, the future would not be easy.

The new Alemán government, they said, must resolve the property title issue (see "Sorting Out the Land-Reform Mess") and put legal guarantees in place to ensure investor confidence.

"The new government has about 18 months [until mid-1998], and if they don't have policies in place by then, investors will go somewhere else," said Baker.

Tom Carter is a Foreign Desk reporter for the **Washington Times.**

Article 12   *Current History*, February 1997

Do Panama's preparations to assume control of the canal in 2000 constitute a new framework for democracy and ascension to membership in the global economy? Or, as evidence of its incremental movement toward authoritarianism suggests, are these efforts merely the dictator's new clothes?

Panama: Tailoring a New Image

STEVE C. ROPP

In his most recent best-selling spy thriller, *The Tailor of Panama*, John le Carré paints a bleak picture of a country struggling to come to grips with the rapid approach of the millennium. His lead protagonist is Harry Pendel, a tailor of English origin who turns his modest shop in Panama City into a "listening post" for British and American neo-imperialists. Operating in a sea of corrupt local politicians, opposition groups, drug dealers, and influence peddlers, Pendel purports to have discovered a plot by Asian corporate interests to gain control of the canal following its reversion to Panama. Reports of Pendel's findings to Washington eventually lead to "Operation Safe Passage," a fictional follow-up to America's real-life 1989 invasion, "Operation Just Cause."

Le Carré's gloom and doom stands in sharp contrast to the positive vision the Panamanian government and the ruling Democratic Revolutionary Party (PRD) are promoting. Panama is optimistic because the United States will soon turn over a veritable treasure trove of prime real estate that includes housing, hospitals, schools, port facilities, and airports. The government plans to convert these facilities into export-processing zones, educational institutions, and ecotourism centers (there are, for example, proposals for the construction of a "City of Knowledge" that will draw students and professors to Panama from all corners of the globe).

Which of these visions of Panama's future is correct? Will the country continue to struggle politically and economically with the legacy of 20 years of military dictatorship between 1968 and 1989? Or will its leaders find creative ways of dealing with the challenges presented by the new millennium?

For Panama, the turn of the century is much more than just a magic millennial date. It is the point at which concrete developments will take place, developments that are built into the terms of the 1976 Panama Canal Treaties and Panamanian domestic law. First, and most important, Panama will inherit the canal and its associated real estate. Second, United States troops are scheduled to leave the country. And third, a new Panamanian president will take office in September 1999, a scant four months before the canal transfer.

As a prelude to these events, Panama must deal with a number of problems that have plagued it since the 1989 United States invasion. These include finding ways to strengthen a political system that is stalled somewhere between authoritarianism and democracy; completing the economic transition from a closed to a more open capitalist economy; and dealing with the negative international image that has persisted since the days of General Manuel Antonio Noriega.

OUT WITH THE OLD—IN WITH THE . . . ?

Panama's political health must be charted against a background of developments that followed the 1989 invasion. Guillermo Endara, the country's first postinvasion president, managed to complete his term despite several coup attempts, the collapse of his ruling coalition, and a precipitous drop in public support.

Given the obvious fragility of Panama's new democracy, many observers were expecting the worst from the May 1994 presidential and legislative elections. Six candidates ran for president, supported by a cast of 16 political parties. Popular disgust with the inability of politicians to deal with national problems during the Endara years, as well as rapidly changing alliances among various fragmented parties, seemed to point toward fraudulent elections.

STEVE C. ROPP *is a professor of political science at the University of Wyoming. He is cofounder of* INTERPAX, *a private academic research facility that is examining emerging patterns of cooperation and conflict around the Pacific Rim.*

However, the 1994 elections turned out to be surprisingly free and fair—judged by most observers to have been among the cleanest in Panama's short history. Endara refused to use the economic and organizational resources of the government to favor his coalition's candidates and accepted defeat at the hands of the opposition.

Thus, the good news was that Panama had experienced one of its few Costa Rican-style elections. The more disturbing news was that the elections also resulted in the return to power of the PRD, a party that had been closely associated with the preinvasion military regime. Not only did it manage to restore one of its own to the presidency, but it also gained effective control of the National Assembly.

President Ernesto Pérez Balladares has many ties to the country's predemocratic past. An economist trained at the University of Notre Dame and the Wharton School of Finance at the University of Pennsylvania, he became secretary general of the PRD in the early 1980s. He participated in the 1984 presidential elections, first as campaign manager for a retired military officer, Rubén Darío Paredes, and then as a candidate in his own right. Forced into a brief retirement because General Noriega had different plans for the presidency, Pérez Balladares reemerged to manage the 1989 campaign of Noriega's handpicked presidential candidate.

Since assuming office in the fall of 1994, Pérez Balladares has governed Panama with a measure of efficiency. Nevertheless, there are indications that his government is still struggling with the legacy of its authoritarian past. Indeed, recent developments suggest that Panama has not fully completed the transition from authoritarianism to democracy and remains in political limbo.

THE THREADS OF DICTATORSHIP

The "politics of continuous transition" are clearly reflected in the fact that Panama has yet to significantly alter its constitution, which was imposed by the military in 1972. Although some important changes were made in 1978 and 1983, the constitution still retains undemocratic provisions. During Endara's presidency an effort was made to amend the constitution by popular referendum in order to enhance liberties and demilitarize politics. However, the overly complex basket of constitutional changes failed to spark voter enthusiasm and came to be associated with the president's failed efforts to revive the economy. As a result, they were rejected in November 1992 by a margin of two to one.

Furthermore, the political opposition is increasingly fearful that the PRD is intent on preserving its grip on power, as was its military-dominated predecessor. During 1996, Democratic Revolutionary Party activists launched a number of trial balloons to assess the popular climate for altering the constitution to allow a second successive presidential term. In March, Vice President Tomás Gabriel Altamirano Duque suggested that Pérez Balladares was the only Panamanian leader with sufficient will and stature to lead the nation into the twenty-first century.

If the PRD chooses to follow the path to civilian dictatorship charted by Alberto Fujimori of Peru, it will face significant obstacles. The National Assembly would first have to pass legislation authorizing a constitutional amendment that would then have to be approved in a national referendum. Sensing that Panamanians might not be willing to approve a second presidential term, the PRD's latest strategy has been to suggest linking these changes in the constitution and electoral code to other, more popular initiatives.

Although the primary threat to democratic governance is a possible "soft" civilian authoritarianism, renewed militarism cannot be entirely ruled out. Panama's military has been formally abolished through legislative action, but there are several national problems that might lead to its resurrection. Postinvasion Panama has one of the highest rates of violent crime in the world, especially in major urban areas. This, of course, concerns not only Panamanians but also foreign visitors. The country also remains vulnerable to drug trafficking, particularly along the Colombian border. Democratic Revolutionary Party legislators in the National Assembly, who remain sympathetic to the military, have used these problems and associated vulnerabilities to argue for the rearming of Panama's police, the Public Force, and for the creation of a new quasi-military elite unit within the force.

The career of retired Colonel Eduardo Herrera Hassan is emblematic of Panama's possible movement toward renewed militarism. A relative of legendary populist leader General Omar Torrijos, Herrera maintains close ties to members of the former military institution. After participating in an aborted coup attempt against the Endara government in 1990, Herrera was sentenced to several years in prison. He has since emerged to lead a new populist party that plans to field candidates in the 1999 elections.

CRASH DIET

Panama is also struggling with a shift to a more open economy. As has been the case in other Latin American countries, Panama's political discourse during the 1990s has been dominated by the central issue of productive restructuring. By the late 1980s, the alternative models of state-led economic growth that framed global political debate for most of the twentieth century—state capitalism and communism—had been discredited. Panamanian politicians joined the hemisphere-wide rush to institute economic reforms that would restore the globally competitive economic position their country had maintained until the mid-1970s. These reforms included lowering tariffs, increasing labor productivity and reducing the size of various government bureaucracies.

While Endara was president, the nation made little headway toward productive restructuring. It was only after Pérez Balladares's election that the government began serious economic reform. As president, Pérez Balladares explicitly sought to follow the development path of the so-called Asian tigers (Taiwan, Singapore, Hong Kong, and South Korea). In adopting an economic strategy that called for a dramatic lowering of tariff barriers and domestic wages to make Panamanian products more competitive in international markets, Pérez Balladares sought to emulate Asian success in encouraging export-led growth. His administration also placed great emphasis on attempts to gain membership in the World Trade Organization, the North American Free Trade Agreement, and the Asia Pacific Economic Cooperation group.

Immediately following his inauguration, Pérez Balladares publicly made the case for adopting drastic economic measures to increase Panama's global competitiveness. In early October 1994, the cabinet council approved a new government economic plan that included a five-year timetable for reducing the public sector through an inclusive process of public consultation. At the same time, Economic Minister Guillermo Chapman suggested that some changes in the progressive 1972 labor code would be necessary.

Although the Pérez Balladares administration did make some attempts at broad consultation, it soon became clear that the government was intent on imposing its new economic policies no matter what the short-term cost in public support. The absence of a populist dimension to the government's economic plan could be seen by the lack of an explicit safety net for the poor and the lack of any clear indication that savings derived from the downsizing of the public sector would be used to support social development. While the government denied that its plan for productive restructuring was dramatically different from the economic plans that the PRD had supported in the past, the plan clearly constituted a major change in economic (and hence class) orientation.

By the spring of 1995, battle lines had been drawn between the government and large sectors of the public around the issue of reforming the labor code. The government was especially insistent on allowing Panamanian companies to freely hire and fire workers, and the question of who would pay for contributions to a new dismissal fund (created by the government's labor reform bill) became a particularly contentious issue. Opposition to the reform process was led by powerful unions associated with banana workers and the urban construction industry.

When the PRD-dominated National Assembly attempted to revise the labor code in August 1995, matters came to a head. Following an initial debate on August 4, there were strikes and riots in Panama City in which four people died and hundreds were detained by the police. Some 49 labor unions went on strike, and received broad support from business and professional organizations, students, and opposition political parties. Labor unrest continued following legislative approval of the reforms one week later.

While the Pérez Balladares administration has pushed its economic reform agenda with tenacity and vigor, it has little to show for its efforts. The nation's economic growth rate hovers at around 2 percent (a full percentage point below the regional average), and unemployment remains stubbornly high (between 13 and 15 percent). One major factor leading to short-term growth stagnation and unemployment is the administration's current effort to pay off the nation's massive commercial debt. The government reached agreement with its creditors early in 1996 to restructure this debt within the general guidelines of the Brady Plan, but it required freezing public expenditures for all but the most basic services.[1] Meanwhile, Panama continues to suffer from one of the most unequal patterns of wealth distribution in all of Latin America, and half the population lives in dire poverty.

In sum, Panama's crash diet may be working, but the new suit of clothes is hanging rather loosely from the country's emaciated frame. The result of all this economic distress has been a series of strikes in the public and private sectors over the past several years. As for the architect of economic reform, President Pérez Bal-

> *Panama has not fully completed the transition from authoritarianism to democracy and remains in political limbo.*

---

[1]In 1989, the Brady Plan, named for United States Treasury Secretary Nicholas Brady, proposed that banks holding outstanding loans from Latin American countries should forgive a portion of the debt in exchange for guarantees that the remaining debt would be paid.

ladares seems willing to stay the course, although he may be dismayed by his declining public support. Not only does his agenda come under regular assault by opposition political parties, it is also attacked by members of his own PRD.

TAKING A GOOD LOOK IN THE MIRROR

Panama's current political and economic problems are compounded by a negative image abroad that has plagued the country since it was ruled in the 1980s by General Noriega. It is "a Casablanca without heroes, a hotbed of drugs, laundered money and corruption," as le Carré puts it. Its image as a safe haven for shady businesses is so bad that Russians actually use the word "Panama" to refer to any bogus corporation established for illicit purposes.

Since the early 1990s, public officials have made restoring the image of the country as a stable democracy a priority. However, they have often been hindered in this effort by seemingly endless quarrels between the various political parties and between the three branches of government. For example, certain Democratic Revolutionary Party legislators have engaged in a vigorous campaign to put opposition-appointed Supreme Court magistrates on trial for purported crimes. These machinations are especially troubling because they appear remarkably similar to those witnessed in the years before the military seized power in 1968.

General Noriega's extensive involvement in drug trafficking and money laundering during the 1980s intimately associated the country with corruption. Part of Panama's problem in this regard is geographic in that the isthmus is located close to the major cocaine-refining facilities and drug-trafficking routes of the Colombian cartels. As home to a substantial banking community and one of the world's largest free trade zones, Panama is an extremely attractive place for traffickers to do business.

Drugs in transit to the United States and Europe arrive via Panama by sea and air, passing through the country's major ports or some 200 small landing strips in the San Blas Islands and Darien. Much of the money laundering is done through the purchase of major urban construction projects (hotels, condominiums, office complexes), a process that has created a real estate glut in Panama City. For the past three decades, the Colón Free Zone has offered an attractive option for money launderers, including the Cali cartel, which used the area extensively in the early 1990s.

The perception of Panama as a hotbed of drugs, coupled with the country's willingness to serve as home for bogus corporations, threatens to undermine legitimate activities in the Colón Free Zone and in the country's large banking sector. In 1996 the National Banking Com-

mission was forced to take over and liquidate the Agro-Industrial and Commercial Bank after it lost some $50 million in investors' funds. This case sparked concern in the international community about Panama's ability to oversee some 100 financial institutions—especially since the Banking Commission has fewer than 70 employees.

"Narcoscandals" have also spilled over into the political arena. In May 1996 *The Economist* reported that President Pérez Balladares may have received illegal donations from the Cali cartel during his 1994 election campaign. Following further allegations of possible wrongdoing in the *Miami Herald* and *New York Times,* it was discovered that the president's campaign committee had indeed received some $50,000 from a businessman associated with the cartel. By admitting that he had unknowingly received these donations, Pérez Balladares avoided invidious comparisons with Colombia's beleaguered president, Ernesto Samper. However, his personal avoidance of "Samperization" did the country little good as it struggled with its larger image problems.

Panama faces one more major difficulty when it comes to restoring the view that it is a stable and economically progressive democracy. Following the 1989 invasion, and partly as the result of the abolition of Panama's brutally effective Defense Forces, crime and violence became pervasive. Weapons of all kinds remain widely available, kidnappings of Panamanians and foreigners are common, and street crime has assumed major proportions. In the war against Panama's large criminal element, 34 policemen were killed in 1995 alone. Restoring Panama's image of tranquillity without simultaneously restoring the military to power will not be easy.

CARE TO TRY ON A KIMONO?

Panama's difficulties in dealing with ongoing domestic political and economic transitions are further complicated by its rapidly changing relationship with other countries and "actors" within the international system. Panama is becoming involved in a complex pattern of cooperation and conflict along the eastern edge of the Pacific Rim. To some extent this involvement represents a return to the pattern of multiple relationships with great powers that influenced isthmian developments during the late nineteenth century. But today, the locus of these relationships has shifted from the Atlantic to the Pacific, and their patterns are much more complex, involving not only the region's great powers but broader transnational economic interests.

Of the great powers involved, the United States remains the most important and influential. American interests have changed in minor ways since the canal treaties were negotiated two decades ago, but the most salient concerns remain the same. First, there is a continuing interest in the efficient and secure operation of the canal, given that some 70 percent of United States seaborne trade passes through it. Second, the United States remains interested in Panama's political stability and believes that democratic government is stability's best guarantee.

Under the terms of the 1977 canal treaties, the United States is obligated to turn over large amounts of property, including 12 military installations, to Panama before the year 2000. The remaining 7,000 American military personnel are scheduled to leave by that date, and the headquarters of the United States Southern Command will be moved from Panama to Miami, Florida. However, a majority (70 percent) of Panamanians have consistently indicated that they would like some bases to remain, provided that the United States pays rent.

Panama's crash diet may be working, but the new suit of clothes is hanging rather loosely from the country's emaciated frame.

From the standpoint of the Clinton administration, some residual military presence is desirable, both as a guarantor of Panama's political stability and to help fight the drug war. In particular, there is considerable interest in retaining access to Howard Air Force Base, from which numerous intelligence sorties are flown each year in the war against narcotraffickers. Although President Pérez Balladares has indicated he would like to turn Howard into a multilateral drug antitrafficking center, and an interagency working group has been formed in the State Department to examine American options, nothing is assured; bureaucratic consensus concerning the desirability of a continued American presence in Panama would have to be reached in Washington. Panama's political parties would also have to agree not to turn the issue of a continued United States military presence into a political football prior to the 1999 elections.

Although the United States retains great influence on the isthmus, Japan has also emerged as a major player. As the canal's second most important customer and a country that was highly influential during the Noriega years, it remains extensively—if somewhat cautiously—involved in Panama's affairs. This involvement has led to a certain amount of tension between the United States and Japan, as the multinational construction and shipping companies of both countries compete in the effort to modernize the canal and its associated port facilities. Such tensions lay just below the surface in the deliberations of the Tripartite Commission, formed in 1985 by Panama, the United States, and Japan to discuss future canal modernization.

Because Japan is frequently portrayed by novelists such as le Carré as Asia's great conspiratorial power, it is easy to overlook the significant role played by Asia's smaller, newly industrialized economies—especially Taiwan. For example, Panama and Taiwan are currently in the process of establishing at the former Fort Davis a major export-processing zone similar to the one set up by the Taiwanese at the former Subic Bay United States naval base in the Philippines.

Taiwanese businessmen have expressed considerable interest in creating an export platform for light industrial goods in Panama. But the relatively high cost of local labor suggests that this is not Taiwan's primary concern on the isthmus. Rather, Taiwan's increasingly autonomous national development has led to the rapid growth of homegrown multinational corporations that are extending their reach into all of the world's regional maritime shipping and transportation centers.

The key player in Taiwan's effort to create a global network of marine transportation facilities to support its worldwide manufacturing activities is the Evergreen Marine Corporation. Owner of the world's largest container shipping fleet, it is currently constructing a container terminal in Colón at the Atlantic terminus of the Panama Canal. As a rapidly expanding global megacorporation, Evergreen's marine operations are closely linked to the People's Republic of China through Hong Kong and through Taiwan's southern port of Kaohsiung. Once a planned Taiwan-China transshipping center is completed in Kaohsiung—already the third-busiest container port in the world—Evergreen will likely consolidate its paramount position in world container shipping.

Because of the imminent withdrawal of United States military and civilian personnel from Panama and the increasing role of Asian powers in the eastern Pacific, all the region's countries and their corporate allies are caught up in a complex dance involving both cooperation and competition. Cooperation is manifest in the efforts the world's major countries have made to ensure that there is continued universal access to the canal within a stable regional framework. Competition over Panama is most pronounced between Taiwan and China, and between Taiwan and a "triumvirate" of Japanese, South Korean, and Chinese corporate interests. These tensions more broadly indicate concern that the Taiwanese may monopolize transshipment activities around the canal. In a certain sense, the curious overlapping patterns of cooperation and conflict that have been apparent in East Asia for some time are now spilling over into Panama and Central America.

FINAL FITTING

Panamanians are a remarkably energetic and practical people, capable of adapting rapidly to new economic circumstances. The past two governments have come up with a number of innovative ideas for future use of the various resources and facilities that will revert to Panama in three years. It seems likely that some of the best of these ideas (such as canal and port modernization and eco-tourism development) will eventually come to fruition.

Yet recent political developments suggest that we should remain somewhat skeptical about the prospects

for a procedurally sound Western-style democracy in Panama. There are troubling indications that the country may be moving toward a new form of authoritarian civilian rule, rendered superficially legitimate by the need for highly centralized national decision making in a time of rapid economic change.

To the extent that Panamanians come to view their country as an emerging "Tiger of the Eastern Pacific" rather than as a more traditional member of the Western Hemispheric community, they may be willing to accept this essentially Asian perspective on "guided democracy." However, such a change in viewpoint seems highly unlikely in the short run. The result may well be a considerable amount of political turmoil that could vastly complicate the canal transfer process.

Article 13   *The Economist*, October 12th–18th, 1996

Remapping South America: MERCOSUR

The end of the beginning

THINK back 20 years, and the southern part of South America was both an economic backwater and an armed camp. Its countries were ruled by military dictatorships, eyeing each.other with suspicion and hostility, even threats of war, across borders sealed against all but a trickle of trade. Think back just seven years, and the dictatorships had given way to civilian democracies, but (Chile apart) the region's economies remained wedded to beggar-thy-neighbour protectionism, and were prostrated by inflation, instability and debt.

And now look five years ahead. Barring accidents, by 2001 an integrated, growing and relatively open market of at least 240m people, with an output of well over $1 trillion, will stretch from the Brazilian north-east to Chile's Pacific coast, over what can be called (taking some geographical liberty with Brazil) South America's southern cone.

At its heart, Brazil and Argentina, which between them account for more than half of Latin Americas's GDP, should have a common foreign-trade policy and, for all but a handful of prod-

ucts, a common external tariff, with increasingly convergent, and market-friendly, macroeconomic policies. United with them in a customs union will be their small neighbours Paraguay and Uruguay. And most, maybe all, of the rest of South America will be linked to this core by free-trade agreements.

As investors, both local and foreign, exploit the potential for growth, scale and specialisation offered by this new market, this southern cone will be emerging as an agribusiness and mining superpower, with a diversified and modernised manufacturing industry fueled by cheap and abundant energy. It will have forced its way back on to the world economic and business map, after an absence of two generations, and be preparing, led by a once self-doubting but already confident Brazil, to take its place, with the rest of Latin America, the Caribbean, Canada and the United States, in a free-trade area, starting around 2005, that will embrace the entire western hemisphere.

That, at least, is the prospect. Some of it has happened already. The big push

Mercosur has achieved surprisingly swift success. But there is plenty more to do, writes Michael Reid

came from the formation of the southern common market, Mercosur (in Spanish; Mercosul in Portuguese), by Argentina, Brazil, Paraguay and Uruguay in 1991. True, some of the change began, and would have gone on, anyway. Latin American economies could not stay stuck for ever in the age of state industry, state intervention and isolated markets. And Mercosur is only one in a web of international agreements—31 of them, by the count of ECLAC, the United Nations Economic Commission for Latin

Four members and a friend

1995	Population m	GDP $bn	GDP per head $	Total exports $bn	Total imports $bn
Argentina	34.3	282.7	8,250	21.0	20.0
Brazil	156.0	676.0	4,350	46.5	49.7
Paraguay	4.9	8.9	1,800	2.0	3.4
Uruguay	3.2	17.2	5,400	2.1	2.7
Chile	13.9	67.3	4,850	16.0	14.7

Sources: EIU; National statistics

America and the Caribbean—signed since 1990 to liberalise trade within the region. Meanwhile, older but moribund sub-regional groups, such as the Andean Group—soon to be "Community"—are reviving. Yet Manuel Marin, the European commissioner who handles relations with the region, is right to call Mercosur the "hard kernel" of its integration.

This is the world's fourth-largest integrated market, after NAFTA (the North American free-trade area), the European Union and Japan. It is a dynamic one. Intra-Mercosur trade has soared; combined GDP, despite ups and downs, has grown by an annual average of 3.5% since 1990; and at $5,000 its income per head is 30% above that of Latin America as a whole. Above all, Mercosur is seen throughout the region as the leader in the field.

It is still not yet a full free-trade area, let alone a customs union, applying a common external tariff; its "common market" tag expresses only an aspiration—toward free movement not just of goods but of services, capital and labour—not fact. Even so, this is the world's most ambitious scheme of regional integration since the birth of the European Economic Community in 1957. Mercosur offers a framework and a timetable (and a snappy brand-name that has become an attractive visiting-card in the rest of the world). And it has won political commitment: despite some backsliding and a few tense moments, its members, by and large, have stuck to their undertakings and kept the process moving.

It is too early to say with confidence that Mercosur is irreversible. Much can yet go wrong: Latin America's history has seen many visionary schemes for integration that foundered on local rivalries, economic turbulence, outside meddling or their own flawed economic assumptions. But there are two basic grounds for optimism. The first is that Mercosur is the creation of democratic governments; it can fairly be seen not as a short-term expedient but as a long-term project for integration between the peoples they represent. Second, it is based on a commitment to trade liberalisation, and is being taken forward by governments pledged to broadly sound macroeconomic policies that have tamed inflation. Earlier integration schemes, such as the Latin American free-trade association of 1960, did increase trade among members, especially in manufactures, through the granting of selective bilateral preferences. But their intention was only to widen protected markets, in an ultimately doomed effort to make import-substitution work better. In contrast, Mercosur's integration is predicated on market opening and export-based growth; "open regionalism", as it is known.

The clearest single measure of Mercosur's progress is the growth in trade that it has prompted. From $4 billion in 1990, trade among its four members more than tripled to $14.5 billion by 1995. There is plenty of room for more: in 1995, intra-group trade amounted to only 1.6% of Mercosur's GDP, compared with 4.5% for the NAFTA countries and 14% for the EU. Trade has flowered partly because the end of inflation, followed by economic growth, produced consumer booms, first in Argentina and then in Brazil. But another reason is that Mercosur has lifted artificial barriers that had long restrained commerce between those two countries. Between them, they account for 97% of Mercosur's GDP, and they have at last recognised that they are natural trading partners.

The assumptions changed in Asuncion

When in 1494 Queen Isabel of Castile and King João II of Portugal made the Treaty of Tordesillas, fixing a boundary between their respective empires at a point 370 leagues west of the Cape Verde islands, they created what turned out to be one of history's less porous frontiers. Though groups of marauders, and then settlers, pushed Brazil's frontier further west into the Amazon, the Mato Grosso and to the river Uruguay, there it came to rest. While ex-Spanish South America fractured into separate countries after

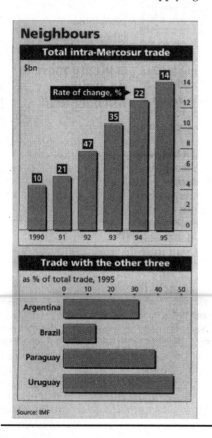

What Mercosur has done

The free-trade area

In a transition phase between 1991 and 1994, Mercosur's members cut tariffs sharply on trade with each other; today most goods go tariff-free inside Mercosur, though there are some far-from-trivial exceptions: cars and sugar (which are subject to special arrangements) and groups of products considered sensitive by each member, 950 items for Uruguay, 427 for Paraguay, 221 for Argentina and 29 for Brazil. Internal tariffs on these products are to be cut progressively to zero by 2000 (1999 for Brazil and Argentina), by which time cars and sugar are supposed to be brought into the free-trade scheme. But, unlike NAFTA, Mercosur as yet lacks agreements to achieve eventual free trade in services, or to deal with such issues as intellectual property and government procurement.

The customs union

Against most expectations, at the end of 1994 Mercosur agreed to embark on the second stage of its integration project: to create a customs union, in which, as in the European Union (but not in NAFTA) members apply a common external tariff (CET) to imports from third countries. From January 1st 1995, a CET set at 11 different levels, from zero to 20%, was applied to most imports. In this case, a larger group of products has been temporarily excluded: each country was allowed to exempt 300 items (399 for Paraguay), whose tariffs will converge (through annual increases or decreases) at the CET by January 2001 (2006 for Paraguay, which will have to raise its tariffs). A second group of products also is subject to special arrangements: tariffs on imported capital goods are to converge by 2001 at a CET of 14%, and on computers and telecommunications equipment at 16% by 2006. During 1995, two further changes were made. To sup-

port its anti-inflation plan, Brazil was allowed temporarily to cut tariffs below CET levels on 150 products (since reduced to ten), while the others were allowed to do this for 50 products. Secondly, because of global financial markets' concern over fiscal and balance-of-payments deficits in developing countries after the Mexican crisis, Argentina imposed a general 3% duty on imports from outside Mercosur, besides raising its tariffs on capital goods and telecoms equipment; while Brazil increased its list of CET-exempt products by 150 for a year, and raised tariffs on consumer electronics and cars.

Towards a common market

In December 1995, Mercosur agreed a five-year programme under which it hopes to perfect the free-trade area and customs union. This involves standardising many trade-related rules and procedures, and moving towards harmonising its members' economic policies. But since there is no commitment to allow free movement of labour, creating a true common market remains a fairly distant aspiration.

Free-trade agreement with Chile

During 1996 tariffs on most Mercosur/Chilean trade will be cut on both sides by 30%; from 2000 they will then fall to zero over four years. A small group of Chile's food and agricultural imports from Mercosur will have special treatment: tariffs on most of these will start falling in 2006 and reach zero by 2011, though wheat, flour and sugar will retain their existing tariffs (from zero to 31%, depending on world prices) until at least 2014. To qualify for tariff preferences, goods must have Mercosur or Chilean content of at least 60%.

---

achieving independence in the early 19th century, Brazil remained united. In the south, there were two bits of unfinished business. A struggle between Brazil and Argentina for control of the territory north of the river Plate was settled when Uruguay emerged as a buffer state, after British mediation. And Brazil, Argentina and Uruguay ganged up in the 1860s in a terrible war which humbled an expansionist Paraguay.

Thereafter, the two big neighbours paid remarkably little attention to each other (except on the football field). Argentina rose as an agricultural power, and then declined; Brazil got on with the business of filling its huge territory with people and industry. Until 1985, apart

from a couple of border encounters, only three Brazilian presidents had ever visited Argentina, and only two Argentine rulers had made the trip the other way. Sporadic attempts to increase bilateral trade bore only modest fruit, in the face of military and political mistrust

That changed when civilian governments took charge again—in Argentina in 1983, in Brazil in 1985—after long periods of military rule. The two new presidents, Raul Alfonsin and Jose Sarney respectively, signed agreements aimed first at strengthening democracy and reducing military tensions; by allowing mutual inspection of nuclear facilities, for example. But they also tried to revive sick and still-protectionist

economies through selective bilateral trade preferences, in the form of sectoral agreements, while maintaining restrictions on imports from other countries.

The process then underwent a vital change: the election of Carlos Menem in Argentina in 1989, and of Fernando Collor in Brazil in 1990, brought to power governments intent on trade opening and economic reform. They scrapped import bans and quotas. In place of notions of managed trade and industrial policy, when Mercosur was born in 1991, under the Treaty of Asuncion (capital of Paraguay), it was as an instrument to achieve free trade among members and to seek the efficiencies needed for competition in the world economy. The ear-

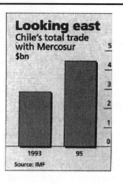

Looking east
Chile's total trade with Mercosur $bn
Source: IMF

lier agreements had involved negotiating exceptions to general tariff protection. The Mercosur treaty turned this process inside-out, requiring automatic and progressive tariff cuts, and allowing protection only that was both selective and temporary.

The decision in 1994 to proceed to a customs union involved a second debate as to how open Mercosur should be. Argentina, like Uruguay and Paraguay, had low tariffs on capital goods; one of its aims in opening its economy was to allow its firms cheap access to imported technology. Brazil, in contrast, wanted to protect its own capital-goods industry. In the event, the agreed common external tariff (CET) was a compromise: Argentina and the others agreed to raise tariffs, Brazil to bring them down. Today, Mercosur's average trade-weighted external tariff is 14%—well below that of any of its members (except Paraguay) in 1990, and broadly comparable to current Latin American norms.

A customs union should help to deepen Mercosur's internal free-trade area: it obviates the need to determine the national origin of goods traded between members. But, as free-traders object, Mercosur's external tariffs vary widely from low to high, so distorting

relative prices. Chile—Latin America's fastest-growing economy, and one that liberalised trade earlier and more thoroughly than did others—offers a contrast. Though Chile's external tariff of 11% is only slightly lower than Mercosur's, it is applied uniformly to almost all imports (bar the rising number that come in tariff-free, under bilateral trade deals). This has prevented Chile from becoming a full Mercosur member. Still, the free-trade agreement that Mercosur reached with Chile last June, though highly complex, underlines its relative openness. Mercosur is close to a similar deal with Bolivia, and talks are due with the Andean Group as such this month, to start setting a framework for individual deals with its other members (Colombia, Ecuador, Peru and Venezuela).

Trade, politics and diplomacy

Some of the rise in trade within Mercosur represents a diversion of trade from outside sources: for instance, the sale of cars between Brazil and Argentina; or, more deliberately, Brazil's decision to buy oil from Argentina rather than Iraq. But the rise in intra-group trade has gone hand-in-hand with an accelerating rise in Mercosur's trade with the rest of the world. Economists agree that, overall, Mercosur has been more trade-creating than trade—diverting, the test of whether regionalism is open or closed. It has had other benefits too: without the growth in its exports to Brazil, Argentina would have suffered even worse than it did from the knock-on impact of Mexico's 1994–95 currency collapse.

While Mercosur's exports to much of the rest of the world are dominated by primary products, trade liberalisation has helped to create local markets for

manufactures. These (especially cars and car parts, chemicals and machinery) make up a sizeable part of intra-group trade: almost half of Argentina's $5.6 billion of exports to Brazil last year, and almost 85% of the $4 billion of goods that Brazil sent in return. Much of this is intra-industry trade, as similar firms, or branches of the same firm, swap products or components, taking advantage of the specialisation made possible by a bigger market.

This process is helped along by the hefty foreign investment that Mercosur countries are attracting, some from each other, but more from outside. Outside direct investment within Mercosur has risen sharply. It totaled around $6 billion in both 1994 and 1995, and is likely to go higher this year, as multinationals, especially in the car, chemical and food industries, upgrade existing plants, build new ones or enter a region that they used to ignore.

Mercosur has also brought political gains. Democracy and military detente were a precondition of success in the project, but have also benefited from it. Brazil and Argentina have moved from renouncing their incipient nuclear-weapons programmes to conducting joint military exercises. Brazil's elderly aircraft-carrier (which lacks planes) has exercised with the airmen of Argentina's navy (whose aircraft-carrier has been mothballed for several years). For the first time, small units from the two armies are due shortly to conduct a joint training exercise in peacekeeping.

But for Mercosur, Paraguay would this year almost certainly have gone back to military rule, setting a dangerous precedent for Latin America. When in April a rebellious general moved against President Juan Carlos Wasmosy,

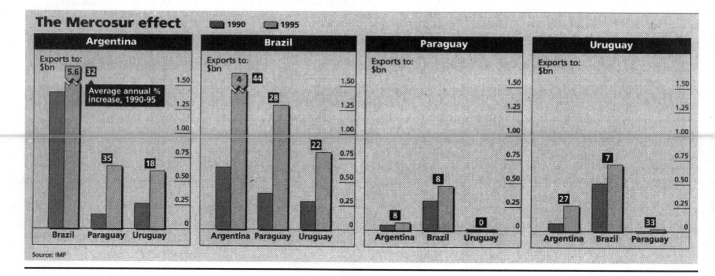

The Mercosur effect ■ 1990 ■ 1995
Source: IMF

Mercosur foreign ministers descended on Asuncion and demonstrated to the upstart that he would face diplomatic and economic isolation. Mercosur's presidents promptly agreed that, as in the EU, democracy should be a formal condition of membership. Revealingly, elements of Chile's right-wing opposition, close to General Pinochet and the armed forces, cited this as a reason to oppose their country's deal with Mercosur.

Another indicator of Mercosur's effectiveness is its diplomatic pulling power in the wider world. Last December, it signed a framework agreement with the EU, its largest single source of external trade and investment. The deal is not all that some enthusiasts in Mercosur hoped for, but it sets a tentative target of free trade by 2005. It now looks increasingly likely that the planned western-hemisphere free-trade area will involve an agreement between NAFTA and Mercosur. And the Japanese, during a visit to the region by their prime minister, Ryutaro Hashimoto, in August, expressed interest in starting a dialogue with Mercosur.

In sum, Mercosur has got off to a surprisingly good start. Yet this survey will argue that if it is to continue to prosper, it faces tougher challenges than those it has surmounted so far. The first is the maintenance of macroeconomic stability, open trading regimes and economic growth in Brazil and in Argentina; for while Mercosur can contribute to all of these, it cannot flourish without them. The second is to make an integrated market a reality by improving transport links and customs procedures, standardising or demolishing a mountain of rules and regulations, and striking the right balance between the nation state and common-market institutions. All of these issues are likely to test its members' commitment to their common project.

A lopsided union

NOBODY (except in France, maybe) can doubt that Germany is the European Union's paramount member. Yet its primacy is relative. Brazil, by contrast, towers over Mercosur, rather as the United States dominates NAFTA. That could be a problem. Post-1945 Germany had strong political reasons to embrace European integration. And though not all its citizens agreed, the United States had strong geopolitical motives, as well as business ones, for drawing Mexico under its wing: it wanted more influence over a large and potentially unstable neighbour. In contrast, Brazil and Argentina have never fought a war, nor does either see the other as a source of instability. That may make integration between them easier, but, at first sight, it also makes the need for it less compelling.

Ask a reasonably well-informed inhabitant of São Paulo what Mercosur means for Brazil, and he is likely to reply "not much". Ask the same question of a north-easterner, and he will answer that Mercosur is simply irrelevant. Its name doesn't help: Brazilians tend to assume that it concerns only the south of their country. Repeat the question in Buenos Aires, and you have more chance of an enthusiastic answer. Paraguay and Uruguay, as is often the fate of small countries, had little choice: once Brazil and Argentina, their main trading partners, got together, they could not afford to be excluded.

One reason for Brazil's relative aloofness from Mercosur is that it is a genuinely global trader. Despite its recent growth, Brazil's trade with its three Mercosur partners made up only 15% of its total trade in the first half of this year. The equivalent figure for Argentina was 28%; indeed, the Brazilian state of São Paulo has now displaced the United States as the largest single outlet for Argentina's exports. The markets for Brazil's exports are more widely spread: last year 27% went to the EU, 21% to NAFTA, around 18% to Asia. So Brazil's paramount commercial interest lies in the maintenance of an open, multilateral world trading system.

Not that Brazil is a gung-ho exporter. Though some of its companies have long been successful that way, its total trade, albeit twice what it was in 1990, still is equivalent to only around one-seventh of GDP; in Chile, the comparable figure is over 45%. This is the natural arithmetic of any big country; but that does not alter the truth that Brazil is still, in consequence, fairly inward-looking. Facing a large and usually growing home market, and obstacles to selling abroad, its firms have tended to grow sideways, becoming conglomerates, rather than to push up their core business through exports. For an Argentine firm, Mercosur more than triples its domestic market; for a Brazilian one, the expansion is not even half. Marcelo Telles, of Brahma, a Brazilian brewer, remarks that the growth in his country's beer market in 1995 (an exceptional year, it's true) was equal to Argentina's entire consumption.

Still, Brazil is Mercosur's giant, and has had a big say in shaping it. It is Brazil that most wants a wider, rather than a deeper, Mercosur, and so has pushed for other countries to be associated with

Brazil is Mercosur's dominant power, yet much of Brazil doesn't much care

it. In contrast, this worries Uruguay, whose small industries make goods much like those of, for example, Chile. Yet in the new can-do spirit now abroad in South America, the response of Uruguay's president, Julio Maria Sanguinetti, to a development that he was unable to stop was to lead a group of businessmen on a sales trip to Chile in August.

A triumph of minimalism

On the other hand, Brazil is naturally reluctant to cede sovereignty to smaller countries. Argentina has often cited the EU as a model; Brazil insists that Mercosur should be a union of nation states, with a minimum of supranational institutions, and decisions taken by consensus. It has a tiny permanent secretariat in Montevideo, Uruguay's capital, but decision-making rests with an inter-governmental Common Market Council, made up of the member countries' foreign and finance ministers—and in practice more often with the national presidents, at their twice-yearly meetings. Beneath the council, the groundwork is done by a group of civil servants from half-a-dozen ministries, and the central banks, in each country. But these individuals are not permanently seconded to the group. There is no Mercosureaucracy, no southern-hemisphere Brussels, no parliament (and, because the group speaks only two, fairly similar, languages, no army of interpreters or Babel of translated documents).

That is less natural than it looks. Jose Botafogo, in charge of international economic relations at Brazil's foreign ministry, points out that this pragmatism is "absolutely new" for countries with 500 years of legalistic, Iberian cultural baggage. One reason why earlier efforts at Latin American integration failed was that they began by erecting complex structures of baroque extravagance, unrelated to the real needs of those who actually do the trade.

But minimalism carries an opposite cost. Even Mercosur's smallest disputes have tended to go up for settlement by national presidents. That risks generating political heat. And big brother Brazil has felt free to act unilaterally when it chose. When last year it suddenly raised tarrifs on some car imports, and when this year it required textile imports to be paid for within 30 days rather than 180, it at first failed to exempt its partners. Barely had Mercosur agreed on its deal with Chile than Brazil, in July, temporarily put up tariffs on toys from 20% to 70%, to the loud dismay of Chilean toymakers. Such things may happen because one Brazilian ministry acts without consulting others; only the foreign ministry and, to some extent, the finance ministry are indoctrinated in the need to take Mercosur into account on a wide range of issues.

Yet Brazil has also shown flexibility. It did not insist on a weighted voting system inside Mercosur. It agreed to compromise on a lower common external tariff than it originally wanted. It has acquiesced as its former trade surplus with its Mercosur partners has become a deficit (thanks largely to the 1995–96 recession, and its aftermath, in Argentina). And it has generally been careful to keep in step with Argentina on Mercosur issues, just as Germany's understanding with France has been the backbone of the European Union.

A passport to the world

Brazil is flexible because it has powerful long-term motives for wanting Mercosur to work. Gabriel Porcile, an economic historian at the Federal University of Parana, in southern Brazil, argues that for the past half-century Brazil and Argentina have shown bursts of interest in integration whenever they have felt excluded from changes in world trade patterns. Five years ago, the prospect of NAFTA, the Maastricht treaty cementing European union, the rise of South-East Asia and of China in world trade, and the difficulties in concluding the Uruguay round of global trade talks all combined to produce such a sense of exclusion.

This was sharpened by Brazil's declining weight in world trade: its share of total world exports fell from 1.9% in 1984 to 0.9% a decade later. Half a century of import-substitution had left many Brazilian companies ill-equipped to compete elsewhere. Brazil's total exports to the EU may be bigger than those going to Mercosur, but much of the European figure is accounted for by raw materials. It is Brazil's neighbours who represent the fastest-growing export market for its manufactures. Brazil's leaders see Mercosur as offering both a test-bed and greater room to manoeuvre, in preparing Brazilian business for worldwide competition, as well as adding to the country's diplomatic weight. "With regional integration, we're going to be able to take part more actively in world trade and world decision-making in the next century," says President Fernando Henrique Cardoso.

Yet Brazil has also found rapid trade opening more painful and harder to digest than have its neighbours, and the government faces intermittent domestic pressure for selective protection. Brazil is now pushing for a common Mercosur regime of safeguards against dumping. Such instruments are allowed by the World Trade Organisation; indeed, Mercosur exports have been victims of their, sometimes arbitrary, application by the United States. But all anti-dumping measures risk becoming a back-door route to renewed protectionism. Brazil's wavering may be temporary, a conse-

quence of the political difficulties Mr Cardoso faces in pushing through certain economic and other reforms—and of the costs that the lack of such reforms places on business. But it shows that support for open trade policies is less than wholehearted.

Like the EU, Mercosur is largely the creation of determined political leaders and far-sighted diplomacy. But it does not provoke much opposition in society at large, except to some extent in Paraguay and Uruguay. That is partly because in Brazil and Argentina the pain of adjusting to Mercosur has been less than that of their own unilateral trade opening. But as Monica Hirst, a Brazilian political scientist based in Buenos Aires, points out, it is also because Mercosur attracts support from the centre-right and centre-left alike, and across generations. For older people and for centre-leftists, it is politically attractive, as the fulfillment of long-held dreams of Latin American integration. A younger generation of technocrats, and people on the centre-right, see its economic charms, based as it is on open trade and free markets. This is a happy combination. But broad though public support is for Mercosur, it remains shallow. Mercosur has a joint parliamentary committee, but political parties in the member countries have few cross-border links. As Mercosur starts to produce losers as well as winners, opinion may become more polarised.

Slowly, Mercosur is starting to promote growing interdependence. In southern Brazil, universities, chambers of commerce and agricultural co-operatives are all forging close links with their counterparts in north-eastern Argentina. Even in Brazil's north-east, Chilean fruit farmers have been invited to bring their know-how in quality control and marketing, and textile factories are sending T-shirts to Argentina. Petrochemicals plants in the northeastern state of Bahia are busily swapping products with distant partners. Not surprisingly, in the new market-based model of integration, it is business that is starting to turn Mercosur into a reality. . . .

(continued)

Getting the government books in order

MERCOSUR'S better-than-expected start owed much to economic reform in both Argentina and Brazil. The end of hyperinflation, first in Argentina in 1991, and then in Brazil in 1994, triggered consumer booms, while privatisation has attracted foreign investment. Argentina's economy grew at an annual average rate of over 7% between 1991 and 1994. In 1993, after three years of recession, Brazil began to revive, as the government speeded up the liberalisation of imports. The recovery accelerated from mid–1994, with the launch of an anti-inflation plan, and a new currency, the *real*, devised by Mr Cardoso, finance minister until he resigned in April of that year to move forward to a presidential candidacy. In both 1994 and 1995, economic growth exceeded 4%, reaching a quarterly peak in the first quarter of 1995, at 10.4% over the same quarter a year earlier. In both countries, the lowering of tariffs was an important instrument in achieving price stability, by forcing local producers to compete with cheaper imports. And so Mercosur began to work, as first Brazilian firms and then Argentine ones found booming markets next door.

Then came the "tequila effect". The bungled devaluation of Mexico's currency in December 1994, and its subsequent collapse, caused global moneymen to retreat in panic from much of Latin America. Argentina was hit hardest. Under the "convertibility" plan launched by its economy minister, Domingo Cavallo, in 1991, its peso is fixed by law at par with the dollar, and the supply of coin and notes is tightly linked to the level of foreign reserves. So, as reserves shrank, the money supply shrank too. Mr Cavallo stuck to his guns, refusing to abandon convertibility,

but the cost was high: the economy slid by 4.4% last year, and is recovering only slowly. Brazil did not escape, though there a sharp rise in interest rates was intended mainly to cool its overheated economy. In both countries, the monetary squeeze exacerbated frailties in the banking system, concealed in the past by high inflation.

Both economies have been in low gear this year: Brazil may achieve modest growth of 2.5–3%, Argentina probably even less. This is not enough: 16–17% unemployment in Argentina and widespread poverty in Brazil call for sustained growth nearer 5–6% a year. Reform and trade opening will help. But in both countries the economy is held back by a structural, and politically rooted, constraint: the need to balance the public sector's accounts, and to create a more efficient state. Until state reform is accomplished, investors will continue to have doubts about the permanence of macroeconomic stability—and about the ability of either country to withstand further external shocks; for instance, a sharp rise in global interest rates.

Take Argentina first. At around 2.5% of GDP, its fiscal deficit is smaller than Brazil's, and that of many West European countries. But its "convertibility" restraints deny it an exchange-rate policy, and most of a monetary one too. Fiscal policy is the only economic tool left. And a deficit, albeit small, has a disproportionate effect in increasing the cost of credit for the private sector. Mr Cavallo first tried to deal with this by lowering taxes, hoping in time to raise revenues through economic growth. In July he changed tack and announced cuts in welfare spending. The angry reaction, especially from the unions linked to President Menem's Peronist party, per-

Both Brazil and Argentina have fought off inflation, but have yet to achieve fiscal balance

suaded the president to sack his star minister.

Roque Fernandez, the new economy minister, had an uneasy start. In a package hurriedly announced days after a general strike, he proposed a bundle of tax rises, meant to pull in at least $4 billion next year (this year's deficit is heading for $6.6 billion). He also proposed to tackle two longer-term problems: to set a ceiling on the share of tax revenues that goes to provincial governments, and to lessen the deficit in the state pension system, by raising the retirement age for women to 65. Yet critics complained that this did nothing to cut central-government spending, nor did it leave a margin to boost exports by further reductions in payroll taxes and so in wage costs. The package was later greatly diluted by Peronist legislators, though Mr Menem went on to float other plans, for privatising trade-union health schemes and loosening labour laws.

This fiscal fight has turned into the toughest political battle Mr Menem has faced in seven years as president. If he wins it (so appeasing the IMF and thus the financial markets), Argentina's prospects should brighten, at least in the medium term. By 1998, a new system of private pensions should have accumulated $15 billion in funds available for

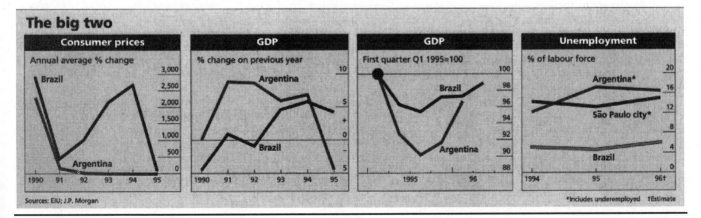

The big two

| Consumer prices | GDP | GDP | Unemployment |

Sources: EIU; J.P. Morgan

*Includes underemployed †Estimate

long-term investment. Thanks largely to exports, notably to Brazil, manufacturing output has been growing healthily in recent months. With a record harvest also on its way, Alieto Guadagni, the industry minister, reckons that Argentina is on the verge of a new agro-industrial golden age. But if Mr Menem loses—and he is hampered by widespread public anger at government corruption—Argentina's economic and political stability may be among the casualties.

Brazil's government has more policy options, but in a more complex political environment. His new *real* apart, Mr Cardoso's 1994 plan tamed inflation by relying first on keeping the *real* high, to cheapen imports, and then on high interest rates and tight money to restrain consumption. That, says Gustavo Franco, a central bank director, was the only way to speedy price stability, given that reaching fiscal balance takes longer. Now the *real* is being lowered gently against the dollar (though not at a pace that matches inflation), and monetary policy has been cautiously relaxed, though the resulting rise in consumer debt means that any sharp rise in interest rates, to meet some shock, could bring some banks nasty problems. Still, these are instruments that Argentina lacks; and, together with foreign-exchange reserves of some $60 billion, they give Brazil more time to carry out its fiscal adjustment. But adjust it must, if it is both to keep inflation down and achieve sustainedly higher growth.

When critics point this out, the economic team responds, with justifiable irritation, that they are preaching to the converted. The problem the team faces is that much fiscal spending is mandated by the constitution, which can be changed only by a 60% vote in each house of Congress. In principle, President Cardoso has the votes; in practice, he often does not.

Critics argue that he was elected on a mandate to stabilise the economy, and then tarried too long in exercising it. Last year he pushed through constitutional amendments ending state monopolies and allowing foreign investment in telecommunications, oil and mining. But Congress is yet to approve constitutional changes allowing reforms of taxation, the civil service and pensions, which are essential for long-term fiscal health. The government has now persuaded Congress to scrap a rule that facilitated small minorities' wrecking amendments to constitutional bills. It is preparing for a fresh attempt at reform after this month's municipal elections.

Meanwhile, the government is trimming spending and making such piecemeal changes as it can; for instance, a recent law to exempt exports, capital goods and energy from local sales taxes. Overall, says Pedro Malan, the finance minister, it reckons its measures will cut this year's fiscal deficit to 5% of GDP (from 7.4% last year), and push 1997 growth to 4.5%. As in Argentina, growth will be partly due to foreign direct investment, attracted notably by privatisations in electricity and telecoms; Mr Malan expects at least $7 billion of that this year and as much next.

Outsiders underestimate at their peril the Brazilian capacity for creative improvisation. Yet they are right to point to a worrying rise in the government's internal debt, and the lack of control on spending by state governments. And the political climate for continued reform may yet deteriorate. Thanks to a sophisticated system of indexation, Brazilians were less traumatised by inflation than were Argentines. Brazil's elite is correspondingly less convinced than Argentina's of the need for fiscal rectitude. And the constitutional reform that Mr Cardoso currently appears most excited by is one that would allow him to stand for reelection in 1998—for whose approval Congress might well seek to exact a fiscal price.

Nevertheless both Mr Cardoso and Mr Menem (twice) owe their posts to economic stability. Neither man will jettison it lightly. That augurs well for Mercosur, since nothing would damage it more than a round of competitive devaluations. But increasingly Mercosur, and the trade opening that lies behind it, will demand agile governments that are able to ease the process of adjustment, and to afford (or get private finance to help them afford) the investments in infrastructure required to extract full advantage from an expanded market.

The race to bridge borders

TALK to a public official in southern Brazil, Argentina or Chile about Mercosur, and sooner rather than later he will probably refer you to a map. Indeed, Jaime Lerner, an architect who is governor of the Brazilian state of Parana, himself drew a detailed one in his Curitiba office for your reporter. Mercosur has awoken century-old dreams of linking the southern cone from the Atlantic to the Pacific in many ways and at many points. Not surprisingly, each Brazilian state, each Argentine province and each Chilean region, not to speak of Paraguay and Bolivia, wants its own cross-border route. But the distances and costs involved are immense, and nature has placed formidable obstacles in the way; not least, the Andes. It will take quite a while before

there is a prospect of sufficient traffic to justify some of the costlier schemes.

Yet improvements in Mercosur's transport and its energy links are vital. History, and military mistrust, caused Latin American countries to turn their backs on each other. Rather than joining up, each one's transport system grew on its own, linking the national production and consumption centres to national ports. Railways were built with different gauges, so that no Brazilian train has ever entered Argentine territory, nor vice versa; cargoes such as Brahma's beer, which goes by rail, have to be unloaded and reloaded, at a cost in time and money.

Progress is fastest in energy integration. The earlier building of giant bi-

If trade is to continue to grow, infrastructure must keep pace

national dams on the rivers Parana and Uruguay means that only a small investment is needed to link Mercosur's electricity systems (though their different frequencies do not help). Privatisations in Argentina and Peru have enabled Chile's ambitious electricity firms to win large slices of power generation in those

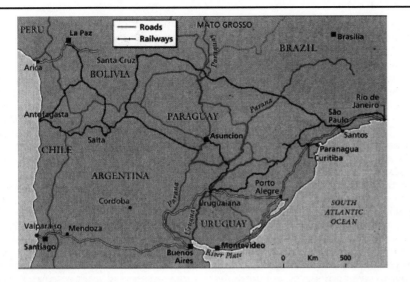

countries; they are likely buyers when Brazil follows suit. Bruno Philippi, chairman of Chilgener, one such firm, reckons that in ten years' time there could be an interconnected grid for the seven southern-cone countries (the Mercosur four, plus Chile, Bolivia and Peru), with a single multinational regulator ensuring efficient use of capacity—something that Western Europe is only now getting towards. A network of transcontinental gas pipelines is well underway: Chilgener is a partner in a consortium that is building one from Argentina's natural-gas fields to Santiago. Another consortium is starting work on a pipeline to bring Bolivian gas to São Paulo.

Ports, roads and railways

Transport links are less advanced. Many airports are saturated, and many ports, at least in Brazil, require radical reform and expansion; Brazilian businessmen condemn São Paulo's port of Santos as the least efficient and most expensive big port in the hemisphere. Road and railway networks are groaning under the sharp increase in trade. Three-quarters of all terrestrial trade between Brazil on the one hand, and Argentina and Chile on the other, travels across a single bridge over the river Uruguay. On an average day, between 300 and 700 trucks cross the bridge, but only after a delay, often, of at least 24 hours at the customs post there; and once through, they face long journeys on often poorly maintained single-carriageway roads before they approach the main cities. There are

two other bridges on the 1,000-kilometre (620-mile) Brazil-Argentina border. One carries little traffic; the other, completed a year ago, is still not in use because of a dispute involving customs workers.

Things are not much better on the main route between Chile and Argentina. The number of lorries travelling between the two countries has more than trebled in the past ten years, but 90% of them (or 300 a day) use a road between Santiago and Mendoza that climbs above 3,100 metres (10,000 feet) and in winter is often blocked by snow. Trains stopped running in 1984 on the trans-Andean railway between these two cities.

There have been some improvements, though, both in border procedures and in roads: in the 1980s, according to an ECLAC study, a lorry took up to two weeks to go from Santiago to São Paulo; now it can get there and back in less than 11 days. This owes much to the development of larger transport firms, using more efficient operating methods. The car makers have been the pioneers in cutting through red tape: Volkswagen has a road shuttle of 150 trucks a day moving components between its plants in São Paulo and Buenos Aires, a journey that used to take a week and now takes three days.

Enrique Iglesias, president of the Inter-American Development Bank (IDB), reckons that, if their economies grow at an annual average of 5%, the seven southern-cone countries need to invest $20 billion a year in infrastructure to keep pace. Some big projects are under way. The IDB and the World Bank are fi-

nancing the upgrading of the main road south from São Paulo, doubling its width, as part of a medium-term plan to build a superhighway linking Rio de-Janeiro and Buenos Aires (perhaps, eventually, via an expensive bridge across the estuary of the river Plate). Landlocked Bolivia has at last completed a decent paved road to link La Paz to its nearest port, Arica, in far-northern Chile. An addendum to Chile's agreement with Mercosur commits Chile and Argentina to invest $150m each in improving cross-border links.

Private capital can help. A new road bridge over the river Uruguay is being built, and will be operated, by private investors. Brazil and Chile are privatising their railway systems, as Argentina and Bolivia have already done. In Parana, Mr Lerner plans to privatise a railway that runs inland from the Atlantic port of Paranagua, on condition that the new operators invest $150m to extend it towards Paraguay and Argentina. He reckons that this railway could eventually link up with others in either of those countries to provide a multi-modal link with Chile's Pacific ports.

But most of the money for transport improvements will have to come from governments. "All processes of physical integration have to be done with public money, because it's a bet on the future," says Ricardo Lagos, Chile's minister for public works. He, like Mr Lerner, is a practical and respected man with a map. Both have their eyes on Brazil's 25m-tonne soya crop, much of which is exported to Asia. Much of the soya is grown in Parana. Some 10m tonnes come from Mato Grosso. That state is about as near to Arica as to Santos—and, as Mr. Lagos notes, Japan is 14,500km from Arica, but 19,000 from Santos. He favours a $700m road to link Mato Grosso via Santa Cruz, in Bolivia, to Arica. But others too are eyeing that soya crop: Paraguay's President Wasmosy dreams of navigational improvements to turn the Paraguay-Parana river system into "a Mississippi that doesn't freeze"; environmental and feasibility studies for that project are under way. Though choice is a fine thing, public money is scarce. The governments need to get together with users and work out which among the competing routes deserve priority.

(continued)

The road to a single market

WHEN the Brazilian firm of Sadia exports its chickens and frankfurters to Argentina, they leave home with a sanitary certificate from Brazil's health ministry. When they reach the border, they face two further inspections, by Argentina's health and agriculture ministries. While today the border police often operate round-the-clock, officials from other state bodies may be present only for eight or ten hours a day. That, laments Luiz Fernando Furlan, Sadia's chairman, means that the extra checks can take up to two days, days that come off the products' shelf-life. Sadia must also pay Argentina's value-added tax at the border, rather than when the products are sold to consumers. Were it selling them to an import wholesaler, they would have to be paid for neither in Argentine nor Brazilian currency but in dollars. And any foreign-exchange transaction in a Brazilian bank requires much form-filling in quadruplicate.

Mr Furlan quickly adds that Argentina's red tape is not uniquely dense. Indeed, Brazil's is worse. There, importers can wait up to six months just to register for sanitary certificates. The IDB has found that in the Mercosur countries a journey of 100km (62 miles) that crosses any frontier costs 40% more than one that does not. If Mercosur's opportunities are really to be grasped, it needs not just tariff-cutting but harmonisation of rules on many things from intellectual property to antitrust and the environment; and clearer mechanisms, such as NAFTA has, for the settlement of disputes.

Through joint working parties, the four members are moving to tackle these non-tariff questions. The most urgent task is to simplify border procedures. With luck, Mercosur should introduce a single customs document, valid for exports to all members, by next year. Mutual recognition of sanitary certificates, and a common register of products and common technical standards, should come by 1998 (it is hoped; as the EU has shown, dilly-dallying about standards is a great way for closet protectionists to delay competition). The sooner change comes, the better. Big firms have found ways to cut through the red tape, but for small ones it is much harder. "Big companies can be multi-modal. The small guy who has a truck can't get across the river," says Marcos Azambuja, Brazil's ambassador in Buenos Aires. Harder to change is the mentality of customs officials. In Brazil, they are part of the tax department, reflecting their traditional function of levying tariffs rather than assisting trade.

Equally urgent is improvement in the mechanisms for settling trade disputes. In 1991 Mercosur drew up a procedure, involving an ad hoc arbitration tribunal, but it has never been tested. In practice, disputes have been settled politically, by the Mercosur presidents themselves. Until now, this system has worked: to safeguard the whole project, the presidents have been prepared to compromise and, when need be, rewrite the rules. But this carries a cost, in reducing certainty. Until a tested and politically-neutral dispute-settlement mechanism is in place, investors thinking of setting up in, say, Uruguay, cannot be certain of guaranteed and barrier-free access to the Brazilian market.

If it is to deserve its name as a common market, Mercosur will also have to move to open up trade in services, especially financial services, and to tackle such difficult issues as harmonisation of tax and of macroeconomic policies. Its members are unlikely to feel ready to do any of this soon. The central banks have held preliminary talks about harmonising bank regulatory systems, and finance officials have similarly discussed their tax regimes. But the differences are wide. Uruguay, for example, has a large off-shore financial business and a liberal corporate-tax regime. Brazil (and Chile) has exchange controls, while the others do not.

Banco Itau, a large Brazilian private-sector bank, has moved vigorously into retail banking in Argentina, with ten branches so far and plans for 35 by 1998. But it is an exception. Brazil's central bank has indicated it would allow banks from other Mercosur countries to come in. But Brazil is unlikely to agree to a full-scale financial opening, or to freeing trade in services, until its programme of

Mercosur needs less red tape, but more common rules

stabilisation and economic reform is consolidated. On this, says Jorge Campbell, Argentina's chief Mercosur negotiator, diplomatically, "There is a difference of emphasis, rather than a clash." Nevertheless, at Brazil's prompting, Mercosur rejected a Chilean request to include trade in services in its association agreement. Here too the EU offers a warning: for all its supposed good intentions and zeal for integration, directives opening up cross-border sales of financial services had to wait till the 1990s, and in the real world there are problems still.

Harmonisation of macroeconomic policies within Mercosur so far extends no further than the exchange of information. That is useful. When he sacked Mr Cavallo, Mr Menem sent an envoy by private jet to brief Mr Cardoso before the news was made public. And at least policies are headed in broadly the same direction. But Argentina's fixed exchange rate could yet prove a problem: neither the peso nor the *real* is yet solid enough to play a role like that of the D mark or the dollar.

As for policy co-ordination, Mercosur, like the EU, will probably find that the hardest part of living together. The only thing that rivals it is allowing free movement of labour. Although the four Mercosur countries now issue a special businessman's visa, Uruguay and Argentina will resist giving the mostly poor and unskilled citizens of Brazil's north-east the right to work, let alone settle, in their richer countries. Yet Mercosur's members cannot afford to let it turn into an instrument that makes already unequal societies more unequal. That makes its new, non-tariff agenda an urgent necessity. But this deepening process will be all the more complex because Mercosur is already growing wider.

(continued)

And now, the hemisphere

IF MERCOSUR is seen as a significant actor within Latin America and beyond, that is only partly thanks to its own achievements. It also has much to do with congressional obstruction on trade matters in Washington, and the failure of the Clinton administration, relatively uninterested in Latin America—beyond Mexico and Cuba—to overcome it.

The 1990 "Initiative of the Americas", in which President George Bush proposed a free-trade area from Alaska to Tierra del Fuego was welcomed by a new generation of Latin American leaders, bent on trade liberalisation and export-led growth. In the past, says Miguel Rodriguez, who heads the trade unit of the Organisation of American States, Latin Americans would come to Washington pleading for non-reciprocal deals; now many are prepared to grant the United States complete access to their own markets in return for a similar opening of the American one. And these days they feel let down.

Mr Clinton fought hard to get congressional approval for NAFTA. But he has been unable to deliver on its promised extension to Chile (or to Central America and the Caribbean). And his modest interest in Latin America has taken him—unlike his three immediate predecessors—no further than Miami. Still, there, in December 1994, he invited the leaders of 34 western-hemisphere countries, all except Cuba. They assembled, and agreed to negotiate, by 2005, a Free Trade Area of the Americas (FTAA) to be implemented over a further ten years.

Eight days later, Mexico devalued its peso. Mr Clinton arranged a bail-out. His voters did not like that, nor the way Mexico's trade deficit with their country soon became a surplus. Hopes of winning "fast-track" authority from Congress for talks with Chile were scuppered. That procedure allows Congress to accept or reject a deal as a whole, but not to amend it; and without fast-track—as the Chileans well knew—trade negotiations with the United States are a waste of time. Rebuffed, Chile reversed its earlier decision to stand aloof from Mercosur.

Some believe that even Argentina, had it been promised a trade deal by the United States, might at one time have abandoned Mercosur. Its doubts were high in early 1994, with Brazil's inflation above 40% a month, and Luis Inacio Lula da Silva, a left-winger, poised to win its coming presidential election. But no offer came from Washington, Mr Cardoso launched his anti-inflation plan and won the presidency. And Mercosur bloomed.

A wider Mercosur, and then?

So Mr Clinton has helped Mercosur to consolidate, and to exercise a growing attraction in South America. But its widening was also partly inevitable. The adoption of a common external tariff meant that members' bilateral preferences granted earlier to other Latin American countries had to be renegotiated. Carlos Mladinic, trade chief at Chile's foreign ministry until he was recently appointed agriculture minister, points out that half Chile's trade with Mercosur markets enjoyed such preferences, which would have expired but for last June's deal.

Though Brazil's diplomats talk less loudly than they used to of building a South American free-trade area, that appears still to be the goal. After Chile, Bolivia seems set to become the next Mercosur associate; then, if the framework talks go well, other Andean Group members. Mr Cardoso says he would like to invite all five Andean presidents to Mercosur's next presidential meeting in December.

This quest for a wider grouping is not just concerned with South American trade, however. It has a political motive that stretches wider, towards the United States. How exactly is a hemispheric free trade area to be built? At Miami, the participants agreed to set up technical working groups, 11 in all, to prepare the ground. These have vigorously collated and analysed the current rules and procedures in the hemisphere's patchwork of trade agreements. But negotiation is not their job, and there is no consensus on how to make further progress.

The United States at first seemed to favour moving ahead by the selective extension of NAFTA; some countries would prefer a multilateral negotiation to create a kind of 34-country mini-WTO; others see existing groupings such as Mercosur and the Andean Group as building blocks to be fitted together with NAFTA. All is possible, but the best bet today is that the main negotiation will be between NAFTA, led by the United States, and a widened Mercosur, led by Brazil. The Brazilians, whose market is the main attraction for the United States, naturally want as many allies as possible.

When? Mr Clinton's trade officials say they want the next meeting of the hemisphere's trade ministers, due to be held in the Brazilian city of Belo Horizonte next May, to fix a date for proper FTAA negotiations to start. Brazil has appeared reluctant, but Mr Cardoso now says he too favours fixing a date. More difficult is what to negotiate.

The United States wants any deal to go beyond existing commitments under the WTO, NAFTA and other regional groups. It wants things like product standards, investment protection and customs procedures treated as "early action" items; in the main talks, it would stress such issues as intellectual property and market-opening for services. Brazil, still digesting the political and economic consequences of its trade opening, is uneasy about accepting more stringent rules than those of the WTO, especially in services. It sees the FTAA as a tool to remove barriers against its exports to the United States. For though most Latin American exports face low or no tariffs there, for some the barriers are higher. A fierce tariff protects Florida's growers from Brazilian juice; Brazil's privatised steel firms face anti-dumping duties, a legacy of their state-owned past. Many of Argentina's farm exports are subject to quotas.

In the end, two things are likely to determine the pace and form of the FTAA talks. First, will the new administration in Washington secure fast-track authority from Congress next year? Though fast-track could be of broad scope, it is

Selling to Uncle Sam
Exports to United States as % of total
1995

	0	10	20	30	40	50
Venezuela						
Colombia						
Bolivia, Ecuador & Peru						
Mercosur						
Chile						

Source: IMF   *'total' excludes intra-group

likely—if it is granted at all—to be used in the first instance for talks to extend NAFTA to Chile. Peter Allgeier, at the office of the United States trade representative, says that while fast-track is not necessary to start the FTAA talks, its existence would influence those talks.

Indeed it would. It might do more. By signalling seriousness in Washington about opening trade, and a real prospect of progress, fast-track authority could dampen enthusiasm for association with Mercosur among the Andean countries. The United States' market matters far more to them than does the Brazilian one; a fact that may also make them less-than-solid allies for Mercosur when the real bargaining starts.

Sceptics, however, doubt that early, or perhaps any, fast-track authority will be forthcoming. Protectionism is alive and well on Capitol Hill, and likely to be still more so if the Democrats regain control of the lower house there. "The gap between the freetrade rhetoric of the leaders of both American parties, and their tendency to abandon it when faced with any problem, mean that the credibility of the United States in this matter is relatively low," says Alejandro Foxley, president of Chile's ruling Christian Democrats and a former finance minister. Some Chileans would put it more forcibly.

Two-way attraction

The second factor which may change the equation is the future performance of the Mercosur economies. Peter Hakim, of Inter-American Dialogue, a Washington think-tank, argues that if Brazil were to grow at over 5% for three or four years, the United States' interest in a deal with Mercosur would soar. On the other side, Mercosur would be strengthened and Brazil itself would feel far more self-confident about sitting down to haggle with the United States. Since, along with Mercosur, the United States is the Brazilians' main market for manufactured exports, they have much to gain there from an FTAA. In turn, progress towards an FTAA could push the EU into freer trade—notably, into relaxing its barriers to Mercosur's agricultural exports—for fear that the United States would otherwise gain privileged access to the South American market. And Brazil's skilled diplomats need no telling how advantageous it is to be negotiating simultaneously with rivals who can be played off against each other.

But the Mercosur countries and their associates also have business at home to think of: the further development of their own grouping.

Article 14

The Economist, August 9th, 1997

Bolivia

An example in the Andes

LA PAZ

Bolivia has been Latin America's unlikely pacesetter in innovative structural reform. Will its new president, a former dictator, go forward—or back?

LANDLOCKED, isolated by its Andean heights, savannas and tropical jungles, small (7.5m) in population, Bolivia rarely attracts much outside attention. Yet it has often led its neighbours in political creativity. Its 1952 revolution both anticipated a regional wave of nationalist statism with a state takeover of the tin mines—at the time its main source of wealth—and produced a successful agrarian reform that granted land to Amerindian farmers, so helping

to spare Bolivia the kind of rural violence suffered by Peru and Colombia. Then, in 1985, Bolivia turned its back on many of these policies. After Chile, but before most of Latin America, it tamed inflation by embracing free markets and open trade.

For the past four years under President Gonzalo Sanchez de Lozada, a Californian-educated mine-owner who as a minister pushed through the 1985 stabilisation plan, Bolivia has made a bold and innovative effort to deepen its commitment both to the market and to democratic governance. Its experiment is of more than local interest.

Why? First, its reforms—notably, large-scale privatisation, educational reform and decentralisation of government—are ones that many observers, not least the World Bank, see as vital if Latin America is to complement its new economic stability with faster growth and greater equity. Second, Bolivia is very poor and socially backward. Most of its people are Amerindians, long denied even a share in either prosperity or power. Sceptics say free-market reforms are likelier to hurt than help such people. Will Bolivia prove them wrong? Third, after four years of Mr Sanchez de Lozada, Bolivians appear to have tired of change. The new president, sworn in (for five years, thanks to a constitutional change) on August 6th, is General Hugo Banzer Suarez, who ruled the country as a dictator in the 1970s. Conservative in economics as in politics, he could put reform into reverse. Will he?

Probably not. General Banzer came first in the presidential election at the start of June, but with only 22.3% of the vote. That threw the decision into Congress. There, this week, he won comfortably but only by putting together a disparate coalition whose constituent parties share little but their dislike of Mr Sanchez de Lozada. The latter's candidate came second in June, and, in all,

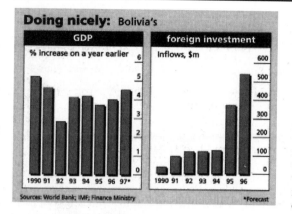

Doing nicely: Bolivia's

GDP — % increase on a year earlier

foreign investment — Inflows, $m

1990 91 92 93 94 95 96 97*

Sources: World Bank; IMF; Finance Ministry   *Forecast

three-quarters of those who voted then chose parties that favour market economics; and of those who did not most backed Condepa, a party speaking for Amerindians that has joined the general's coalition.

The coalition resembles that of 1989–93, under President Jaime Paz Zamora, when General Banzer's Democratic Nationalist Action (ADN) party ran economic policy. That regime did not reverse its predecessor's changes, nor, said President Banzer at his inauguration on August 6th, will he: more concern for social justice, but no turning back the free-market clock. Even if he wished to do that, he faces external constraints. Like a few other poor countries, Bolivia can hope to see some of its foreign debt written off if—but only if—it goes on taking the World Bank's medicine.

A new way to privatise

For most of its history, Bolivia has been a byword for instability and military coups. In the decade after civilian rule was restored in 1982, it managed to establish democracy and defeat hyperinflation. But stability did not bring prosperity.

In Mr Paz Zamora's four years, annual growth averaged 3.9%—but the population rises at over 2% a year. Average income is only $800, some 20% of adults are illiterate and life expectancy is only 60 years; in Peru, no paradise, average income is $2,300, illiteracy 10% and life expectancy 69. Poverty is worst in the countryside, still home to two out of five Bolivians; there, two-thirds of women are illiterate, and one child in three is chronically malnourished.

Growth has been held back by low saving and low investment (even now, foreign aid pays for half of public investment). The cornerstone of Mr Sanchez de Lozada's economic reforms was an attempt to jump-start private investment

through an unorthodox method of privatisation which he christened "capitalisation". This covered Bolivia's five main state companies, in telecoms, electricity, transport, and oil and gas. The state ceded a 50% shareholding and management control to foreign investors, in return for explicit investment pledges; these totalled $1.7 billion, to be spent within seven years. Since the foreigners were supposed to deposit money for their entire programme at the start, they had an incentive to put it to work fast.

Foreign investment is indeed climbing quickly, and privatisation is expected to act as a magnet for more. Oil and gas offer one big prospect. Work has begun on a $1.9 billion pipeline from eastern Bolivia to Sao Paulo in Brazil, 3,150 kilometres (1,950 miles) away. A market thus assured, it is hoped that private-sector firms will drill around 50 deep wells a year, five times as many as the state-owned oil company managed. The Brazil pipeline alone should add almost one extra point to Bolivia's growth rate. Another boom area could be agro-industry, notably soya products. These have displaced minerals as Bolivia's main export, but, centred around Santa Cruz, to develop further they need better transport links.

The sums are not huge. But they are big in relation to Bolivia's economy.

Given fiscal prudence from his successors, Mr Sanchez de Lozada reckons Bolivia could achieve Asian growth rates. Juan Antonio Morales, governor of the (newly independent) central bank, is more cautious, suggesting that a stable 5.5% is feasible.

Sharing the benefits

But the capitalisation idea went wider, and had wider aims than improving investment and infrastructure. One was to soften hostility to privatisation by giving Bolivians at large a stake in its returns. Large minority holdings in the "capitalised" firms have been put into a trust fund on behalf of the Bolivian people (more precisely, those over 21 at the end of 1995). Secondly, it is hoped that the gradual sale of these holdings will, in time, stimulate the local capital market.

Several Latin American governments are studying Bolivia's capitalisation programme. Yet has it worked? Privatisation remains unpopular there. One reason is that the government, to attract investors, reckoned it had to offer them monopolies, lasting up to seven years. Electricity tariffs have risen; the new owners of the airline and railway companies have been slow to improve services. Besides, some critics argue, conventional privatisation might have been just as effective in attracting foreign investment, and on less onerous terms.

That smacks of hindsight. Earlier governments had not privatised anything

Sector/firm	Foreign investor	$m*
Electricity		
Guarachi	Energy Initiatives (USA)	47.1
Corani	Dominion energy (USA)	58.8
Valle Hermoso	Constellation Power (USA)	33.9
Telecoms		
Entel	STET (Italy)	610.0
Railways		
ENFE	Cruz Blanca (Chile)	39.1
Aviation		
Lloyd Aero Boliviano	Vasp (Brazil)	47.5
Oil and gas		
Andina	YPF/Perez Companc/Pluspetrol (Argentina and Spain)	264.8
Chaco	Amoco (USA)	306.7
Transportadora Boliviana de Hidrocarburos	Enron (USA) and Shell (Britain/Netherlands)	263.5
Total		**1,671.4**

Who bought what?
Bolivia's privatised firms

Source: Finance Ministry   *Amount of pledge investment in return for 50% shareholding

much. Mr Sanchez de Lozada, with his capitalisation, did—and, suggests Arturo Valenzuela, a political scientist at Georgetown University in Washington, who advised him, he might not have managed it otherwise. Congress might have balked at selling out to foreigners without provisions to give Bolivians some palpable benefit.

What form that benefit should take is controversial. The citizens' trust fund is being managed by two Spanish-led private-sector consortia brought in to set up a new private pension scheme. Mr Sanchez de Lozada decided to use this fund to pay all Bolivians over 65 an annuity, called a "solidarity bond", or bonosol. In May (just before the election, critics noted) each received a payment of $248—for many, says the ex-president, the biggest capital sum they will ever see, the equivalent of a pair of oxen or a milch cow. The bonosol, he says, "gives back to the people what belongs to the people."

Paternalism, retort his critics. They argue that anyone who reaches 65 in Bolivia is privileged by definition—miners rarely live beyond 45, for example, while life expectancy in poor rural areas is 55 (though much more for those who survive their first five years). Critics say the money would be better put into the new private pension system, or into forms of social investment—education, health, road schemes—aimed specifically to benefit the poorest.

Whether or not the bonosol is poor economics, it may turn out to have been good politics. "I'm not saying we'd scrap it," says Jorge Quiroga, the new

vice president, though he notes a risk that the trust fund will be quickly exhausted. Indeed. Capitalisation assumes that it will benefit from a future rise in the market value of privatised firms. But to pay the bonosol the fund may have to sell shares before the hoped-for gains materialise. The investment pledged by STET, Italy's telecoms giant, to win control of its Bolivian equivalent, Entel, values Entel shares at $90; the shares granted to Entel workers now sell in an over-the-counter market at a mere $40.

The bonosol was one part of a broader attempt by Mr Sanchez de Lozada to redistribute income and opportunity. In another change, this one widely popular, he decentralised government responsibilities and revenues, creating 311 municipalities, some based on Indian communities. Municipalities' share of government revenues has increased almost fourfold, and mayors have been put in charge of health posts and schools. New indirectly-elected councils are to supervise spending by regional authorities. An education reform pushed through by Victor Hugo Cardenas, the outgoing vice-president, an Amerindian, aims to improve teaching and has introduced the principle of bi-lingual primary schooling.

Worries ahead

Will it all work? With luck, Mr Sanchez de Lozada's reforms will boost economic growth, and may even improve the distribution of its fruits. Yet he has left wor-

ries for his successor—and watchers outside.

One concerns the regulation of the privatised firms. All the new investment came at a price, in the form of complexity and potential conflicts of interest. For the new pension-fund managers, for example, Bolivia's main attraction is the commissions they get for administering the capitalisation fund. Someone must check that the foreign owners of the former state firms do not dress up their investment to meet their promises. The outgoing government has set up independent regulators, who are supposed to balance the interests of consumers and investors. In a country where democratic institutions remain relatively weak, politicised regulation would be the quickest way to give privatisation an even worse name. Whatever else he may decide to change, General Banzer would be well advised not to meddle in these arrangements.

Another worry goes wider: corruption. A recent 52-country survey by a German lobby group put Bolivia second only to Nigeria on that score. Though privatisation has reduced the potential for fiddling in the awarding or fulfilment of government contracts, the outgoing government did little to reform the customs, police or judiciary. At American urging, those who will run the new one have promised to crack down on one source of corruption, the cocaine trade. Yet neither General Banzer's ADN, nor its main partner, Mr Paz Zamora's party, has a spotless reputation on corruption or cocaine.

Article 15   *The Bulletin of the Atomic Scientists, November/December 1996*

Brazil: The meek want the Earth now

Millions of poor Brazilians, led by the Landless Workers Movement, want to settle on idle land. Could it lead to civil war?

By FÁBIO L. S. PETRAROLHA

When hundreds of Brazilian demonstrators protesting the glacial pace of government-sponsored land reform blocked traffic on a highway near their camp (called Eldorado dos Carajás) last April 17, the Brazilian government agreed to send 50 buses to take them to Marabá. There, they were told, they would be able to negotiate with the ministry for agrarian reform.

Instead, it was the military police, not buses, that arrived. The police shot tear gas into the crowd, and then opened fire with machine guns. The demonstrators fled in all directions, seeking shelter in the underbrush or in nearby huts. The police followed in pursuit, still shooting. In a matter of minutes, 19 demonstrators had been killed and another 45 wounded. Another 50 are still listed as missing—witnesses say the police hid a pile of corpses of women and children in a truck.

As luck would have it, a television reporter and cameraman were among those caught in the traffic jam created by the demonstration. Their recording of this massacre was the first time that the Brazilian public had seen for themselves the violence that has frequently been visited on the "Landless Workers Movement" (*Movimento do Trabalhadores SemTerra*) It was, according to a report by the state of Pará's state's attorney's office, a premeditated police crime.

Months after the tragedy, questions remain. The police had removed their badges before arriving at the site of the slaughter; none of the shooters have been identified. There is also speculation about the source of their weapons: Only 85 guns had been issued, but all 155 members of the force were said to be armed. Meanwhile, a peculiar justice has been done: Four demonstrators who shot back (although none of the police were hit) have been under investigation.

Facing the thugs

The Landless Workers Movement is a 12-year-old grassroots group that organizes controversial land occupations to help dispossessed farm workers and those longing to escape from the slums to establish small agricultural encampments on Brazil's vast tracts of privately owned but idle land.

This movement cannot be easily shrugged off. Hundreds of thousands of workers have become involved, and it enjoys the support of the Unified Workers Central (CUT), which represents more than 20 million workers, and of the Labor Party, the principal opposition party. Landless Workers are even among the characters of a popular television soap opera, "*O Rei do Gado*" ("King of Cattle").

In a typical occupation, several hundred workers and their families—squatters—live in temporary tent communities while beginning to cultivate a parcel of land that has been targeted for takeover. About 44,000 families are currently squatting on various tracts of land.

In many cases, the occupiers will be dispersed. Thugs hired by private landowners, the police, or the two together, often raid the camps and drive the squatters out. Beatings are common and the mass murder of occupiers is not unknown—more than 1,700 have been killed in the last decade, according to the CUT.

The landless are willing to risk their lives because—if they are lucky—eventually their possession of the land will be accepted as a fait accompli and the government will follow the mechanism established in Brazil's 1988 constitution to purchase the land from its original owner (usually at highly inflated prices), delivering title to the occupiers. Nearly a half-million Brazilians have been resettled in this manner.

Two Brazils

Brazil is not a poor country. It ranks ninth among the world's nations in gross domestic product. By 2015, Brazil's economy—which already surpasses that of Russia—will be the sixth largest in the world, according to a prediction by the British finance ministry.

Fábio L. S. Petrarolha, a Brazilian sociologist and economist, writes for several newspapers in Brazil. He was a Bulletin visiting fellow in 1996.

But the results of Brazil's enormous economic growth have been mixed. The poorest 40 percent of the population receive only 7 percent of the total income. The result: a paradise for the few; a nightmare for the many.

Economists sometimes call Brazil "Belindia" because its development resembles a peculiar mixture of India and a cosmopolitan European state like Belgium. Brazil's upper class shares the lifestyle of the industrialized world. Yet by most development measures, Brazil is a Third World nation. According to the U.N. Human Development Index, Brazil lags behind countries like Mexico, Colombia, Venezuela—even Albania—in education, life expectancy, and other indicators of standard of living.

Tracy Ann Breneman, a U.S. historian and specialist on Brazil (a "Brazilianist," as we call foreign researchers who study the country), points out that the "two Brazils . . . live in very different worlds. They walk on the same land, they speak the same language, but they eat at different tables."

If the inequality in income is startling, the inequities of land distribution are even more striking. Fewer than 1 percent of all landowners control nearly half of the countryside. The Brazilian state itself owns another 600 million unused acres. A non-governmental human rights organization, Brazil's Service of Justice and Peace, estimates that 450 million acres of land suitable for agriculture lie idle, most having never been cultivated.

Nonetheless, as farming has been modernized, millions of peasants have lost jobs on the large estates where they once lived and worked. As a result, Brazil—a country that is larger than the continental United States but has only 60 percent of the U.S. population (and a growth rate that has declined sharply in the past decade)—now has an estimated 12 million landless peasants, many of whom have flocked to the cities in search of work.

Once there, these migrants find they have merely traded rural poverty for urban misery, joining millions in a desperate competition for a dwindling number of jobs. According to the Brazilian Institute of Geography and Statistics, in recent years the job supply has been decreasing by more than 1 percent a year.

With little in the way of social welfare or public housing, every rise in unemployment expands Brazil's 3,500 slums. And Brazilian slums are much worse than their North American second cousins. They are filled with shabby one-room shacks piled on top of one another, precariously built from wood, cardboard, or whatever their owners can scavenge in the streets. One slum in Rio—the *Favela da Rocinha*—is the largest in South America, with over 300,000 inhabitants. Meanwhile, Brazil's planning ministry predicts that the housing crisis will only worsen.

The perverse combination of lack of housing and the high rate of unemployment has not only swollen the population of Brazilian slums, it has given rise to new forms of violence. Many of the unemployed turn to crime, and Brazil's cities have become exceptionally dangerous places. A phenomenon of the 1990s is that of the *arrastões*, mobs of as many as 300 poor people who leave the slum as a group and fall like an avalanche on a neighborhood or beach, stealing everything they can. Even the police are helpless against them. As Brazilian President Fernando Henrique Cardoso said in a recent radio address, "Violence is taking our liberty away from us. We must be able to walk in the streets again, to lean out of our windows without being shot by a stray bullet."

Non-Brazilians are generally familiar with only one part of this story—the tragic lives of Rio's homeless street children and how some have been murdered by the police, a story that has been reported extensively in the international press.

Making a bad situation worse are the government's recently imposed anti-inflationary policies, which Brazil was pressured to accept by the International Monetary Fund. Although the government's austerity plan has brought a soaring inflation rate (nearly 47 percent a month in June 1994) under control, this has come at considerable cost: Interest rates in the 25-percent range have stifled entrepreneurial activity as funds have moved to financial instruments. Meanwhile, foreign goods have flooded the market, choking domestic production, dampening employment opportunity, and further straining the lives of the poor.

As Adolfo Perez Esquivel, a Chilean Nobel Peace Prize-winner and president of an international Catholic human rights group, concluded on a visit in September, these "economic policies are increasing marginalization, poverty, the ranks of the excluded, [and] the lack of money to fund a dignified life."

Coronelismo

The roots of Brazil's lopsided land policies date back to the 1530s, when King Dom João III of Portugal divided his South American colony into 15 immense tracts of

---

The two Brazils "live in very different worlds. They walk on the same land, they speak the same language, but they eat at different tables."

The poorest 40 percent of Brazil's population receives 7 percent of total income. The result: A paradise for the few, a nightmare for the many.

land (*capitanias hereditárias*), which he distributed to 13 settlers (*donatários*). Each was granted not only title to the land, but also unlimited hereditary power to make laws and enforce them. These *donatários* then doled out portions of their lands as rewards to their followers.

Over the centuries, a culture of *coronelismo* took root. "*Coronelismo*" derives from the "colonels" (*coronéis*)—the original landowners, most of whom held military titles. For centuries, the *coronéis* ruled Brazil.

By the early twentieth century, the rural elite remained dominant by controlling a government that only appeared to be freely elected. They chose which candidates would run for political office, and they determined the outcome of elections—either by buying votes, employing physical violence or fraud, or a combination of these methods, aided by the fact that each individual's vote was a matter of public record. The secret ballot was not introduced until 1934.

Since the agrarian oligarchy could elect whomever they pleased, they believed and expected—correctly—that the country would be governed according to their interests. Because the economy was predominantly agricultural, there were no countervailing powers or the means to oppose them. And their methods of maintaining dominance were notoriously violent.

The *coronéis'* hegemony went unchallenged through the 1920s. Beginning in the 1930s, however, and accelerating especially after World War II, Brazil experienced an intense period of urbanization and industrialization. The oligarchy saw its political and economic monopoly diminished, although its traditional practices still flourished in the poorest parts of the country, where the elite continued to rule like feudal barons.

No longer all-powerful, they remained a force to be reckoned with. Even in today's electoral politics, as political scientist Ricardo Tavares points out, the "rural states in the North—mainly the Northeast—elect proportionally more members of the National Congress than the industrial and more populous states of the South and Southeast."

A dream deferred

Even as their relative power was fading, the traditional agricultural elite fiercely protected their historic control of the countryside.

In March 1964, then-president João Belchior Marques Goulart held a rally in Rio de Janeiro that was to be the opening move in his effort to enact a wide-ranging series of measures aimed at improving the lives of the Brazilian poor. Although Goulart's "basic reforms" addressed other popular issues like extending the right to vote to previously disenfranchised groups, the centerpiece of his program was agrarian reform. At the rally—which was broadcast on radio and television and attended by more than 200,000 people—Goulart signed a decree authorizing the government to purchase unused (or under-used) farms that were larger than 1,200 acres.

The oligarchy's response was swift. Within weeks the conservative Brazilian elite mounted a military coup that deposed Goulart and ended any prospect of reform in rural Brazil.

The coup ushered in one of Latin America's bloodiest dictatorships, a violent 23-year reign that rivaled the Chilean and Argentinian regimes of the period.

During those years, censorship was severe—at one point the media were warned not to report political kidnappings. Sometimes a don't-report warning came before the victim had been snatched. Persecution, imprisonment, mass murder, torture, and a growing list of the "disappeared" were features of daily life.

Today, 10 years after the end of the dictatorship—and to a large extent because of the great concentration of wealth that occurred during the regime—the issue of access to land has become more critical than ever.

The dream renewed

If Goulart's dream of agrarian reform is coming true today, it is certainly coming about in an unusual way. Agrarian reform is a stated goal of the government, and a mechanism is enshrined in the reform constitution, but it is the de facto occupation of land by the Landless Movement that is driving what has been a lengthy process.

Brazilian peasants had begun organizing in the early 1960s in an effort to gain the right to claim legal title to land they had been squatting on or where they had lived as tenant farmers for many years. Their action was prompted in part by the large-scale depopulation of the traditional large farms, or *latifúndios*, which, as they became mechanized, were expelling large numbers of workers. The peasants' political pressure certainly played a role in Goulart's decision to take on land reform.

When Goulart was overthrown by the military, the new government declared that it had been forced to take action. The dictators always referred to the coup and their regime as "a democratic revolution" that had saved Brazil from what it termed "the communist threat."

It was a time of exceptional economic growth. In 1973, for example, gross domestic product grew 14 percent. The "Brazilian Miracle" had an annual average growth rate exceeding that of fast-growing Japan.

The military rulers were firm believers in "trickle-down" economics. One explained the policy: "We want the rich to be richer, so that the poor can be less poor." The trouble was, very little trickled down, and the lower classes lost ground. According to the World Bank, Brazil's distribution of income became the most skewed on the planet.

As the years of the dictatorship wore on, new organizations were formed to aid the peasants. The National Confederation of Agricultural Workers had been established in 1963, but its major growth occurred during the military regime. In 1975, the progressive wing of the Brazilian Catholic Church adopted agrarian reform as a priority and established the Pastoral Land Commission. In 1979, the Labor Party was founded, and other movements formed an alliance with it—rural unions, trade unions, various landless organizations, and human rights groups.

But it was only in the first half of the 1980s, as Brazil's economic miracle ran out of steam and the immense international debt that had fueled the expansion came due, that the dictatorship foundered, eventually losing support—even of the elites who had helped to establish it. Grassroots protests became too big to control. A new government was inevitable.

It was in this environment that the organizations that most prominently work for agricultural reform today were established—CUT's National Department for Rural Workers, and especially the Landless Workers Movement.

"Democratizing" the land

Founded in 1984, the Landless Workers Movement first took action in the three most southern states—Rio Grande do Sul, Santa Catarina, and Paraná—but the organization's activities have since spread throughout the country. Many of the current occupations are in the northeast.

The decision to occupy an area is usually made by a local rural union, which turns to the national office of the Landless Movement for help. Occupations are dangerous; they may end in expulsion or slaughter. The movement draws rural workers, of course, but it also attracts the urban poor, whose lives are so desperate that they readily volunteer, whatever the risk. All of the occupiers know that the chance of benefiting from reform is slim to zero unless they take direct action. "It is necessary to occupy, because this is the only way to achieve agrarian reform in Brazil," said Cícero Pereira Neto, one survivor of the 1995 police massacre at the Corumbiara landless camp, where a dozen were killed but others are still missing.

Occupations usually occur in regions with a long tradition of land disputes. In addition, the land to be occupied must be idle or under-used, and therefore legally eligible for reform. A group of regional landless workers first organize themselves through a local rural labor union. Meetings are held to decide the details of the occupation. If the local union is an affiliate of CUT, the workers will probably receive political support from that organization. In addition, the action may be endorsed by the Labor Party and by the Pastoral Land Commission.

The Landless Workers Movement provides transportation, tents, agricultural tools, and seeds. But even more important, the Landless organization provides people. The organization has more than 5,200 "professional militants" who organize occupations and work for "democratization of the land" within the political system.

The movement maintains a permanent and frequently updated file of the names of families living in urban slums who want to participate in farmland occupations. Once a decision to occupy a tract of land is made, workers may come from all over the country to participate.

Many of those recruited from the slums believe that taking part in an occupation is the least immoral option open to them. "Those who submit themselves to land occupations are desperately trying not to become criminals in cities. So, they struggle for land. It is a shame for this country that they have to do that," says Nilmário Miranda, a federal deputy and member of the National Congress's Commission for Human Rights.

If the idea of moving back to the countryside renews the hopes of the jobless, the reality they face on arrival is daunting. Once on the land, they begin cultivating the soil in order to harvest the crops they will need for survival. There is always the danger of expulsion. And in the majority of occupations that occurred in 1995, the lives of the squatters were directly threatened by the local landowner, the police, or both.

Professional militants

Neither the Landless Workers Movement nor the Brazilian government can definitively answer the question of how many people have participated in occupations. But between 1986 and 1995, 139,000 families eventually received the legal right to the land they settled on. An additional 44,000 families are engaged in current occupations. Adding in those who have lost their lives in the struggle, it is not unreasonable to estimate that in the last 10 years about 700,000 people—men, women, and children—have been directly involved in occupations.

During the last decade, the Landless organization itself has grown powerful—and some say, rich. The organization has no single leader, but is managed by a national

> *Some Brazilians believe that the media have purposely underreported the movement's activities in order to discourage potential support and participation.*

board of coordinators. The board's 65 members are drawn from 21 of the 26 Brazilian states and from the federal district. The board makes general policy decisions, which are implemented by a 15-member national board of directors. The directors are drawn from the movement's "professional militants"—individuals who have participated in previous occupations, and who have gained the respect of the peasants. For instance, one director, José Rainha, has often been described in the newspapers and on TV as "the leader of the Landless Workers Movement," even though such a position does not exist.

A similar structure exists on the state level. And within various regions of the states there are further administrative and operational subdivisions or *regionais*. The boards in each state decide how many of these *regionais* they want. The state of São Paulo currently has five.

Individual occupations are aided by local organizers—encampment co-ordinators who function on the local level. Each of the coordinators deals with a different area of concern—education, nutrition, health, production, conflict negotiation, and the press. In addition, the workers who participate in each occupation elect their own representatives.

As the movement has grown, it has diversified. In Sarandi, the Landless Movement produces 30,000 liters of milk a day. In the city of Dionísio Cerqueira, it operates the Conquista da Fronteira, a cooperative factory that produces 1,200 pairs of jeans a month. The movement also supports cooperatives in other ways. In Veranópolis, the movement runs—in cooperation with the Ministry for Education!—a school that teaches cooperative techniques. Most of these entrepreneurial activities are in the south, where the movement has existed the longest and is the best organized.

According to the newspaper *Folha de São Paulo*, the Landless Workers Movement has an operating budget of millions of dollars a year. One percent of everything that is produced at settlements that now own their own land

goes to the organization. Felinto Procópio, one of the directors of the movement in São Paulo, insists that these contributions are voluntary. "Nobody is forced to support [the movement], but the peasants want to do it," he says.

A pivotal bear

It is difficult to gauge public opinion about the Landless Workers. The mass media often refer to the organization as "land invaders." In contrast, some Brazilians believe that the media have purposely underreported the movement's activities in order to discourage potential support and participation. Nonetheless, many Brazilians have a positive image of the organization, which they believe has demonstrated concern for social justice, and which has struggled for reform in a disciplined and non-violent manner.

However, the events of this year may be straining the organization's ability—and willingness—to maintain discipline and practice non-violence. Over the past 12 months, the Landless Movement has organized a greater number of occupations and received more attention from the media than ever before. But two initiatives—one public and one private—have resurrected institutions that menaced earlier activist organizations during the military regime.

The military dictatorship's intelligence agency, which engaged in a wide range of secret—and repressive—activities, was closed in 1989. That was considered one of the last, but most important steps in Brazil's transition to democracy. This year, however, President Cardoso has established the *Agencia Brasileira de Inteligéncia*, or ABIN. Gen. Alberto Cardoso, the minister of military affairs who was charged with establishing ABIN, has said the agency's role is to keep an eye on "potentially dangerous" popular organizations "so that they should not be politically manipulated." That was widely viewed as a veiled accusation that the Landless Workers was vulnerable to a communist fifth column.

At the same time, the *União Democrática Ruralista* (UDR), a landowner-run paramilitary organization that was disbanded in 1994, has been reborn. When he was asked if farmers should be able to use armed militias against occupiers, the UDR's provisional president, Roosevelt Roque dos Santos, replied: "Those who own shops, banks, or factories keep private armed security in order to care for and defend their property. Farmers should not be prevented from protecting their property either."

Many outside the movement deride the organization's members as communists, although the Landless Movement has consistently argued that agrarian reform is a necessary condition for democracy, as well as a way to solve hunger and high rates of unemployment. Surprisingly, a June survey of landless workers carried out by a private polling organization, Datafolha, found that

Some groups will occupy a parcel of land, but leave when the police arrive. They return again as soon as the police go away.

those polled were about evenly divided in their support of Labor and the more conservative ruling coalition.

A new phenomenon is the occupation of city buildings. The economics ministry's building in São Paulo has been occupied, but more frequently buildings that house branches of the Institute for Colonization and Agrarian Reform are the targets. These urban occupations get media attention more readily than rural activities, and they are probably safer—the military police may be reluctant to pay the stiff political cost that another highly visible assault on occupiers might bring with it.

The Landless Worker's slogan is "Occupy, resist, and produce. Agrarian reform is everybody's struggle." In an effort to avoid direct confrontation, some Landless Workers employ an "occupy-deoccupy" tactic: Hundreds or thousands will occupy a parcel of land, but when the police arrive, they leave. As soon as the police go away, they return.

Alternative landless groups are not necessarily as pacifist. None is nearly as big as the Landless Workers, but some are far more radical, and growing rapidly. Several groups add "defend" to their slogans, shorthand for their willingness to pursue armed confrontation. In the state of Bahia, the "Fighting for Land Movement," which has settlements with about 6,000 people, is affiliated with the Communist Party of Brazil, whose own land reform efforts of the 1970s failed. "We are better prepared in theoretical terms. We want socialism and are Marxist-Leninist," says Marcondes Nunes Machado, one of the group's leaders.

Another smaller but more militant organization is the "Landless Democratic Movement," which also characterizes its proclivity to fight as "self-defense." One of this group's leaders, João Baptista da Fonseca, believes that "agrarian reform will not be completed under capitalism." This group has seven encampments that house about 3,200 people.

Additional movements have split off from the Landless Workers. Some are directly supported by CUT, the rural union, which announced on July 1 that it would openly promote land occupations throughout the countryside.

When public sympathy for the Landless Workers swelled after the April massacre, President Cardoso appointed a new minister for agrarian policies to accelerate government land purchases and redistribution. Minister Raul Jungmann claims to have transferred more than two million acres in his first 100 days in office. Still, with more than 62 percent of arable land described in the *Land Atlas of Brazil* as "*improdutivas,*" all the landless who wish to become settlers could be accommodated.

Dividing the land is not a total solution. A more effective reform would also provide workers with start-up help. As a matter of fact, statistics show that the places where settlers are established have less access to infrastructure and receive fewer subsidies from the government than other areas. As a result, the occupiers may be more likely to be unsuccessful and find themselves forced to sell their new property.

Brazil could thus repeat the example of Venezuela's failure, where, ironically, agrarian reform ultimately resulted in land ownership being concentrated in fewer hands. Despite the reforms of the last decade, the *Land Atlas of Brazil* reveals that Brazil's pattern of land ownership is nearly identical to that of 56 years ago. Landowners are usually greatly overcompensated for expropriated land; often they use the money to buy more, with the result that they have more land than they did before.

The long and violent tradition of *coronelismo* and the more recent military regime have perpetuated the perverse slogan of a 1920s president, Washington Luís, who said: "A social issue is a case for the police." Today, however, with modern communications—and a free press—organizations like the Landless Workers can rally opposition. And the Landless Workers Movement is much more prominent than even a few years ago.

There is always the danger that the present turmoil may turn into a bloody civil war. The reestablishment of ABIN and the UDR, two anti-democratic institutions, indicates how desperately the powerful oligarchy will fight to maintain its historical privileges. But they face not only the Landless Workers, an organization that has increased in size and consolidated its political influence, but also smaller and more radical groups.

In recent months the Landless Workers have met with Mexico's Zapatista guerrillas to "exchange experiences," and they are training urban people for mass occupations in areas of the countryside where UDR is strongest. The situation is tense, and both landowners and some landless organizations are developing paramilitary apparatuses for future battles. Even the Landless Workers seem to be preparing for violent confrontation. "We are going to take over estates for keeps in future—and we will take up arms to fight if any landowner tries to keep us out by force," José Rainha, one of the movement's national directors, recently proclaimed.

If strong social policies that result in meaningful and lasting reform and rescue significant numbers of the poor are not promoted, Brazilian democracy may be in grave danger. The oligarchy could form another alliance with the military, establishing a new dictatorship. Alternately, an all-out war between the haves and have-nots cannot be ruled out. The question is: How long can a slow process of reform, punctuated by occasional massacres, continue? Not indefinitely.

Article 16   *Multinational Monitor*, April 1997

Conquering Peru

Newmont's Yanacocha Mine Recalls the Days of Pizarro

by Pratap Chatterjee

CAJAMARCA, Peru—A new dirt road connects this city to the picturesque village of Negritos Altos some 14,000 feet up in the Andes of northern Peru, allowing heavy vehicles to drive through for the first time.

But for Negritos resident Frederico Carrasco, this road, which allows him to travel to the city 30 kilometers away in two hours, is no cause for celebration. Days before this past Christmas, Minera Yanacocha notified him that bulldozers would come down the road to tear down his house.

Yanacocha (which means "black lake") is the largest gold mine in South America. It is operated by Denver-based Newmont in a joint venture with a Peruvian mining company, Buenaventura. Newmont owns a 51.4 percent of Yanacocha, Buenaventura owns 43.6 percent and the International Finance Corporation, the private sector arm of the World Bank, owns 5 percent.

Last year, Yanacocha produced 811,400 ounces of gold for roughly $107 an ounce, a production cost that is less than half that of most major gold mines in the world. If all this gold was sold at the 1996 average international market price of $390 an ounce, the company would have made $317 million, or a net profit of $230 million.

Land grab

Not much of this trickled down to Carrasco, who was paid $540 a hectare for a 42-hectare plot of land last August. Land in Negritos costs more than $2,000 a hectare on the open market, so Carrasco can only buy a fraction of the land he once had.

And, compared to some of his neighbors, Carrasco was lucky. Yanacocha paid another farmer, Nicholas Cruzado, $42 a hectare for 332 hectares of land in the neighboring village of Combayo in November 1992, for example.

Cruzado used the money to buy a 12-hectare plot of land, which is too small to support his 13-member family. He has had to sell off 250 animals ranging from cows to pigs to make ends meet. His son Mario works on nearby farms for $1.40 a day.

"There is very little I can do. Yanacocha has bought legal title to the land. The farmers should have come to me before they sold their property," says Jorge Malca, a lawyer who works for the Catholic church and helps represent local people. So far, seven of the more than 50 farmers who have sold their land to Yanacocha have asked for legal help to sue the company.

Some farmers appear to have stronger cases but they have yet to seek Malca's help. David Cueva, a farmer in

© 1997 PRATAP CHATTERJEE
Hiriberto Ventura, a leader of Peasant Patrol in Negritos Altos.

the neighboring village of Yanacancha Grande, says the company simply took 26 hectares of his 211-hectare property without paying for it.

Nicholas Cotts, Yanacocha's manager of environmental affairs, says that the company recognizes "fair-value prices" for all its land transactions. "Approximately 95 percent of the land purchases conducted by Minera Yanacocha have been conducted under full knowledge and in direct negotiation with the land owner. In other cases expropriation was used at the request of and in complete cooperation with the landowner," he wrote to *Multinational Monitor*.

Yanacocha's toxic burden

Two hours horse ride away from Yanacancha Grande, it is possible to see distant deep brown furrows which scar the grassy hills as well as a gray plateau of mine waste built up next to the mine.

Yanacocha mining engineers explain that they loosen up the rocky hills with daily dynamite blasts. Earth movers then scoop up 20-ton loads of the debris and dump them in trucks that carry 85 tons at a time. The trucks take the ore, which contains less than two grams of gold per ton, to Yanachoca's heap leach facility. There it is piled on thin plastic liners, and drenched with a cyanide solution. The cyanide dissolves the gold and carries it to collection ponds, leaving behind mountains of tailings.

Concerns about heap leaching have been triggered by the lethal impact of cyanide. A teaspoonful of a two-percent solution of cyanide can kill a human adult. Cyanide blocks the absorption of oxygen by cells, effectively causing the victim to "suffocate." Levels of two parts per million are considered lethal to humans; concentrations as low as five parts per billion can inhibit fish reproduction.

Mining companies insist that cyanide breaks down when exposed to sunlight and oxygen, rendering it harmless. Scientific studies show that cyanide swallowed by fish will not "bio-accumulate," which means it does not pose a risk to anyone who eats the fish. But other scientists say that if the cyanide solution is very acidic—and mining often turns local water acidic simply by exposing previously buried sulfide ores to air—it could turn into cyanide gas, which is toxic to fish.

"The attitude [is] if you don't see corpses, everything is okay," writes Philip Hocker, president of the Washington-based Mineral Policy Center, in his paper, "Heaps of Gold, Pools of Poison." "There is good reason to suspect that a compound as aggressive as cyanide in lethal doses also has serious health effects in long-term chronic exposures at low levels."

Local communities have reacted angrily to the effect of these deadly chemicals on their lives. Hiriberto Ventura, a leader of Rondas Campesinos (Peasant Patrol) in Negritos Altos, says that last August, five community members died after using plastic containers, discarded by the company, to collect water. The containers were apparently used to store cyanide.

Just three years ago, local rivers teemed with trout, says another local resident, but today the rivers are lifeless. "When the rains come, the water runs off the tailings into the rivers, making them turbid. If the horses and cows drink the water from the rivers, they get stomach problems and sometimes die," he says.

Not surprising, says Mary Mueller, an environmental scientist in Colorado. Mueller points out that mining waste invariably contains heavy metals that are just as toxic as cyanide. Copper and sulfate concentrations exceeding one part per million can cause stomach and intestinal problems in humans and kill animals like horses. Lead and mercury can kill humans.

Local residents receive little in exchange for the toxic burden they are forced to bear. Local mayors say that Newmont employs almost none of the local residents. Not one of the 1,800 people in Yanacancha Grande has been able to get a job with the company, according to local residents. And Francisco Llanos, the mayor of Combayo, says that a mere 10 people in his village of 4,936 people have jobs with Yanacocha. These jobs pay $5.60 a day.

Those who are employed at Yanacocha toil under dangerous conditions. In one week in late 1996, five people were killed in three separate incidents: a Newmont geologist was killed when an unstable rock face collapsed; three men employed by a sub-contractor were asphyxiated by a diesel engine they started up to keep warm after working late; and another contractor's employee died when a truck rolled on him.

Yanacocha's Cotts says concerns about the mine's operational practices are unwarranted. To ensure water supplies are not poisoned, the company monitors approximately 120 water sources on a regular basis, he says. He says that Yanacocha maintains a herd of 60 sheep and alpacas at the site which have never shown any signs of contamination. A 1994 investigation into deaths of local cattle showed that the animals had died of "liver fluke and related indigenous diseases," he claims.

Company representatives also point out that Yanacocha follows the same environmental standards that Newmont would employ in the United States. That may be less comforting than it sounds. Newmont had a permit revoked in 1990 for its uranium mine on land near Spokane, Washington. The company lost the permit for ignoring repeated government demands to take care of 15.5 billion liters of acidic water in pits that threatened to leak into the Columbia River.

Yanacocha officials also say that they maintain an "open door policy" for "any and all" to visit the site and inspect safety facilities.

Llanos and others say that this is not true. They say their written requests for an opportunity to meet with the mine management have gone four months without a response. They have also travelled to the mine, where they have been refused entrance.

Company officials also claim that Yanacocha has contributed heavily to the local community, spending $3 million in 1995 on roads, schools and providing free hot lunches to local children.

Critics are skeptical of these efforts, pointing out that the roads were built for the mine. And while the mine site has satellite telephones and private generators, none of the villages surrounding the mine—Combayo, Yanacancha Grande and Negritos Altos—have telephones, regular electricity, running water or sewage facilities.

Ephrain Castillo, a Catholic priest who has been providing the local villagers with agricultural services, food and legal help, says, "People here are very poor. The mine promises to change things," but excludes local people from sharing in the economic riches it generates.

Hernan Herrera, Cajamarca city manager, calls the mine a "detonator" for commerce and economic growth. But even Herrera complains the mine has not created as many jobs as expected, while crime has increased and street prostitution has cropped up near the central city plaza.

The new conquest

In the same plaza in 1532, Pizarro, the Spanish *conquistador*, tricked Atahualpa, the last Inca king, into an ambush that led to the collapse of the empire that stretched across Ecuador and Peru.

One of Atahualpa's final acts was an attempt to buy off the Spanish by offering them a room full of gold and two rooms full of silver. The Spanish accepted the gold, but then murdered Atahualpa and razed the rest of the city to the ground.

Last year alone, Yanacocha mined roughly one and a half times as much gold as the Incas turned over to Pizarro. Like the Spanish before them, Yanacocha has considerable financial support from outside the country. The International Finance Corporation and private banks

like the Union Bank of Switzerland put up approximately $41 million in start-up costs for this venture. Also like the Spanish before it, Newmont exports all of its gold to Europe. Half of the gold goes to Johnson Matthey in Britain and the other half to Switzerland.

Unlike Pizarro, Newmont has not brought cannons or cavalry to rout angry natives. Instead it insured the mine for hundreds of millions of dollars against political risk (such as nationalization or political violence) with policies underwritten by the World Bank's Multilateral Investment Guarantee Agency and the U.S. government's Overseas Private Investment Corporation (OPIC).

Thanks largely to Yanacocha, Newmont declared a $94 million profit for 1996. More of the same is expected by company executives, who are extremely bullish about future profits from Peru. Tom Conway, Newmont Peru chief executive, recently said, "We are really blessed with this deposit. We expect gold to just scream out of there."

Dozens of international companies are now flocking to Peru in an attempt to emulate the success of Yanacoha. Some 240 new sites are under active exploration all over the country. The new climate in Peru is also attracting oil and gas companies such as Chevron, Mobil and Shell. Mineral exports (including petroleum and its by-products) now constitute 51.3 percent of Peru's total export income.

One of the new investors in Cajamarca is a Canadian company called Cambior. Cambior plans to begin extracting copper on a 3,000 hectare claim called La Granja.

Cambior already has a bad name on this continent. Just two years ago, a Cambior gold mine in Guyana, on the eastern side of Latin America, spilled 2.5 billion liters of cyanide and destroyed the local river system [see "Courting Disaster in Guyana," *Multinational Monitor*, November 1995]. Like Yanacocha, the mine had political risk insurance from the World Bank but no local person could claim relief from this insurance. It is only intended for the opposite purpose—to repay the company if locals or the government infringe on or take over the company's operations, not to compensate local residents in the event, now being repeated at Yanacocha, that they are injured by the insured company.

Article 17   *The Chronicle of Higher Education,* October 24, 1997

Cuba Today: Instant Antiquity

By Tony Mendoza

CAMUS once observed that the only paradises are those that are lost. I agree. During 37 years of exile (and 37 years of American winters), I have increasingly remembered Cuba, where I was born and raised, as paradise.

People born on islands shouldn't move to the Midwest. Every winter I had memories of Cuba that seemed to revolve around the climate. I remembered Varadero Beach, where my entire family on my mother's side spent the three summer months at my grandfather's house. I especially remembered the porch overlooking the ocean. I ate breakfast there every morning, always on the lookout for the large fish—sharks, barracudas, tarpons—that glided close to the surf in the early morning to feed on sardines. After a morning of water skiing and spearfishing, I would return to the porch. There, on a soft, comfortable sofa, I would stretch out after lunch and nap. I can still feel the strong breeze that came in from the sea, and hear the hypnotic sounds of the surf. I wanted to see that porch again, and go swimming in front of the house.

Last year, while on sabbatical, I flew to Havana—my first trip back since 1960, when I left with my family. I was 18. Now, I wanted to confirm my memories and to satisfy my curiosity about life in socialist Cuba. In the 21 days of my visit—the maximum allowed to returning exiles—I shot 80 rolls of black-and-white film and recorded, on tape or in my diary, conversations with more than 200 Cubans.

Passengers on the flight had warned me that I was going to find a ruined Havana, but I was still surprised by what I saw. Havana reminded me of the set for the movie *Brazil*; the same old factories that had lined the airport road during the 1950s were still there, rusting away in the tropical sun, and still in use. People rode bicycles everywhere, reminding me of old newsreels of Asian countries. My cabdriver drove me past 1940s- and 1950s-model cars; I felt as if I were in a time warp. In the residential area where I used to live, the Vedado, an affluent neighborhood in pre-Castro days, the lush gardens I remembered were wildly overgrown or barren. The

buildings were even more depressing. Havana's architecture is pseudo-Greek and Roman, and after 37 years of socialism, the buildings seemed to be exact copies of the ruined monuments of Greece and Rome. Instant antiquity.

The overwhelming message I got from talking to Cuban citizens is that very few people are happy with socialism, with the Revolution, or with Fidel. Among the older people to whom I spoke, almost everyone stated that at one time they had supported the Revolution, but that 37 years of hardships were enough. They wanted change, but they also seemed resigned. I heard this expression often: *Esto esta de madre, pero no hay quien lo tumbe.* This is terrible, but it can't be overthrown. The overwhelming feeling among Cubans, expressed by virtually everyone, is that as long as Fidel is around, nothing will change. While issues dealing with the absence of the most basic freedoms came up often in conversations, the problem that continually grates on people is more fundamental: Most Cubans work for the state, which pays an average salary of $8 a month. On that pay, it's not possible to eat two meals a day.

Since nobody in Cuba can make it on their official salary, how do people survive? It's simple. Everyone has to *resolver*: to solve. It's one of the most commonly heard words in Havana. How are you? *Aqui, resolviendo.* One hears about *la busqueda,* the search. And another phrase, *Hay que inventarsela*: One has to invent. All these words refer to the many creative and mostly illegal ways to make ends meet, so common that they have become part of the economic fabric of life.

Most Cubans do a lot of *resolviendo* at their places of work. If you're offered a job in a ministry, before you take the job you need to know how you can solve your problems in that job. Maybe the job has a product that gets distributed, and some of that product can get diverted and distributed among the workers and managers. After all, the government never tires of reminding everyone that in Cuba, everything belongs to the people.

Construction outfits solve many problems for their workers. Lumber, concrete blocks, and steel re-bars can be sold easily on the black market. Food-distribu-

tion outfits are even better; the family diet will improve spectacularly if you are employed in a food warehouse. At a gas station, gasoline can easily get siphoned from the tanks, without going through the meter, and be sold privately. Cubans are so busy doing *biznes* that Cuba is probably the most capitalistic and entrepreneurial country in the world. A crude word for all this illicit economic activity is stealing, but Cubans don't use that word. There is a joke that socialism has only two fundamental problems: lunch and dinner.

One evening, I started a conversation with a man who was fishing. He said that he had been a party militant since the 1960s, but that he no longer believed in the Revolution. "The idea behind Marxism is very beautiful," he said. "It seduced me. But it has a great error. It doesn't work. The flaw is this idea that we are all the same, that we have the same needs, that we should be paid the same. *Not true!* See these hands? They are different from every other pair of hands. See these eyes? *Also different!* This brain of mine? *Different!*"

He picked up momentum and got louder as he went through every remaining part of his body. I started to worry for my physical safety; this man was losing it.

"For 39 years, I've been working like a dog for this Revolution," he went on. "Thirty years of volunteer work, 30 years of sacrifice. *What for? What for?* We have nothing here. I don't have anything. I have the shirt on my back, this pair of pants, these shoes. That's all. But all these scums around me, the black marketers, the illegal vendors, the good-for-nothings with relatives in Miami, who haven't done s— for the Revolution, they are going great. They have dollars. It's not fair. *It's not fair!*"

Then, suddenly, he started crying.

After the fall of the Soviet Union and the end of Soviet subsidies to Cuba, the socialist government was forced to allow some self-employment. One sees many private restaurants, one-man repair shops, vendors, and taxis. But the best-paid self-employed workers in Cuba are the *jineteras.* In the old days, prostitutes were called *puntas,* but that word has a seedy and dishonorable connotation. *Jineteras* are different: They have college degrees. Their activity is seen by Cubans as entrepreneurial rather than immoral. If a *jinetera* has a "date" every night, she can easily make $2,000 a month, tax-free, which in Cuba is a fortune. A brain surgeon would have to do brain surgery in Cuba for eight years to earn an equivalent amount.

Fidel never tires of repeating in his speeches how the Yankees had transformed pre-revolutionary Cuba into a gambling den and a brothel, and how the elimination of casinos and prostitution during the first days of 1959 revealed the high moral character of the Revolution. Times are different now. I saw *jineteras* everywhere in Havana, always dressed in black like New York artists. I'm assuming that the high moral character of the Revolution has come down a few notches, because I didn't see any jineteras getting arrested. Cuba desperately needs tourists, for their dollars; right now, tourists are coming mostly for sex.

Jineteras accosted me every day. I turned down their services, but I did want to know how they felt about their lives. One group of women, left alone during dinner by their three Italian companions, told me that they earn $25 to $50 an evening, which typically includes dinner and dancing. They see their activity as a date with a $50 tip. One of the women in the group was finishing her medical internship. She said it was very tempting to earn $50 in one night, eat a good dinner, talk to foreigners, find out how the rest of the world lives, have fun. She buys whatever she wants and she helps her family. When I asked her if her parents knew how she earned those dollars, she said: "Of course they know. How else in Cuba am I going to make this kind of money and buy the things we are buying?"

"Are they upset?"

"Not really. *Hay que resolver.* I'm supporting the entire family."

"Are you afraid of AIDS?"

"No. There is no AIDS in Cuba. I wouldn't dream of having sex without a condom. Nobody here does it without condoms."

"So, what do you think about the Revolution?" I asked her.

She looked at me as if I were from Mars. My apartment was two blocks from the ocean, and I liked to start my day sitting on the sea wall, drinking coffee and staring out to sea. I noticed a man equipped with fins, mask and snorkel, a spear gun, and a tiny buoy trailing behind him, swimming straight out every morning until he disappeared. I used to spearfish, so I was interested in what he was doing. One day I caught him before he went out. He was an impressive-looking 55-year-old man, with long, white hair, a carefully trimmed beard, and a bronzed, muscular body.

"I see you swimming out every morning. How far do you go?" I asked him.

"Depends. Some days I snorkel by the wall. What I do is I retrieve fish hooks and nylon lines, which I sell. When I go for fish I swim out seven miles. At other times, I go looking for bodies. I find bodies even further out, 10 miles out."

He continued, "Between Varadero and Camarioca there is a trench, about 10 miles out. Rafters [people trying to escape to Miami] who drown at sea get brought back by the current, and they get caught in this trench. I dive down there for the jewelry. I find gold medallions, rings, and I sell them.

"Don't bodies float?" I asked.

"When the lungs fill up with water, they sink. Usually I find only the skeletons. And the rings are still there."

"Do you do this often?"

"I used to, but lately, no. There haven't been too many rafters since the United States started returning them. So I've been going fishing."

I asked him why he fishes so far out to sea. He replied that the shore is "fished out" and what fish there are are polluted.

"Aren't you afraid when you are so far from shore, alone, without a raft? What if you get a cramp?"

"No, I believe in destiny. I'm going to die when destiny decides." He told me how he catches sharks, to sell. "I'm never scared at sea, because I'm among beings that give me sustenance, give me life. I've been spearfishing for 40 years. I'm at home in the water. I'm more scared when I get on land. People, I don't understand them. They do strange things, they say strange things. I look at

their faces and they look terrible. I trust fish more.

I WAS APPALLED by what I saw in Cuba. When you walk the streets you see faces that are as devastated as the buildings. People look depressed, beaten down. They stare into the distance, as if in a trance, as they wait for buses or in endless food lines, or when they sit on the sea wall, staring intently toward the horizon, toward Miami. All conversations in Cuba ultimately deal with "the situation." No other thoughts or concerns are possible. The liveliness, humor, wit, and energy that I have always associated with Cubans are mostly gone.

The most vital Cubans I found were also the most rabidly anti-Castro—the self-employed workers. This segment is fomenting economic growth, capitalism, and political independence, paving the way for the transition everyone outside Cuba seems to want. The restaurant owner pays the man who brings him fish, the repair man, the woman who makes the desserts. Those workers in turn support others. None of them will ever again work for the miserable wages the government pays, or go to the plaza to listen to Fidel. Right now, these independent Cubans are supported by Canadian and Italian tourists. The United States should eliminate travel restrictions to Cuba and let Americans go to Havana, too, with their video cameras, their thoughts and opinions—and their dollars.

And, along with the tourists, let's send logistical support, money, food, and medicine to dissidents, churches, and charities. Let's send artists and musicians and academics. But no matter what America does, time seems to be running out on the Castro regime. No one can predict when and how it will end, but the joke one hears in Havana, that socialism is the economic system between capitalism and capitalism, seems destined to become reality.

Tony Mendoza is an associate professor of art at the Ohio State University. "Cuba: 1996," an exhibition featuring 54 of his photographs and 20 text panels, is at the university's Hopkins Hall Gallery through November 7, 1997.

Article 18   *The New Republic*, September 29, 1997

Haiti's deteriorating democracy.

ISLAND OF DISENCHANTMENT

By Charles Lane

PORT-AU-PRINCE

The Haitian police who stumbled upon Eddy Arbrouet one night last May thought he was a dangerous bank robber, but they probably didn't know just how dangerous until Eddy and his gang opened fire. Amid the hail of heavy-caliber bullets, one cop dove for cover under a pile of banana leaves; another radioed for reinforcements. Help arrived and, miraculously, the police escaped. But Eddy Arbrouet remains at large and—at least for now—the police dare not tackle him again.

This obscure underworld episode would be of no interest outside Haiti except for one fact: Eddy Arbrouet is also wanted for the August 1996 murder of Antoine Leroy and Jacques Fleurival, two right-wing opponents of the U.S.-backed Haitian government. A pile of evidence links Arbrouet to the murders—and other evidence suggests that he was acting in collaboration with senior officers of Haiti's Presidential Security Unit, the American-trained and -financed corps of official bodyguards who protect Haiti's president, René Préval. Haitian officials deny that any such conspiracy existed. But U.S. officials and other sources familiar with the incident say the killing was one in a series carried out by political hit men who appear to have been operating from within the National Palace.

The mere existence of such a systematic campaign would of course raise new questions not only about Préval, but also about his predecessor, Jean-Bertrand Aristide, who remains Haiti's most influential leader behind the scenes. It would therefore also represent a significant failure in the Clinton administration's Haiti policy, which the administration has been touting as a foreign policy triumph. Three years ago, when the U.S. dispatched 23,000 troops to expel the brutal Haitian Army, the FADH, from the power it had usurped from Aristide in a 1991 coup, the objective was not merely to restore a president but to build democracy as well. Aristide, who had seemingly endorsed mob violence against some political foes during his seven-month presidency before the coup, promised the U.S. that "national reconciliation," not vengeance, would follow his return to office. But with Arbrouet still at large, and twenty-six political murders since 1995 still officially unsolved, that promise—and hence the promise of democratic rule—seems unfulfilled.

It's true Haiti endured worse while the FADH was in control. The FADH and its "attachés"—a latter-day incarnation of François "Papa Doc" Duvalier's murderous Tontons Macoutes—killed hundreds, perhaps thousands, and so far nobody has been made to pay for these crimes, either. Nor can it be said that U.S. policy in Haiti has achieved nothing. For two centuries, Haiti has been the poorest and most violent society in the Americas. In that context, $2 billion in U.S. aid, plus contributions from Canada and the European Union, has purchased some development—most palpably illustrated by the fact that the flow of Haitian boat people to the U.S. has largely ceased. Préval's succession of Aristide was the first time that one elected Haitian civilian had finished his term and peacefully transferred power to another. An elected, boisterous parliament is in place. A new U.S.-trained Haitian National Police has begun to tackle crime. (See "Cop land.") New roads have been built and more are planned. The U.S. has shown the world it will not permit a successful military coup in this hemisphere.

But the Clinton administration has achieved less than it might have, and almost nothing irreversible. Not even the withdrawal of U.S. forces is total; some 500 soldiers and Marines remain, ostensibly to build roads and dig wells, but also to prevent a coup or other major threat to stability. The withdrawal of the last 1,300 U.N. peacekeepers from Canada and Pakistan, first set for March 31, has been twice postponed. The new date is November 30, but since the new National Police still cannot keep order, American officials are scrambling to preserve a foreign security presence after that.

While most Haitians still live in dire poverty, the government has moved slowly on critical economic reforms such as privatizing corrupt and inefficient state companies—reforms upon which foreign aid largely hinges. Prime Minister Rosny Smarth resigned on June 9, fed up with resistance to the reforms from Aristide's party, which controls the lower house of parliament. No successor has been approved by parliament, so the government is at a standstill. It cannot even conduct new business with foreign lenders or investors.

The Haitian electoral process has also collapsed. Turnout was less than 10 percent in elections to choose new local governments and one-third of the twenty-seven-member national Senate on April 6. While in Haiti for nine days, I did not meet a single Haitian who voted, except for politicians themselves. What voting took place was tainted by massive irregularities. The Aristide-leaning Provisional Election Council, for example, tried to guarantee victory for pro-Aristide Senate candidates by excluding blank ballots from the vote count, a maneuver the Organization of American States declared illegal. Aristide's Senate candidates also benefited from highly visible—and highly intimidating—armed protection from presidential bodyguards. All parties except Aristide's refuse to recognize the April 6 results or to participate in runoffs, which have been indefinitely postponed. On August 19, the United Nations announced it would provide no further aid to elections in Haiti "until the credibility and transparency of the electoral process are re-established."

And then there are the political murders, for which no one has yet been convicted, or even formally charged, and which remain a source of quiet tension between the United States and Haiti. The Clinton administration has informed Préval that the Leroy-Fleurival investigation is a test case of Haiti's commitment to the rule of law; it has done so largely because Republicans in Congress have made clear *they* see Haiti's response to the murders as a test of the Clinton administration's policy. And so it is. Haiti has always been a country where the powerful and the well-connected are unaccountable—where they can literally get away with murder. If that has not changed, then nothing really has.

The trail of blood that leads to Eddy Arbrouet's hideout began at 3:45 in the afternoon of March 28, 1995, on a busy street in Port-au-Prince. Mireille Durocher Bertin and a client, Eugene Baillergeau Jr., were sitting in their car, stuck in a traffic jam, when two assailants opened fire on them with a 9 mm pistol and a 5.56 mm machine gun. Both died on the spot. (This account of the murders in Haiti, and the subsequent investigations, is based on interviews with Haitian and U.S. government sources, law enforcement sources in both countries, congressional hearing records and internal U.S. government documents.)

Coming soon after Aristide's restoration to power, the murder of Bertin and her associate sent a chill through Haiti: Bertin, an attorney for members of the traditional elite, was one of Aristide's leading critics. Shortly before her death, she had sent a letter to U.S. military authorities, who were in control of the island at the time. Written

on behalf of the right-wing Mobilization for National Development Party (MDN), the letter accused an Aristide government intelligence operative named Patric Moise of being involved in a plot to kill 100 members of the right-wing elite.

Her letter was one reason U.S. military officials were not entirely surprised by her murder. Another was that nine days before the killing, a Haitian employee of the U.S. forces had made a startling statement to his American boss: Moise had asked him to assist in a plan to kill Bertin. Mondesir Beaubrun, then Aristide's minister of interior, had purportedly offered Moise $5,000 to carry out the hit. The U.S. Army immediately arrested five suspects, including Moise, catching four of the alleged conspirators in an Isuzu Trooper owned by the Ministry of Interior, a car Moise said Minister Beaubrun had lent to him. (Beaubrun denies plotting; he now lives in the Dominican Republic.)

But then U.S. officials made a strange decision. Rather than warn Bertin about the plots directly, they asked Aristide and his Minister of Justice, Jean-Joseph Exume, to warn Bertin. (Some U.S. embassy officials had argued that U.S. officials should warn Bertin directly, but they were overruled by the U.S. Ambassador, William Swing, according to a General Accounting Office report about the affair.) Exume claims he did warn her, but she didn't heed him. Bertin's family says Exume merely told her she might be arrested, and said nothing of the murder plot.

Whatever the case, U.S. officials were palpably alarmed when Bertin showed up dead despite what they thought was a good-faith understanding that Aristide and his justice minister would protect her. With President Clinton set to arrive for a triumphal visit to Haiti on April 1, Ambassador Swing asked Aristide to invite FBI agents to help crack the case. Aristide, evincing great dismay at Bertin's death, agreed. By dawn of the day after the murders, the first FBI agents were picking up bullet fragments at the scene of the crime.

The FBI quickly discounted theories that the murders had been related to a robbery, drug trafficking or a family dispute. Instead, the investigators said, the most likely scenario was that a second group of government hit men had taken over after the U.S. nipped the Beaubrun-Moise plot in the bud. Among the leads were radio conversations intercepted by the U.S. military the day of the killing; in which two men appeared to be talking about following Bertin's car. The two men were Joseph Medard, then the deputy chief of Aristide's bodyguards, and Lieutenant Pierre Lubin of the Interim Public Security Force (IPSF), the police force that Aristide selected—and financed with U.S. money—to help American troops keep order during the transition. The FBI began trying to question Medard, Lubin and several other officials of the IPSF and the National Palace.

Suddenly, FBI agents found themselves in the position of having to investigate the very government officials who were supposed to help them solve the case. The Haitians were not accommodating. Haitian officials told the FBI agents they could not investigate the Bertin case unless they also agreed to investigate twenty killings by the ousted military regime. In May, FBI agents saw Haitian government vehicles parked menacingly near the home of a key witness. Witnesses told of threats from the IPSF. On June 7, the FBI interrogation of one IPSF agent was disrupted by a heavily armed group of other IPSF agents. Ambassador Swing sent the State Department a cable saying that "the FBI investigation of the Bertin assassination is at a standstill due to lack of [Haitian government] cooperation."

The FBI called for a high-level meeting between American officials and Aristide. At the meeting, on July 3, 1995, the Haitian president implied that he shared American concerns, promising that the FBI would have unfettered access to anyone it wished to interview. Aristide's sole and seemingly reasonable condition: that those interviewed by the FBI have access to attorneys. The American officials agreed. Through Ira Kurzban, his Miami-based American lawyer, Aristide arranged for fifteen IPSF and National Palace officials to be represented by two Miami defense lawyers, at a cost of $120,000 to the Haitian taxpayer.

The result was more frustration for the FBI. The Miami lawyers said the FBI could only interview the Haitians if the lawyers could make and keep verbatim transcripts. The FBI refused: it almost never permits persons it questions in the U.S. to keep a transcript, for the obvious reason that this could compromise the confidentiality of their preliminary investigations. This was a particular concern in the Bertin case, where the FBI felt it was seeking to interview a group of possible co-conspirators. Feeling double-crossed by its supposed Haitian partners, the FBI withdrew from Haiti on October 13, 1995.

After the FBI quit, the Bertin case was assigned to the Haitian police force's new Special Investigations Unit. The unit consists of a small U.S.-funded team of Haitians working under the direction of an American adviser with forensic support from the FBI. At Haitian insistence, the unit is also looking into killings by the ousted military regime; but it has had plenty of new business. Indeed, the suspicious killings continued while the FBI was still in town.

Michel Gonzales, a prominent Haitian airline executive, lived with his horses on forty acres in the Port-au-Prince exurb of Tabarre. He rented the property from the wealthy, conservative Debrosse family. Gonzales's next-

door neighbor was a powerful Haitian, too: Aristide. On two occasions around the time of Aristide's return to Haiti, Aristide's advisers, Jean-Marie Cherestal and Leslie Voltaire, asked U.S. officials to obtain the land for Aristide's use, according to two U.S. sources familiar with the events. The request was refused. (Voltaire denies this; Cherestal could not be reached.) At that point, Gonzales's friends say, visitors began arriving and telling Gonzales pointedly to get out. He didn't. On May 22, 1995, two men on a motorbike shot Gonzales dead in front of Aristide's place, while Gonzales's wife and daughter—both American citizens—looked on in horror. No one in Haiti is quite sure now who owns the property, but it appears to be vacant.

Two days after the cops found Gonzales dead, Michel-Ange Hermann, a former colonel in the FADH, was gunned down. And in the run-up to the national elections, assassins felled two minor Senate candidates: Leslie Grimar, an auto parts dealer, and Max Mayard, a former general with the FADH. An FBI inspection of shell casings found at the Bertin, Hermann, Mayard and Grimar murder scenes has established that the bullets were all fired from the same gun. They also match shell casings found at the Leroy-Fleurival homicide scene. Which brings us back to the case that made Eddy Arbrouet the most wanted man in Haiti.

The summer of 1996 was a politically tense period in Port-au-Prince. U.S. intelligence developed reliable information that Haitian rightists and ex-FADH officers were arming for a coup against President Préval. Shots were fired at the National Palace. On August 17, Préval's police tackled the threat by rounding up nineteen former FADH members at the headquarters of the same party with which Bertin had been associated, the MDN. Three days after that, Leroy and Fleurival were killed.

Within hours of the shooting, the U.S. Embassy in Port-au-Prince had convincing evidence that several presidential bodyguards had been present at the crime. (*The Los Angeles Times* has reported that the evidence consisted of intercepted radio conversations among the bodyguards.) Police found a Taurus 9 mm pistol next to Leroy's body. The serial number on the Taurus identified it as property of the presidential bodyguards.

Even more damning evidence about Arbrouet's ties to the National Palace has emerged since then. Arbrouet was a paid informant for the presidential bodyguards, working directly for the top officer, Joseph Moise. Arbrouet had both an entry pass to the National Palace and a government-issued gun. On August 5, 1996, the National Police arrested Arbrouet after he attempted to rob an armored truck in Cap-Haitien. But, according to a non-U.S. diplomat in Port-au-Prince familiar with the case, Arbrouet was released from jail after one of the presidential bodyguards called the National Police in

Cap-Haitien and ordered his release. Fifteen days later, Leroy and Fleurival were dead. Bullet shells gathered at the murder scene matched shells from the Glock 9 mm pistol Arbrouet used in the failed holdup.

Ambassador Swing did not yet know all of this when the bodies of Leroy and Fleurival showed up on August 20, 1996. But what he did know caused him to rush to Préval and urge him to take action against the killers in his midst. Préval balked. Ambassador Swing summoned National Security Adviser Anthony Lake and Deputy Secretary of State Strobe Talbott, who—upon arriving in Port-au-Prince on August 30, 1996—told Préval he could lose American support unless he purged his bodyguards. Only then did the true reason for Préval's hesitation become clear: according to senior U.S. officials, he feared he would be killed himself if he took on the bodyguards, most of whom were selected by, and primarily loyal to, Aristide. (Préval has since publicly denied this.)

The highly unstable situation posed a threat not only to the physical survival of the president of Haiti, but also to the political survival of the president of the United States, who was running for re-election at the time. The Clintonites tried to handle the dilemma by dispatching forty-six American bodyguards to watch Préval's back while he began the delicate process of removing the ten bodyguards who were suspected of having knowledge of, or a role in, the killings. Moise, the top officer, was one of the first to be suspended at U.S. insistence. But Préval dragged his feet about firing the men, and delays cropped up in the Haitian investigation.

Leroy's body was in handcuffs when police discovered it; those handcuffs have now disappeared from the custody of the Haitian judicial authorities. At one point, the State Department heard a rumor that senior Haitian officials had tried to coach eyewitnesses to the killings. That prompted Clinton to send Préval a letter on December 12, 1996, warning that U.S. aid to Haiti was at risk. By then, the Clinton administration was also responding to pressure from New York Congressman Benjamin A. Gilman and other Republican critics on Capitol Hill. After months of Republican threats to cut off aid, and several more administration démarches to Préval, the last of Préval and Aristide's bodyguards suspected of involvement in the case were finally kicked off the government payroll by July 30 of this year. Not that they were treated too harshly: each walked away with a severance package equal to four months' salary.

Today, a security detail from the State Department still watches Préval. Arbrouet is a fugitive, though his whereabouts are an open secret: he's in Leogane, an hour's drive from Port-au-Prince. He has been spotted driving around Port-au-Prince in a new Fiat. Arbrouet has even gone on the radio to claim that anything he did was on the orders of Pierre Denize, chief of the National Police. Though probably untrue, the claim shows Arbrouet understands his best protection from arrest is the fear Haitian officials have of what he might say if he's ever captured alive.

U.S. officials say the National Police SWAT team now has weapons heavy enough to match Arbrouet's arsenal, and that a new attempt to bust him will be made. But just how eager are the Haitian authorities to take on Arbrouet? I asked Ambassador Swing when we could expect an arrest. "The wanted posters are up in the police stations," he replied. I didn't see any—not even at National Police headquarters. In Jacmel, just down the road from Leogane, a detective told me he'd never heard of Arbrouet. Really? I asked. Oh yes, he suddenly recalled, there had been a poster in his station for a while, "but it mysteriously disappeared."

Since the Leroy-Fleurival killings, Aristide and Préval's traditional right-wing enemies have been, in the words of one U.S. official, "quiescent." Yet the Aristide forces still face opposition from some of their former allies, and it is Aristide's determination to triumph over these opponents—rather than bargain with them—that has precipitated the current electoral crisis.

Lavalas, the loose popular coalition Aristide first rode to electoral victory back in 1990, has fractured into two separate political parties. The Lavalas Political Organization (OPL) is, as its name suggests, an organized, internally democratic political party. OPL wants to get ahead by playing ball with Haiti's international patrons: supporting economic reform and privatization, strengthening the role of the parliament and the courts. The OPL's leaders broke with Aristide in late 1995, when he maneuvered, unsuccessfully, to extend his term, in violation of the Haitian Constitution. OPL controls the Haitian Senate.

As its name suggests, Aristide's party, Fanmi Lavalas—Creole for "the Lavalas family"—is organized around Aristide as the personalistic leader who decides all major questions, in consultation with a small inner circle. Though Aristide and his supporters denounce U.S.-backed economic reforms as unfair to the poor, it's not clear what they support—except their own access to traditional sources of power and patronage. The tainted April 6 elections were, in part, a bid by Aristide to get control over the Senate by hook or by crook. Among the "winning" candidates was Jean-Marie Fourel Celestin, an Aristide crony whose reputation for corruption reportedly contributed to the Haitian Senate's decision to reject him when Aristide tried to nominate him as police chief in 1995.

All the key issues in Haitian politics—the future of the economic reforms, the prime ministership, control of the Senate, the credibility of elections themselves—hinge on the struggle between OPL and Fanmi Lavalas. "The hour is late in Haiti," concluded a June 26 House International Affairs Committee report on the situation that was signed not only by Gilman, the Republican chairman, but also by ranking Democrat Lee Hamilton of Indiana. Stung by rising bipartisan concern, the administration has dispatched a parade of high-level emissaries, including former National Security Adviser Lake, to urge Aristide to cut a deal.

But the effort is not going well. Aristide has little incentive to negotiate. After all, he "won" the April 6 vote; and, with U.S. acquiescence, the installation of local governments, of which he controls a plurality, is moving forward. On August 26, the Fanmi Lavalas-dominated lower house of parliament rejected Préval's U.S.-supported choice for prime minister, a political unknown named Ericq Pierre. Préval barely lifted a finger to help Pierre; he seems cowed by Aristide, whom he served as a loyal subordinate throughout his entire previous career in politics.

Perhaps the Clinton administration will orchestrate some face-saving solution. Even if it does, a short-term political arrangement is no substitute for institutional development. Aristide is committed to a politics of personalistic leadership and haphazard "mass action." In deference to his de facto power, U.S. officials still deal with him almost as a head of state. When U.N. Ambas-

Cop land

By all accounts, Haiti's new National Police Force is the best-trained and best-qualified force in the island's history. The Clinton administration talks up its success, and this year alone the U.S. will subsidize the force's training to the tune of $6.5 million. But for all the progress, the police force remains susceptible to the influence of Haitian figures whom the U.S. government suspects of corruption and political violence against opponents of former President Jean-Bertrand Aristide. And that is bad news in a country where the establishment of a clean, apolitical and effective police force is a prerequisite for real democracy.

Among the most controversial figures hovering around the new police is Dany Toussaint. As a major in the FADH, the now-defunct Haitian military force, Toussaint was one of Aristide's few early supporters in that force and is reputed to have rescued Aristide during the 1991 coup. Aristide, with U.S. approval, placed Toussaint in charge of the country's temporary police force after the U.S. intervention in 1994. But later the FBI soured on Toussaint; the Bureau came to believe that Toussaint had frustrated, rather than facilitated, its investigation of the murder of Mireille Durocher Bertin, Aristide's right-wing political opponent, in 1995.

Citing intelligence that allegedly linked Toussaint to incidents of political violence, the U.S. eventually told the government of President René Préval (who succeeded Aristide) to keep Toussaint out of the new National Police that replaced the interim police at the end of 1995. Then, in August of last year, Joseph Sullivan, the State Department's top Haiti official, sent a letter to the Immigration and Naturalization Service instructing that agency to block Toussaint's entry into the United States because of American intelligence that the Aristide confidant had "participated in extrajudicial killings."

Sure enough, this January the Immigration and Naturalization Service arrested Toussaint at the Miami airport. Toussaint was held for two days and questioned about the Bertin case by the FBI; he has since claimed an FBI agent told him that "he knows I am not the triggerman but they would like me to cooperate with them." Toussaint refused the purported offer; his U.S. lawyer, Ira Kurzban, says Toussaint is the innocent target of an intimidation campaign by U.S. officials frustrated by their own fruitless investigations. Kurzban says that the intelligence on Toussaint is tainted by the CIA's longstanding anti-Aristide bias. Eventually, U.S. authorities had to let Toussaint go, first from detainment and then from the country. He returned to a hero's welcome from Aristide supporters.

The forced stay in the U.S. did prevent Toussaint from running for Senate in Haiti's April 6 elections, but he has prospered in other ways. Now acting as chief of security and intelligence for Aristide's party, he also runs a large force of private security guards, a firing range where customers pay to shoot high-caliber guns and a new company called Dany King's Police and Security Supply. Located at No. 2 Rue Lamarre, in the upper-class Port-au-Prince suburb of Pétion-Ville, the establishment is the only place in Haiti where members of the underequipped police force can buy vital supplies. A Haitian security-industry source told me that some equipment on sale in Toussaint's shop was originally donated to Haiti by Taiwan. Several cops complained to me about the prices: it costs almost a day's pay to get an iron-on shoulder patch that identifies the wearer as a police officer.

Toussaint, of course, isn't just making money. His business lets him infiltrate the very police from which the Clinton administration has tried to exclude him. In what is supposed to be the first apolitical force in Haitian history, former President Aristide's security chief clearly has in-

sador Bill Richardson visited Port-au-Prince in July to cement local support for an extension of the U.N. troop presence, his key meeting was with Aristide. It had to be: "popular" organizations linked to the former president were staging violent demonstrations against the very foreign troops that had reinstated Aristide. Anti-U.N., anti-American graffiti remain daubed in red on the whitewashed walls of Port-au-Prince and its surrounding slums, reminders that nothing important can be decided without Aristide and his forces.

Perhaps the writing on the wall is also a sign that Clinton administration policy in Haiti needs a review, beginning with a reassessment of the U.S. relationship—past, present and future—with Aristide. Aristide's image has been defined by polarized perceptions ever since he

burst on the scene as the fiery priest-tribune of Haiti's poor and oppressed after the 1986 collapse of the Duvalier regime. To the Haitian poor and liberal Democrats in the United States, especially the Congressional Black Caucus, he was gentle *Titid*—"little Aristide"—a prophet, a Caribbean Martin Luther King. To the Haitian elite and many conservative American Republicans, he was an unhinged communist rabble-rouser.

A more realistic view of Aristide begins with a journey down the finest paved highway in Haiti, the new 15th of October Boulevard. Named for the date in 1994 on which U.S. troops brought Aristide back in triumph, the road runs seven miles from the elite enclave of Pétion-Ville to the heavily guarded compound in Tabarre where Aristide, defrocked by his longtime foes in the Roman

fluence. Walk into any police station in Port-au-Prince, and you'll see a bright red, white and blue sticker on the wall proclaiming that "Dany King Supports the Haitian National Police."

One piece of good news is that the force's chief, Pierre Denize, seems to be one of Haiti's brighter lights—a man tough on both malfeasance in his own ranks and crime in the streets. Denize has professionalized the force. Now recruits must pass an entrance exam, and undergo four months of training with a strong emphasis on human rights. Already, Denize has expelled 135 cops on charges ranging from incompetence to brutality—a major feat in a country whose security forces have traditionally stolen and killed as they pleased.

But even Denize has his questionable side. He owns Cobra, a company that provides armed protection to those with enough money to pay. Of course, Cobra's financial success depends upon a public perception that the National Police can't do their job fully—which is precisely the perception Denize is supposed to be eradicating. "Haitians do not have a developed notion of conflict of interest," sighs a Clinton administration official. Indeed, far from discouraging Denize, the government of Haiti hired Cobra to protect Teleco, the state-owned telephone monopoly. Denize, through Burton Wides, Haiti's American attorney, says parliament permitted him to retain a passive interest in Cobra; through Wides, Teleco says Cobra got its contract through competitive bidding. Or relatively competitive: Denize's partner, Serge Calvin, is President Préval's brother-in-law.

Another apparent problem under Denize's leadership is the use of foreign money intended to shore up the island's historically underfunded cops. The United States and other nations underwrite a base wage for police of about $375 per month, on the sound theory that decent pay is the cops' best protection against the lure of bribery. However, police officers complain that unjust or poorly explained payroll deductions reduce their take-home pay by up to 20 percent a month. Dolse Estilien, 38, a member of an anti-gang unit, told me he must contribute two-and-a-half days' pay per month toward a pension for which he will only be eligible thirty years from now—if, unlike the average Haitian man, he lives that long. To date, the National Police have not disclosed how, or if, the pension fund is being invested.

Cops are supplied with a gun, shoes and a single uniform upon their graduation from the police academy. Several of them told me that they are required to reimburse the force for these supplies through more payroll deductions—even though most of the equipment was donated to Haiti from abroad. Bernard Gedner, 35, chief detective in the town of Jacmel, is a capable former math teacher who joined the police for the salary. But he has to pay informants out of his own pocket because he has no intelligence budget, despite the fact that Denize is supposed to have tens of thousands of dollars per month to distribute for that purpose. Detective Gedner told me he has spent some $250 of his own money on extra uniforms and other supplies. And where did he buy them? Where else but Dany King's Police and Security Supply?

CHARLES LANE

Catholic hierarchy, now lives with his American wife and their child. I was not invited in. But Michele Karshan, a leftist American journalist who works as a spokesperson for Aristide and Préval in Port-au-Prince, told me chez Aristide is a modest abode. "The pool is not that big," she said.

Along the road, you pass the headquarters of Aristide's Foundation for Democracy and a giant stone-and-metal monument (in the shape of a rickety sailboat) to the Haitian refugees whose travail had so much to do with Aristide's return to power. You also pass luxury housing developments, car dealerships and factories. Aristide's 15th of October Boulevard has made rural Tabarre into a burgeoning exurb—and someone is making a handsome real-estate fortune as a result. Neither Aristide nor the government ever explained where the funds for the road came from, though it was built not long after Taiwan, grateful for the diplomatic recognition it received from Aristide's government, gave Haiti $20 million to rebuild the congested, rutted main road in the slum of Carrefour. The Carrefour project has barely been started.

What the trip down the Tabarre road suggests is that for Aristide, the child of obscure lower-middle-class parents from the Haitian outback, the ten years since the fall of the Duvalier dynasty have been an improbable, very nearly fatal, journey from the margins of Haitian society to its very pinnacle, from outcast to powerbroker. To rise, he employed neither the nonviolence of King nor the conspiratorialism of Lenin. Rather, his were the traditional instruments of Caribbean politics. His true political antecessors are such figures as Eric Gairy of Grenada, Rafael Trujillo of the Dominican Republic, and even "Papa Doc" himself, who also began his career as an apostle of black pride among the Haitian poor.

Like them, Aristide's greatest asset is his ability to keep his true intentions hidden amid the rapture of his supporters and the rage of his opponents. Aristide is a master orator in the proletarian Creole tongue—barely comprehensible to Americans and Haiti's French-speaking elite—using its subtle, sarcastic poetry to inspire the hopes and inflame the passions of the man in the street, and to weave a web of mystery and charisma around his own persona. He understood the centrality of religion and *fanmi* in Haitian culture, and thus organized his followers, whether orphaned street kids, parishioners or disgruntled soldiers, into a series of interconnected "families," all of them headed by Father Aristide.

He also understood, and accepted, the inevitability and the necessity of violence in Haitian politics. But in contrast to his brutish military opponents, Aristide has deployed violence selectively—and always with plausible deniability—whether he's assembling a shadowy coterie of bodyguards around himself, or using Creole double entendres to incite his supporters to throw burning tires around the necks of his enemies.

And finally, Aristide has known how to handle the U.S. He understands that the bottom-line American concern in Haiti is political and economic instability, and the attendant prospect of a mass migration of poor black people to the shores of Florida. It was this fear, tinged with genuine American pity for the most miserable land in the hemisphere, that Aristide, helped by well-intentioned American liberals, exploited to maneuver Bill Clinton into using the mightiest military in the world to restore him to power. Today, Aristide, still manipulates that pity-tinged fear to get the Clintonites to deal with him.

Or to bluff them. Though Aristide is still the likeliest winner in the presidential election planned for 2000—even if the election is clean—I was struck by the degree to which his popular appeal has faded in the seven long years since the 1990 election, in which he polled 67 percent. In part, he has been brought down to earth by defrocking and marriage. In part, he partakes of Haiti's general political apathy. But also, Aristide is less loved because of the evidence that he is enmeshed in a profoundly violent and corrupt political culture.

I spent an afternoon in Carrefour with a former employee of his government, a well-educated social worker in her thirties. Her whole family supported Aristide before and during the coup period, at considerable risk. But now her elderly father never speaks Aristide's name. Her brother, a shopkeeper, still defends Aristide, but even he didn't vote on April 6. For her part, the social worker found she "could not accept" what she saw within the Aristide administration. "Before the people believed in *Titid* because he had the name of 'Father,'" she told me, her voice dipping to a whisper. "But now they perceive that in a different way, like a mafioso—like a godfather."

On my last full day in Haiti, I visited Çité Soleil, the notorious Port-au-Prince slum where some 200,000 horribly poor people live crammed into five square miles between an industrial park and the Caribbean Sea. As expected, I saw raw sewage running through the cratered streets; tin-roof shacks full of hungry children; sullen, disaffected people, all of whom once supported Aristide, none of whom told me they still vote. "The cost of living is so high right now, plus we have children to feed, and things are getting harder and harder every day," said Wesley Jean, a 26-year-old non-voter who earns $33 a month repairing clothes on a beat-up Singer sewing machine.

I noted, though, that the worst signs of squalor—the garbage; the open sewers; the rampant gang battles on unlit, poorly policed streets—are traceable to governmental failure. The signs of hope and life, by contrast, sprang from two sources. One was the U.S. military: with minimal Haitian government involvement, the American Marines, Navy and Air Force troops have built a school and provide visiting medical services. They have dug freshwater wells and a new road. The benefits are of the kind Haiti's poor can see and feel. "It used to take me all day to go downtown to look for a job," said 33-year-old Lut Fenellon. On the American road, it takes three hours.

The other source of hope is the hard work and creativity of ordinary people themselves: Wesley Jean pumping away at his Singer; shacks converted, brick by individually purchased brick, into more substantial homes; front-stoop snack bars that supply families with untaxed income. It is obvious why so many Haitians prosper as immigrants in the U.S. It is equally obvious they could prosper if their own country had the rule of law.

The story of the Haitian slums, in short, is an old one: good people, bad government. That is still the case after three years of the Clinton administration's politico-military stewardship. Unless the Haitian people and their American patrons find a way to develop Haiti that does not involve paying tribute to corrupt, violent and incompetent elites, the fate of this long-suffering land will probably always be tied, in some form, to the fate of people like Eddy Arbrouet.

Article 19   *Américas*, August 1997

SOARING SCALES of the SILVER BASIN

Born of the street culture of Trinidad's underclass, steelpan music has been embraced by renowned orchestras the world over

by Celia Sankar

A warm and friendly sun smiles down on a white sand beach. Gentle, aquamarine waves roll in. Coconut trees softly sway. And an infectious, melodious beat—a high-pitched ping-pa-ting played on a silver basin—fills the air. You could only be in the Caribbean.

Hollywood directors have so often depended on this image to portray the Caribbean in their films that the scene has become cliche. Still, it is easy to understand why this picture conjures the region for so many people. That silver basin, called the steelpan, has come to symbolize an area from the Bahamas to Trinidad. Adopted throughout the Caribbean, where it is often found at ports of call to welcome visitors, the instrument was born some five decades ago on the island of Trinidad.

The exact date of its origin is uncertain, and no single inventor can be identified. The steelpan emerged out of the slums of Port of Spain, Trinidad's capital, around World War II and is acknowledged to be the only acoustic instrument invented in the twentieth century.

The steelpan, or steeldrum as it is sometimes called, is exactly what its name suggests—a large metal container

Celia Sankar is a journalist based in Port of Spain, Trinidad, and a previous contributor to Américas.

turned into an instrument. Clearly, even before the first save-the-earth campaign, the steelpan presented an impressive example of recycling—from the first biscuit tins, cement barrels, cooking oil tins, old buckets, and dustbins to today's oil drums.

On hearing the steelpan in Puerto Rico in the mid-1960s, Spanish cellist Pablo Casals remarked: "The steelpan music has definite possibilities for enhancing the symphony orchestra." Steelpan musicians have done more than that. They've put together hundreds of instruments to form steel orchestras, which have won over audiences from London's Royal Albert Hall to New York's Carnegie Hall.

Musicians as diverse as jazz drummer Buddy Rich and rock guitarist Carlos Santana have used the steelpan in recordings. A steel band toured France with high-tech French musician Jean Michel Jarre; a Trinidad pannist toured the U.S. with the Duke Ellington Orchestra. And last April, Italian tenor Luciano Pavarotti performed to the accompaniment of the Port of Spain-based Desperadoes steel orchestra at a concert in Barbados.

Apparently pleased, the opera star is arranging for the group to join him on a short tour in the future. Anthony McQuilken, the Desperadoes' manager, says that Pavarotti's management had been skeptical until they heard the

group play. "They had no idea that pan could sound like a full orchestra."

Such pairings seemed inconceivable in the instrument's rough early days, when it was reviled by authorities and associated with bloody, and sometimes fatal, street fights. The steelpan emerged as part of the rebellion of the underclass against oppression. In colonial Trinidad, British authorities outlawed the use of African drums, fearing they would be used to rally slaves to revolt. The slaves' descendants, therefore, developed alternative instruments to accompany their ancient religious ceremonies and their festivities in the pre-Lenten Carnival.

The first was the tamboo bamboo. This was a length of bamboo that was played by beating it with a stick in one hand and pounding it on the ground with the other. For Carnival, bands of tamboo bamboo players roamed the streets providing a rhythmic clatter for revelers to dance to.

By 1937 authorities banned these instruments too. One of their complaints was that the pounding damaged roads. However, it was not only asphalt that got bruised when the heavy lengths of bamboo came crashing down on the ground. Many a tamboo bamboo player limped home with smashed toes. These difficulties led musicians to innovate even further.

They salvaged the large tins used to import a popular brand of biscuits, garbage cans, paint tins, old pots and pans, in fact any object made of metal, and started rapping on them. Port of Spain was filled with the exhilarating, rhythmic din of these new bands.

The first band to hit the streets with all steel was a group that called itself Alexander's Ragtime Band, after a Tyrone Power movie that played in the city's movie houses in the late 1930s. The trend took off, and the steel bands that grew up in the depressed areas in and around Port of Spain took their names from the movies, particularly those with fighting themes: Destination Tokyo, from the Cary Grant film of the same name; Invaders, from Laurence Olivier's *The Invaders;* Renegades, from *Renegades of the Rio Grande* with Rod Cameron; and Desperadoes, from *Desperadoes of Dodge City* with Alan Ladd.

Competition among these bands to sound the best on the road was keen. Soon enough, the unemployed young men of the city's poor neighborhoods discovered that the pans produced different sounds if heated and beaten into different shapes. Two names stand out among these innovators: Winston "Spree" Simon from an area called John John and Ellie Mannette in New Town. Along with others such as Anthony Williams, Neville Jules, and Bertie Marshall, they crafted the instrument, year after year toying with the shape and size of the pan.

Steel band legend has it that it was Simon who first awakened the world to the fact that the pan could provide not only rhythm, as the tamboo bamboo had, but could also play melody. On Carnival day in 1946, it is said, he caused a stir and won applause from even the governor when he paraded down the street playing, among other things, Schubert's "Ave Maria" and "God Save the King" on a fourteen-note pan, which was called a "ping pong."

Mannette and his brother Vernon started the Invaders steel band during World War II. Vernon remembers: "It was for the Allied Victory over Japan Day that Ellie brought out the eighteen-note pan, which he called the Barracuda. It took the town by storm and made all the other bands very jealous. The boys from John John stole the Barracuda pan, and when they were finished studying it and copying it, they hung it on a tree and said that Ellie had to come for it."

And later: "It was in 1945 that Ellie first produced the big pans, from the fifty-five-gallon (oil) drum. Again, the (other) boys were jealous and gave us trouble. But Invaders was one of the better fighting bands, so we were not easy to contend with. If they came at us in the day, we went back for them in the night."

The rivalry went way beyond stealing, copying, and retrieving instruments. Especially at Carnival, if steel bands from the various neighborhoods met on the streets, the musicians would drop their pans and "weapons ranging from sticks, stones, and bottles, to knives and cutlasses were brought to bear with an alarming disregard for human life and property," a 1952 government report stated.

The steel band clashes stained the streets of Port of Spain with blood. In his novel about the steel band movement, *The Dragon Can't Dance,* Trinidad author Earl Lovelace tries to explain the violence: "These were the days when every district around Port of Spain was its own island and the steel band within its boundaries was its army, providing warriors to uphold its sovereignty. Those were the war days when every street corner was a garrison."

Small wonder, then, that the steel bands too were outlawed and the musicians had to be on the run from the police. As they would gather clandestinely in the night to play their instruments, the musicians often had to be ready to disperse quickly as the police raided their yards. The violence and the criminalizing of the instrument brought a stigma upon the steel bands, made up primarily of African men, with a sprinkling of the descendants of indentured workers who came from India to work on the sugar plantations after slavery. Still, some middle-class college boys of mixed European and African parentage and a number of young Chinese men defied social barriers to embrace the music.

The turning point for the steelpan came with the formation of the Trinidad All-Stars Percussion Orchestra (Taspo) in 1951. Formed with the express purpose of bringing together musicians from rival steel bands, Taspo helped to quell the violent antagonism associated with the instrument. It also made the steel band international, as the group went to London and Paris, where they performed to wide acclaim. After that success, more college players entered the movement. And a women's steel band, Girl Pat Steel Orchestra, came into being, consisting of schoolteachers, civil servants, and store clerks. Previous to this, women's involvement was limited mostly to support roles. Mothers and grandmothers allowed steel bands to practice in their yards; younger women danced and waved flags as the bands played, and often were the cause over which fights broke out among the musicians.

The fighting petered out after the 1950s as the bands were filled with players who wanted to make only music, not war. The advent of sponsorship also brought about significant changes. Oil companies such as the giant Amoco and the local Petrotrin, automobile manufacturer Neal and Massy, the West Indies Tobacco Company, and local soft drink manufacturer Solo, among others, began to purchase instruments for the bands and underwrite their overseas tours. They also made ending the violence a condition of their sponsorship.

Yet even today the steelpan has not received full acceptance in Trinidad. A few years ago some Trinidadians of Indian descent were outraged when the instrument was used to play a Hindu religious hymn and then objected strenuously to a Ministry of Culture suggestion that steelpan be added to the secondary-school curriculum, arguing that the Indian harmonium should be included as well. But the steelpan has come a long way. Today, even convent schools run by nuns for the daughters of the middle and upper classes participate in the schools' steel band competition during Carnival.

The long and slow road to acceptance at home, however, contrasts with the manner in which the instrument has been embraced abroad. Some members of Taspo stayed behind in London, where the steelpan took off with the large West Indian community there. By the 1970s the instrument had become mainstream, and it is now taught in schools. Today there are some 160 school steel bands in London.

From London, steelpan players took their silver basins to Europe. Scandinavia, in particular, has been receptive. There are some 150 steel bands in Switzerland alone, one of which came to Trinidad to compete with local bands in a classical music competition for steel bands last October.

"People in Switzerland thought we were crazy to be going to Trinidad," says Wilbert Gill, the Barbados-born director of the band. "They asked how we could go to Trinidad for a competition—Trinidad—where the best pan players in the world are.

"We have much respect for the bands here. I felt they [the Swiss players] must come here and see how the bands perform. That will make my job easier. After being here, they will know what they have to do."

Migration by steelpan players—among them Ellie Mannette in the 1960s—to the United States and Canada has led to the instrument's spread there. North America today has many more bands than does Trinidad. The United States alone has over eight hundred, while Canada has seen the proliferation of bands from Toronto—where there are about a dozen community bands and thirty school groups—to Vancouver and Edmonton.

And while Trinidad only two years ago started a pilot project to teach steelpan playing in the school system (steel bands in Trinidad's schools have tended to be ad hoc creations that crop up for competitions), North American music teachers have for years been finding that the novel and easy-to-learn instrument is excellent for introducing students to music.

The instrument is endorsed at the college level, too, at home and abroad. The Trinidad campus of the University of the West Indies recently began a diploma course in steelpan. Northern Illinois State University offers a bachelor's degree with pan as the major, as does Miami-based Florida Memorial College. The University of West Virginia gave Mannette an honorary doctorate for his contribution to the steelpan's development and spread.

The instrument has also traveled beyond the cultural magnets of Europe and North America. The Nigerian Police Force has a steel band. Orchestras can be found in Australia, South Africa, Iran, and South Korea. In Japan, the town of Fukuno-machi, with a population of fifteen thousand, has established its own steel band. The residents first heard the instrument in 1995 when Trinidad's Renegades steel band performed at an international music festival there. Renegades left some of their pans and one of their members behind, and from this start the Sukiyaki Orchestra took off.

"We have members who are construction workers, plumbers, carpenters, and painters," Mitsugu Yamabe, manager of the Sukiyaki Orchestra, said when they performed at Trinidad's Carnival earlier this year. "We have a love for the instrument and play wherever we can. Our arranger has found a way to fuse the Japanese music with the sounds of the pan. The art form is well received. The Japanese public comes out any time we have a concert."

Swiss and American entrepreneurs have established pan factories in Bern,

Switzerland, and Akron, Ohio. The Swiss factory was started by a former university professor who quit his job to take up the steelpan business full-time. The Ohio plant was established about a decade ago by Ronald Kerns and a partner, both of whom learned to play the steelpan as part of their undergraduate degree in music at the University of Akron. The firm has a one-year backlog of orders and is also building an archive of compositions for the steel band. For the first time, sheet music is being produced for compositions that are performed every Carnival by brilliant but musically illiterate Trinidadians.

"That's our gift to Trinidad and Tobago for creating such a wonderful instrument," Kerns says. "It's better to have someone like me doing this, someone who truly likes the art and the culture and is concerned about preserving it, than have some businessman who knows nothing about the art form just jump on it and get in it for the money."

Despite such declarations of love for the instrument, these developments alarmed Trinidadians. Islanders became wary that the lead in taking the instrument forward could be stolen from them. Within recent years, two steelpan factories were set up on the island to manufacture pans on a large scale for local use and for export. One of them, Trinidad and Tobago Instruments Limited, is largely mechanized. It uses sheets of metal that are pressed into a mold to form the basin of the steelpan. This is then tuned. But at other factories the instrument is mass produced using the conventional technique that continues to be used by small-scale individual pan makers.

It is a long and laborious process of hammering the drums inward to form the basin; creating bumps on the basin to form the notes; making grooves between those welts to separate the notes; cutting the skirt of the drum; burning the pans to harden the steel; tuning the notes; and coating the instrument with zinc to prevent rusting. The tuners, like the majority of Trinidad's pan musicians, are highly skilled but have no formal training in music. By ear, and of late using an electronic tuning device or another instrument, the tuners hammer the welts inward and outward until they get the right sound.

The steelpan remains close to its origins, with the biggest showcase for the instrument being Trinidad's annual Carnival celebrations. The bands do not dominate the street parades as they

once did; today huge trucks transporting deejays and brass bands provide the music for revelers to dance to. But a major part of the Carnival is the Panorama competition.

As many as seventy-five bands, some with more than 150 musicians, play calypsos in this competition. Most bands play calypsos written for the steelpan. The grand master of the art is the veteran calypsonian Kitchener (Aldwyn Roberts), who has been composing for the steel band since 1944. But steel band arrangers of today, such as Len "Boogsie" Sharpe and Ken "Professor" Philmore, now compose their own songs for their bands.

The arranger's role is crucial in a steel band world. The arranger determines what part of the music will be played by the different types of pan—tenor pans, guitar pans, bass pans, and others. Since most of the musicians and arrangers are not trained to read music, the arranging of the music and the learning of the tune are done by ear. For example, in the Carnival's Panorama contest for steel band supremacy, each band plays a ten-minute calypso from memory. Desperadoes and Renegades have together won the Panorama fourteen times in the event's thirty-four-year history.

Several other shows and competitions have emerged in Trinidad to showcase the steelpan, which was formally declared the national instrument in 1992. There's the biennial Pan Jazz Festival; Pan Ramajay allows small ensembles of about ten players to show off their improvisation skills; and the Pan Chutney competition challenges the steel bands, comprising mostly African descendants, to perform the music of Indian descendants.

Every two years there is a classical music festival, which attracts competitors from the Caribbean, North America, and Europe. U.S. classical composer John Corigliano, who came to Trinidad in 1986 to adjudicate at the festival, was so excited about the experience when he returned home that he inspired a friend to make a movie about steelpan.

"He had just come back from Trinidad after judging the show and I remember him telling me, 'If you haven't heard pan play classical music, then you haven't lived,'" Hollywood director David Hess said.

Hess has already begun filming in Trinidad. Entitled *Steel Guns to Steel Drums,* the movie tells the story of the birth of the steelpan. Hollywood, finally, will not just use that silver basin to establish setting, but will pay tribute to Trinidad's gift to the world.

Credits

REGIONAL ARTICLES

Page 140 Article 1. Reprinted by permission of Blackwell Publishers.
Page 150 Article 2. Reprinted courtesy of Cultural Survival, Inc. www.cs.org.

MEXICO

Page 155 Article 3. Reprinted from *World Press Review,* September 1997.
Page 156 Article 4. Reprinted from *World Press Review,* September 1997.
Page 158 Article 5. This article appeared in *The World & I,* August 1997. Reprinted by permission from *The World & I,* a publication of The Washington Times Corporation. © 1997.
Page 161 Article 6. Reprinted courtesy of *The UNESCO Courier.*
Page 163 Article 7. This article appeared in *The World & I,* July 1995. Reprinted by permission from *The World & I,* a publication of The Washington Times Corporation. © 1995.

CENTRAL AMERICA

Page 167 Article 8. © 1996 by the Archaeological Institute of America.
Page 172 Article 9. Reprinted from *The Tico Times,* Central America's Leading English Language Newspaper. www.ticotimes.co.cr.
Page 174 Article 10. © 1997 by the Chronicle of Higher Education. Reprinted with permission.
Page 176 Article 11. This article appeared in *The World & I,* April 1997. Reprinted by permission from *The World & I,* a publication of The Washington Times Corporation. © 1997.

Page 180 Article 12. Reprinted with permission from *Current History* magazine, February 1997. © 1997 by Current History, Inc.

SOUTH AMERICA

Page 185 Article 13. © 1996 by The Economist, Ltd. Distributed by The New York Times/Special Features.
Page 196 Article 14. © 1997 by The Economist, Ltd. Distributed by The New York Times/Special Features.
Page 199 Article 15. Reprinted by permission of *The Bulletin of the Atomic Scientists.* © 1996 by the Educational Foundation for Nuclear Science, 6042 South Kimbark Avenue, Chicago, Illinois 60637, USA. A one-year subscription is $36.
Page 205 Article 16. Reprinted by permission from *Multinational Monitor.*

THE CARIBBEAN

Page 208 Article 17. © 1997 by the Chronicle of Higher Education. Reprinted with permission.
Page 210 Article 18. Reprinted by permission of *The New Republic.* © 1997 by The New Republic, Inc.
Page 217 Article 19. Reprinted from *Américas,* a bimonthly magazine published by the General Secretariat of the Organization of American States in English and Spanish.

Sources for Statistical Reports

U.S. State Department, *Background Notes* (1994–1997).

The World Factbook (1997).

World Statistics in Brief (1997).

World Almanac (1997).

The Statesman's Yearbook (1996–1997).

Demographic Yearbook (1996).

Statistical Yearbook (1997).

World Bank, World Development Report (1997).

Ayers Directory of Publications (1997).

Glossary of Terms and Abbreviations

Agrarian   Relating to the land; the cultivation and ownership of land.

Amerindian   A general term for any Indian from America.

Andean Pact (Cartagena Agreement)   Established on October 16, 1969, to end trade barriers among member nations and to create a common market. Members: Bolivia, Colombia, Ecuador, Peru, and Venezuela.

Antilles   A geographical region in the Caribbean made up of the Greater Antilles: Cuba, Hispaniola (Haiti and the Dominican Republic), Jamaica, the Cayman Islands, Puerto Rico, and the Virgin Islands; and the Lesser Antilles: Antigua and Barbuda, Dominica, St. Lucia, St. Vincent and the Grenadines, St. Kitts-Nevis, as well as various French departments and Dutch territories.

Araucanians   An Indian people of south-central Chile and adjacent areas of Argentina.

Arawak   An Indian people originally found on certain Caribbean islands, who now live chiefly along the coast of Guyana. Also, their language.

Aymara   An Indian people and language of Bolivia and Peru.

Bicameral   A government made up of two legislative branches.

CACM (Central American Common Market)   Established on June 3, 1961, to form a common market in Central America. Members: Costa Rica, El Salvador, Guatemala, and Nicaragua.

Campesino   A Spanish word meaning "peasant."

Caudillo   Literally, "a man on horseback." A term that has come to mean "leader."

Carib   An Indian people and their language native to several islands in the Caribbean and some countries in Central America and South America.

CARICOM (Caribbean Community and Common Market)   Established on August 1, 1973, to coordinate economic and foreign policies.

CDB (Caribbean Development Bank)   Established on October 18, 1969, to promote economic growth and development of member countries in the Caribbean.

The Commonwealth   (Originally the British Commonwealth of Nations) An association of nations and dependencies loosely joined by the common tie of having been part of the British Empire.

Compadrazgo   The Mexican word meaning "cogodparenthood" or "sponsorship."

Compadres   Literally, "friends"; but in Mexico, the term includes neighbors, relatives, fellow migrants, coworkers, and employers.

Contadora Process   A Latin American intiative developed by Venezuela, Colombia, Panama, and Mexico to search for a negotiated solution that would secure borders and reduce the foreign military presence in Central America.

Contras   A guerrilla army opposed to the Sandinista government of Nicaragua. They were armed and supplied by the United States.

Costeños   Coast dwellers in Central America.

Creole   The term has several meanings: a native-born person of European descent or a person of mixed French and black or Spanish and black descent speaking a dialect of French or Spanish.

ECCA (Eastern Caribbean Currency Authority)   A regional organization that monitors the integrity of the monetary unit for the area and sets policies for revaluation and devaluation.

ECLA (Economic Commission for Latin America)   Established on February 28, 1948, to develop and strengthen economic relations among Latin American countries.

FAO (Food and Agricultural Organization of the United Nations)   Established on October 16, 1945, to oversee good nutrition and agricultural development.

FSLN (Frente Sandinista de Liberación Nacionál)   Organized in the early 1960s with the object of ousting the Somoza family from its control of Nicaragua. After 1979 it assumed control of the government. The election of Violeta Chamorro in 1990 marked the end of the FSLN.

Fuegians   An Indian people of the most southern area of Argentina (Tierra del Fuego).

GATT (General Agreement on Tariffs and Trade)   Established on January 1, 1948, to provide international trade and tariff standards.

GDP (Gross Domestic Product)   The value of production attributable to the factors of production in a given country, regardless of their ownership. GDP equals GNP minus the product of a country's residents originating in the rest of the world.

GNP (Gross National Product)   The sum of the values of all goods and services produced by a country's residents in any given year.

Group of 77   Established in 1964 by 77 developing countries. It functions as a caucus on economic matters for the developing countries.

Guerrilla   Any member of a small force of "irregular" soldiers. Generally, guerrilla forces are made up of volunteers who make surprise raids against the incumbent military or political force.

IADB (Inter-American Defense Board)   Established in 1942 at Rio de Janeiro to coordinate the efforts of all American countries in World War II. It is now an advisory defense committee on problems of military cooperation for the OAS.

IADB (Inter-American Development Bank)   Established in 1959 to help accelerate economic and social development in Latin America.

IBA (International Bauxite Association)   Established in 1974 to promote orderly and rational development of the bauxite industry. Membership is worldwide, with a number of Latin American members.

IBRD (International Bank for Reconstruction and Development)   Established on December 27, 1945, to make loans to governments at conventional rates of interest for high-priority productive projects. There are many Latin American members.

ICAO (International Civil Aviation Organization)   Established on December 7, 1944, to develop techniques of international air navigation and to ensure safe and orderly growth of international civil aviation. Membership is worldwide, with many Latin American members.

ICO (International Coffee Organization)   Established in August 1963 to maintain cooperation between coffee producers and to control the world market prices. Membership is worldwide, with a number of Latin American members.

IDA (International Development Association) Established on September 24, 1960, to promote better and more flexible financing arrangements; it supplements the World Bank's activities.

ILO (International Labor Organization) Established on April 11, 1919, to improve labor conditions and living standards through international action.

IMCO (Inter-Governmental Maritime Consultative Organization) Established in 1948 to provide cooperation among governments on technical matters of international merchant shipping as well as to set safety standards. Membership is worldwide, with more than a dozen Latin American members.

IMF (International Monetary Fund) Established on December 27, 1945 to promote international monetary cooperation.

IPU (Inter-Parliamentary Union) Established on June 30, 1889, as a forum for personal contacts between members of the world parliamentary governments. Membership is worldwide, with the following Latin American members: Argentina, Brazil, Colombia, Costa Rica, Haiti, Mexico, Nicaragua, Paraguay, and Venezuela.

ISO (International Sugar Organization) Established on January 1, 1969, to administer the international sugar agreement and to compile data on the industry. Membership is worldwide, with the following Latin American members: Argentina, Brazil, Colombia, Cuba, Ecuador, Mexico, Uruguay, and Venezuela.

ITU (International Telecommunications Union) Established on May 17, 1895, to develop international regulations for telegraph, telephone, and radio services.

Junta A Spanish word meaning "assembly" or "council"; the legislative body of a country.

Ladino A Westernized Spanish-speaking Latin American, often of mixed Spanish and Indian blood.

LAFTA (Latin American Free Trade Association) Established on June 2, 1961, with headquarters in Montevideo, Uruguay.

Machismo The male sense of honor; connotes the showy power of a "knight in shining armor."

Marianismo The feminine counterpart of machismo; the sense of strength that comes from controlling the family and the male.

Mennonite A strict Protestant denomination that derived from a sixteenth-century religious movement.

Mercosur Comprised of Argentina, Brazil, Paraguay, and Uraguay, this southern common market is the world's fourth largest integrated market. It was established in 1991.

Mestizo The offspring of a Spaniard or Portuguese and an American Indian.

Mulatto A person of mixed Caucasian and black ancestry.

Nahuatl The language of an Amerindian people of southern Mexico and Central America who are descended from the Aztec.

NAFTA (North American Free Trade Agreement) Established in 1993 between Mexico, Canada, and the United States, NAFTA went into effect January 1, 1994.

NAM (Non-Aligned Movement) A group of nations that chose not to be politically or militarily associated with either the West or the former Communist Bloc.

OAS (Organization of American States) (Formerly the Pan American Union) Established on December 31, 1951, with headquarters in Washington, DC.

ODECA (Central American Defense Organization) Established on October 14, 1951, to strengthen bonds among the Central American countries and to promote their economic, social, and cultural development through cooperation. Members: Costa Rica, El Salvador, Guatemala, Honduras, and Nicaragua.

OECS (Organization of Eastern Caribbean States) A Caribbean organization established on June 18, 1981, and headquartered in Castries, St. Lucia.

PAHO (Pan American Health Organization) Established in 1902 to promote and coordinate Western Hemisphere efforts to combat disease. All Latin American countries are members.

Patois A dialect other than the standard or literary dialect, such as some of the languages used in the Caribbean that are offshoots of French.

Peon Historically, a person forced to work off a debt or to perform penal servitude. It has come to mean a member of the working class.

PRI (Institutional Revolutionary Party) The dominant political party in Mexico.

Quechua The language of the Inca. It is still widely spoken in Peru.

Rastafarian A religious sect in the West Indies whose members believe in the deity of Haile Selassie, the deposed emperor of Ethiopia who died in 1975.

Rio Pact (Inter-American Treaty of Reciprocal Assistance) Established in 1947 at the Rio Conference to set up a policy of joint defense of Western Hemisphere countries. In case of aggression against any American state, all member countries will come to its aid.

Sandinistas The popular name for the government of Nicaragua from 1979 to 1990, following the ouster of President Anastasio Somoza. The name derives from César Augusto Sandino, a Nicaraguan guerrilla fighter of the 1920s.

SELA (Latin American Economic System) Established on October 18, 1975, as an economic forum for all Latin American countries.

Suffrage The right to vote in political matters.

UN (United Nations) Established on June 26, 1945, through official approval of the charter by delegates of 50 nations at an international conference in San Francisco. The charter went into effect on October 24, 1945.

UNESCO (United Nations Educational, Scientific, and Cultural Organization) Established on November 4, 1946, to promote international collaboration in education, science, and culture.

Unicameral A political structure with a single legislative branch.

UPU (Universal Postal Union) Established on July 1, 1875, to promote cooperation in international postal services.

World Bank A closely integrated group of international institutions providing financial and technical assistance to developing countries.

Bibliography

GENERAL WORKS

Mark A. Burkholder and Lyman L. Johnson, *Colonial Latin America,* 2nd ed. (New York: Oxford University Press, 1994).

E. Bradford Burns, *Latin America: A Concise Interpretive History*, 6th ed. (New Brunswick, NJ: Prentice-Hall, 1994).

David Bushnell and Neill Macaulay, *The Emergence of Latin America in the Nineteenth Century,* 2nd ed. (New York: Oxford University Press, 1994).

Thomas E. Skidmore and Peter Smith, *Modern Latin America*, 4th ed. (New York: Oxford University Press, 1997).

Barbara A. Tenenbaum, ed., *Encyclopedia of Latin American History,* 4 vols. (New York: Charles Scribner's Sons, 1995).

Claudio Veliz, *The Centralist Tradition of Latin America* (Princeton, NJ: Princeton University Press, 1980).

NATIONAL HISTORIES

The following studies provide keen insights into the particular characteristics of individual Latin American nations.

Argentina

Leslie Bethell, *Argentina Since Independence* (New York: Cambridge University Press, 1994).

Nicholas Shumway, *The Invention of Argentina* (Berkeley, CA: University of California Press, 1991).

Bolivia

Herbert S. Klein, *Bolivia: The Evolution of a Multi-Ethnic Society,* 2nd ed. (New York: Oxford University Press, 1992).

Brazil

E. Bradford Burns, *A History of Brazil,* 3rd ed. (New York: Columbia University Press, 1993).

Caribbean Nations

Franklin W. Knight, *The Caribbean: The Genesis of a Fragmented Nationalism*, 2nd ed. (New York: Oxford University Press, 1990).

David Lowenthal, *West Indian Societies* (New York: Oxford University Press, 1972).

Louis A. Perez Jr., *Cuba: Between Reform and Revolution*, 2nd ed. (New York: Oxford University Press, 1995).

Central America

Ralph Lee Woodward Jr., *Central America: A Nation Divided*, 2nd ed. (New York: Oxford University Press, 1985).

Chile

Brian Loveman, *Chile: The Legacy of Hispanic Capitalism,* 2nd ed. (New York: Oxford University Press, 1988).

Mexico

Michael C. Meyer and William L. Sherman, *The Course of Mexican History*, 5th ed. (New York: Oxford University Press, 1995).

Eric Wolf, *Sons of the Shaking Earth: The Peoples of Mexico and Guatemala; Their Land, History, and Culture* (Chicago: University of Chicago Press, 1970).

Ricardo Pozas Arciniega, *Juan Chamula: An Ethnolographical Recreation of the Life of a Mexican Indian* (Berkeley: University of California Press, 1962).

Peru

David P. Werlich, *Peru: A Short History* (Carbondale, IL: Southern Illinois University Press, 1978).

José Carlos Mariategui, *Seven Interpretive Essays on Peruvian Reality* (Austin: University of Texas Press, 1974).

Venezuela

John V. Lombardi, *Venezuela: The Search for Order, The Dream of Progress* (New York: Oxford University Press, 1982).

NOVELS IN TRANSLATION

The Latin American novel is perhaps one of the best windows on the cultures of the region. The following are just a few of many highly recommended novels.

Jorge Amado, *Clove and Cinnamon* (Avon, 1988).

Manlio Argueta, *One Day of Life* (Vintage, 1990).

Miguel Ángel Asturias, *El Señor Presidenté* (Macmillan, 1975).

Mariano Azuela, *The Underdogs* (Buccaneer Books, 1986).

Alejo Carpentier, *Reasons of State* (Writers & Readers, 1981).

Carlos Fuentes, *The Death of Artemio Cruz* (FS&G, 1964).

Jorge Icaza, *Huasipungo: The Villagers* (Arcturus Books, 1973).

Gabriel García Márquez, *One Hundred Years of Solitude* (Penguin, 1971).

Mario Vargas Llosa, *The Green House* (FS&G, 1985).

Victor Montejo, *Testimony: Death of a Guatemalan Village* (Curbstone Press, 1987).

Rachel de Queiroz, *The Three Marias* (University of Texas Press, 1991).

Graham Greene's novels about Latin America, such as *The Comedians* (1966), and V. S. Naipaul's study of Trinidad, *The Loss of El Dorado: A History* (1969), offer profound insights into the region.

CURRENT EVENTS

To keep up to date on the unfolding drama of Latin American events, the following are especially useful.

Current History: A World Affairs Journal
 The Latin American issue usually appears in February.

Latin America Press (Lima)
 A newsletter (48 issues per year) that focuses on human rights and the role of the Catholic Church in Latin America. Available in Spanish as *Noticias Aliadas*.

Latin America Weekly Report (London)
 An excellent weekly review of economic and political developments in Latin America.

Latin American Regional Report (London)
 The Regional Reports are published monthly on Brazil, Mexico and Central America, the Caribbean, the Andean Group, and the Southern Cone.

Update Latin America
 This bimonthly news analysis, published by the Washington Office on Latin America, pays particular attention to human rights problems in Latin America.

PERIODICALS

Americas
 Organization of American States
 17th and Constitution Avenues, NW
 Washington, D.C. 20006
 This periodical by the OAS is published 10 times per year in English, Spanish, and Portuguese.

The Christian Science Monitor
 One Norway Street
 Boston, MA 02115
 This newspaper is published 5 days per week, with news coverage, articles, and specific features on world events.

Commonweal
 Commonweal Publishing Co., Inc.
 232 Madison Avenue
 New York, NY 10016
 This biweekly publication reviews literature, current events, religion, and the arts.

Dollars and Sense
 Economics Affairs Bureau, Inc.
 38 Union Square, Room 14
 Somerville, MA 02143
 Published monthly (except June and August), this magazine offers interpretations of current economic events from the perspective of social change.

The Economist
 25 St. James's Street
 London, England
 This periodical presents world events from a British perspective.

Multinational Monitor
 Ralph Nader's Corporate Accountability Research Group
 1346 Connecticut Avenue, NW
 Washington, D.C. 20006
 This monthly periodical offers editorials and articles on world events and current issues.

The Nation
 Nation Enterprises/Nation Associates, Inc.
 72 Fifth Avenue
 New York, NY 10011
 Published 47 times during the year, this magazine presents editorials and articles dealing with areas of public interest—with special attention given to American politics and foreign policy, social problems, and education. Also covers literature and the arts.

The New Republic
 The New Republic, Inc.
 1220 19th Street, NW, Suite 200
 Washington, D.C. 20036
 Weekly coverage of politics, literature, and world events.

The New York Times
 The New York Times Co.
 229 West 43rd Street
 New York, NY 10036
 A daily newspaper that covers world news through articles and editorials.

Science News
 Science Service
 1719 N Street, NW
 Washington, D.C. 20036
 For those interested in science, this weekly publication gives an overview of worldwide scientific developments.

UNESCO Courier
 7 Place de Fontenoy
 Paris, France
 Published by the UN, the magazine presents extensive treatment of world events by devoting each monthly issue to a specific topic.

The Wall Street Journal
 Dow Jones Books
 Box 300
 Princeton, NJ 08540
 Presents broad daily coverage of world news through articles and editorials.

World Press Review
 The Stanley Foundation
 230 Park Avenue
 New York, NY 10169
 Each month, this publication presents foreign magazine and newspaper stories on political, social, and economic affairs.

Index